Im

Great Priest Imhotep

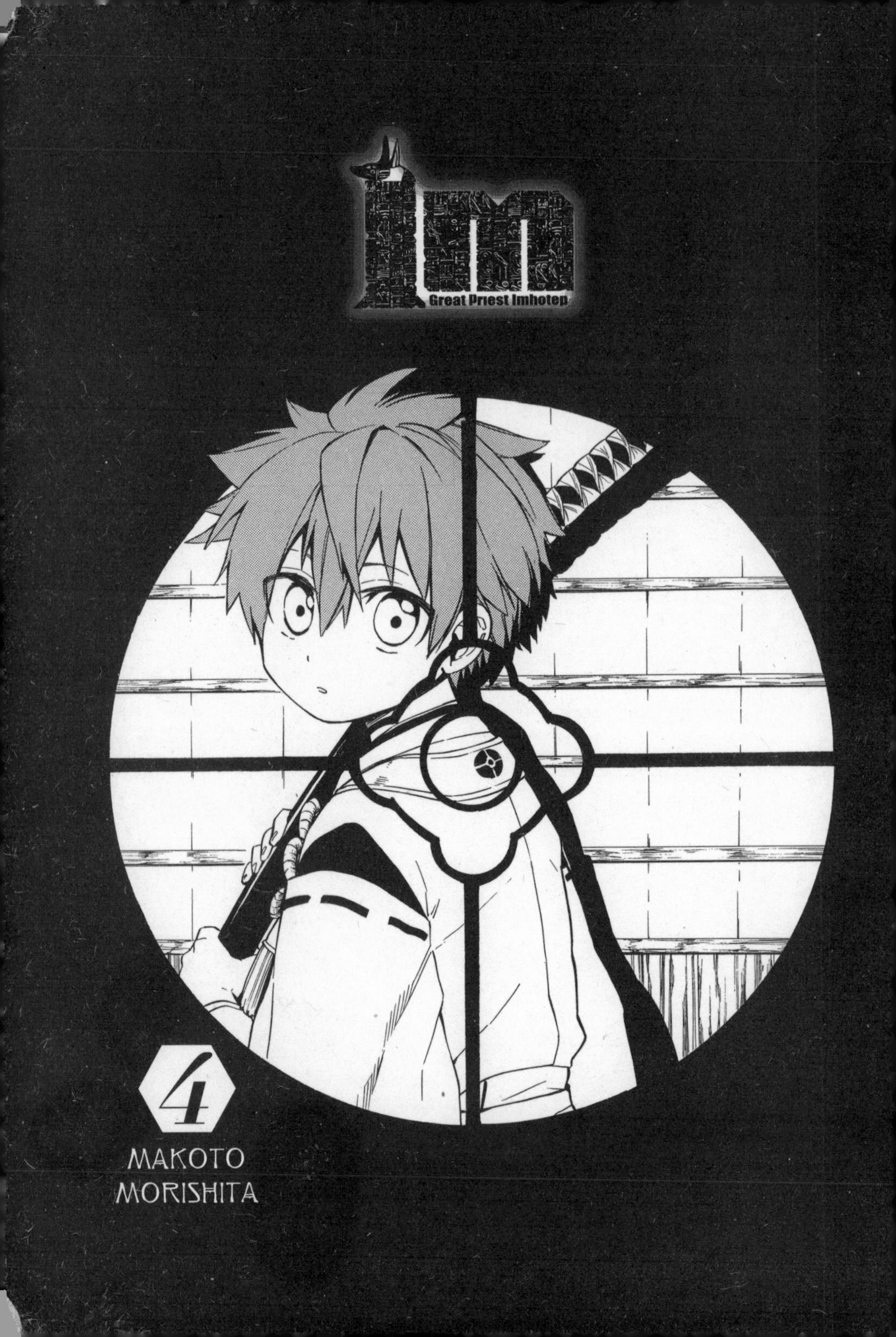

4

MAKOTO
MORISHITA

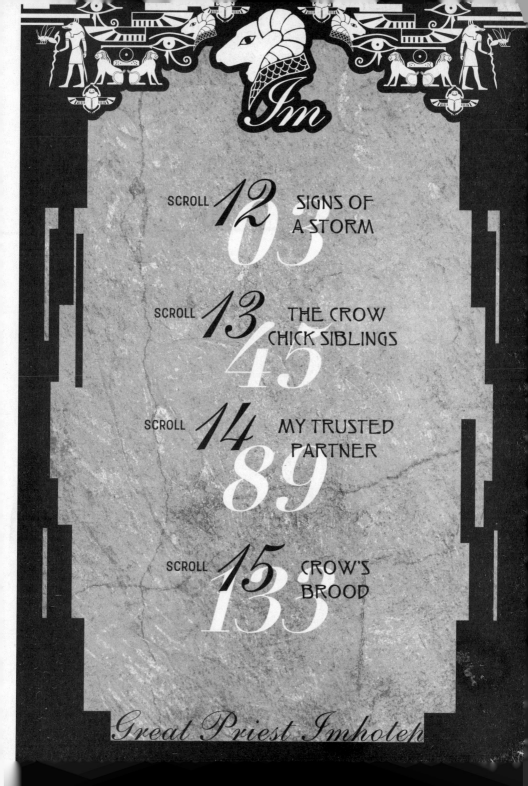

Im

Great Priest Imhotep

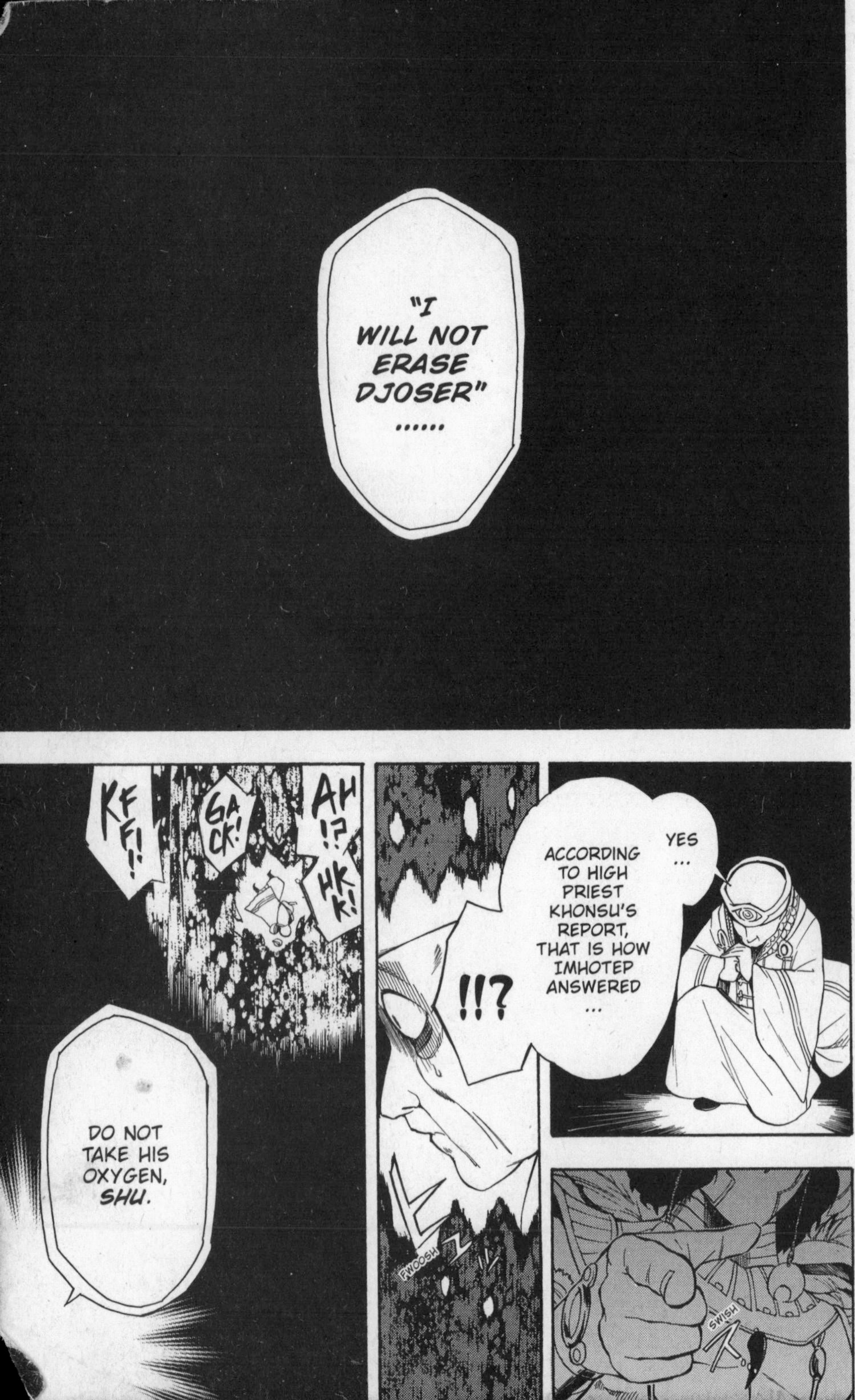
"I WILL NOT ERASE DJOSER" ......
YES ...
ACCORDING TO HIGH PRIEST KHONSU'S REPORT, THAT IS HOW IMHOTEP ANSWERED ...
SWISH
!!?
FWOOSH
AH!? HKK!
GACK!
KFF!!
DO NOT TAKE HIS OXYGEN, SHU.

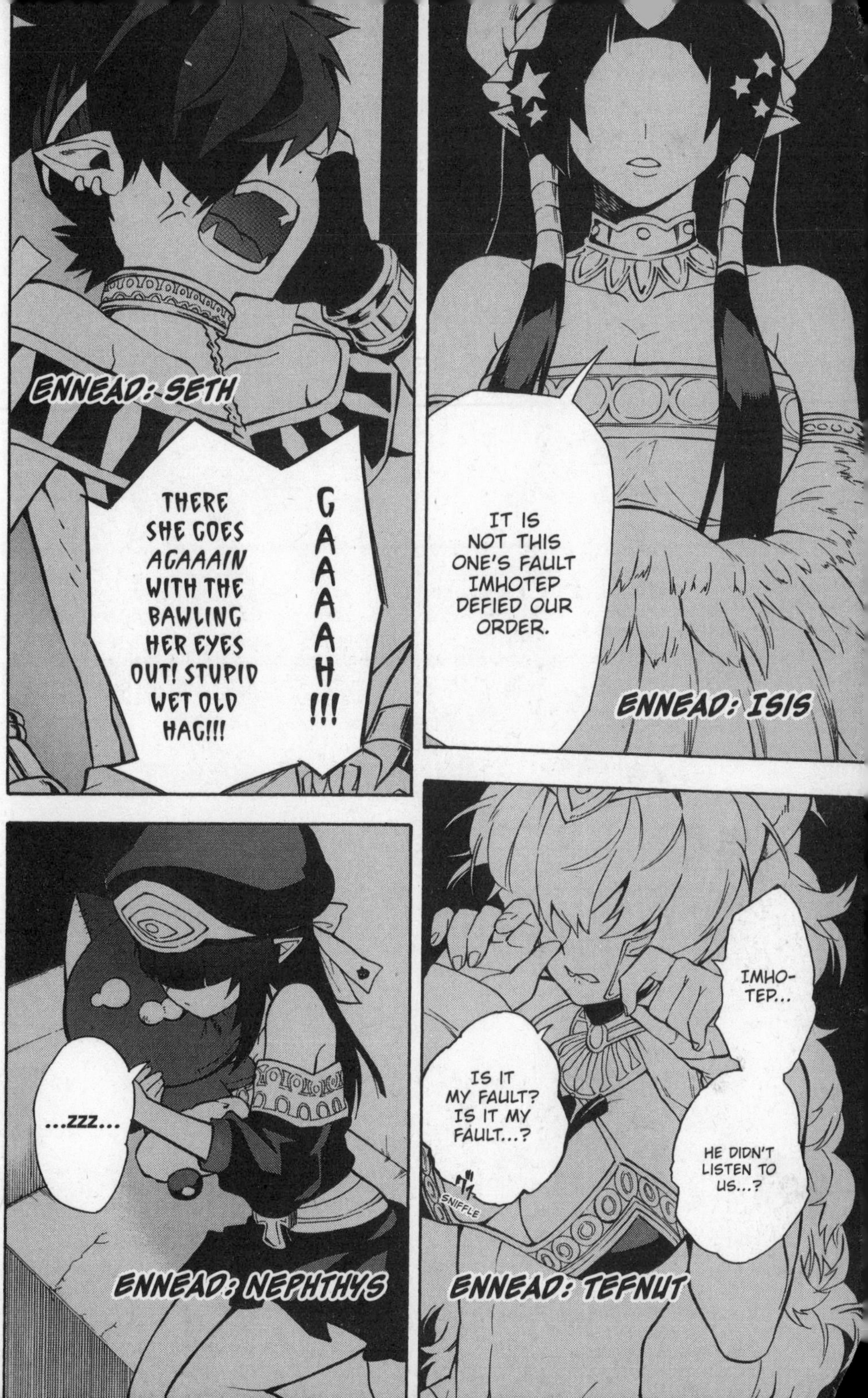
IT IS NOT THIS ONE'S FAULT IMHOTEP DEFIED OUR ORDER.
ENNEAD: ISIS
ENNEAD: SETH
GAAAAAH!!!
THERE SHE GOES AGAAAIN WITH THE BAWLING HER EYES OUT! STUPID WET OLD HAG!!!
IMHO-TEP...
IS IT MY FAULT? IS IT MY FAULT...?
SNIFFLE
HE DIDN'T LISTEN TO US...?
ENNEAD: TEFNUT
...zzz...
ENNEAD: NEPHTHYS

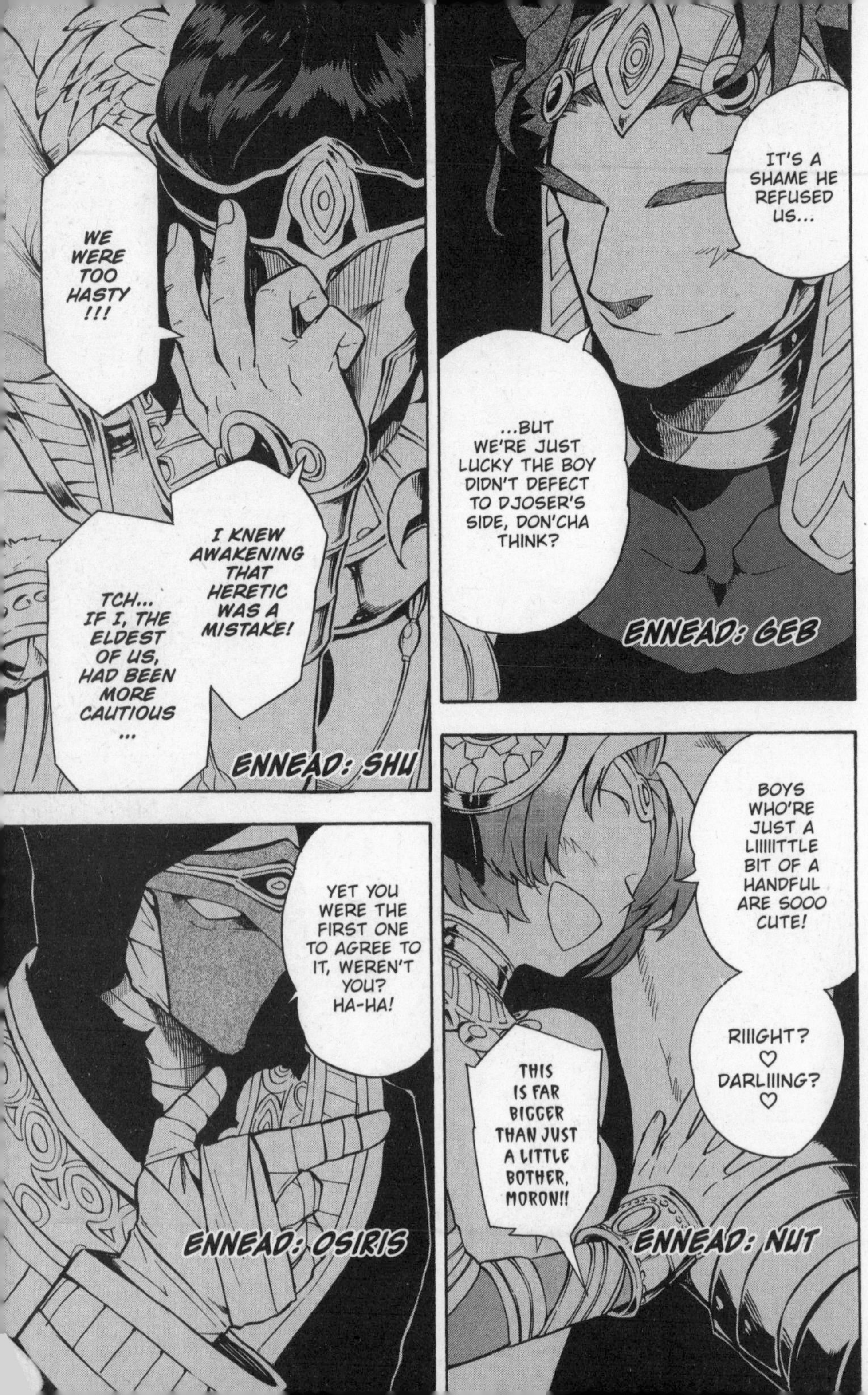
IT'S A SHAME HE REFUSED US...
...BUT WE'RE JUST LUCKY THE BOY DIDN'T DEFECT TO DJOSER'S SIDE, DON'CHA THINK?
ENNEAD: GEB
WE WERE TOO HASTY!!!
I KNEW AWAKENING THAT HERETIC WAS A MISTAKE!
TCH... IF I, THE ELDEST OF US, HAD BEEN MORE CAUTIOUS...
ENNEAD: SHU
BOYS WHO'RE JUST A LIIIIITTLE BIT OF A HANDFUL ARE SOOO CUTE!
RIIIGHT? ♡ DARLIIING? ♡
THIS IS FAR BIGGER THAN JUST A LITTLE BOTHER, MORON!!
ENNEAD: NUT
YET YOU WERE THE FIRST ONE TO AGREE TO IT, WEREN'T YOU? HA-HA!
ENNEAD: OSIRIS

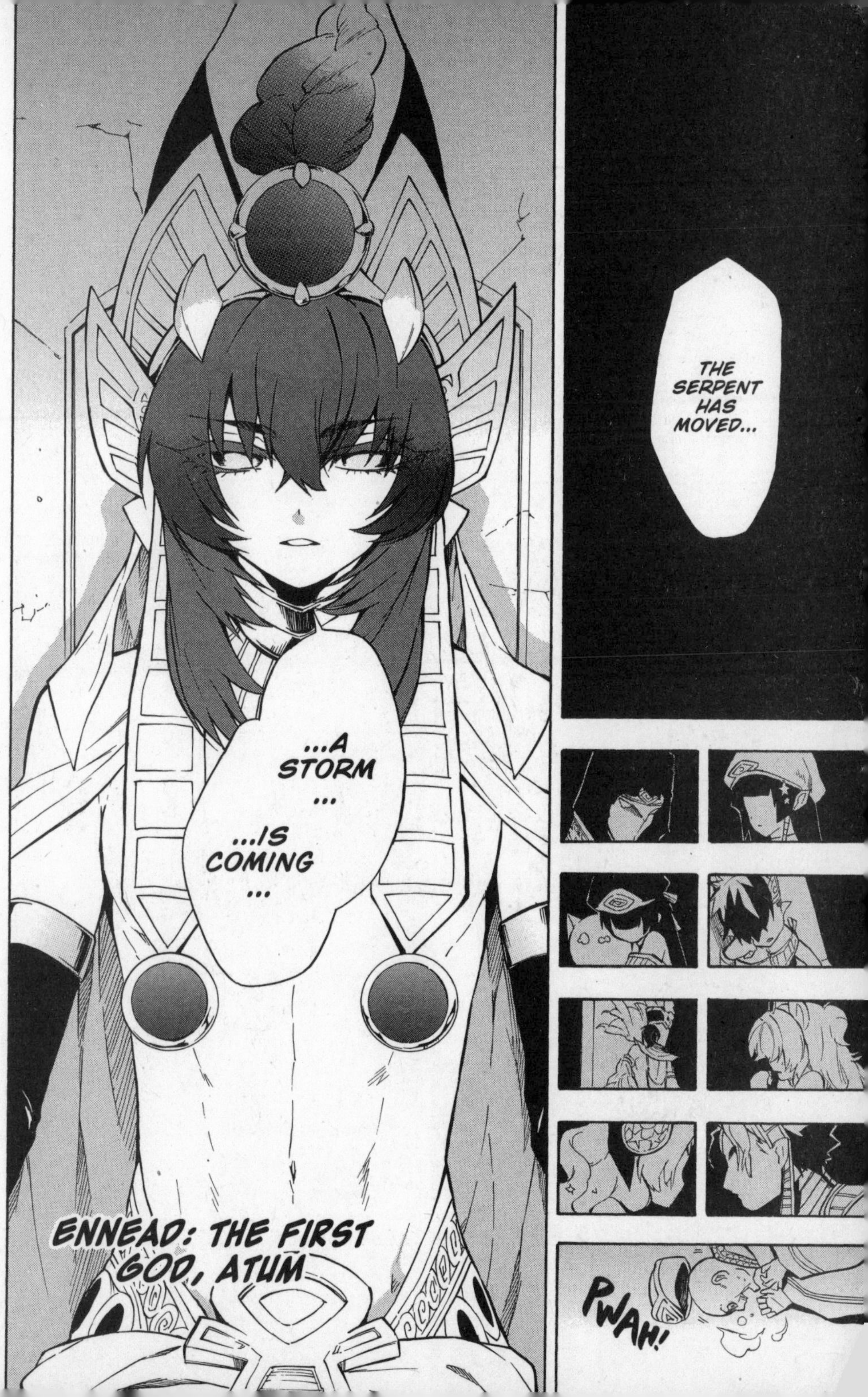
THE SERPENT HAS MOVED...
PWAH!
...A STORM ...
...IS COMING ...
ENNEAD: THE FIRST GOD, ATUM

SCROLL 12: SIGNS OF A STORM

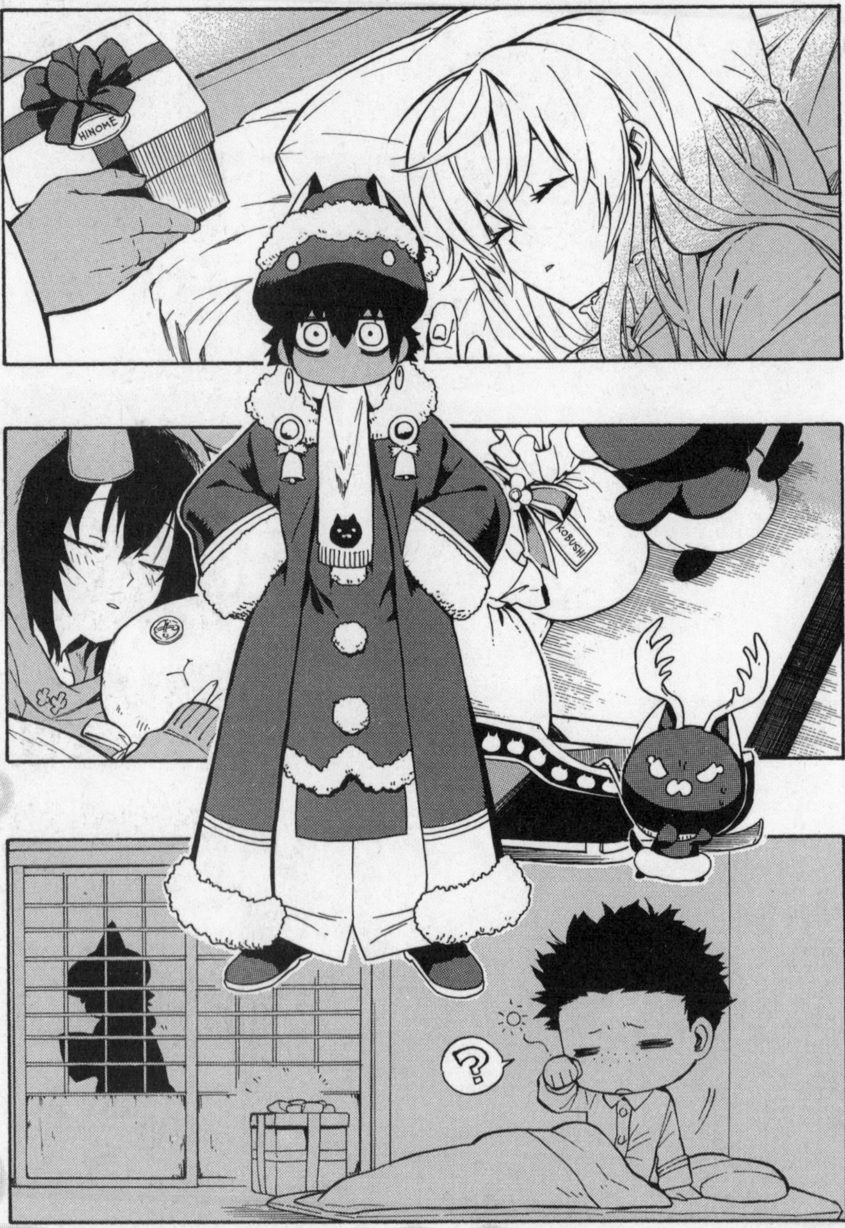
HINOME
KOBUSHI
?

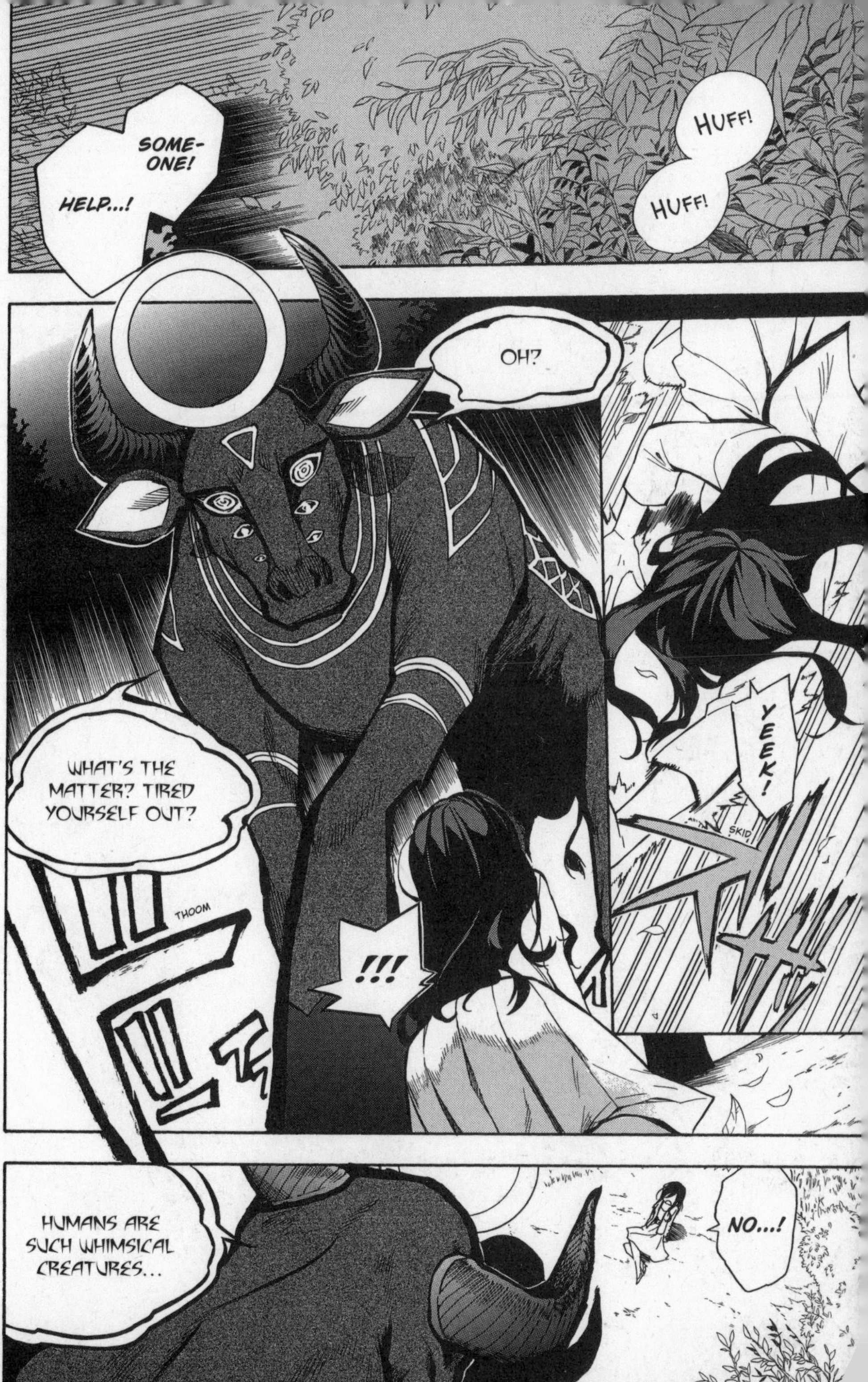
HUFF!
HUFF!
SOME-ONE!
HELP...!
YEEK!
SKID
OH?
WHAT'S THE MATTER? TIRED YOURSELF OUT?
THOOM
!!!
NO...!
HUMANS ARE SUCH WHIMSICAL CREATURES...

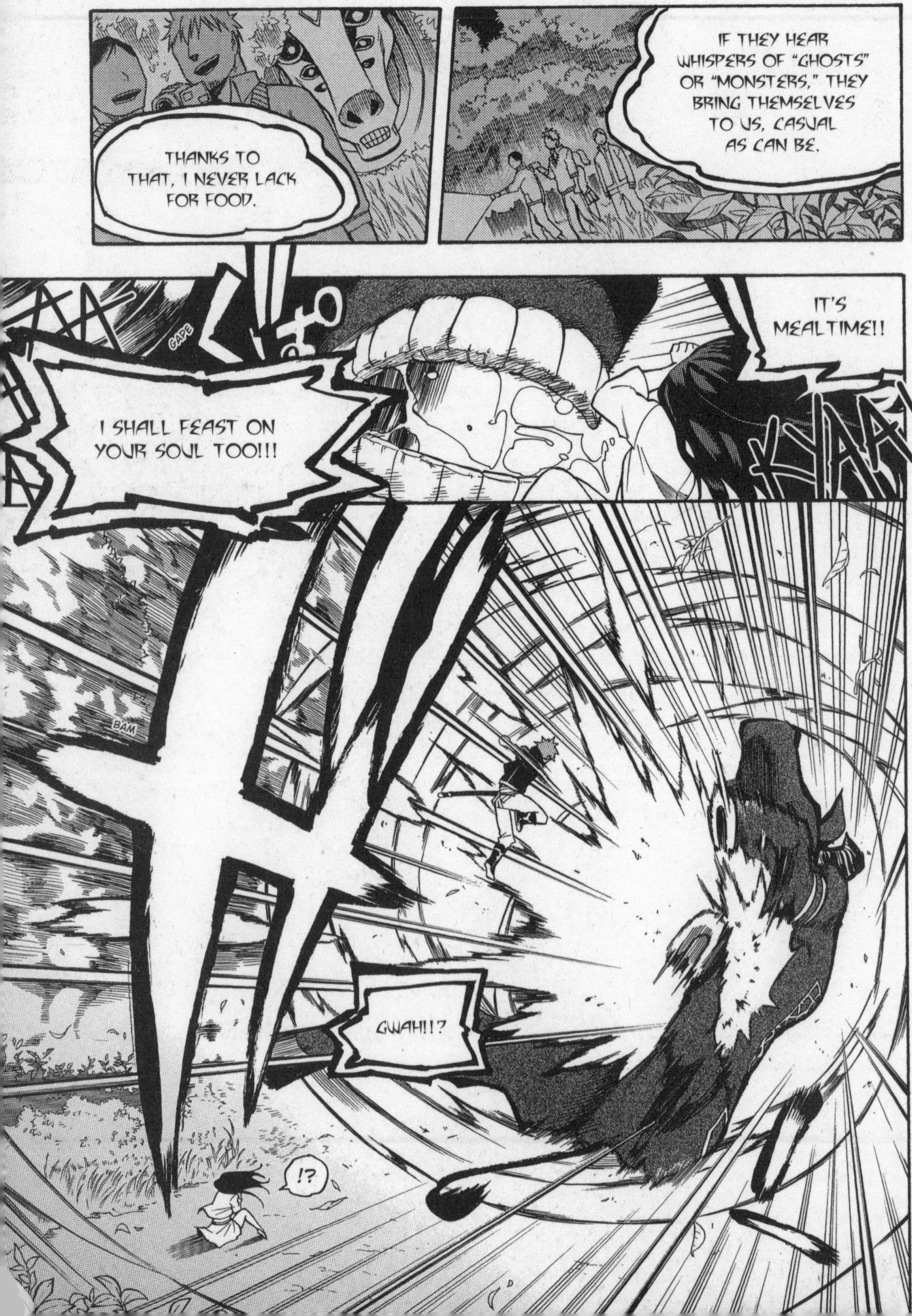
IF THEY HEAR WHISPERS OF "GHOSTS" OR "MONSTERS," THEY BRING THEMSELVES TO US, CASUAL AS CAN BE.
THANKS TO THAT, I NEVER LACK FOR FOOD.
IT'S MEALTIME!!
KYAA!
GAPE
I SHALL FEAST ON YOUR SOUL TOO!!!
BAM
GWAH!!?
!?

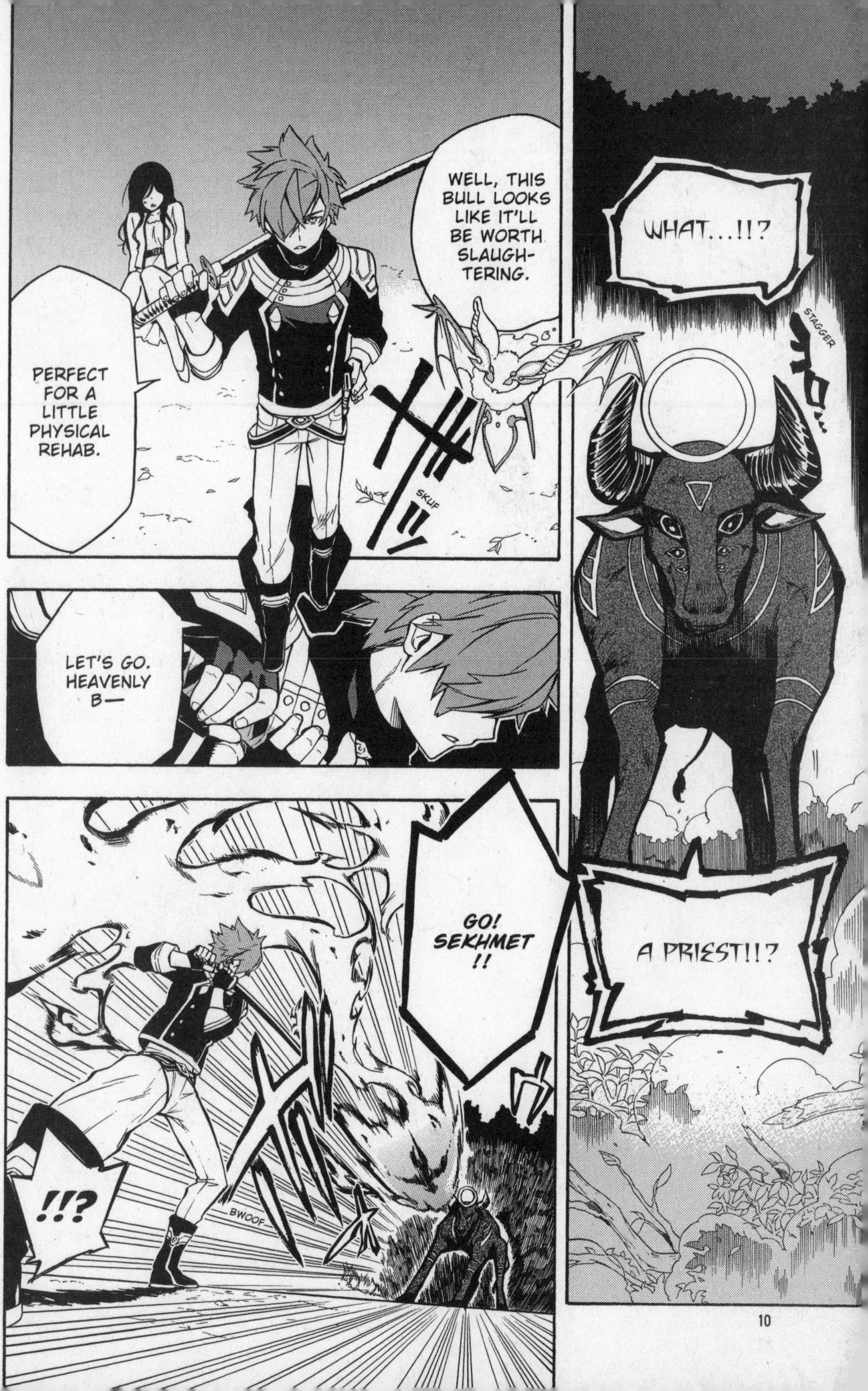
WHAT...!!?
STAGGER
A PRIEST!!?
WELL, THIS BULL LOOKS LIKE IT'LL BE WORTH SLAUGHTERING.
PERFECT FOR A LITTLE PHYSICAL REHAB.
SKUF
LET'S GO. HEAVENLY B—
GO! SEKHMET!!
BWOOF
!!?

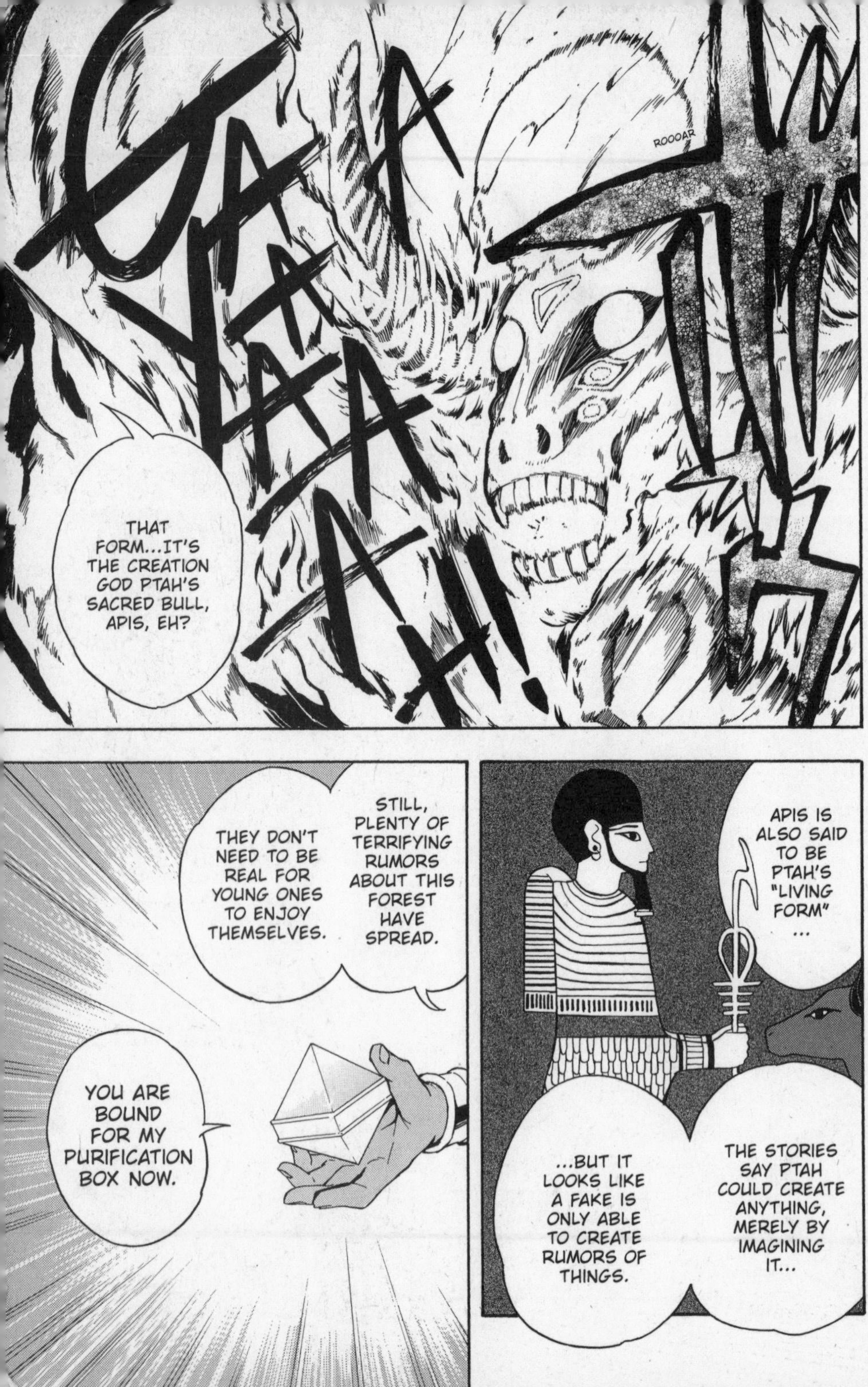
ROOOAR
THAT FORM...IT'S THE CREATION GOD PTAH'S SACRED BULL, APIS, EH?
APIS IS ALSO SAID TO BE PTAH'S "LIVING FORM"...
THE STORIES SAY PTAH COULD CREATE ANYTHING, MERELY BY IMAGINING IT...
...BUT IT LOOKS LIKE A FAKE IS ONLY ABLE TO CREATE RUMORS OF THINGS.
STILL, PLENTY OF TERRIFYING RUMORS ABOUT THIS FOREST HAVE SPREAD.
THEY DON'T NEED TO BE REAL FOR YOUNG ONES TO ENJOY THEMSELVES.
YOU ARE BOUND FOR MY PURIFICATION BOX NOW.

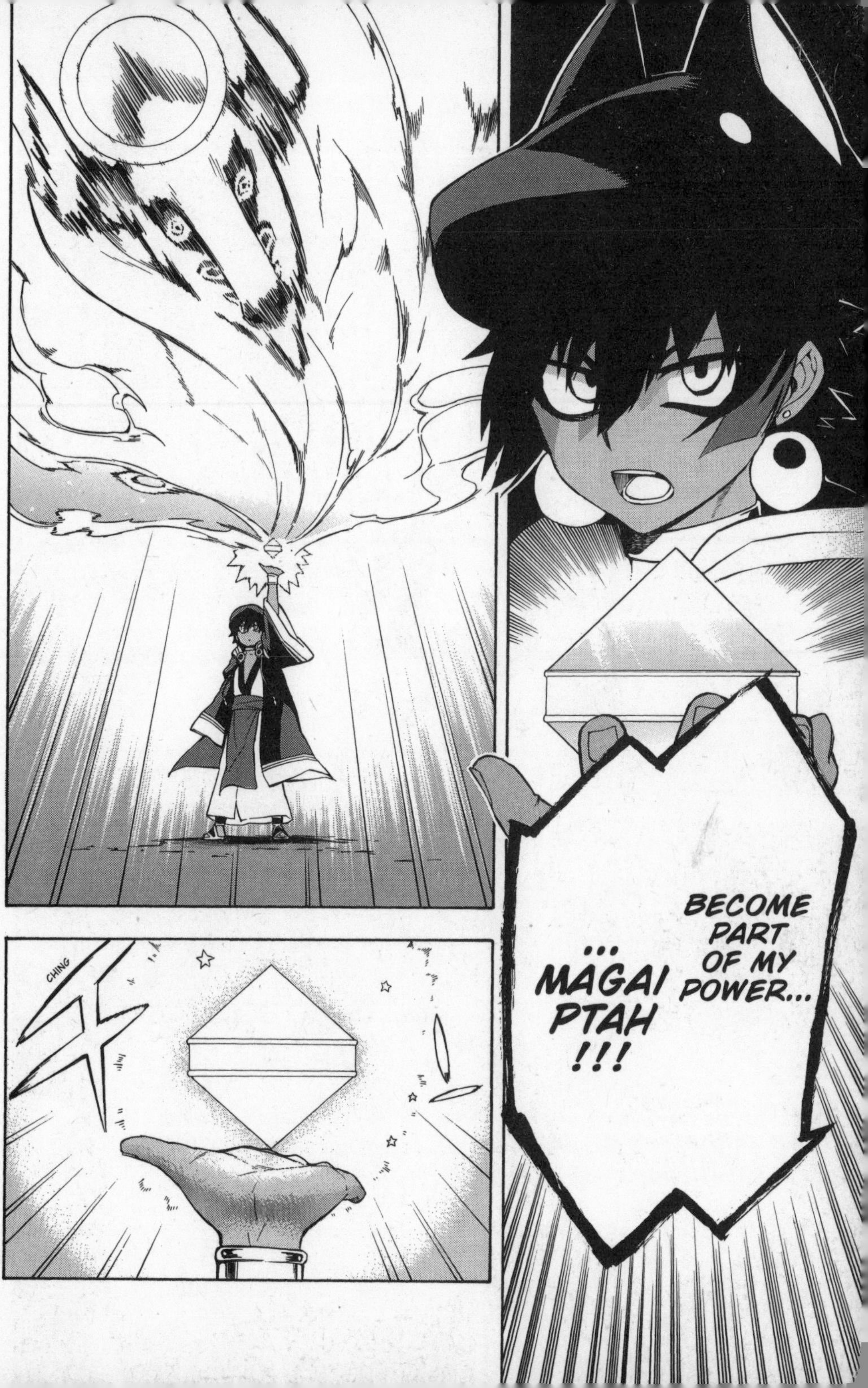
BECOME PART OF MY POWER...
... MÄGAI PTAH !!!
CHING

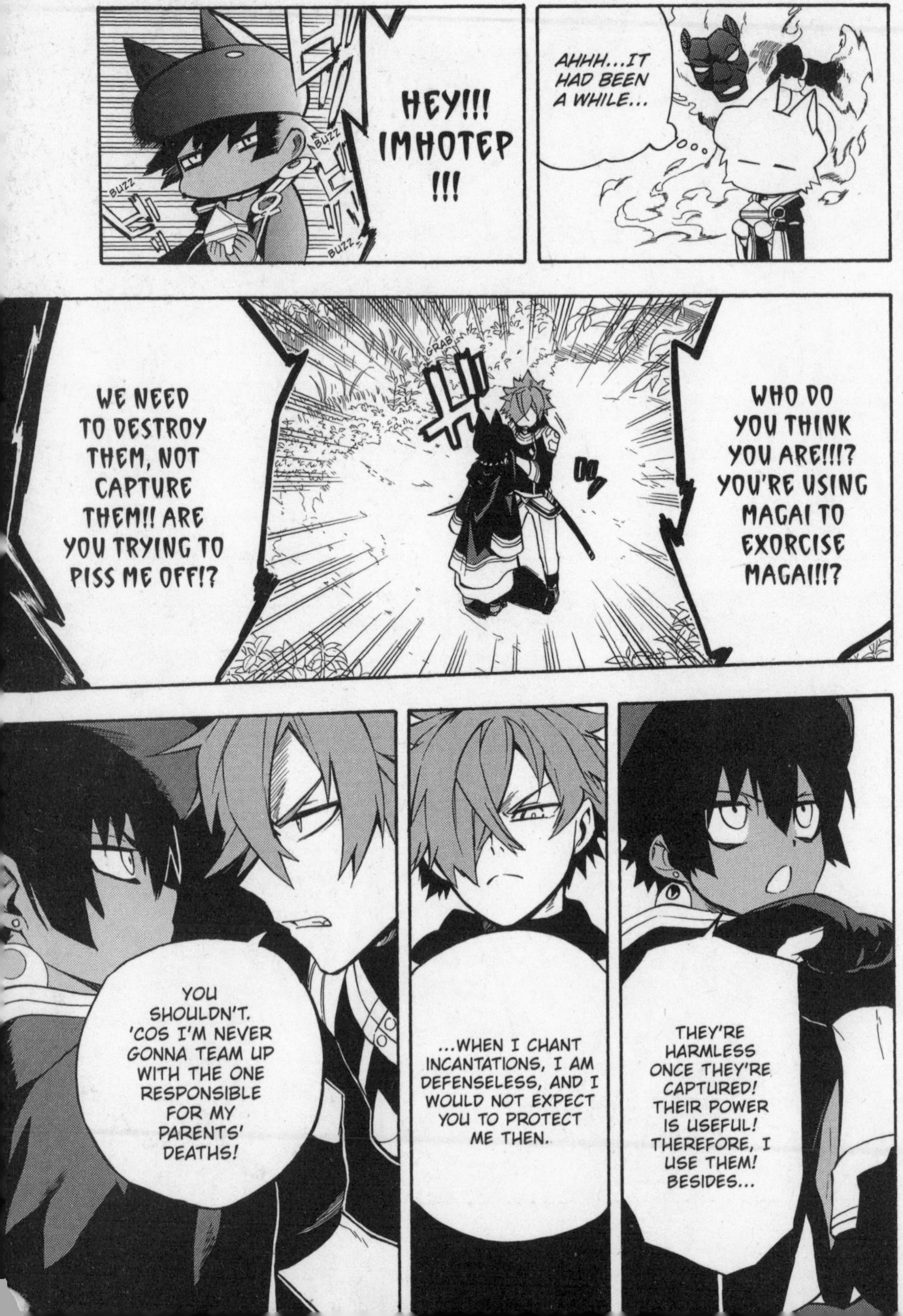
AHHH...IT HAD BEEN A WHILE...
HEY!!! IMHOTEP !!!
BUZZ
BUZZ
BUZZ
WHO DO YOU THINK YOU ARE!!!? YOU'RE USING MAGAI TO EXORCISE MAGAI!!!?
GRAB
WE NEED TO DESTROY THEM, NOT CAPTURE THEM!! ARE YOU TRYING TO PISS ME OFF!?
THEY'RE HARMLESS ONCE THEY'RE CAPTURED! THEIR POWER IS USEFUL! THEREFORE, I USE THEM! BESIDES...
...WHEN I CHANT INCANTATIONS, I AM DEFENSELESS, AND I WOULD NOT EXPECT YOU TO PROTECT ME THEN.
YOU SHOULDN'T. 'COS I'M NEVER GONNA TEAM UP WITH THE ONE RESPONSIBLE FOR MY PARENTS' DEATHS!

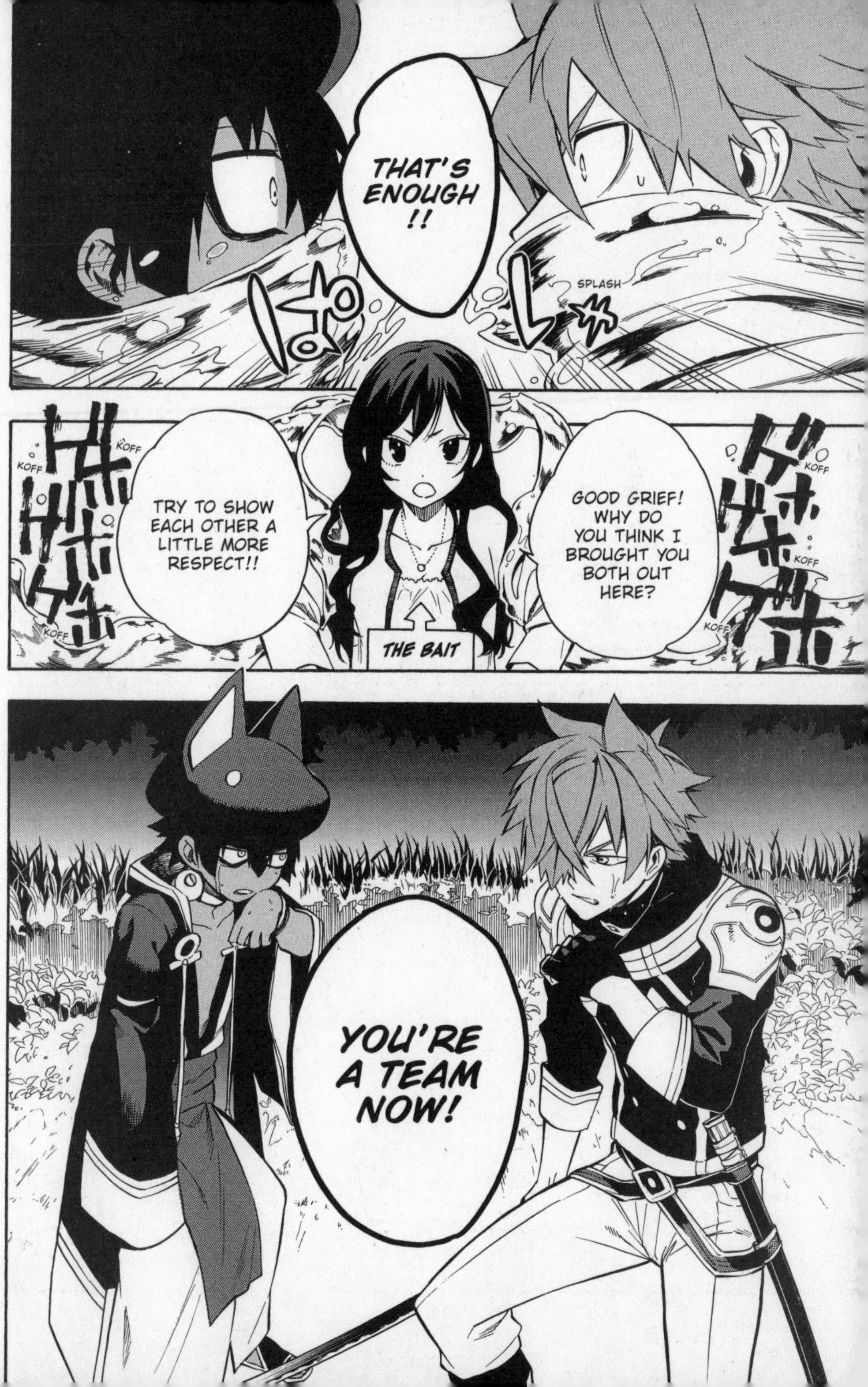
THAT'S ENOUGH!!
SPLASH
GOOD GRIEF! WHY DO YOU THINK I BROUGHT YOU BOTH OUT HERE?
KOFF
KOFF
KOFF
THE BAIT
TRY TO SHOW EACH OTHER A LITTLE MORE RESPECT!!
KOFF
KOFF
KOFF
YOU'RE A TEAM NOW!

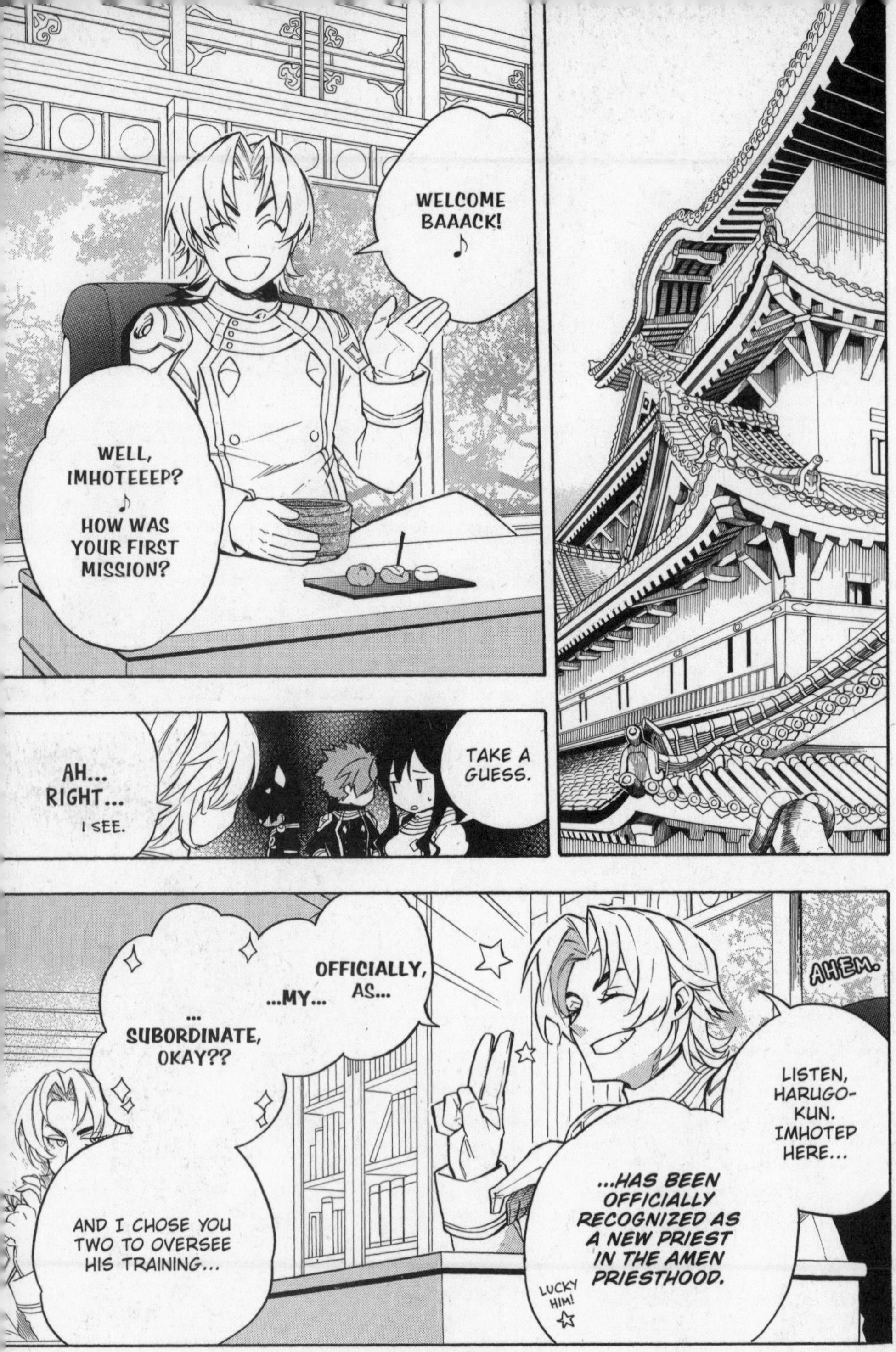
WELCOME BAAACK! ♪
WELL, IMHOTEEEP? ♪ HOW WAS YOUR FIRST MISSION?
TAKE A GUESS.
AH... RIGHT... I SEE.
AHEM.
LISTEN, HARUGO-KUN. IMHOTEP HERE...
...HAS BEEN OFFICIALLY RECOGNIZED AS A NEW PRIEST IN THE AMEN PRIESTHOOD.
LUCKY HIM! ☆
AND I CHOSE YOU TWO TO OVERSEE HIS TRAINING...
OFFICIALLY, AS...
...MY...
... SUBORDINATE, OKAY??

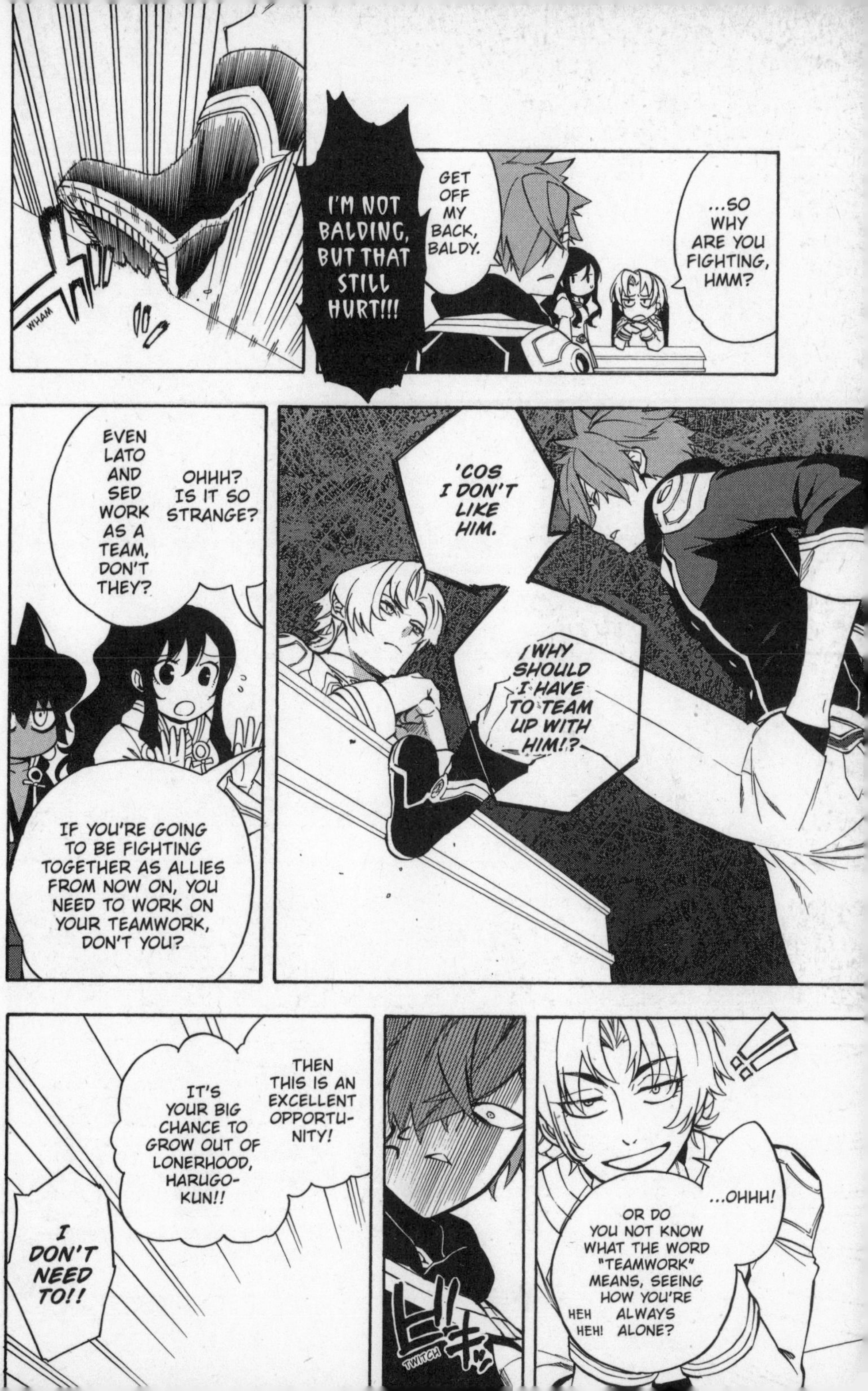
...SO WHY ARE YOU FIGHTING, HMM?
GET OFF MY BACK, BALDY.
WHAM
I'M NOT BALDING, BUT THAT STILL HURT!!!
'COS I DON'T LIKE HIM.
WHY SHOULD I HAVE TO TEAM UP WITH HIM!?
OHHH? IS IT SO STRANGE?
EVEN LATO AND SED WORK AS A TEAM, DON'T THEY?
IF YOU'RE GOING TO BE FIGHTING TOGETHER AS ALLIES FROM NOW ON, YOU NEED TO WORK ON YOUR TEAMWORK, DON'T YOU?
...OHHH!
OR DO YOU NOT KNOW WHAT THE WORD "TEAMWORK" MEANS, SEEING HOW YOU'RE ALWAYS ALONE?
HEH HEH!
TWITCH
THEN THIS IS AN EXCELLENT OPPORTU-NITY!
IT'S YOUR BIG CHANCE TO GROW OUT OF LONERHOOD, HARUGO-KUN!!
I DON'T NEED TO!!

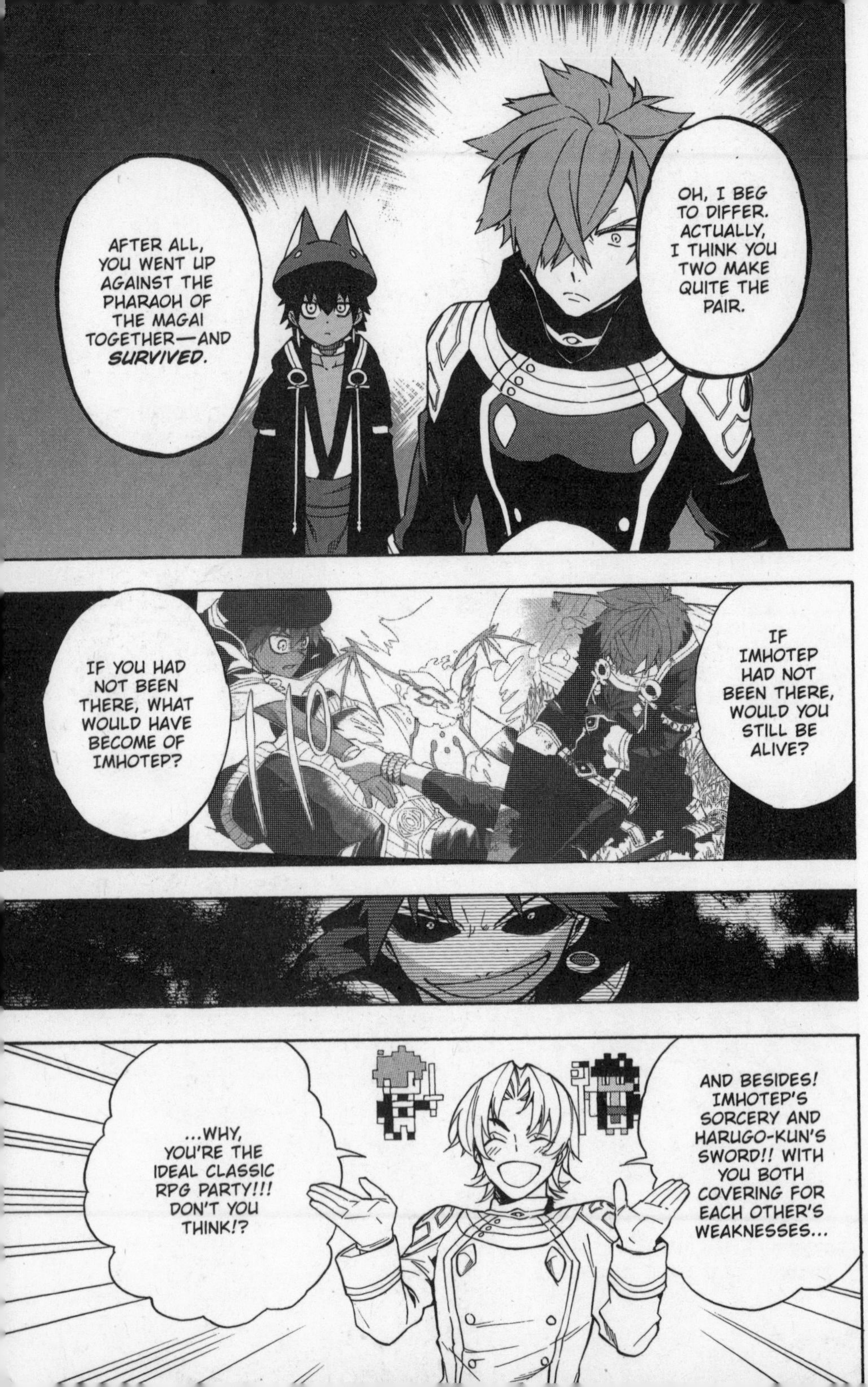
OH, I BEG TO DIFFER. ACTUALLY, I THINK YOU TWO MAKE QUITE THE PAIR.
AFTER ALL, YOU WENT UP AGAINST THE PHARAOH OF THE MAGAI TOGETHER—AND *SURVIVED*.
IF IMHOTEP HAD NOT BEEN THERE, WOULD YOU STILL BE ALIVE?
IF YOU HAD NOT BEEN THERE, WHAT WOULD HAVE BECOME OF IMHOTEP?
AND BESIDES! IMHOTEP'S SORCERY AND HARUGO-KUN'S SWORD!! WITH YOU BOTH COVERING FOR EACH OTHER'S WEAKNESSES...
...WHY, YOU'RE THE IDEAL CLASSIC RPG PARTY!!! DON'T YOU THINK!?

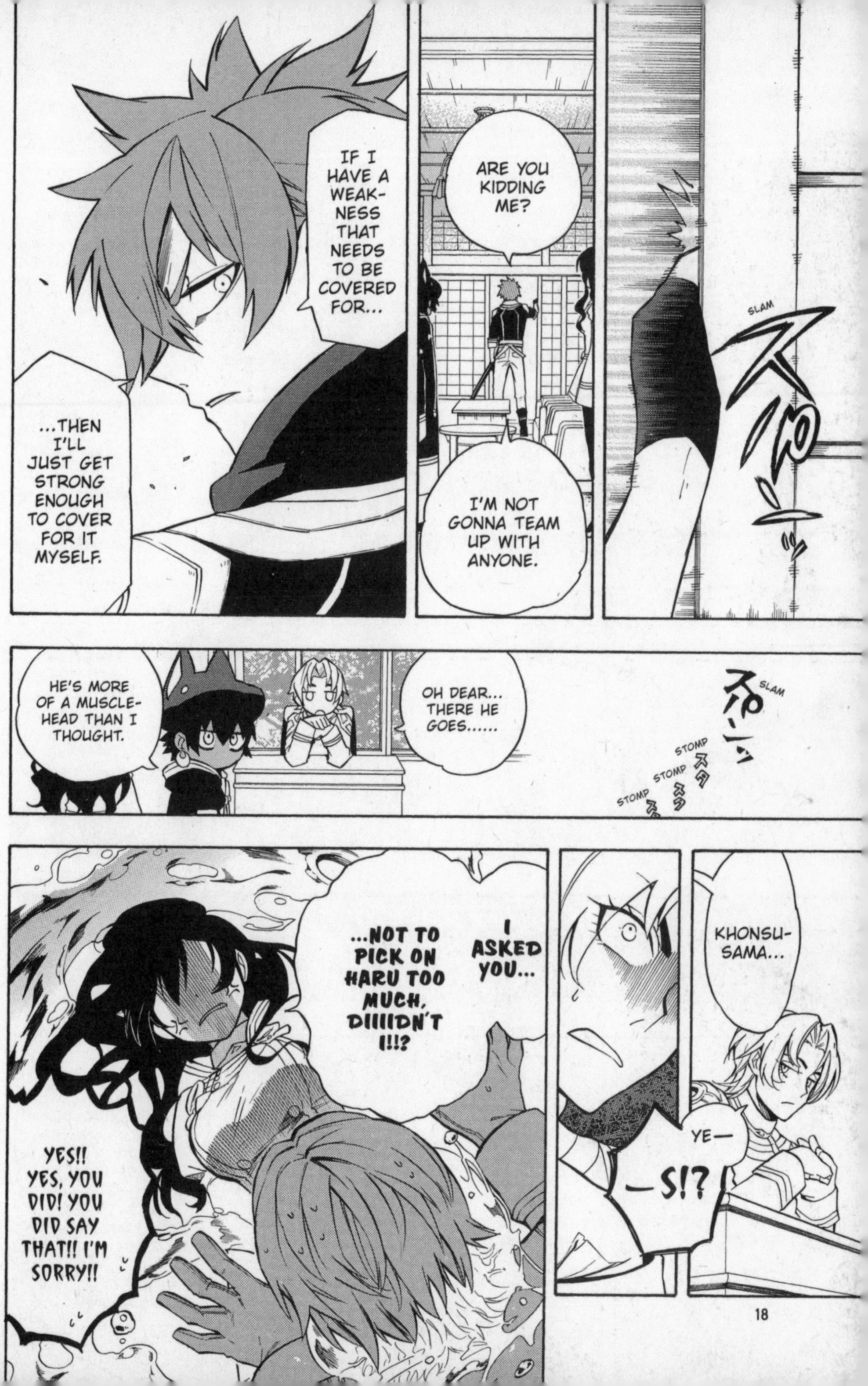
SLAM
ARE YOU KIDDING ME?
I'M NOT GONNA TEAM UP WITH ANYONE.
IF I HAVE A WEAKNESS THAT NEEDS TO BE COVERED FOR...
...THEN I'LL JUST GET STRONG ENOUGH TO COVER FOR IT MYSELF.
SLAM
STOMP STOMP STOMP
OH DEAR... THERE HE GOES......
HE'S MORE OF A MUSCLE-HEAD THAN I THOUGHT.
KHONSU-SAMA...
YE—
—S!?
I ASKED YOU...
...NOT TO PICK ON HARU TOO MUCH, DIIIIDN'T I!!?
YES!! YES, YOU DID! YOU DID SAY THAT!! I'M SORRY!!

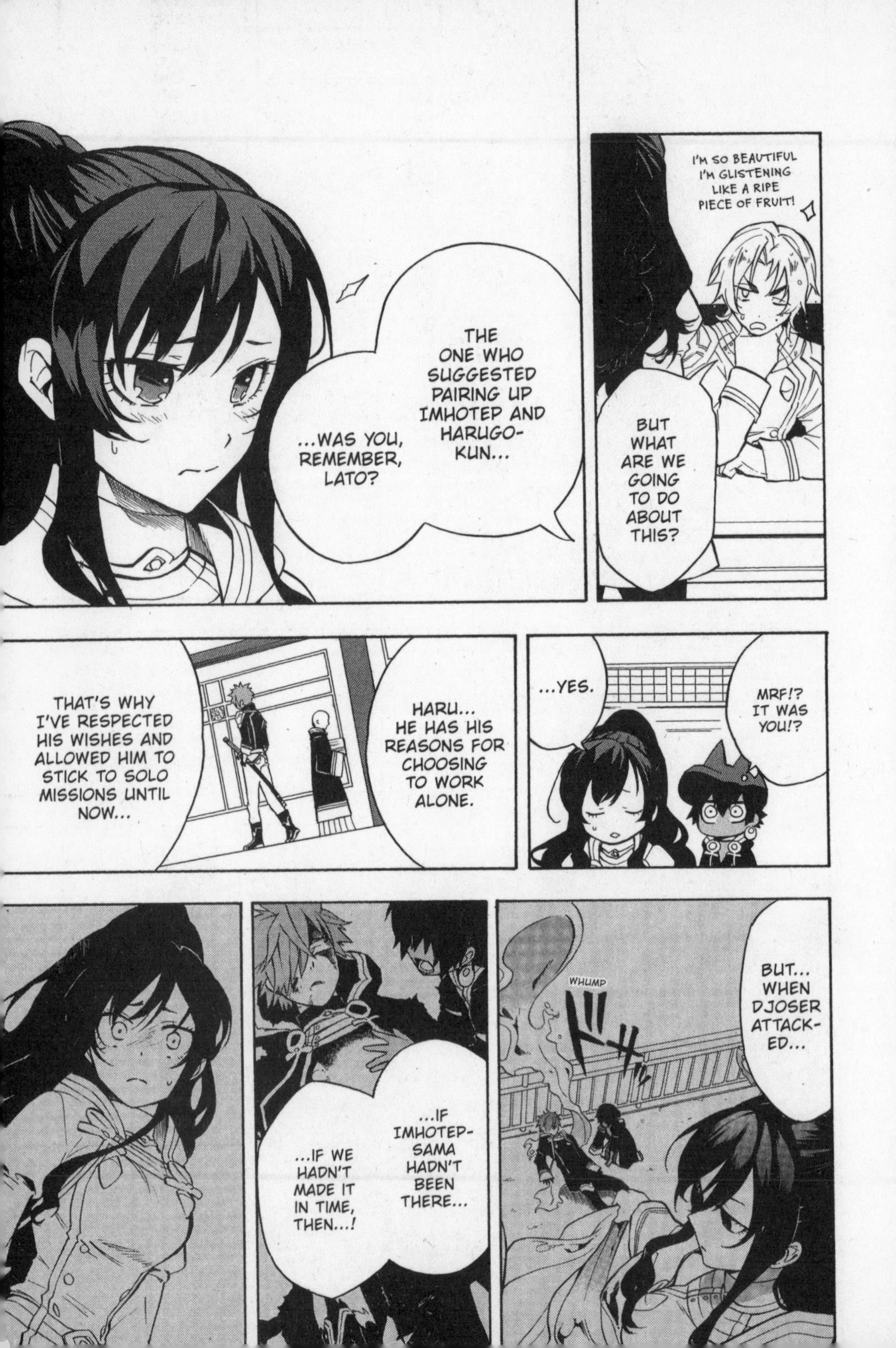
I'M SO BEAUTIFUL I'M GLISTENING LIKE A RIPE PIECE OF FRUIT!
BUT WHAT ARE WE GOING TO DO ABOUT THIS?
THE ONE WHO SUGGESTED PAIRING UP IMHOTEP AND HARUGO-KUN...
...WAS YOU, REMEMBER, LATO?
MRF!? IT WAS YOU!?
...YES.
HARU... HE HAS HIS REASONS FOR CHOOSING TO WORK ALONE.
THAT'S WHY I'VE RESPECTED HIS WISHES AND ALLOWED HIM TO STICK TO SOLO MISSIONS UNTIL NOW...
BUT... WHEN DJOSER ATTACK-ED...
WHUMP
...IF IMHOTEP-SAMA HADN'T BEEN THERE...
...IF WE HADN'T MADE IT IN TIME, THEN...!

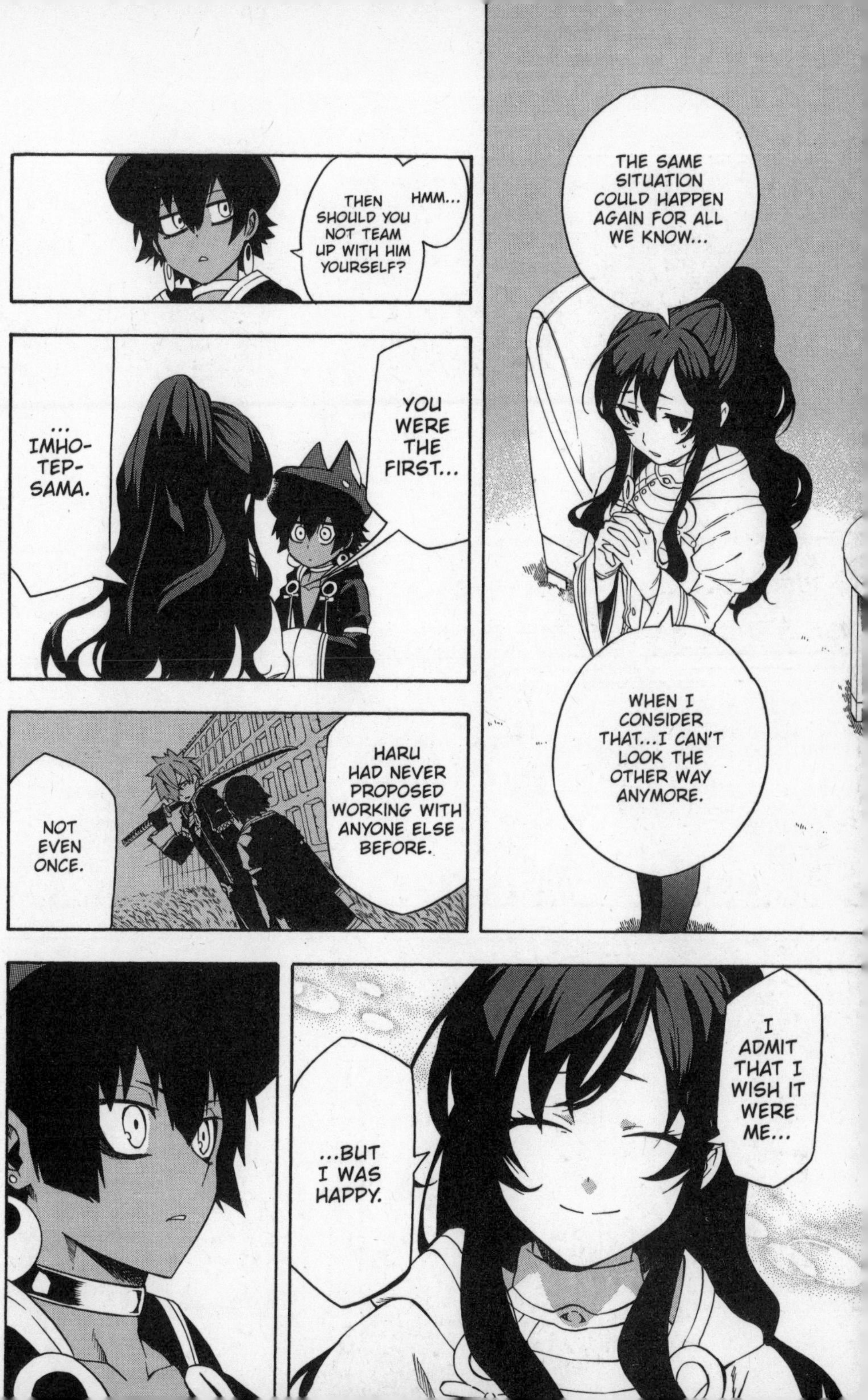
THE SAME SITUATION COULD HAPPEN AGAIN FOR ALL WE KNOW...
WHEN I CONSIDER THAT...I CAN'T LOOK THE OTHER WAY ANYMORE.
HMM...
THEN SHOULD YOU NOT TEAM UP WITH HIM YOURSELF?
YOU WERE THE FIRST...
...IMHOTEP-SAMA.
HARU HAD NEVER PROPOSED WORKING WITH ANYONE ELSE BEFORE.
NOT EVEN ONCE.
I ADMIT THAT I WISH IT WERE ME...
...BUT I WAS HAPPY.

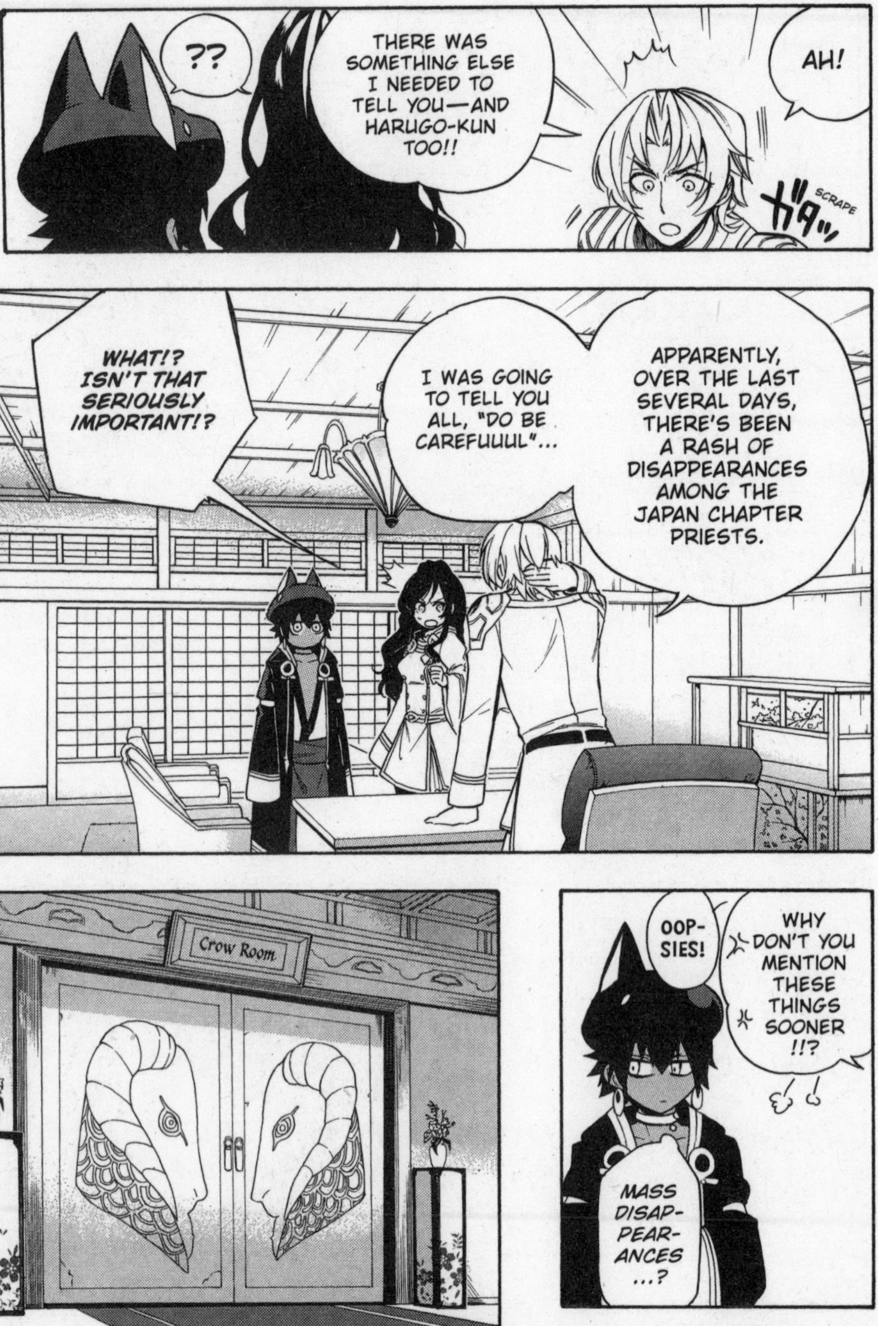
AH!
SCRAPE
THERE WAS SOMETHING ELSE I NEEDED TO TELL YOU—AND HARUGO-KUN TOO!!
??
APPARENTLY, OVER THE LAST SEVERAL DAYS, THERE'S BEEN A RASH OF DISAPPEARANCES AMONG THE JAPAN CHAPTER PRIESTS.
I WAS GOING TO TELL YOU ALL, "DO BE CAREFUUUL"...
WHAT!? ISN'T THAT SERIOUSLY IMPORTANT!?
WHY DON'T YOU MENTION THESE THINGS SOONER!!?
OOP-SIES!
MASS DISAP-PEAR-ANCES...?
Crow Room

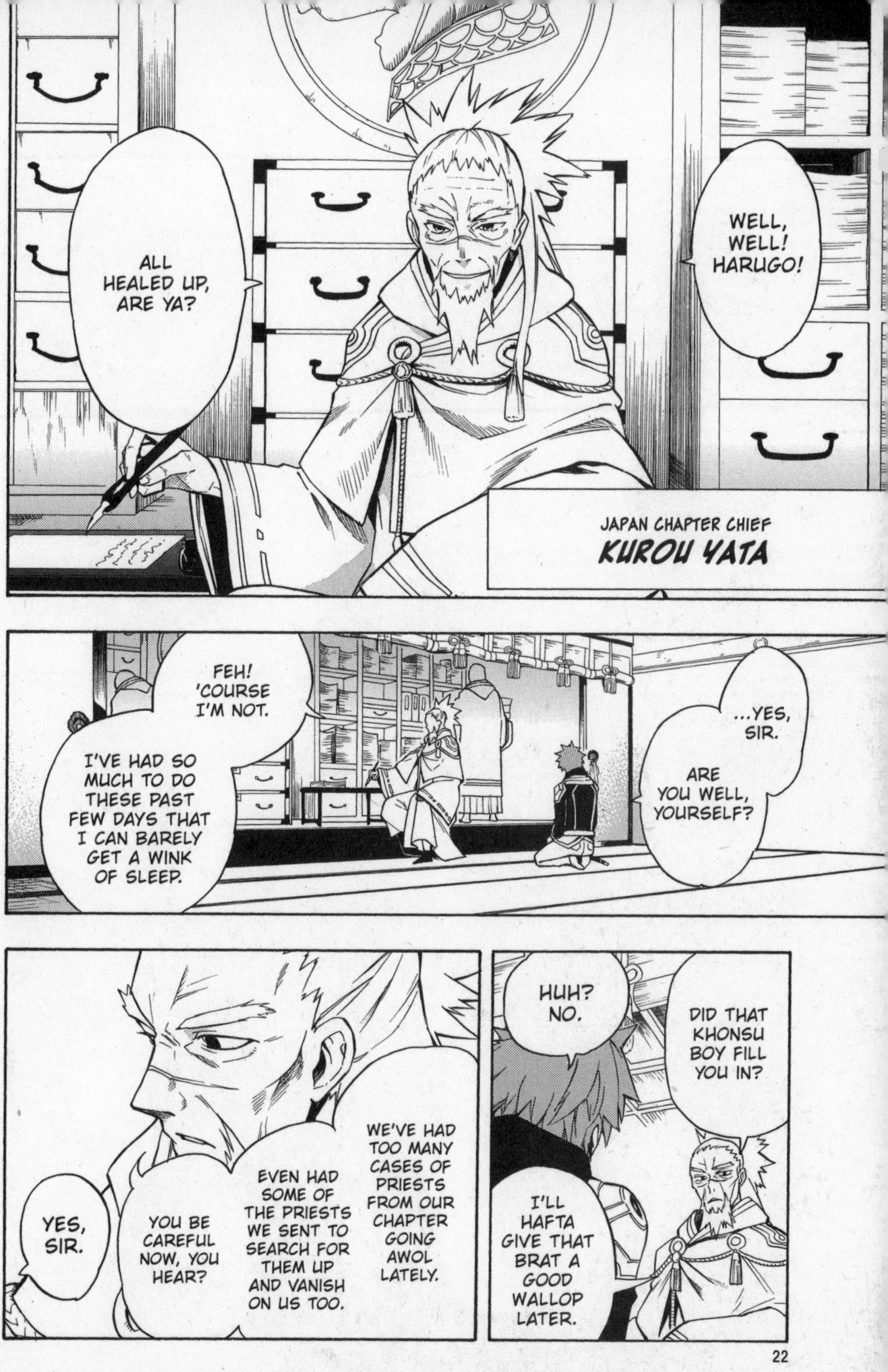
WELL, WELL! HARUGO!
JAPAN CHAPTER CHIEF KUROU YATA
ALL HEALED UP, ARE YA?
...YES, SIR.
ARE YOU WELL, YOURSELF?
FEH! 'COURSE I'M NOT.
I'VE HAD SO MUCH TO DO THESE PAST FEW DAYS THAT I CAN BARELY GET A WINK OF SLEEP.
DID THAT KHONSU BOY FILL YOU IN?
HUH? NO.
I'LL HAFTA GIVE THAT BRAT A GOOD WALLOP LATER.
WE'VE HAD TOO MANY CASES OF PRIESTS FROM OUR CHAPTER GOING AWOL LATELY.
EVEN HAD SOME OF THE PRIESTS WE SENT TO SEARCH FOR THEM UP AND VANISH ON US TOO.
YOU BE CAREFUL NOW, YOU HEAR?
YES, SIR.

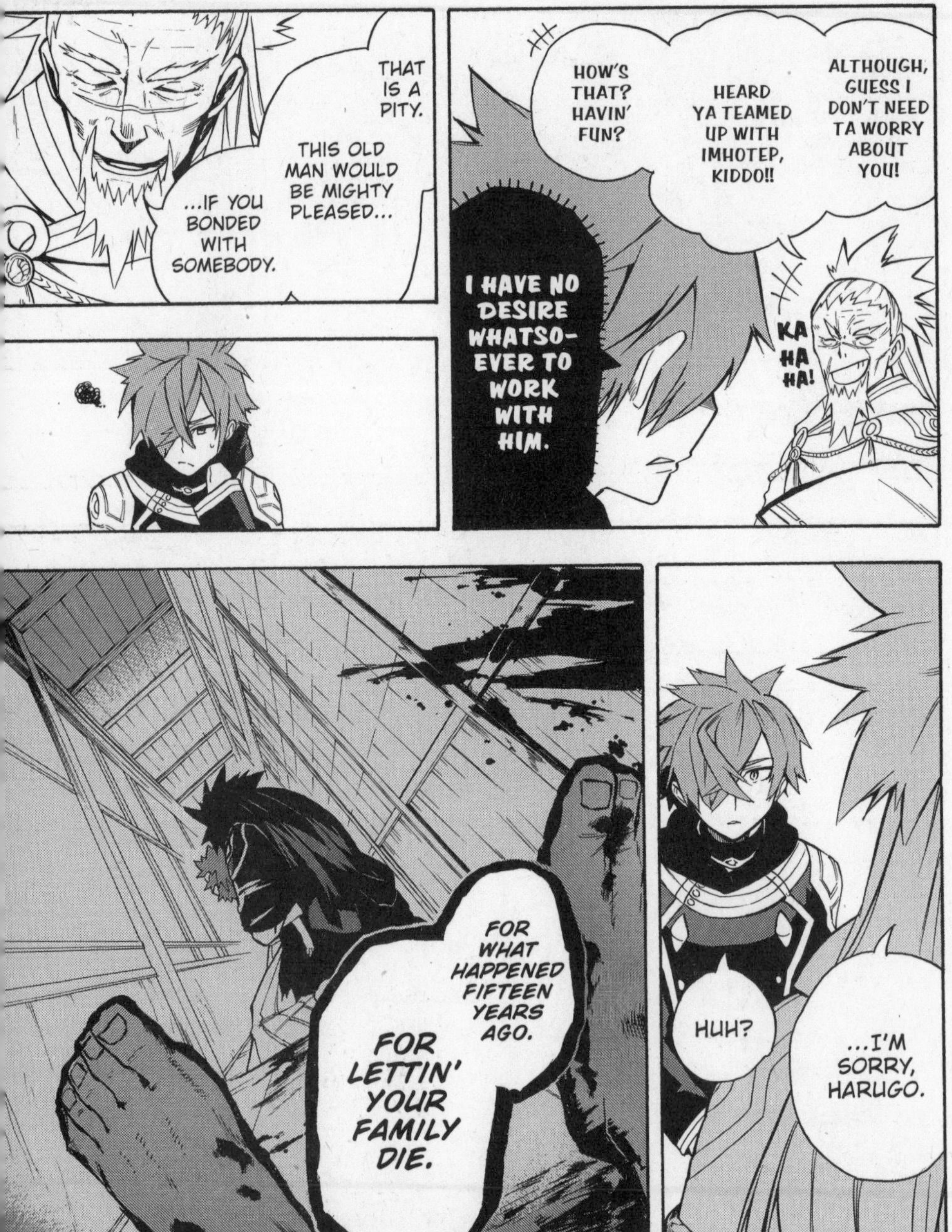
HOW'S THAT? HAVIN' FUN?
HEARD YA TEAMED UP WITH IMHOTEP, KIDDO!!
ALTHOUGH, GUESS I DON'T NEED TA WORRY ABOUT YOU!
KA HA HA!
I HAVE NO DESIRE WHATSO-EVER TO WORK WITH HIM.
THAT IS A PITY.
THIS OLD MAN WOULD BE MIGHTY PLEASED...
...IF YOU BONDED WITH SOMEBODY.
...I'M SORRY, HARUGO.
HUH?
FOR WHAT HAPPENED FIFTEEN YEARS AGO.
FOR LETTIN' YOUR FAMILY DIE.

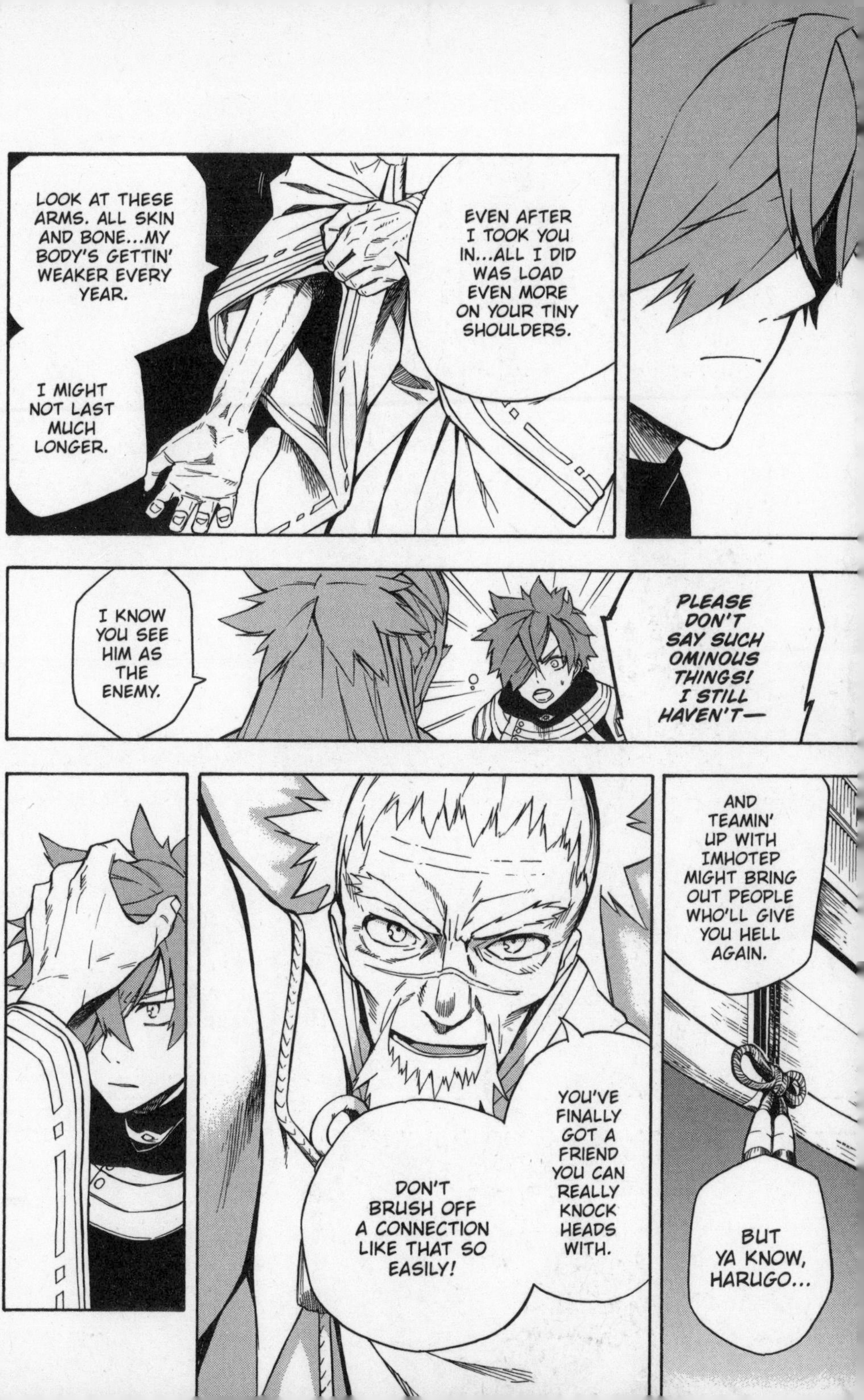
EVEN AFTER I TOOK YOU IN...ALL I DID WAS LOAD EVEN MORE ON YOUR TINY SHOULDERS.
LOOK AT THESE ARMS. ALL SKIN AND BONE...MY BODY'S GETTIN' WEAKER EVERY YEAR.
I MIGHT NOT LAST MUCH LONGER.
PLEASE DON'T SAY SUCH OMINOUS THINGS! I STILL HAVEN'T—
I KNOW YOU SEE HIM AS THE ENEMY.
AND TEAMIN' UP WITH IMHOTEP MIGHT BRING OUT PEOPLE WHO'LL GIVE YOU HELL AGAIN.
BUT YA KNOW, HARUGO...
YOU'VE FINALLY GOT A FRIEND YOU CAN REALLY KNOCK HEADS WITH.
DON'T BRUSH OFF A CONNECTION LIKE THAT SO EASILY!

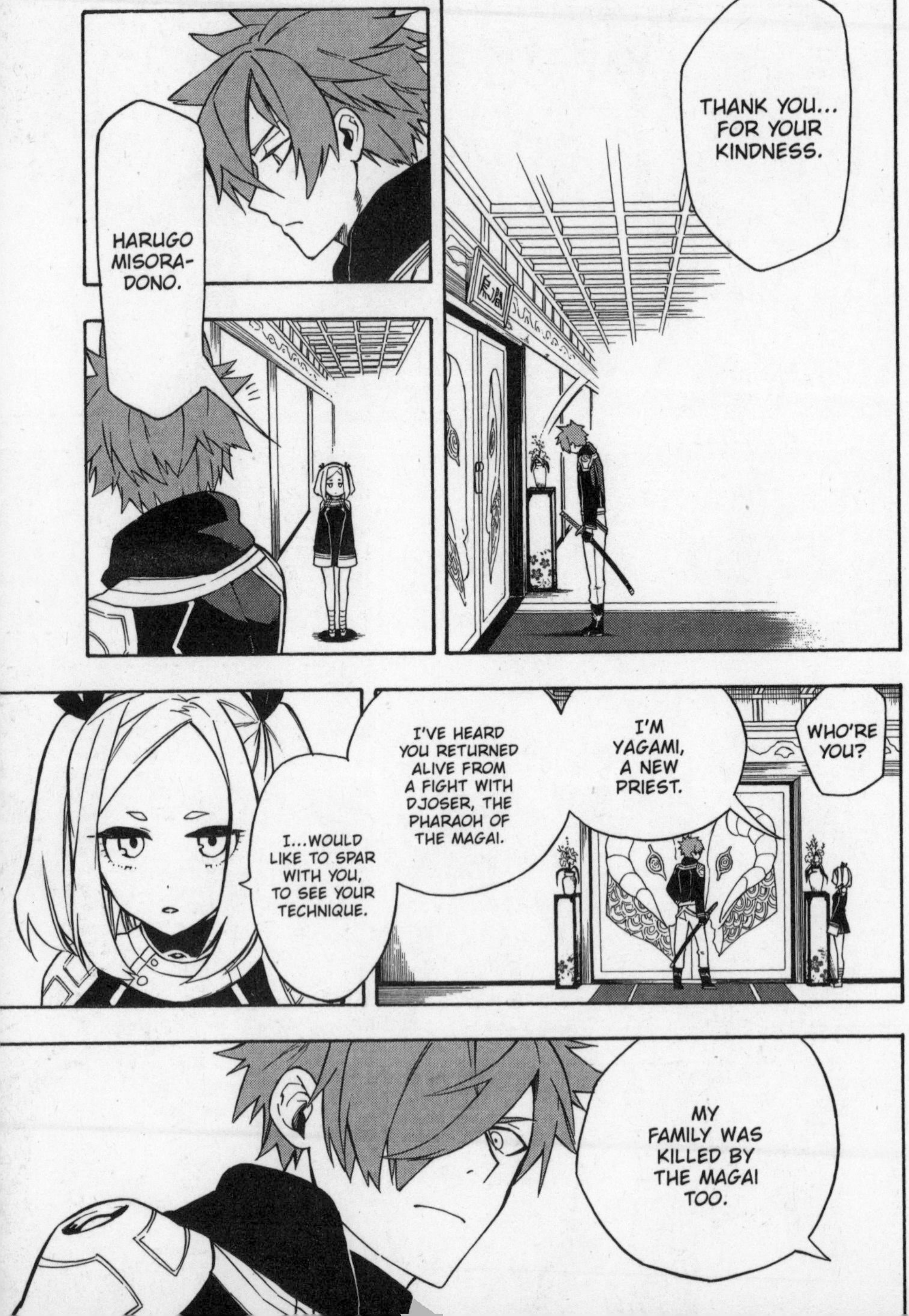
THANK YOU... FOR YOUR KINDNESS.
HARUGO MISORA-DONO.
WHO'RE YOU?
I'M YAGAMI, A NEW PRIEST.
I'VE HEARD YOU RETURNED ALIVE FROM A FIGHT WITH DJOSER, THE PHARAOH OF THE MAGAI.
I...WOULD LIKE TO SPAR WITH YOU, TO SEE YOUR TECHNIQUE.
MY FAMILY WAS KILLED BY THE MAGAI TOO.

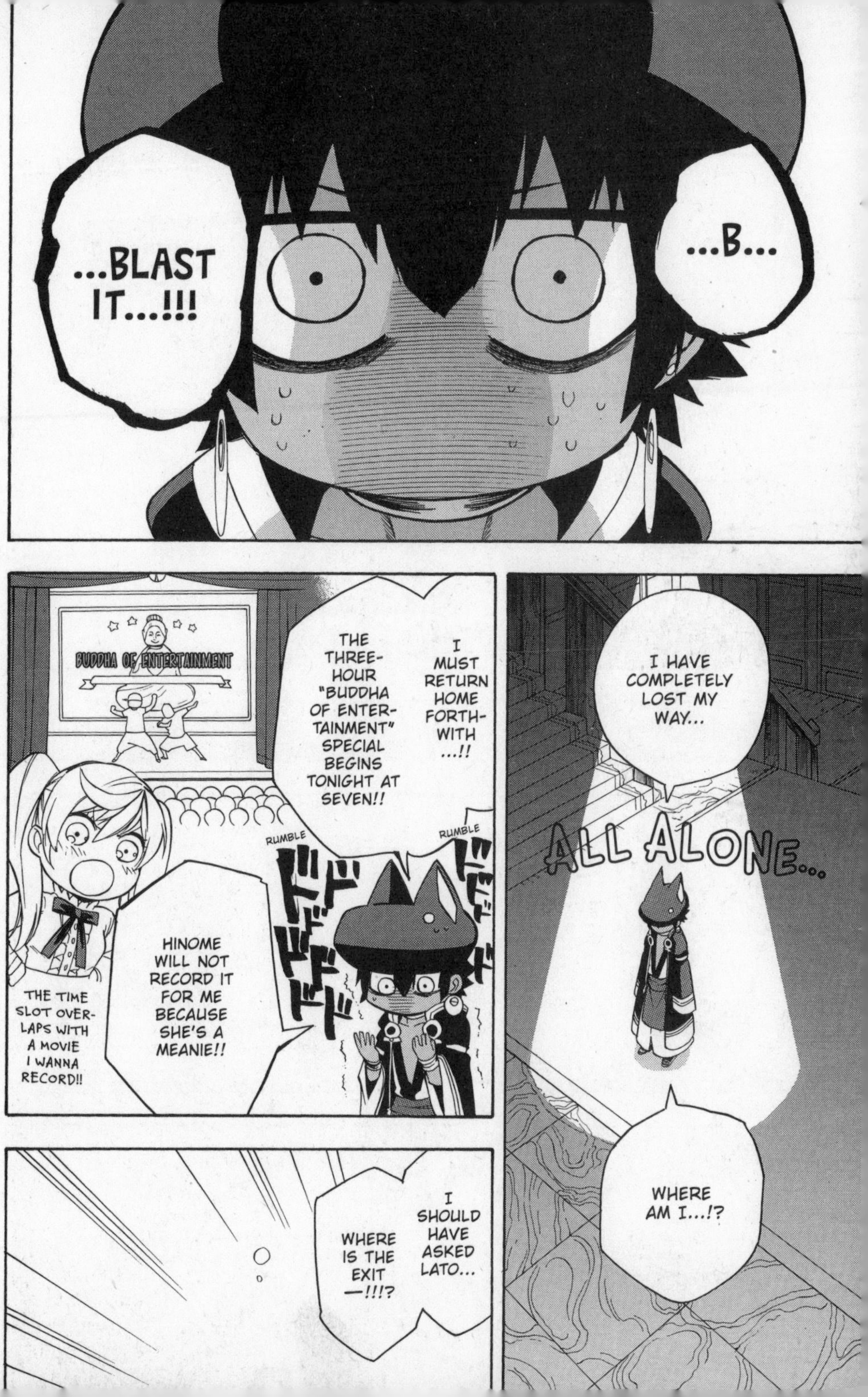
...B...
...BLAST IT...!!!
I HAVE COMPLETELY LOST MY WAY...
ALL ALONE...
WHERE AM I...!?
I MUST RETURN HOME FORTHWITH...!!
THE THREE-HOUR "BUDDHA OF ENTERTAINMENT" SPECIAL BEGINS TONIGHT AT SEVEN!!
BUDDHA OF ENTERTAINMENT
RUMBLE
RUMBLE
HINOME WILL NOT RECORD IT FOR ME BECAUSE SHE'S A MEANIE!!
THE TIME SLOT OVERLAPS WITH A MOVIE I WANNA RECORD!!
I SHOULD HAVE ASKED LATO...
WHERE IS THE EXIT—!!!?

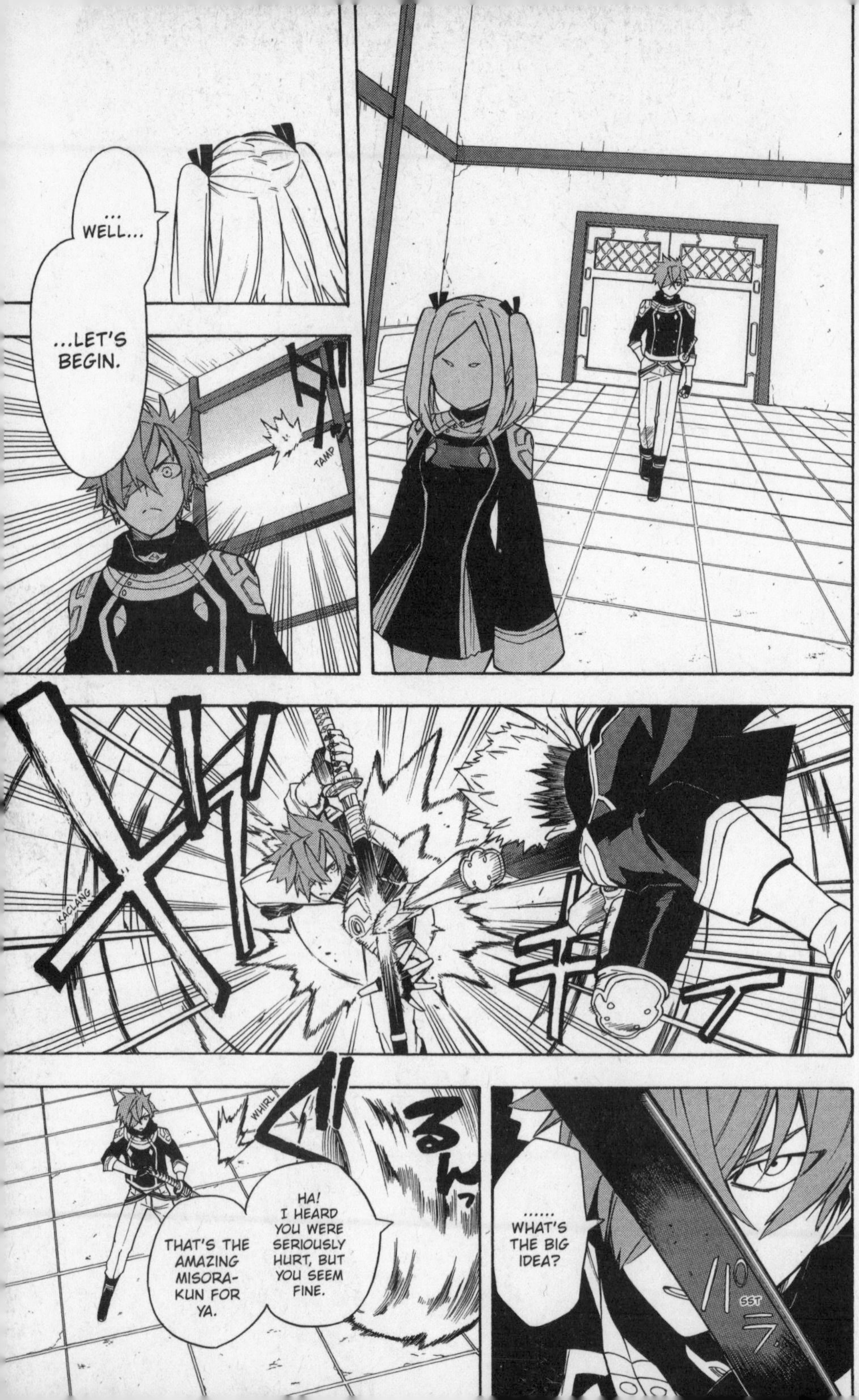
... WELL...
...LET'S BEGIN.
TAMP
KACLANG
...... WHAT'S THE BIG IDEA?
SST
WHIRL
HA! I HEARD YOU WERE SERIOUSLY HURT, BUT YOU SEEM FINE.
THAT'S THE AMAZING MISORA-KUN FOR YA.

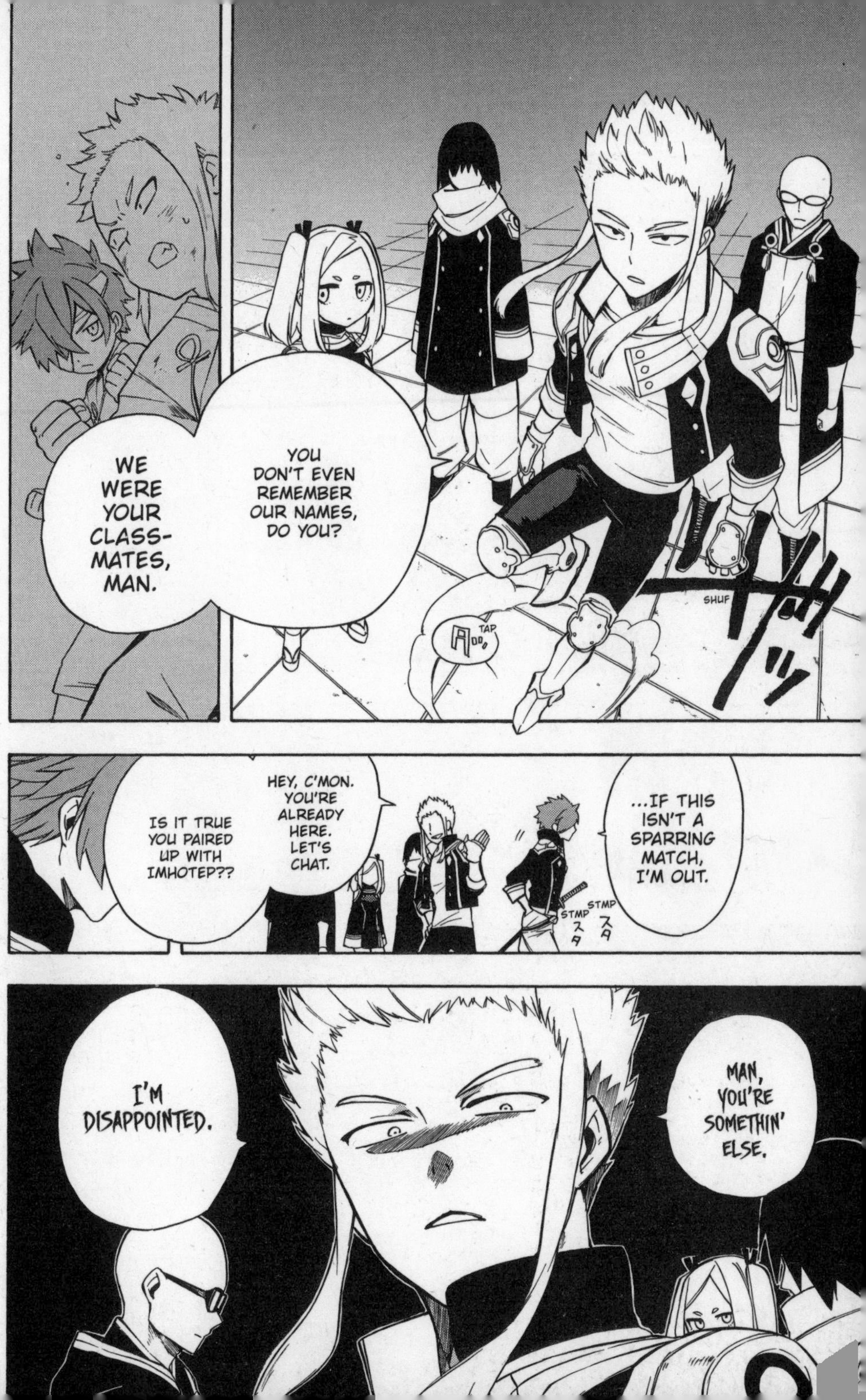
SHUF
YOU DON'T EVEN REMEMBER OUR NAMES, DO YOU?
TAP
WE WERE YOUR CLASS-MATES, MAN.
...IF THIS ISN'T A SPARRING MATCH, I'M OUT.
STMP STMP
HEY, C'MON. YOU'RE ALREADY HERE. LET'S CHAT.
IS IT TRUE YOU PAIRED UP WITH IMHOTEP??
MAN, YOU'RE SOMETHIN' ELSE.
I'M DISAPPOINTED.

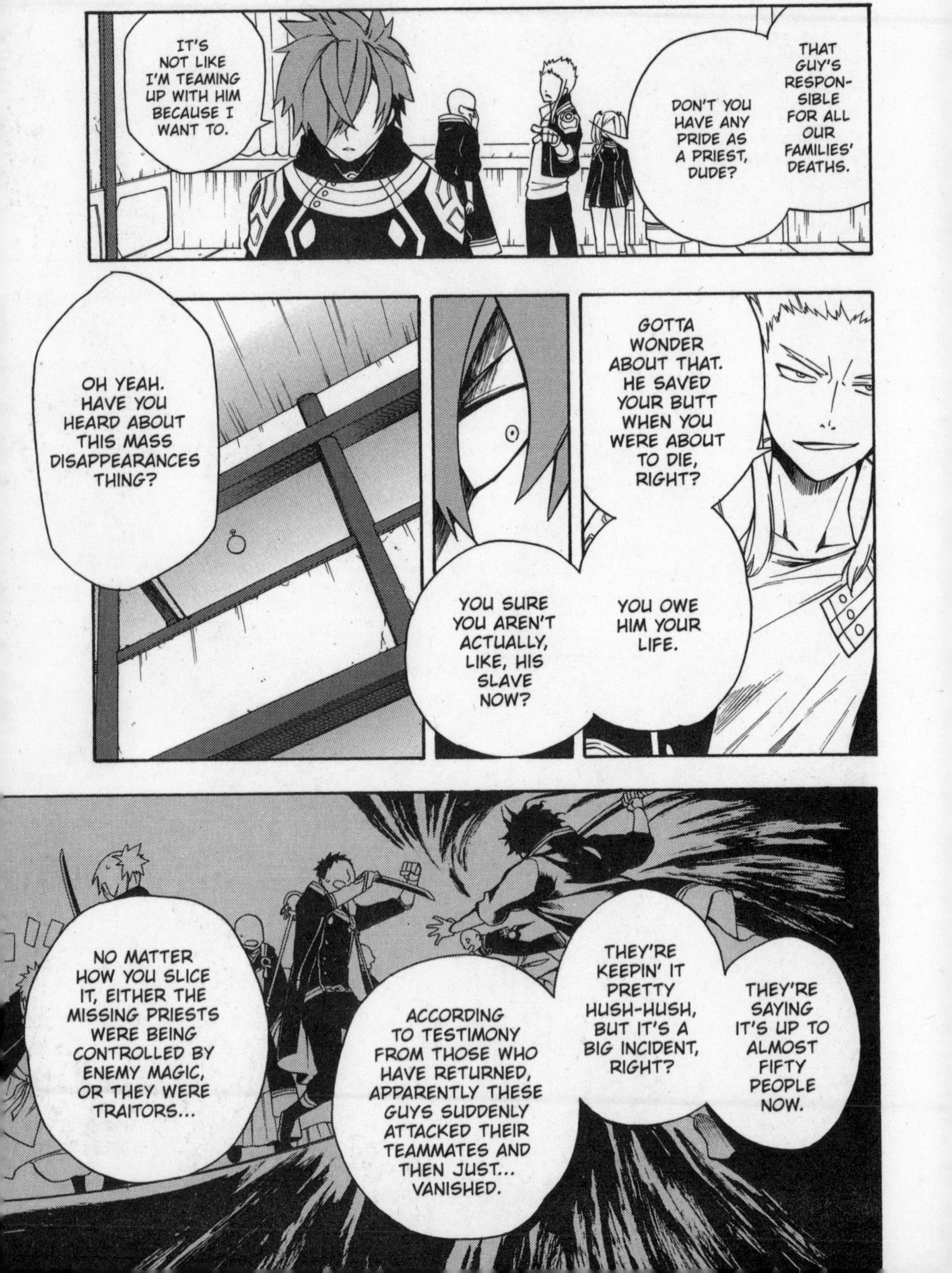
THAT GUY'S RESPON-SIBLE FOR ALL OUR FAMILIES' DEATHS.
DON'T YOU HAVE ANY PRIDE AS A PRIEST, DUDE?
IT'S NOT LIKE I'M TEAMING UP WITH HIM BECAUSE I WANT TO.
GOTTA WONDER ABOUT THAT. HE SAVED YOUR BUTT WHEN YOU WERE ABOUT TO DIE, RIGHT?
YOU OWE HIM YOUR LIFE.
YOU SURE YOU AREN'T ACTUALLY, LIKE, HIS SLAVE NOW?
OH YEAH. HAVE YOU HEARD ABOUT THIS MASS DISAPPEARANCES THING?
THEY'RE SAYING IT'S UP TO ALMOST FIFTY PEOPLE NOW.
THEY'RE KEEPIN' IT PRETTY HUSH-HUSH, BUT IT'S A BIG INCIDENT, RIGHT?
ACCORDING TO TESTIMONY FROM THOSE WHO HAVE RETURNED, APPARENTLY THESE GUYS SUDDENLY ATTACKED THEIR TEAMMATES AND THEN JUST... VANISHED.
NO MATTER HOW YOU SLICE IT, EITHER THE MISSING PRIESTS WERE BEING CONTROLLED BY ENEMY MAGIC, OR THEY WERE TRAITORS...

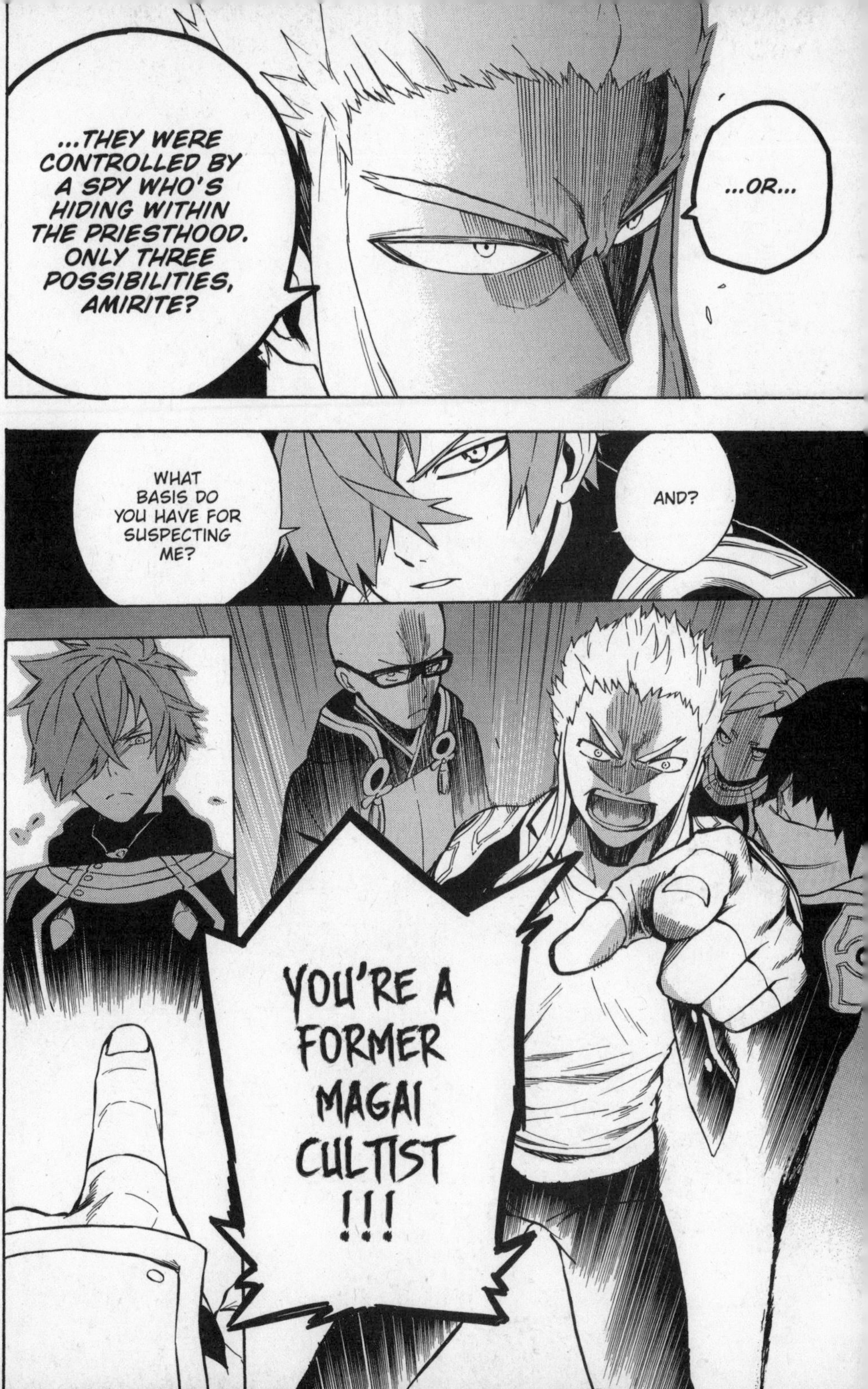
...OR...
...THEY WERE CONTROLLED BY A SPY WHO'S HIDING WITHIN THE PRIESTHOOD. ONLY THREE POSSIBILITIES, AMIRITE?
AND?
WHAT BASIS DO YOU HAVE FOR SUSPECTING ME?
YOU'RE A FORMER MAGAI CULTIST !!!

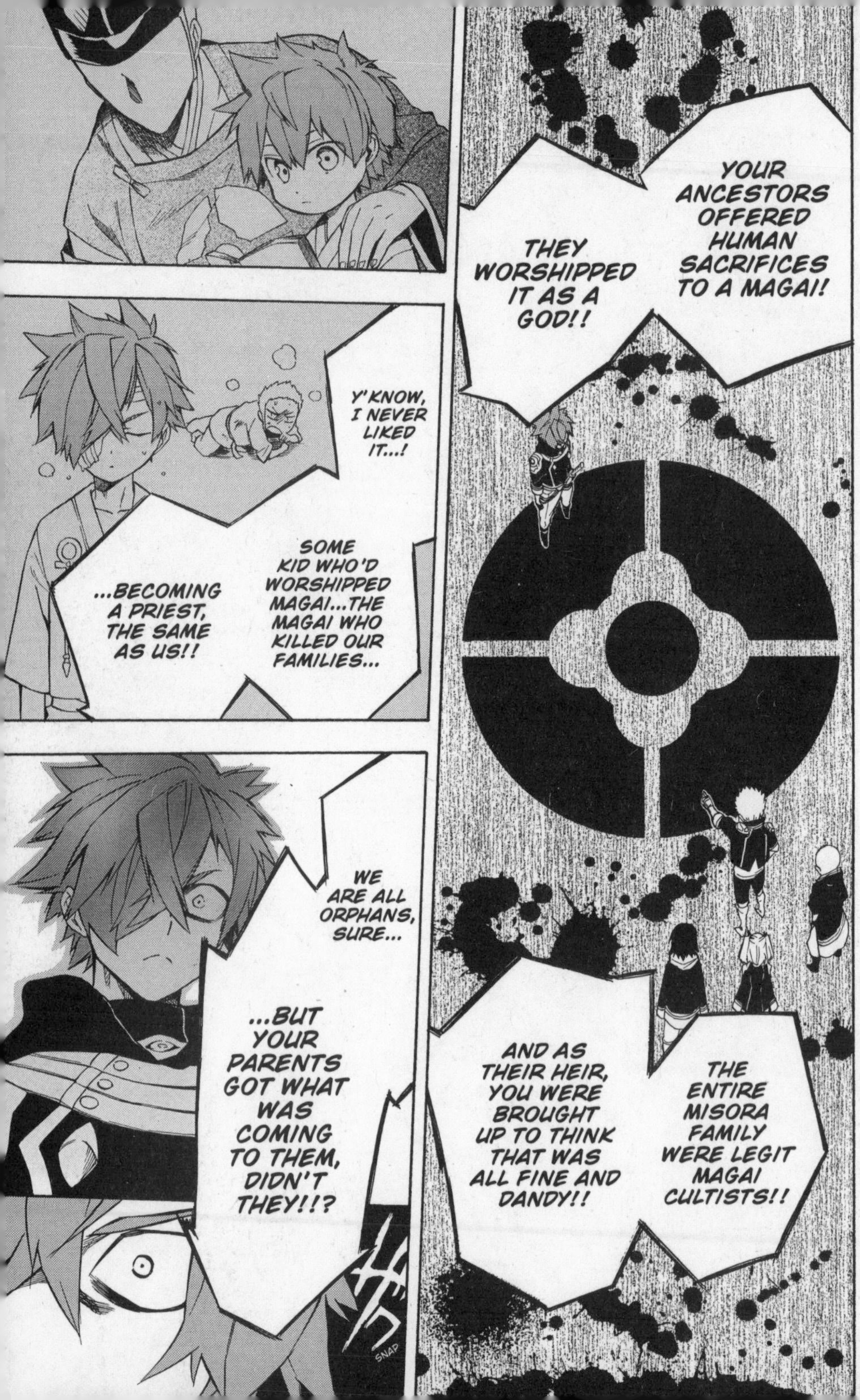
YOUR ANCESTORS OFFERED HUMAN SACRIFICES TO A MAGAI!
THEY WORSHIPPED IT AS A GOD!!
THE ENTIRE MISORA FAMILY WERE LEGIT MAGAI CULTISTS!!
AND AS THEIR HEIR, YOU WERE BROUGHT UP TO THINK THAT WAS ALL FINE AND DANDY!!
Y'KNOW, I NEVER LIKED IT...!
SOME KID WHO'D WORSHIPPED MAGAI...THE MAGAI WHO KILLED OUR FAMILIES...
...BECOMING A PRIEST, THE SAME AS US!!
WE ARE ALL ORPHANS, SURE...
...BUT YOUR PARENTS GOT WHAT WAS COMING TO THEM, DIDN'T THEY!!?
SNAP

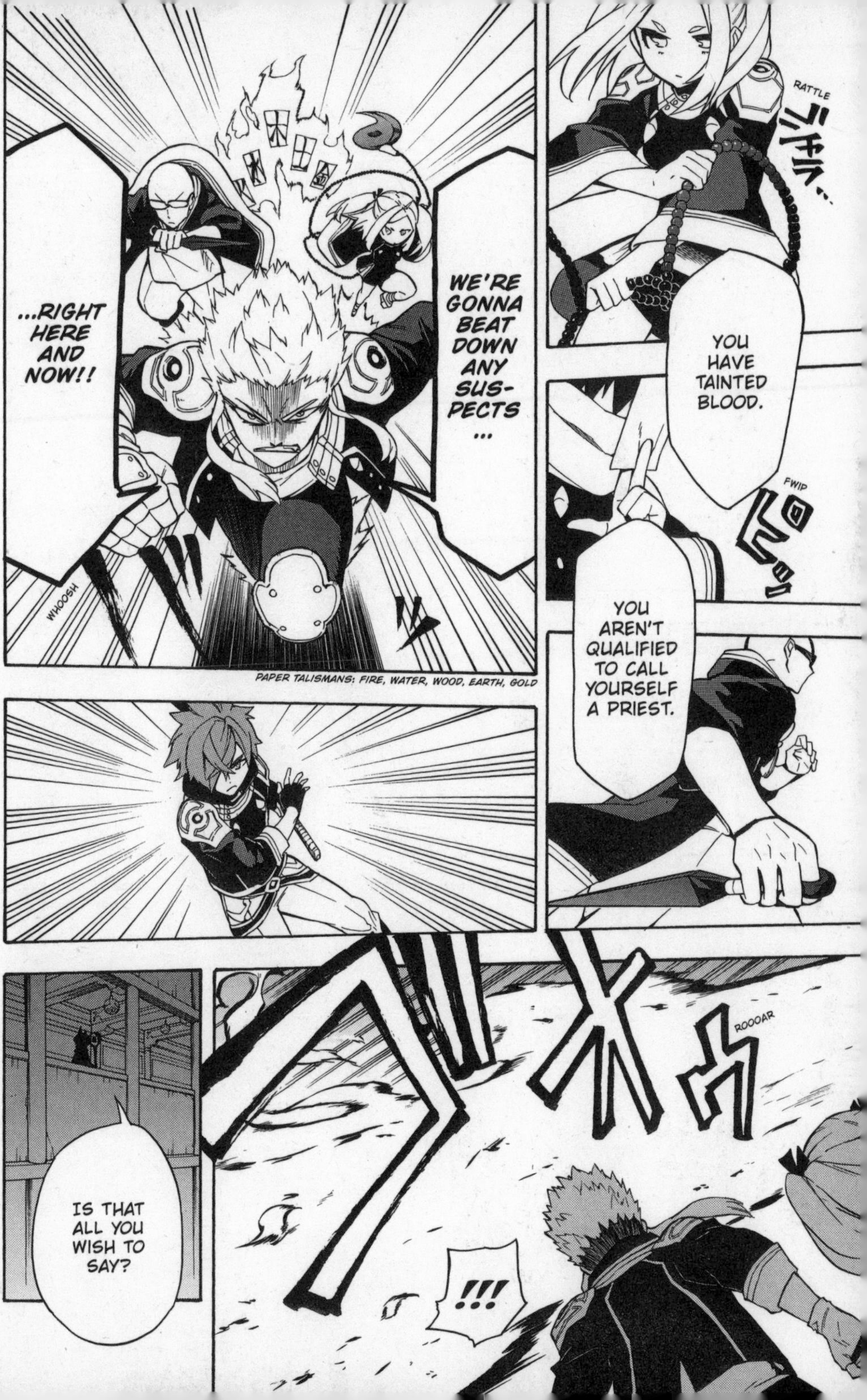
RATTLE
YOU HAVE TAINTED BLOOD.
FWIP
YOU AREN'T QUALIFIED TO CALL YOURSELF A PRIEST.
WE'RE GONNA BEAT DOWN ANY SUS-PECTS...
...RIGHT HERE AND NOW!!
WHOOSH
PAPER TALISMANS: FIRE, WATER, WOOD, EARTH, GOLD
ROOOAR
!!!
IS THAT ALL YOU WISH TO SAY?

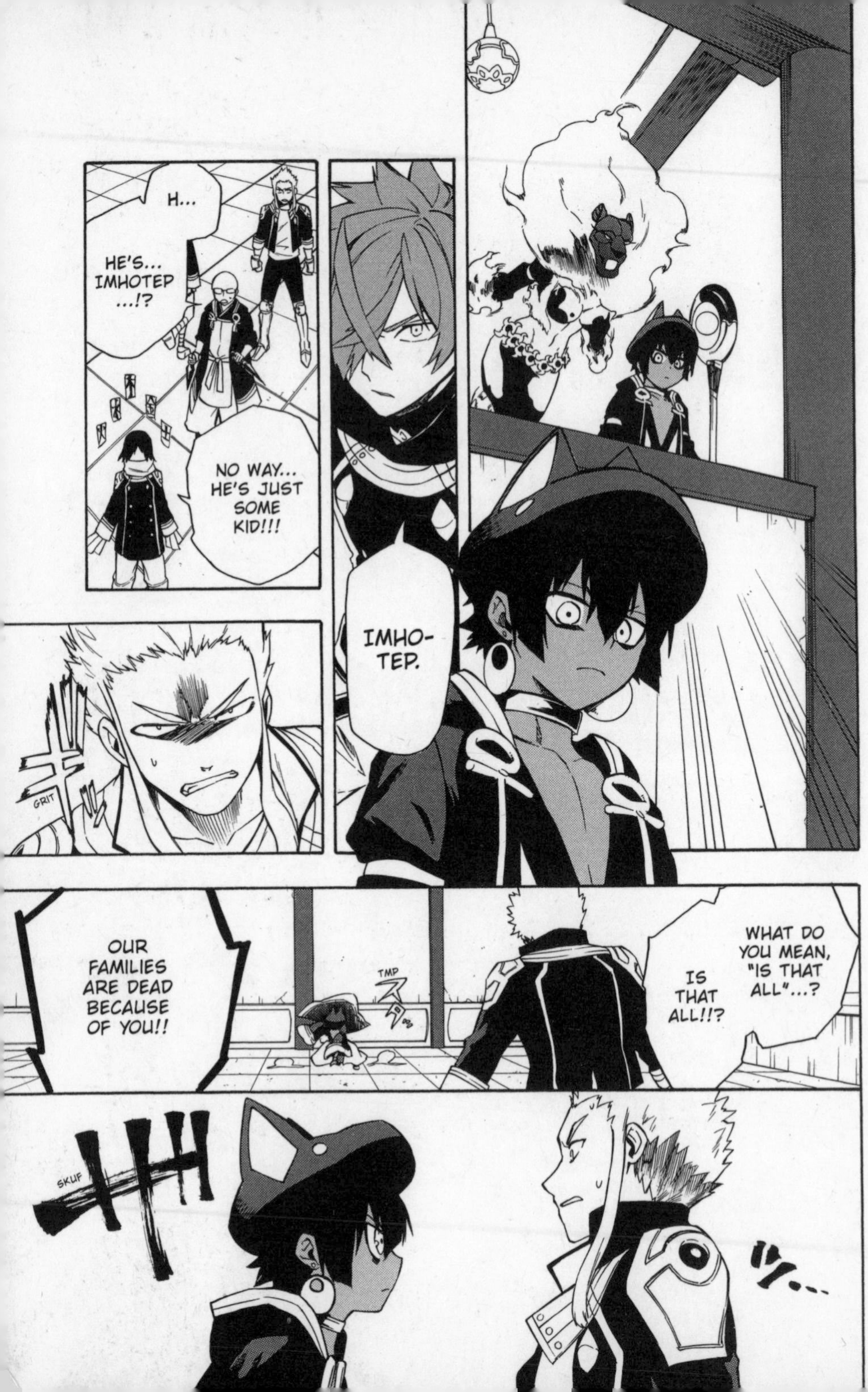
IMHO-TEP.
H...
HE'S... IMHOTEP ...!?
NO WAY... HE'S JUST SOME KID!!!
GRIT
WHAT DO YOU MEAN, "IS THAT ALL"...?
IS THAT ALL!!?
TMP
OUR FAMILIES ARE DEAD BECAUSE OF YOU!!
SKUF

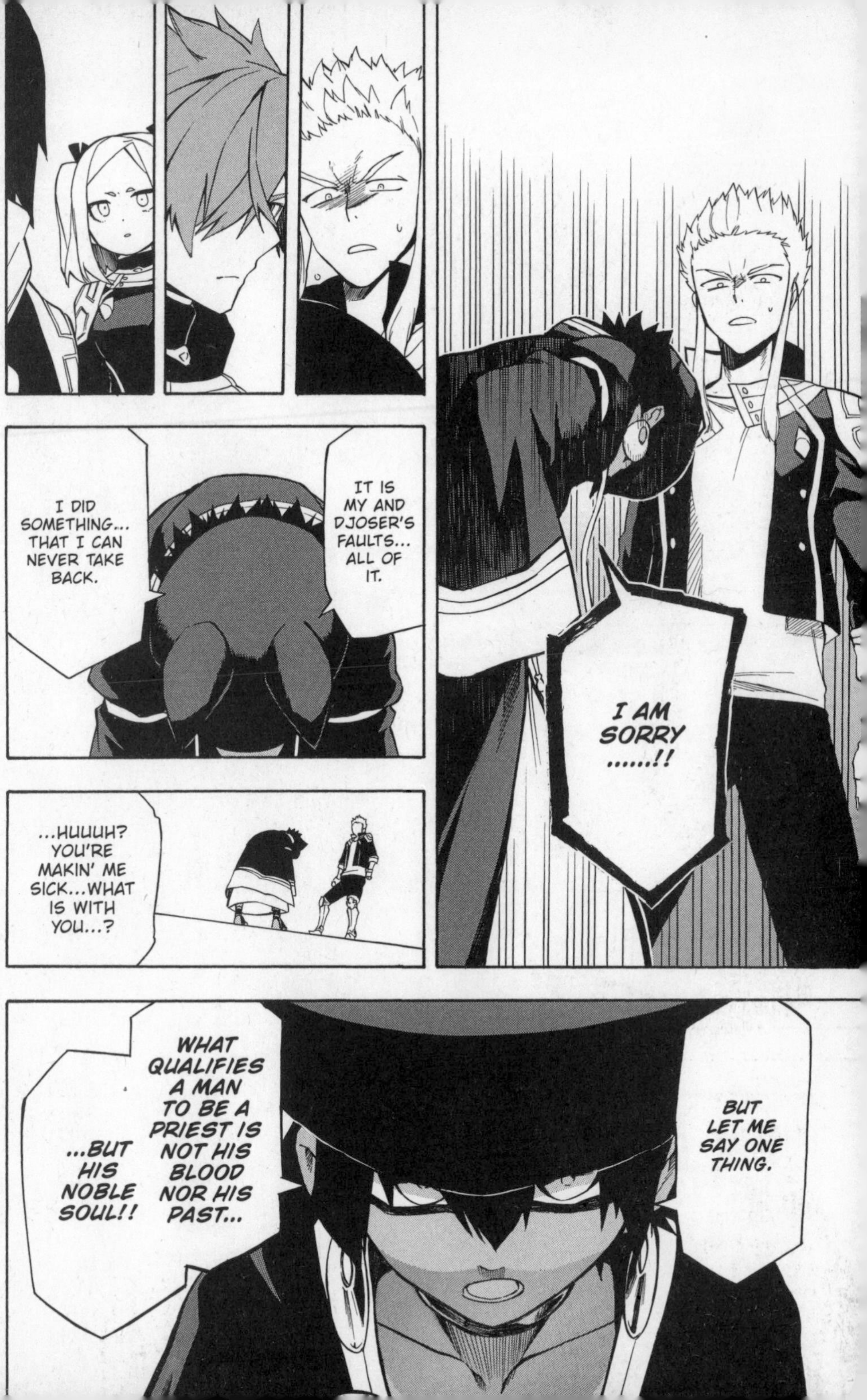
I AM SORRY ......!!
IT IS MY AND DJOSER'S FAULTS... ALL OF IT.
I DID SOMETHING... THAT I CAN NEVER TAKE BACK.
...HUUUH? YOU'RE MAKIN' ME SICK...WHAT IS WITH YOU...?
BUT LET ME SAY ONE THING.
WHAT QUALIFIES A MAN TO BE A PRIEST IS NOT HIS BLOOD NOR HIS PAST...
...BUT HIS NOBLE SOUL!!

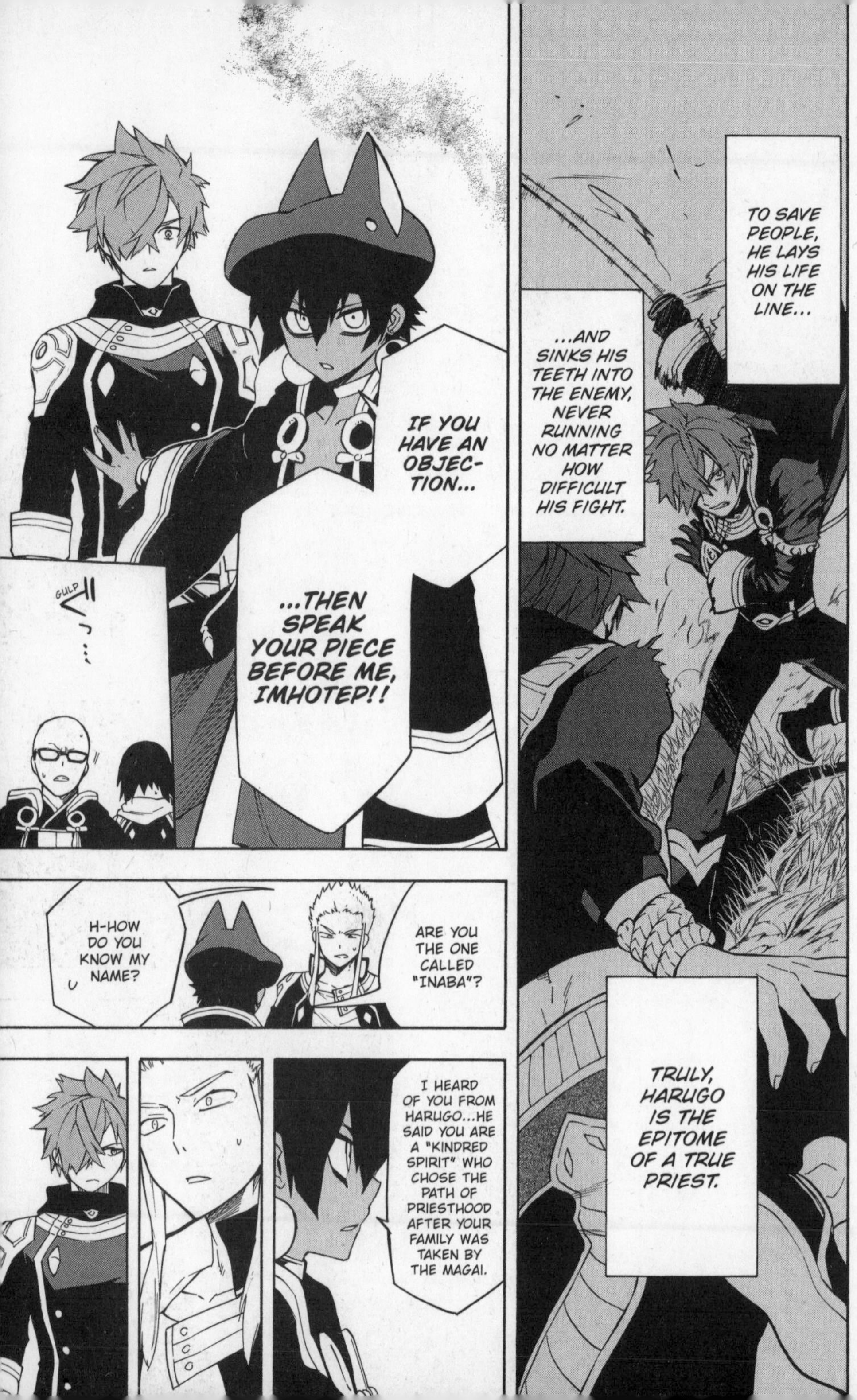
TO SAVE PEOPLE, HE LAYS HIS LIFE ON THE LINE...
...AND SINKS HIS TEETH INTO THE ENEMY, NEVER RUNNING NO MATTER HOW DIFFICULT HIS FIGHT.
TRULY, HARUGO IS THE EPITOME OF A TRUE PRIEST.
IF YOU HAVE AN OBJECTION...
...THEN SPEAK YOUR PIECE BEFORE ME, IMHOTEP!!
GULP
ARE YOU THE ONE CALLED "INABA"?
H-HOW DO YOU KNOW MY NAME?
I HEARD OF YOU FROM HARUGO...HE SAID YOU ARE A "KINDRED SPIRIT" WHO CHOSE THE PATH OF PRIESTHOOD AFTER YOUR FAMILY WAS TAKEN BY THE MAGAI.

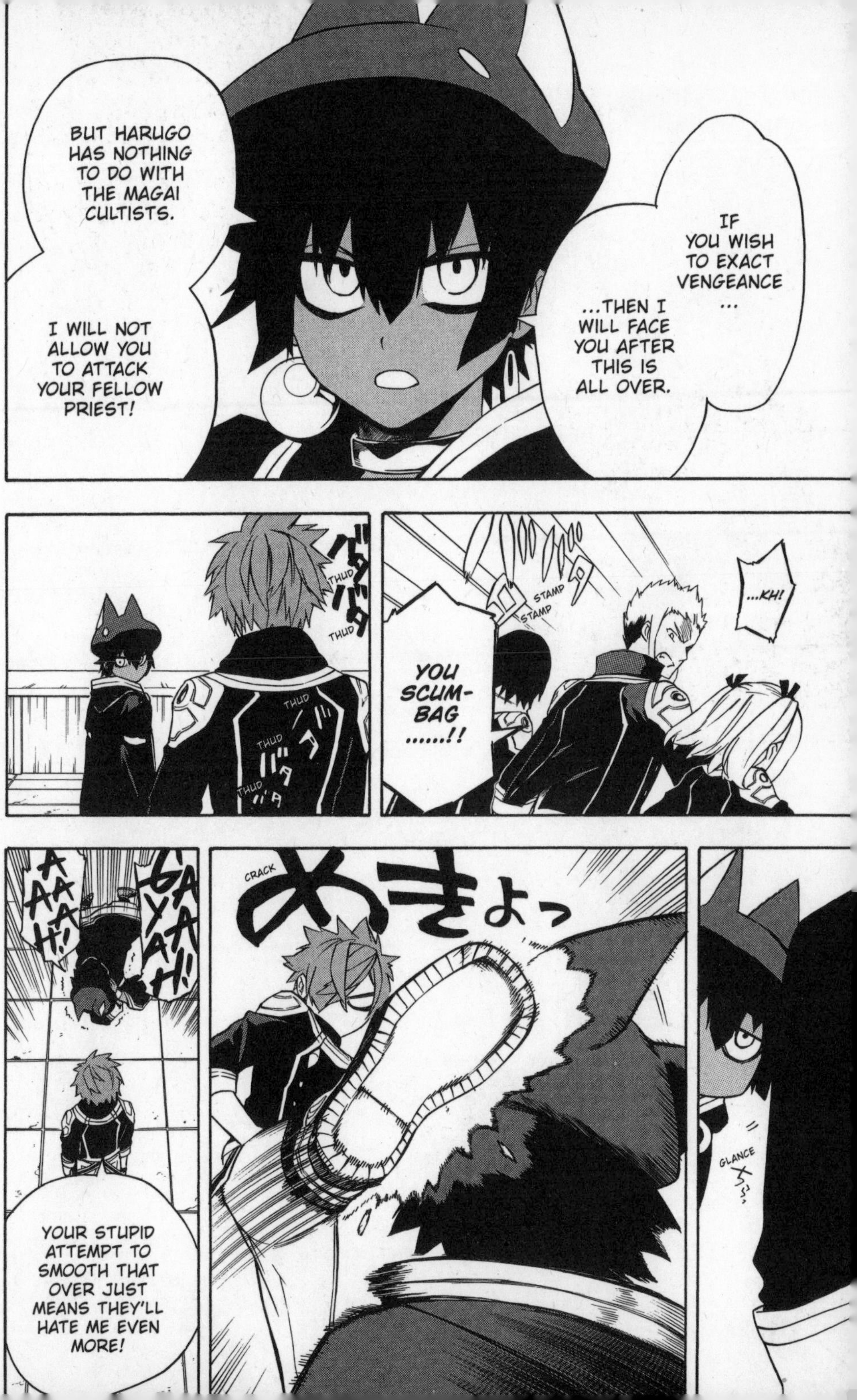
IF YOU WISH TO EXACT VENGEANCE...
...THEN I WILL FACE YOU AFTER THIS IS ALL OVER.
BUT HARUGO HAS NOTHING TO DO WITH THE MAGAI CULTISTS.
I WILL NOT ALLOW YOU TO ATTACK YOUR FELLOW PRIEST!
...KH!
STAMP
STAMP
YOU SCUMBAG......!!
THUD
THUD
THUD
THUD
THUD
GLANCE
CRACK
AAAAH!
GAYAAH!
YOUR STUPID ATTEMPT TO SMOOTH THAT OVER JUST MEANS THEY'LL HATE ME EVEN MORE!

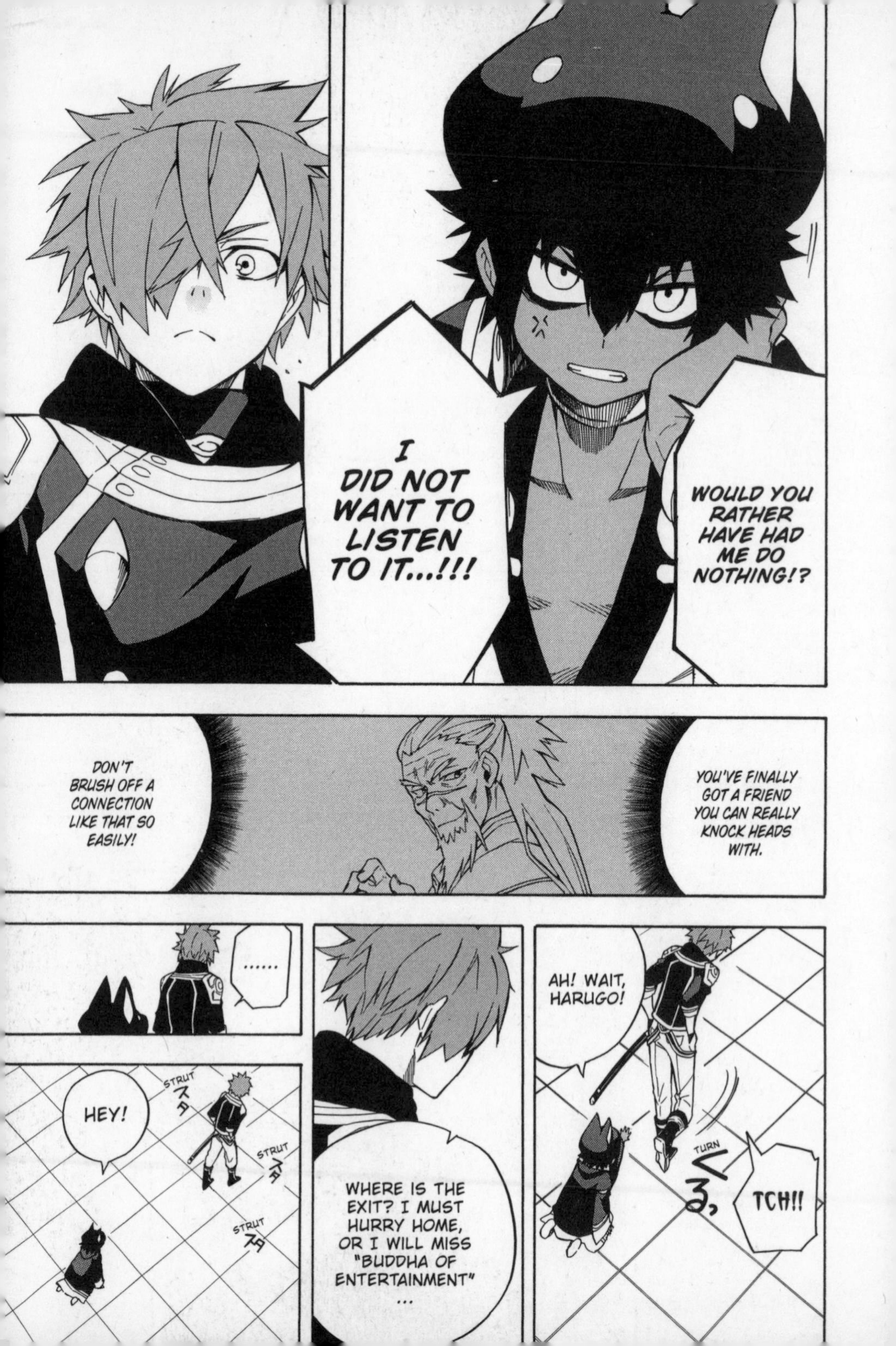
WOULD YOU RATHER HAVE HAD ME DO NOTHING!?
I DID NOT WANT TO LISTEN TO IT...!!!
YOU'VE FINALLY GOT A FRIEND YOU CAN REALLY KNOCK HEADS WITH.
DON'T BRUSH OFF A CONNECTION LIKE THAT SO EASILY!
AH! WAIT, HARUGO!
TURN
TCH!!
WHERE IS THE EXIT? I MUST HURRY HOME, OR I WILL MISS "BUDDHA OF ENTERTAINMENT" ...
......
STRUT
STRUT
STRUT
HEY!

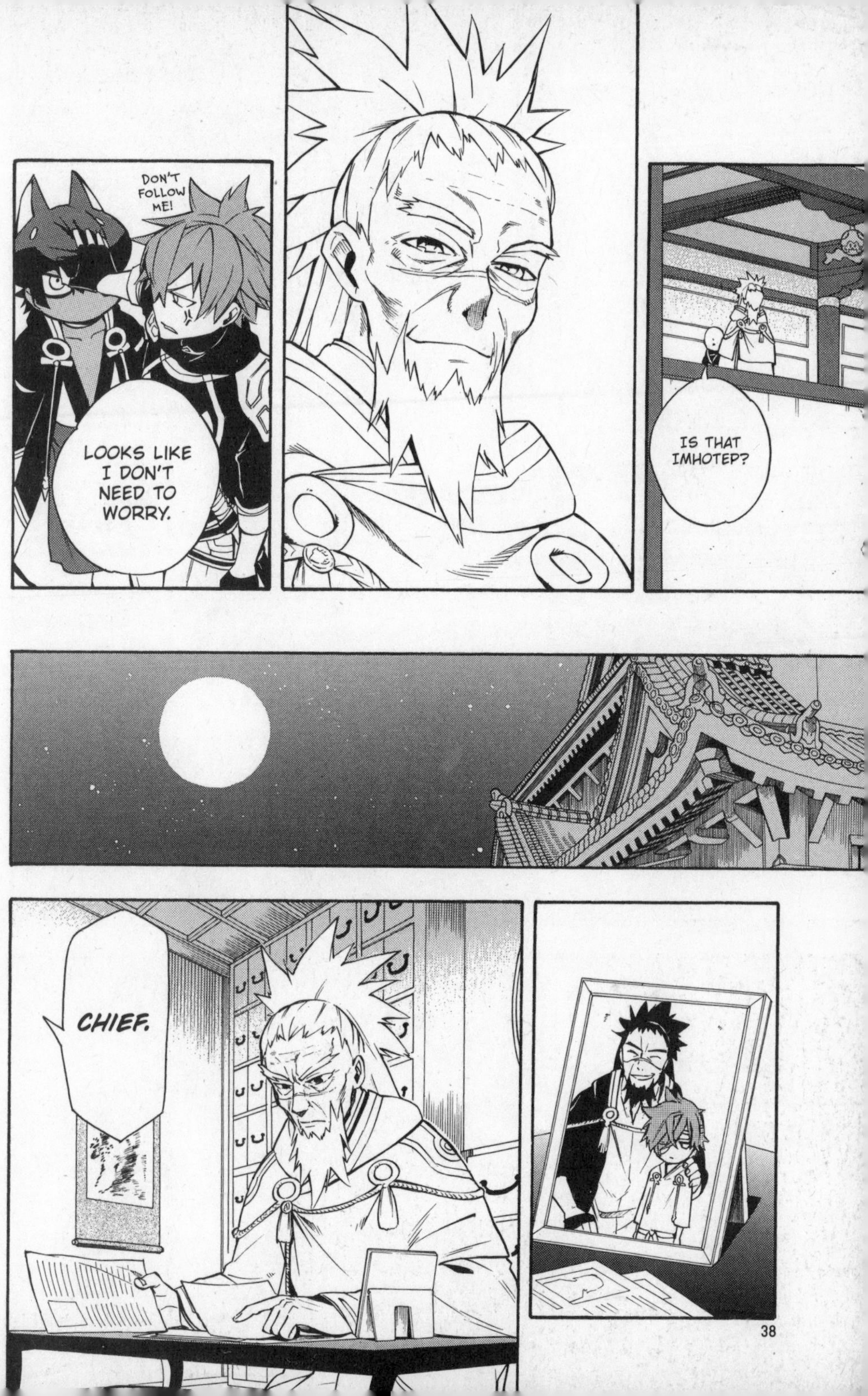
IS THAT IMHOTEP?
DON'T FOLLOW ME!
LOOKS LIKE I DON'T NEED TO WORRY.
CHIEF.

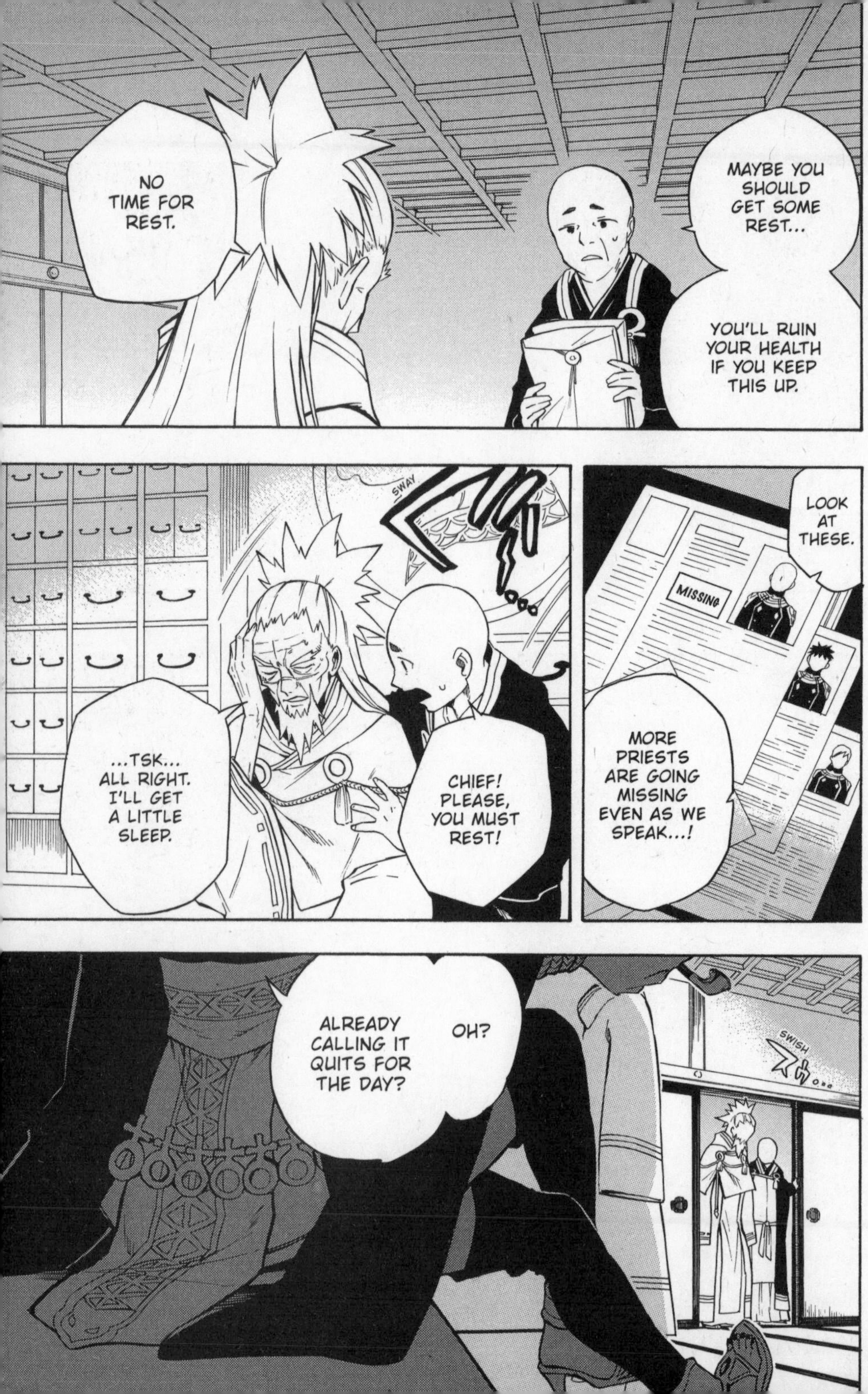
MAYBE YOU SHOULD GET SOME REST...
YOU'LL RUIN YOUR HEALTH IF YOU KEEP THIS UP.
NO TIME FOR REST.
LOOK AT THESE.
MISSING
MORE PRIESTS ARE GOING MISSING EVEN AS WE SPEAK...!
SWAY
CHIEF! PLEASE, YOU MUST REST!
...TSK... ALL RIGHT. I'LL GET A LITTLE SLEEP.
SWISH
OH?
ALREADY CALLING IT QUITS FOR THE DAY?

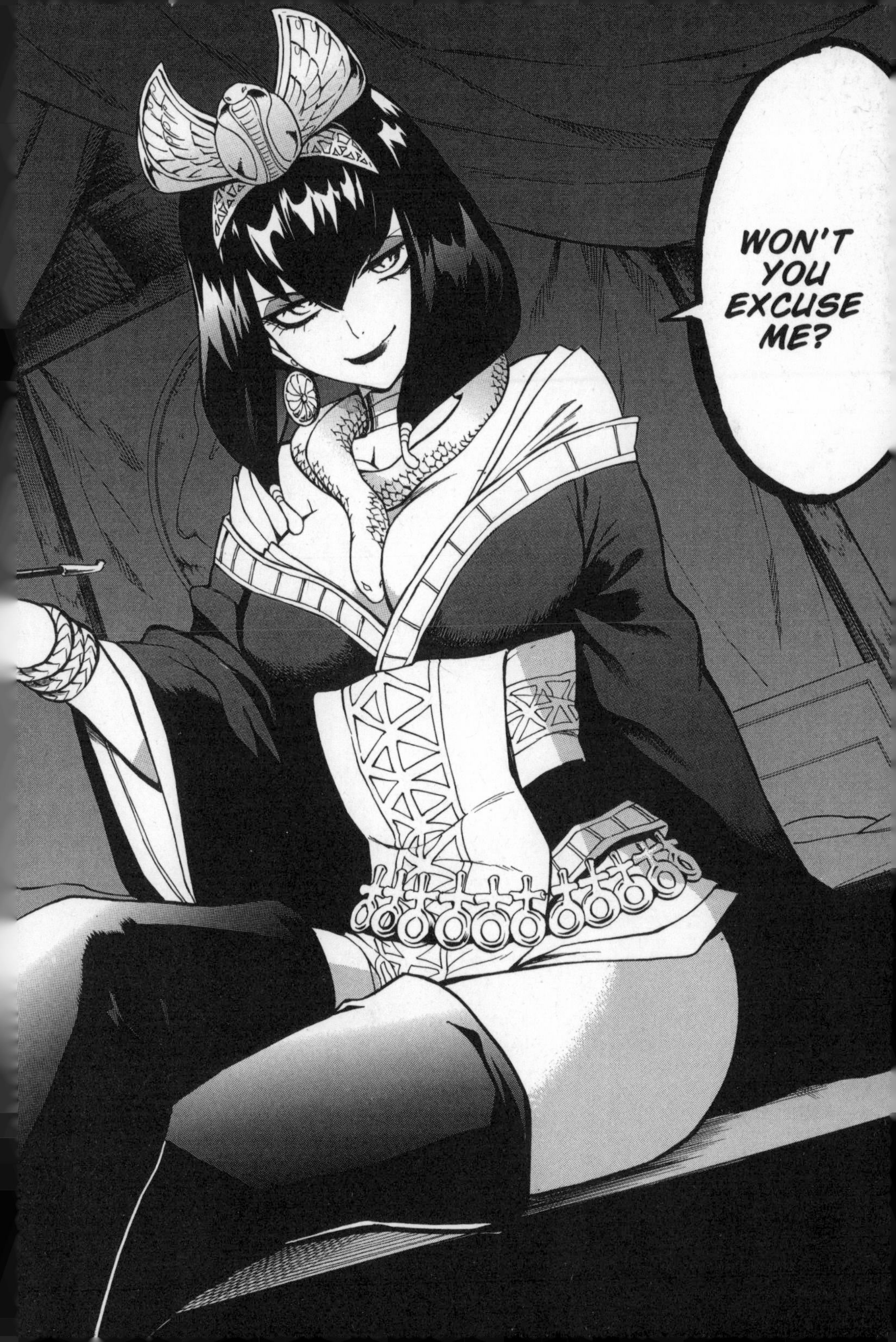
WON'T YOU EXCUSE ME?

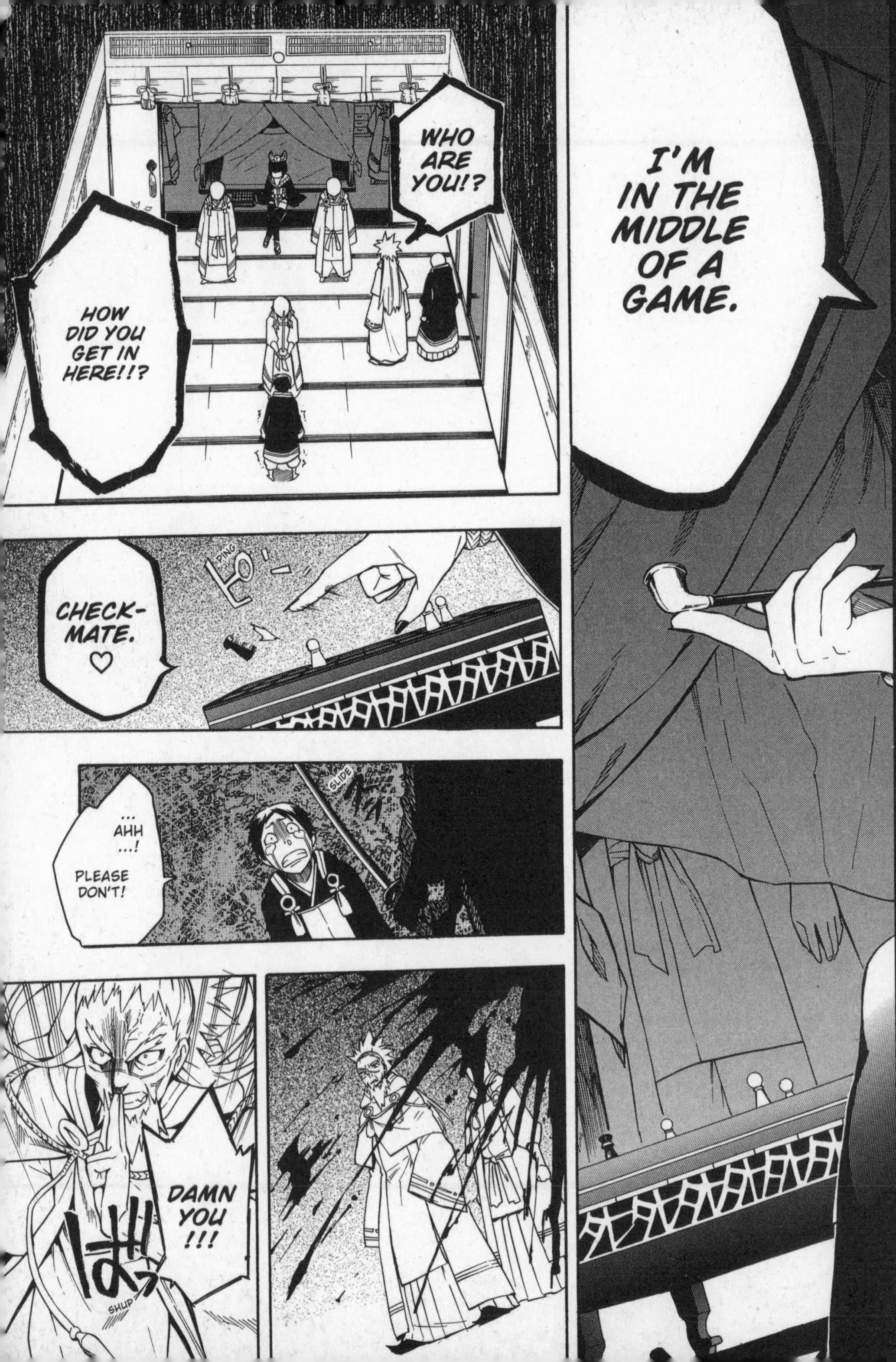
I'M IN THE MIDDLE OF A GAME.
WHO ARE YOU!?
HOW DID YOU GET IN HERE!!?
PING
CHECK-MATE. ♡
SLIDE
... AHH ...!
PLEASE DON'T!
DAMN YOU!!!
はっ
SHUP

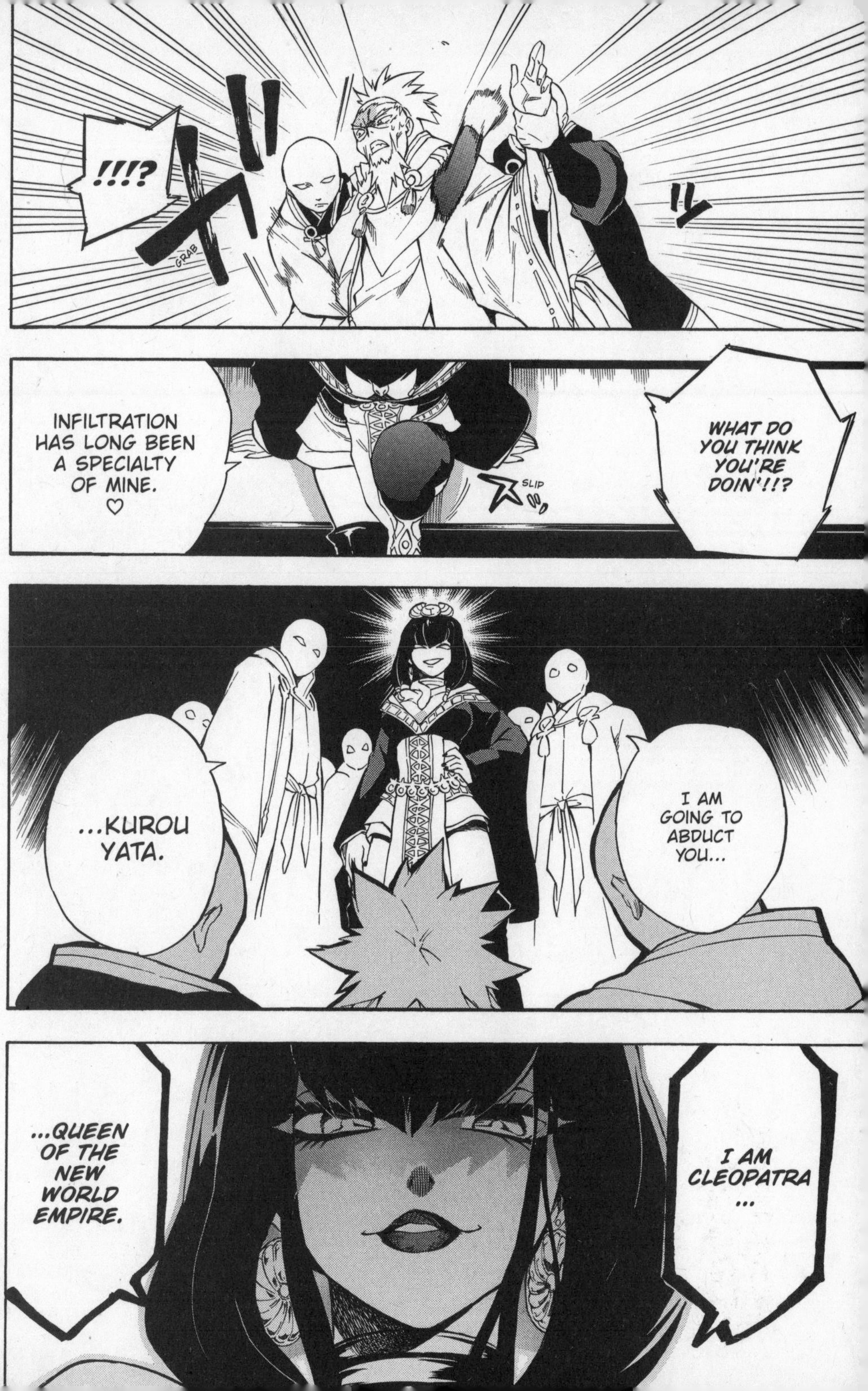
!!!?
GRAB
WHAT DO YOU THINK YOU'RE DOIN'!!?
INFILTRATION HAS LONG BEEN A SPECIALTY OF MINE. ♡
SLIP
I AM GOING TO ABDUCT YOU...
...KUROU YATA.
I AM CLEOPATRA ...
...QUEEN OF THE NEW WORLD EMPIRE.

Great Priest Imhotep

Great Priest Imhotep

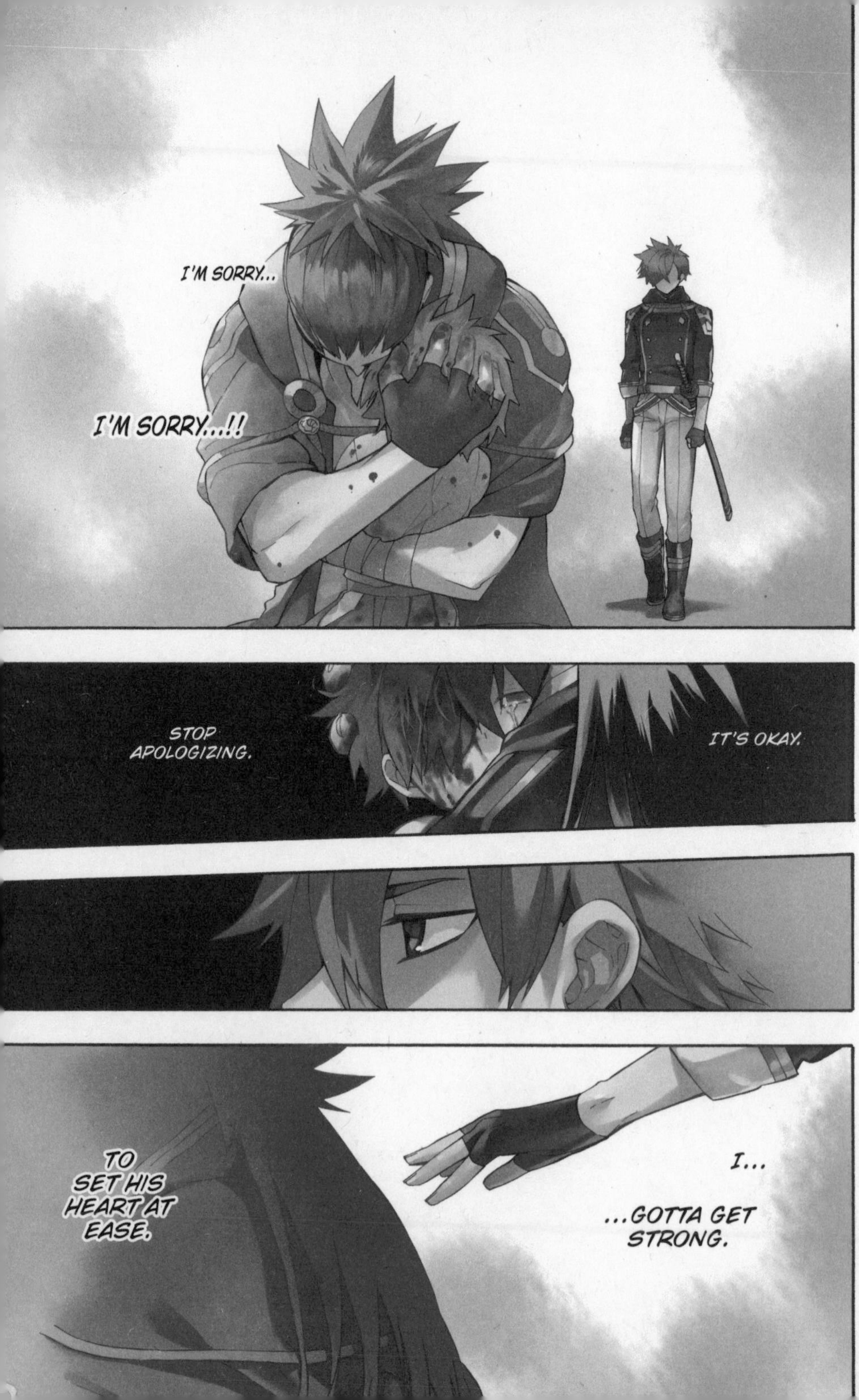
I'M SORRY...
I'M SORRY...!!
IT'S OKAY.
STOP APOLOGIZING.
I...
...GOTTA GET STRONG.
TO SET HIS HEART AT EASE.

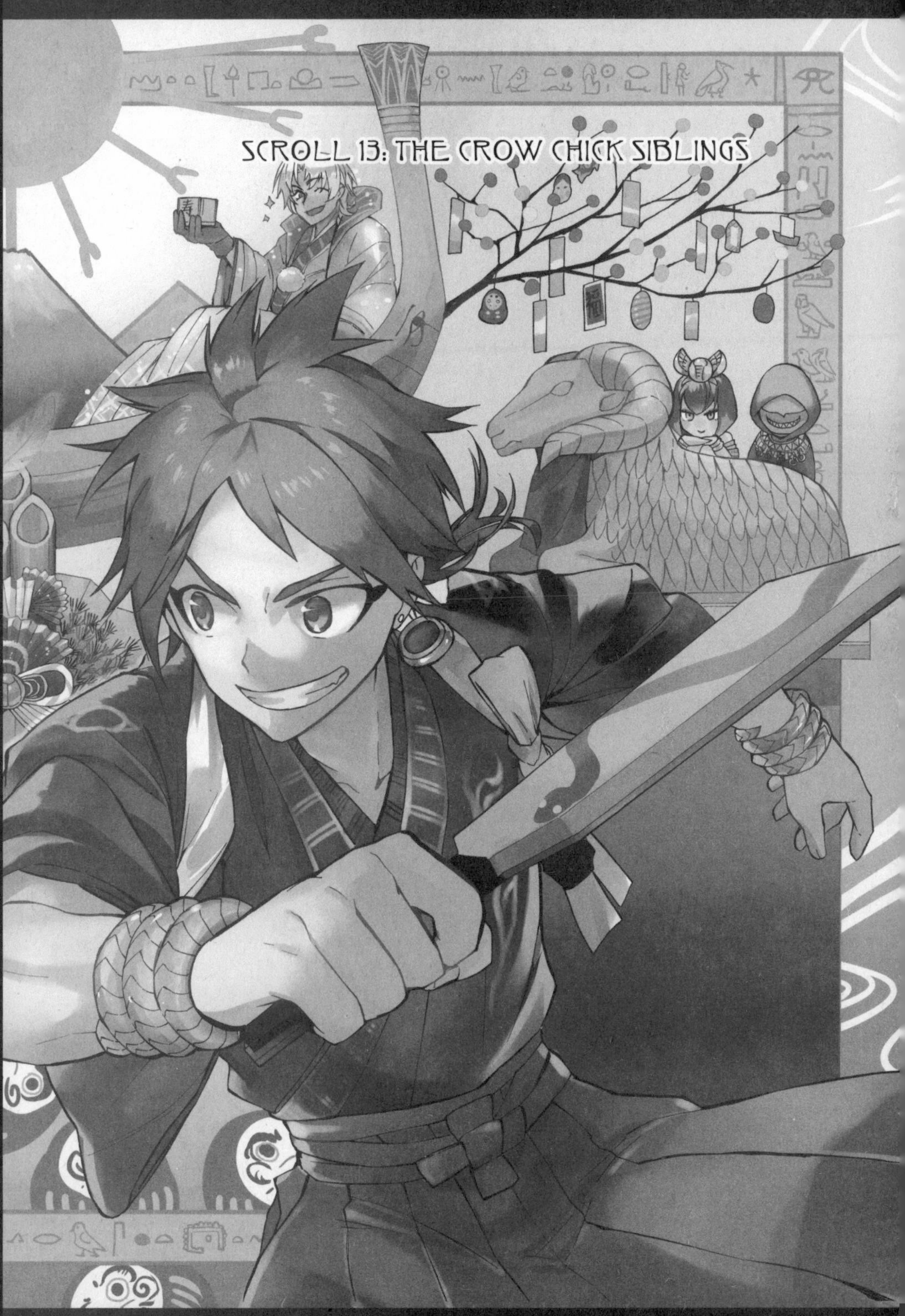
SCROLL 13: THE CROW CHICK SIBLINGS

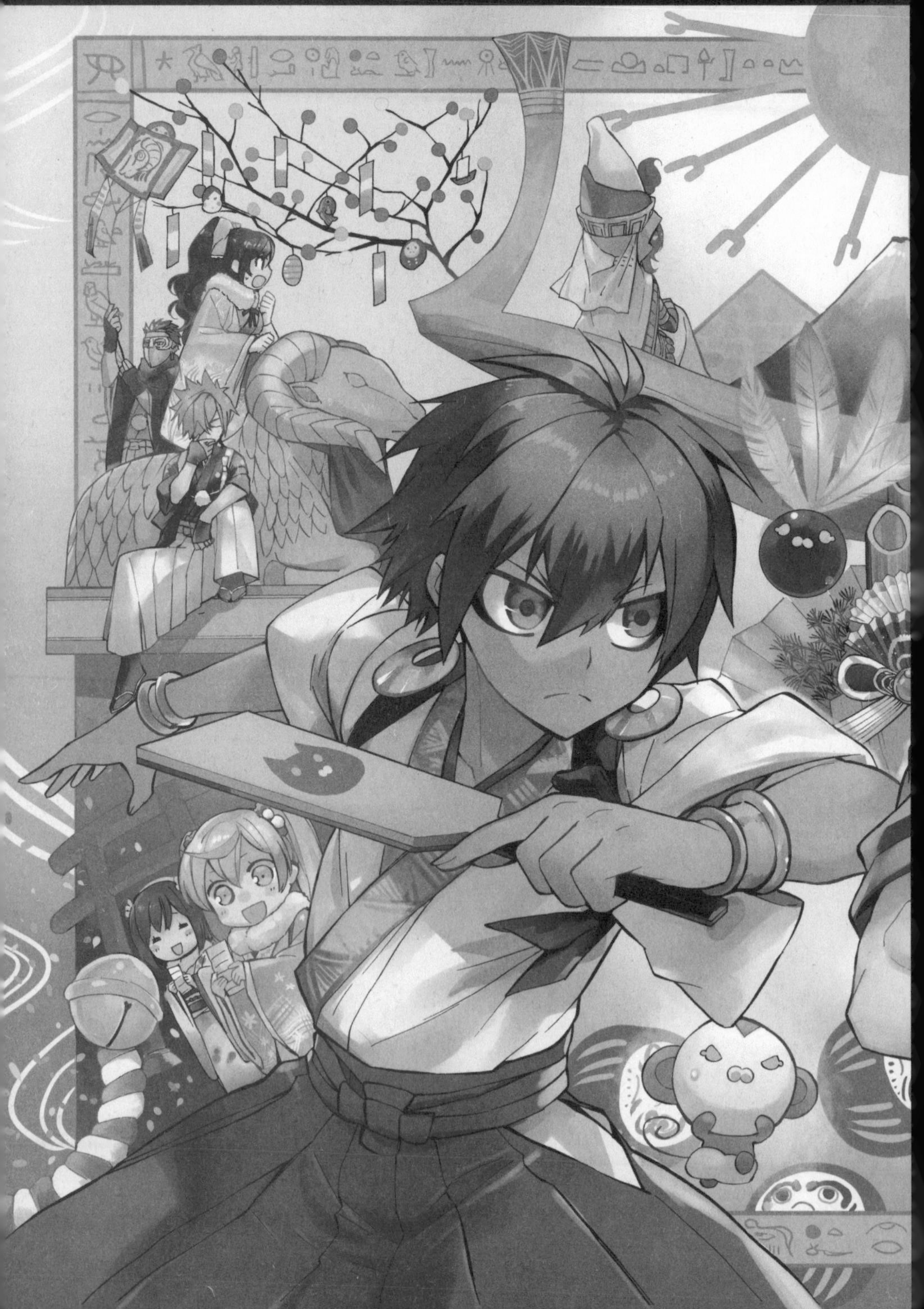

Great Priest Imhotep

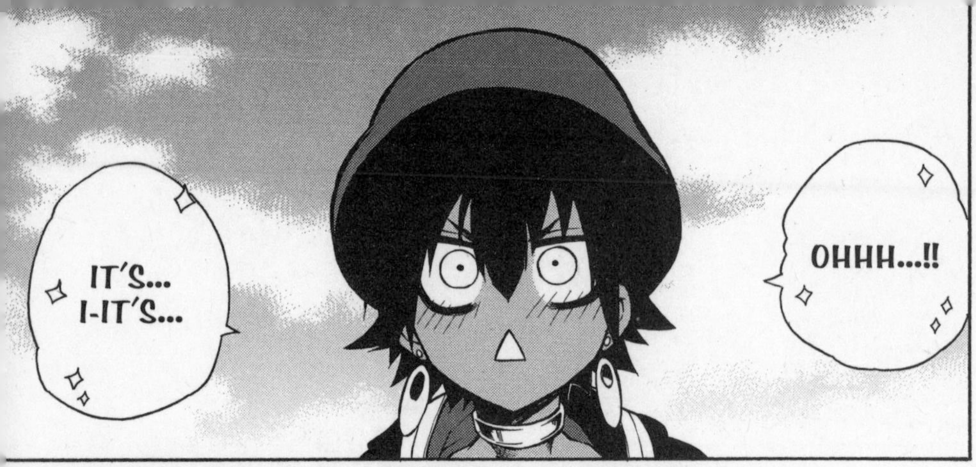
OHHH...!!
IT'S...
I-IT'S...
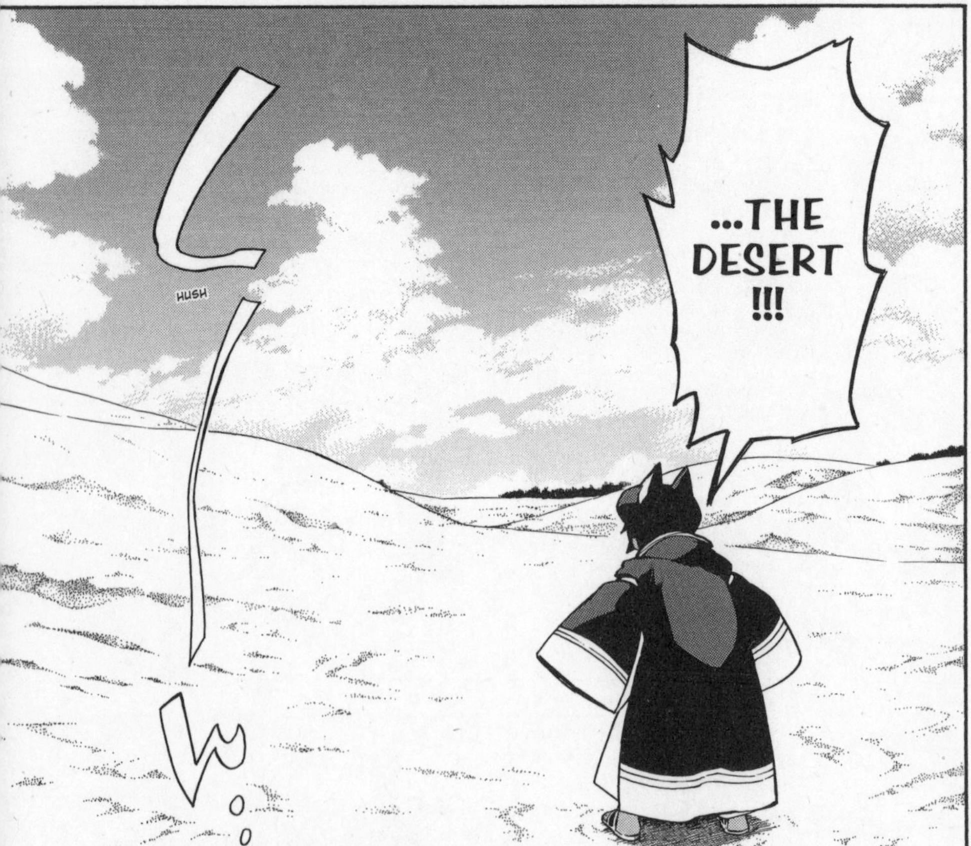
...THE DESERT !!!
HUSH

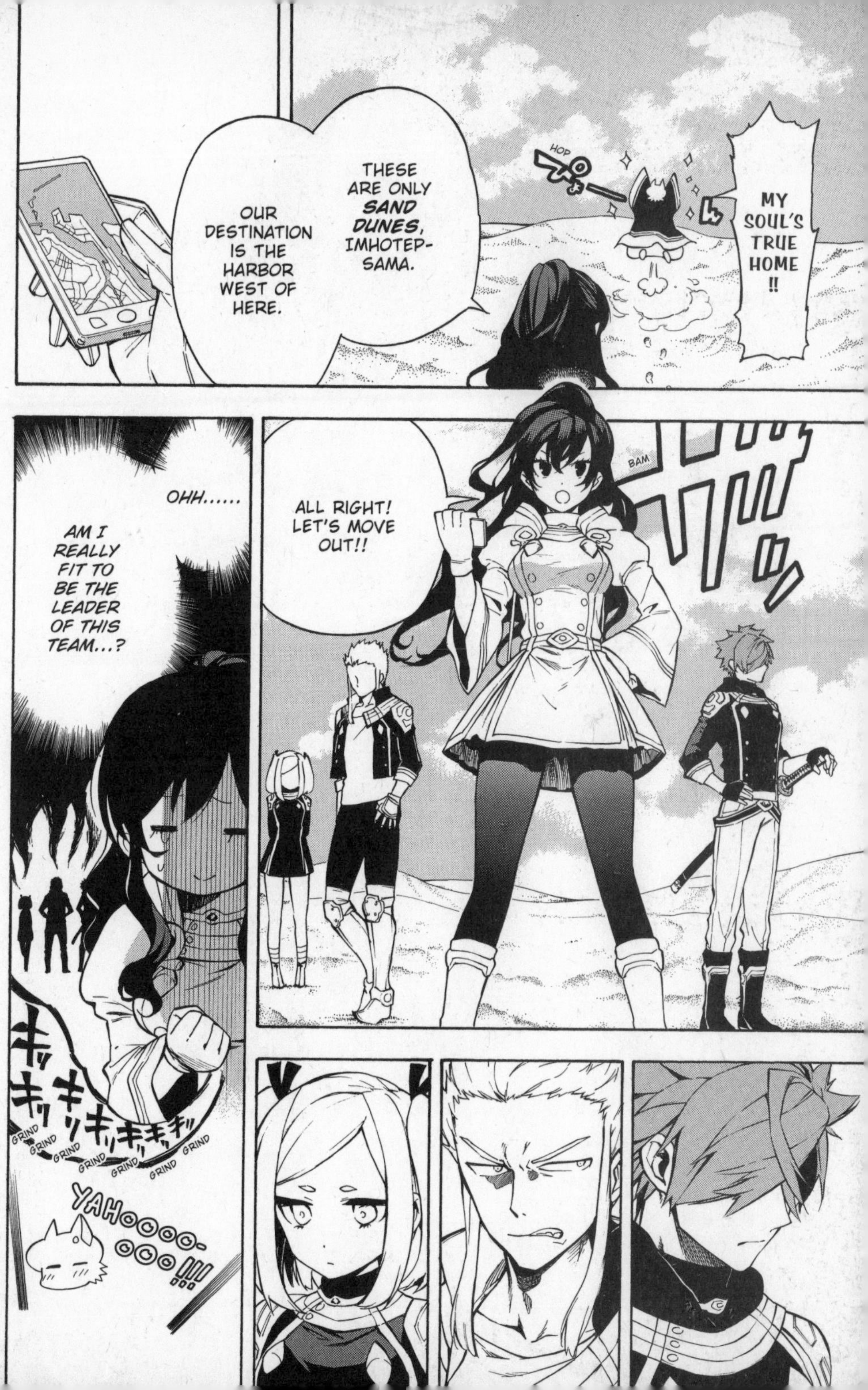
MY SOUL'S TRUE HOME !!
HOP
THESE ARE ONLY *SAND DUNES*, IMHOTEP-SAMA.
OUR DESTINATION IS THE HARBOR WEST OF HERE.
BAM
ALL RIGHT! LET'S MOVE OUT!!
OHH......
AM I REALLY FIT TO BE THE LEADER OF THIS TEAM...?
GRIND GRIND GRIND GRIND GRIND GRIND GRIND
YAHOOOOO-OOO!!!

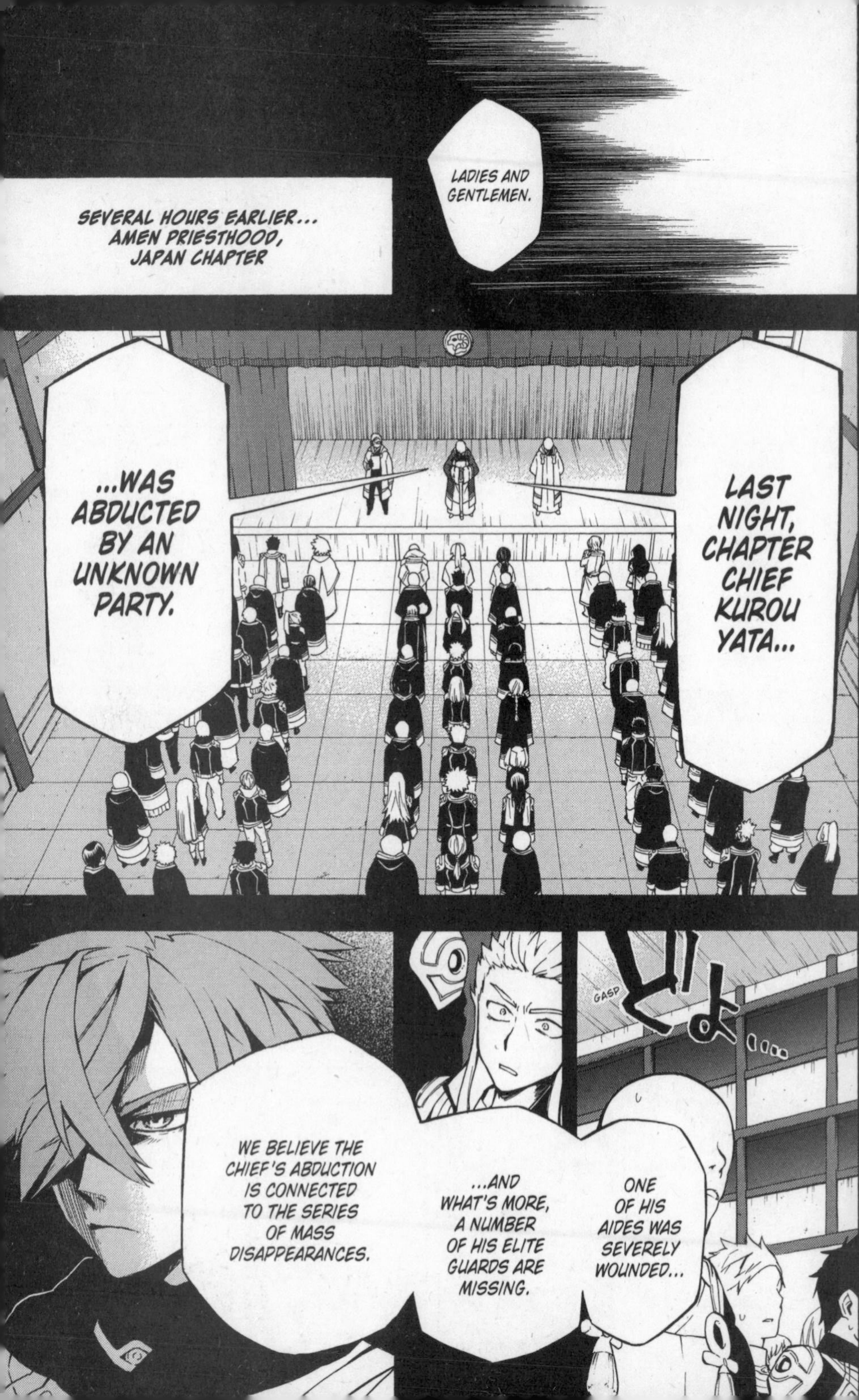
LADIES AND GENTLEMEN.
SEVERAL HOURS EARLIER... AMEN PRIESTHOOD, JAPAN CHAPTER
LAST NIGHT, CHAPTER CHIEF KUROU YATA...
...WAS ABDUCTED BY AN UNKNOWN PARTY.
GASP
...
ONE OF HIS AIDES WAS SEVERELY WOUNDED...
...AND WHAT'S MORE, A NUMBER OF HIS ELITE GUARDS ARE MISSING.
WE BELIEVE THE CHIEF'S ABDUCTION IS CONNECTED TO THE SERIES OF MASS DISAPPEARANCES.

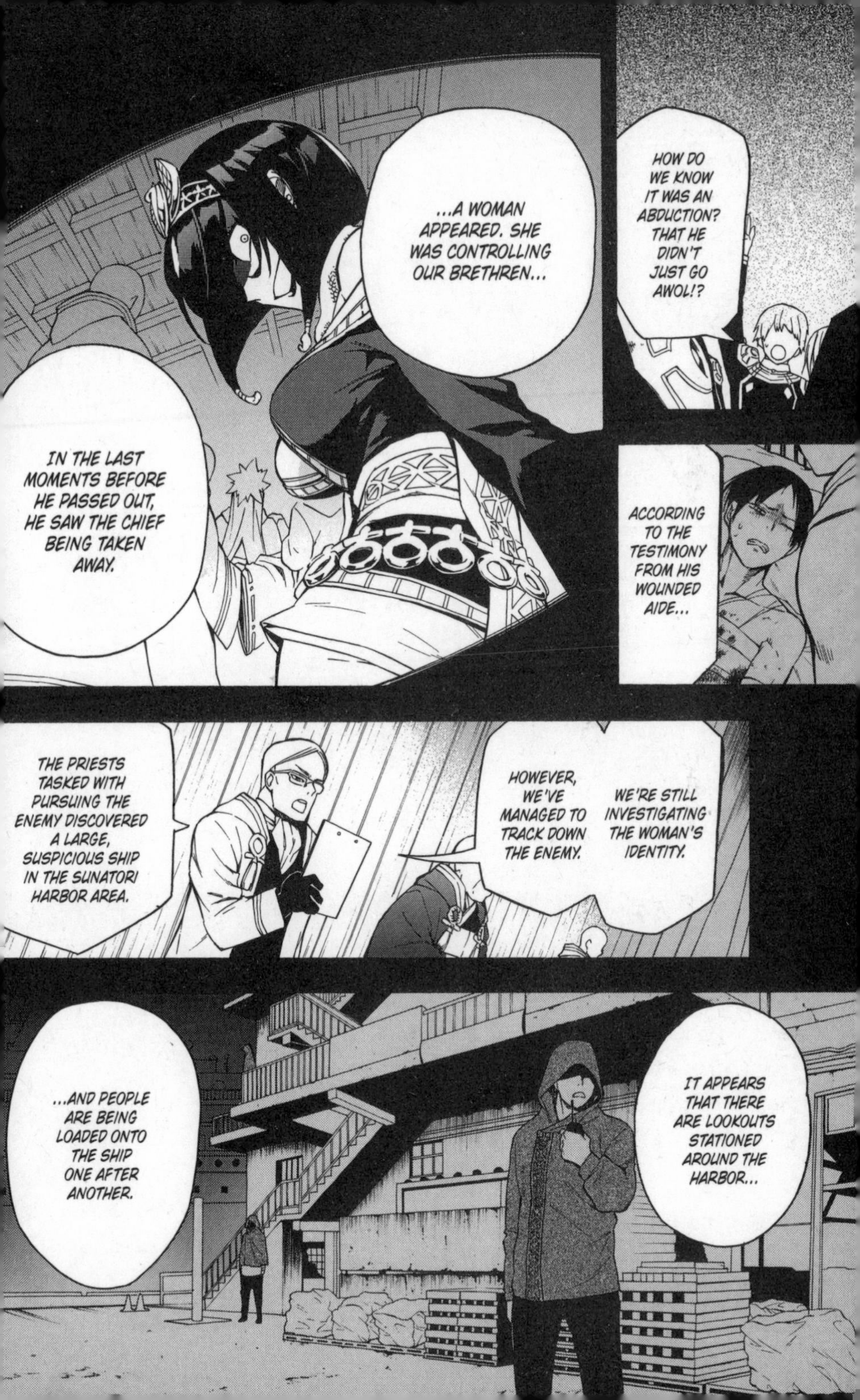
HOW DO WE KNOW IT WAS AN ABDUCTION? THAT HE DIDN'T JUST GO AWOL!?
ACCORDING TO THE TESTIMONY FROM HIS WOUNDED AIDE...
...A WOMAN APPEARED. SHE WAS CONTROLLING OUR BRETHREN...
IN THE LAST MOMENTS BEFORE HE PASSED OUT, HE SAW THE CHIEF BEING TAKEN AWAY.
WE'RE STILL INVESTIGATING THE WOMAN'S IDENTITY.
HOWEVER, WE'VE MANAGED TO TRACK DOWN THE ENEMY.
THE PRIESTS TASKED WITH PURSUING THE ENEMY DISCOVERED A LARGE, SUSPICIOUS SHIP IN THE SUNATORI HARBOR AREA.
IT APPEARS THAT THERE ARE LOOKOUTS STATIONED AROUND THE HARBOR...
...AND PEOPLE ARE BEING LOADED ONTO THE SHIP ONE AFTER ANOTHER.

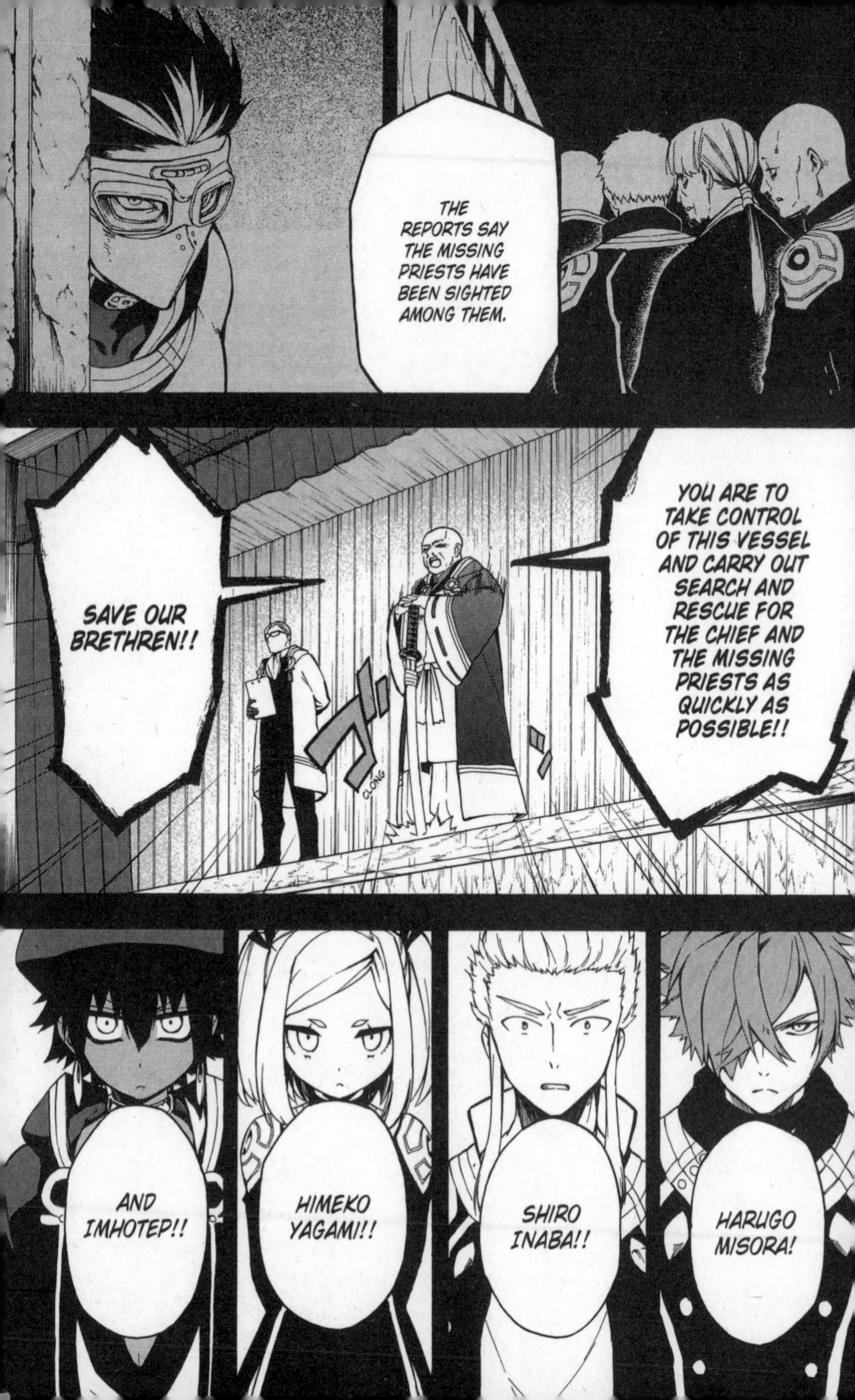
THE REPORTS SAY THE MISSING PRIESTS HAVE BEEN SIGHTED AMONG THEM.
YOU ARE TO TAKE CONTROL OF THIS VESSEL AND CARRY OUT SEARCH AND RESCUE FOR THE CHIEF AND THE MISSING PRIESTS AS QUICKLY AS POSSIBLE!!
CLONG
SAVE OUR BRETHREN!!
HARUGO MISORA!
SHIRO INABA!!
HIMEKO YAGAMI!!
AND IMHOTEP!!

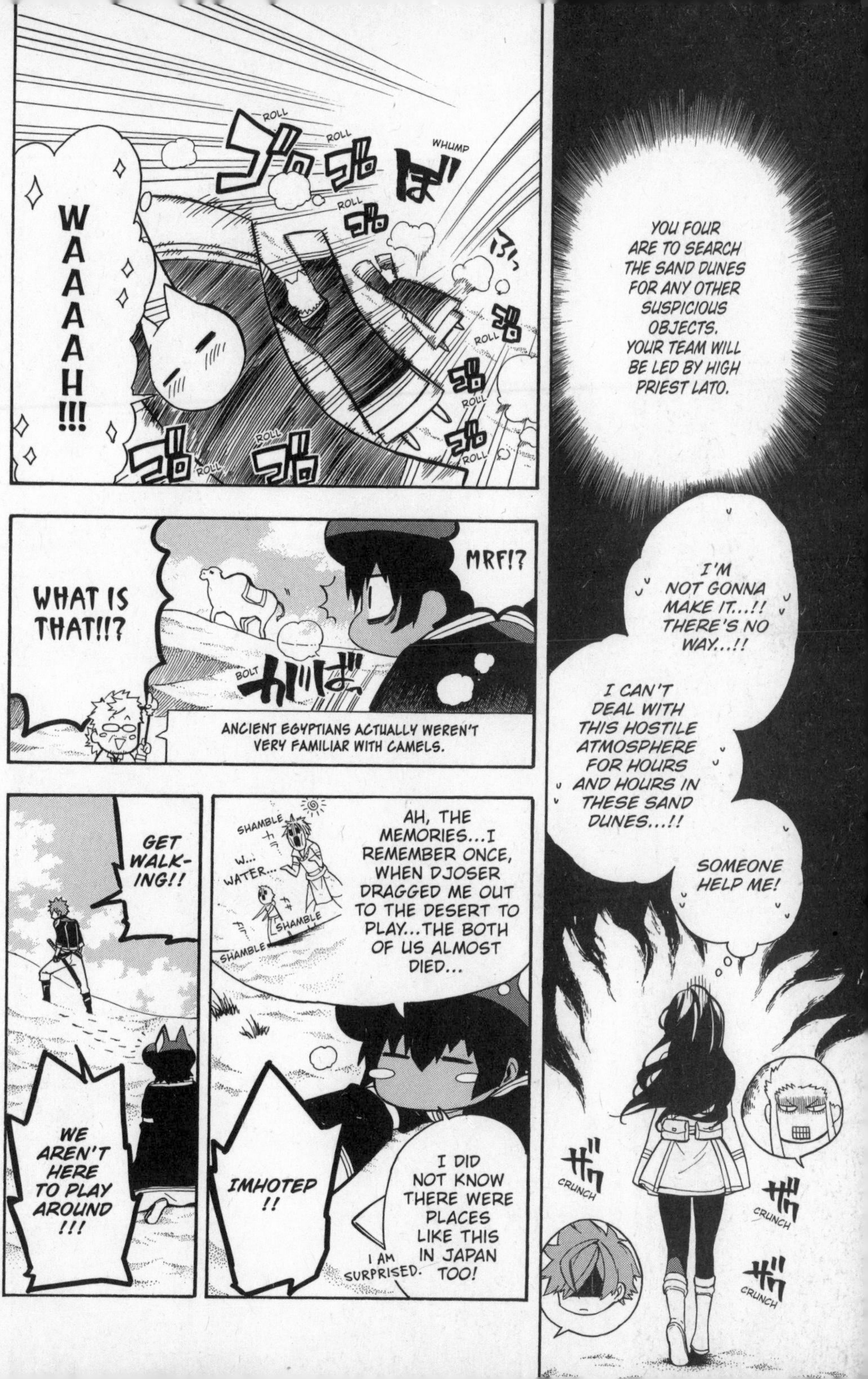
YOU FOUR ARE TO SEARCH THE SAND DUNES FOR ANY OTHER SUSPICIOUS OBJECTS. YOUR TEAM WILL BE LED BY HIGH PRIEST LATO.
I'M NOT GONNA MAKE IT...!! THERE'S NO WAY...!!
I CAN'T DEAL WITH THIS HOSTILE ATMOSPHERE FOR HOURS AND HOURS IN THESE SAND DUNES...!!
SOMEONE HELP ME!
CRUNCH
CRUNCH
CRUNCH
ROLL
ROLL
WHUMP
ROLL
ROLL
ROLL
ROLL
ROLL
ROLL
WAAAAAH!!!
MRF!?
BOLT
WHAT IS THAT!!?
ANCIENT EGYPTIANS ACTUALLY WEREN'T VERY FAMILIAR WITH CAMELS.
AH, THE MEMORIES...I REMEMBER ONCE, WHEN DJOSER DRAGGED ME OUT TO THE DESERT TO PLAY...THE BOTH OF US ALMOST DIED...
SHAMBLE
W... WATER...
SHAMBLE
SHAMBLE
IMHOTEP!!
I DID NOT KNOW THERE WERE PLACES LIKE THIS IN JAPAN TOO!
I AM SURPRISED.
GET WALKING!!
WE AREN'T HERE TO PLAY AROUND!!!

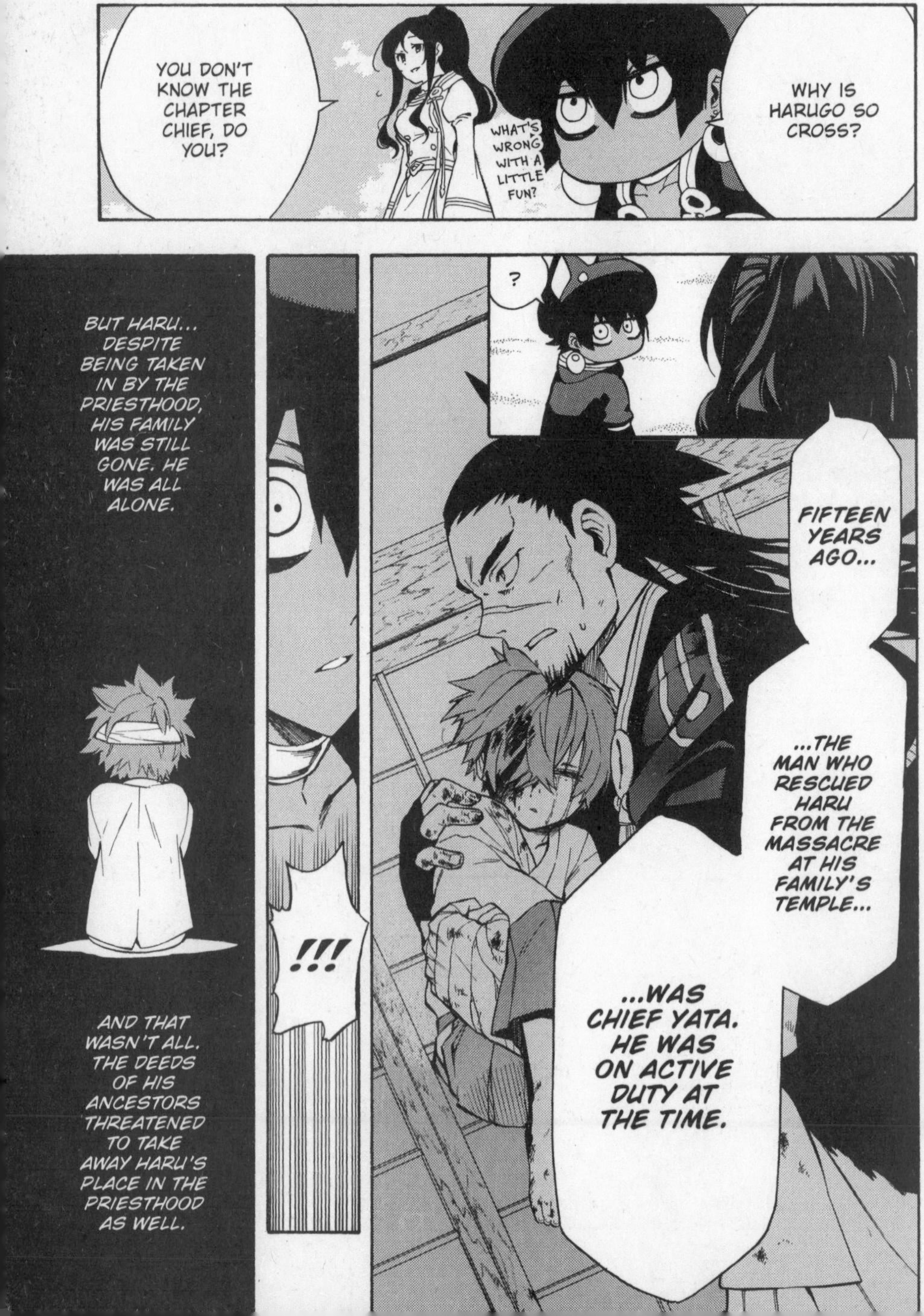
WHY IS HARUGO SO CROSS?
WHAT'S WRONG WITH A LITTLE FUN?
YOU DON'T KNOW THE CHAPTER CHIEF, DO YOU?
?
FIFTEEN YEARS AGO...
...THE MAN WHO RESCUED HARU FROM THE MASSACRE AT HIS FAMILY'S TEMPLE...
...WAS CHIEF YATA. HE WAS ON ACTIVE DUTY AT THE TIME.
!!!
BUT HARU... DESPITE BEING TAKEN IN BY THE PRIESTHOOD, HIS FAMILY WAS STILL GONE. HE WAS ALL ALONE.
AND THAT WASN'T ALL. THE DEEDS OF HIS ANCESTORS THREATENED TO TAKE AWAY HARU'S PLACE IN THE PRIESTHOOD AS WELL.

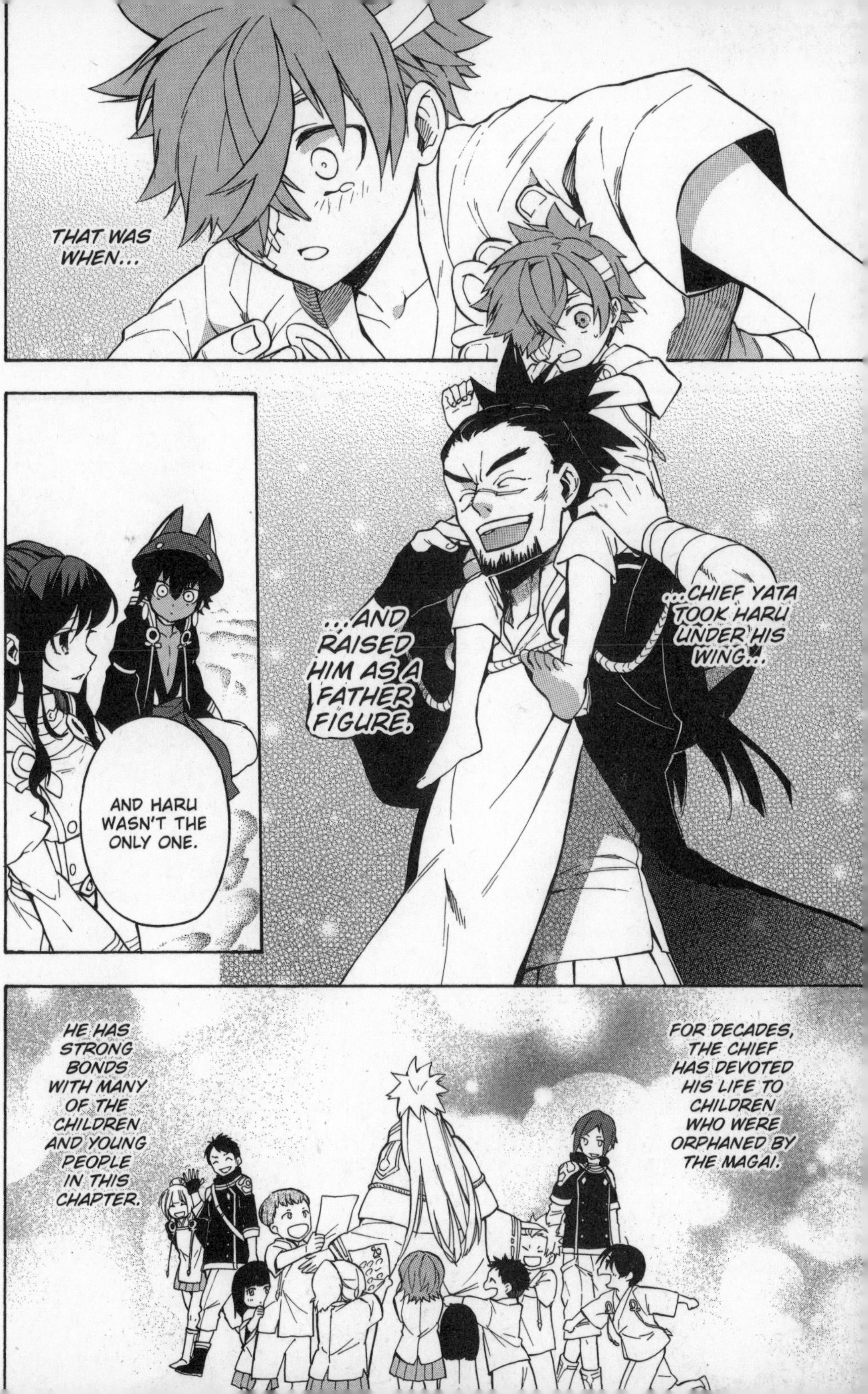
THAT WAS WHEN...
...CHIEF YATA TOOK HARU UNDER HIS WING...
...AND RAISED HIM AS A FATHER FIGURE.
AND HARU WASN'T THE ONLY ONE.
FOR DECADES, THE CHIEF HAS DEVOTED HIS LIFE TO CHILDREN WHO WERE ORPHANED BY THE MAGAI.
HE HAS STRONG BONDS WITH MANY OF THE CHILDREN AND YOUNG PEOPLE IN THIS CHAPTER.

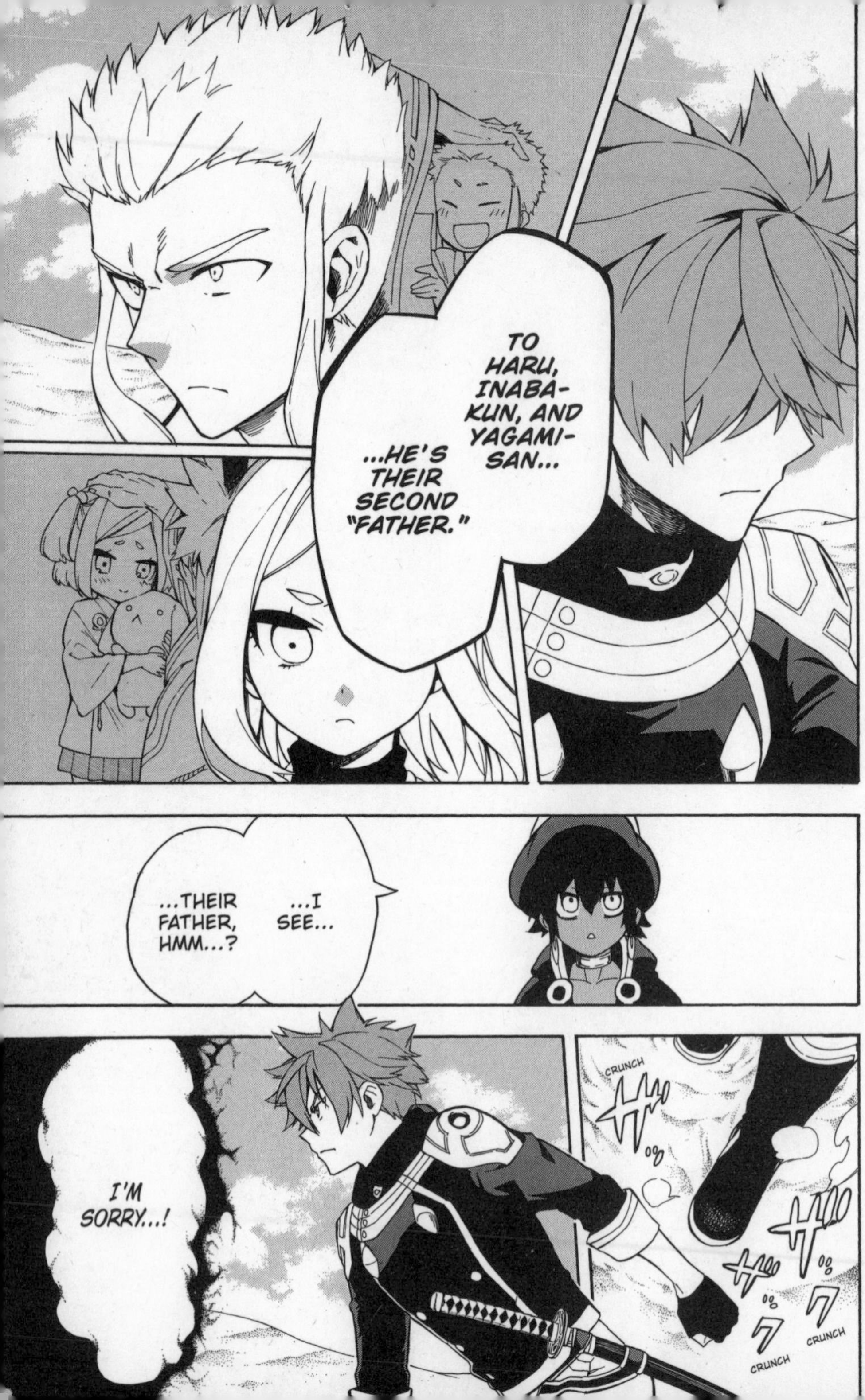
TO HARU, INABA-KUN, AND YAGAMI-SAN...
...HE'S THEIR SECOND "FATHER."
...I SEE...
...THEIR FATHER, HMM...?
CRUNCH
CRUNCH
CRUNCH
I'M SORRY...!

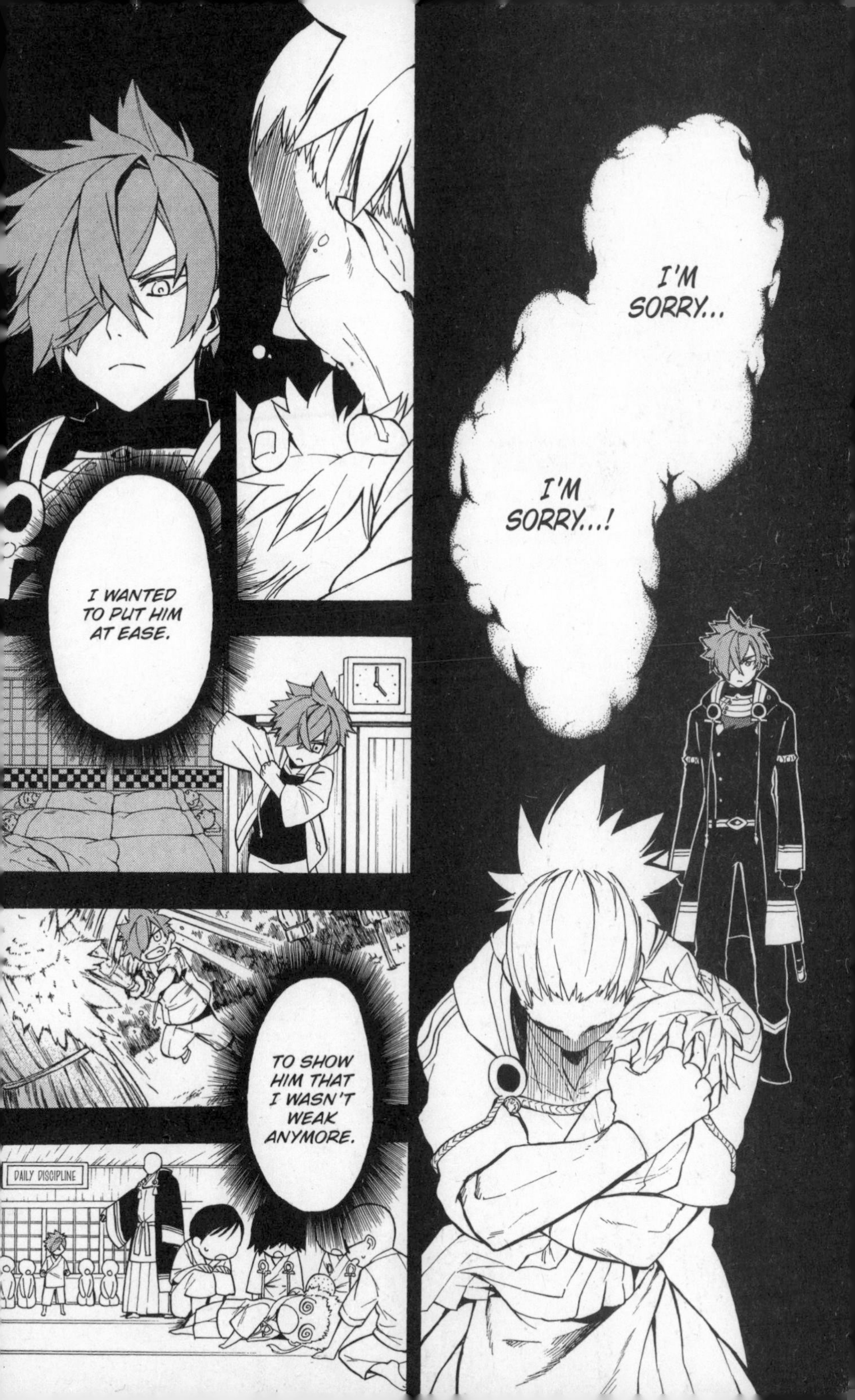
I'M SORRY...
I'M SORRY...!
I WANTED TO PUT HIM AT EASE.
TO SHOW HIM THAT I WASN'T WEAK ANYMORE.
DAILY DISCIPLINE

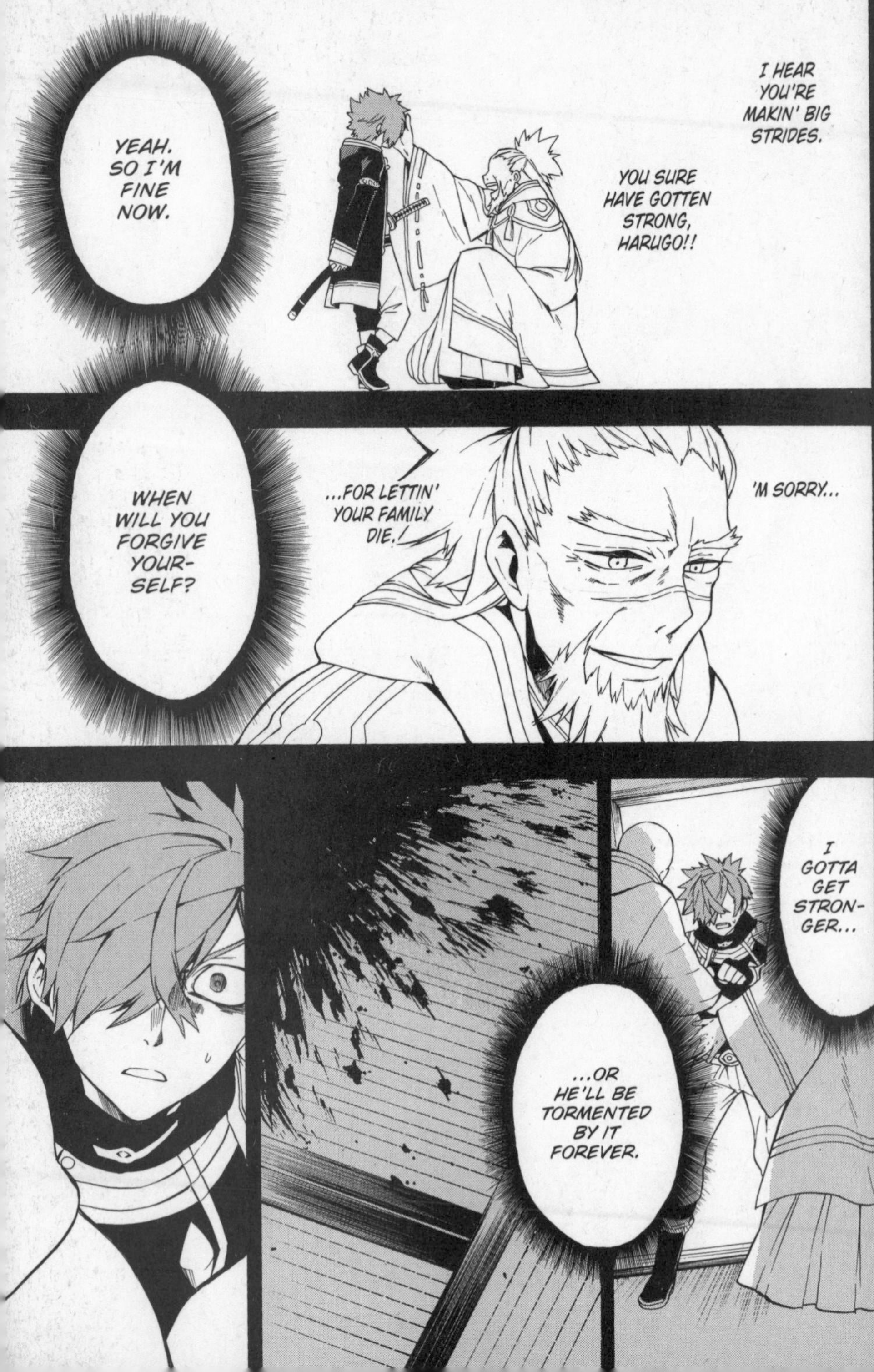
I HEAR YOU'RE MAKIN' BIG STRIDES.
YOU SURE HAVE GOTTEN STRONG, HARUGO!!
YEAH. SO I'M FINE NOW.
'M SORRY...
...FOR LETTIN' YOUR FAMILY DIE.
WHEN WILL YOU FORGIVE YOURSELF?
I GOTTA GET STRONGER...
...OR HE'LL BE TORMENTED BY IT FOREVER.

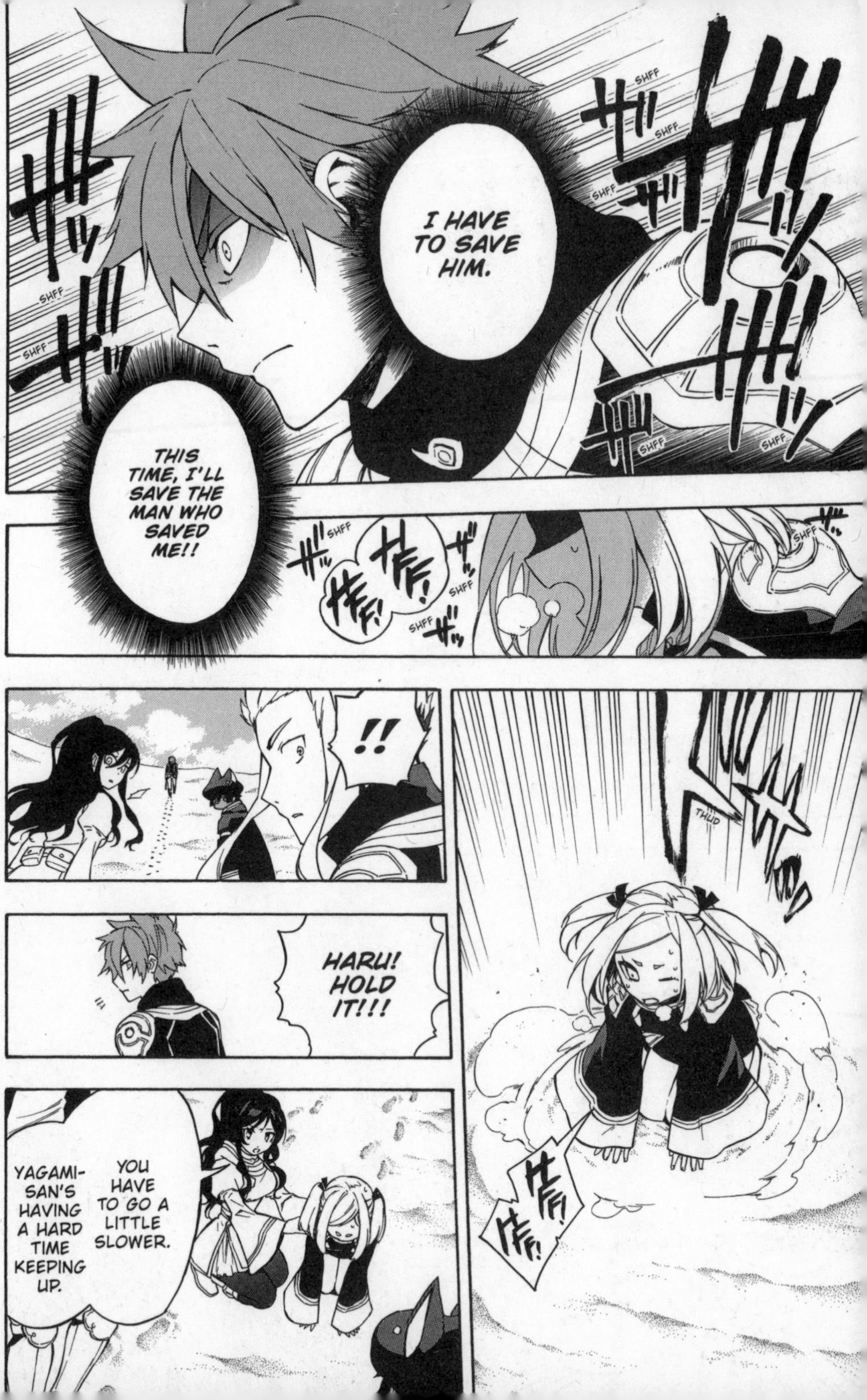
SHFF
SHFF
SHFF
SHFF
SHFF
SHFF
SHFF
I HAVE TO SAVE HIM.
THIS TIME, I'LL SAVE THE MAN WHO SAVED ME!!
SHFF
SHFF
SHFF
SHFF
THUD
!!
HARU! HOLD IT!!!
YOU HAVE TO GO A LITTLE SLOWER.
YAGAMI-SAN'S HAVING A HARD TIME KEEPING UP.

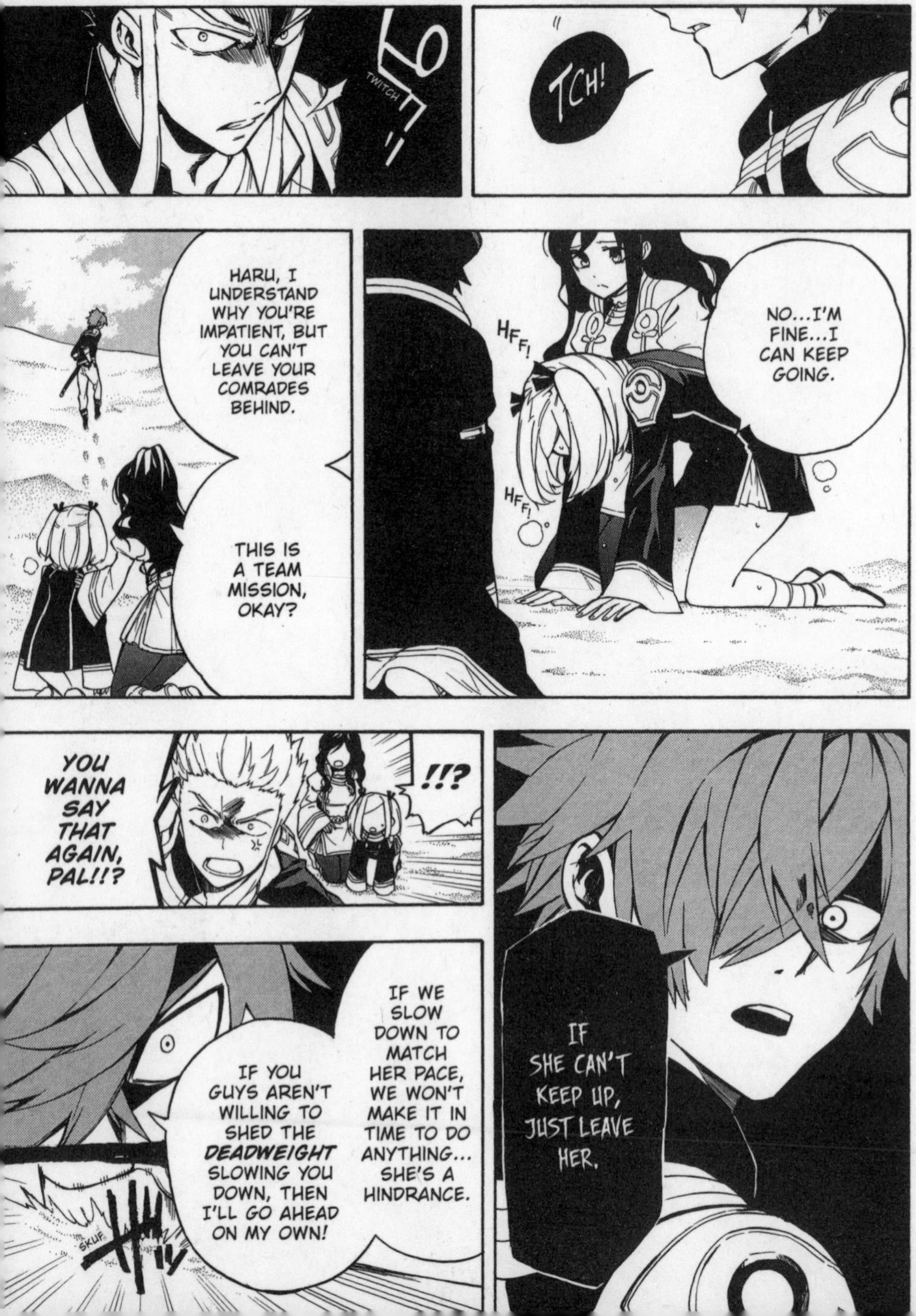
TCH!
TWITCH
HFF!
NO...I'M FINE...I CAN KEEP GOING.
HFF!
HARU, I UNDERSTAND WHY YOU'RE IMPATIENT, BUT YOU CAN'T LEAVE YOUR COMRADES BEHIND.
THIS IS A TEAM MISSION, OKAY?
IF SHE CAN'T KEEP UP, JUST LEAVE HER.
YOU WANNA SAY THAT AGAIN, PAL!!?
!!?
IF WE SLOW DOWN TO MATCH HER PACE, WE WON'T MAKE IT IN TIME TO DO ANYTHING... SHE'S A HINDRANCE.
IF YOU GUYS AREN'T WILLING TO SHED THE ***DEADWEIGHT*** SLOWING YOU DOWN, THEN I'LL GO AHEAD ON MY OWN!
SKUF

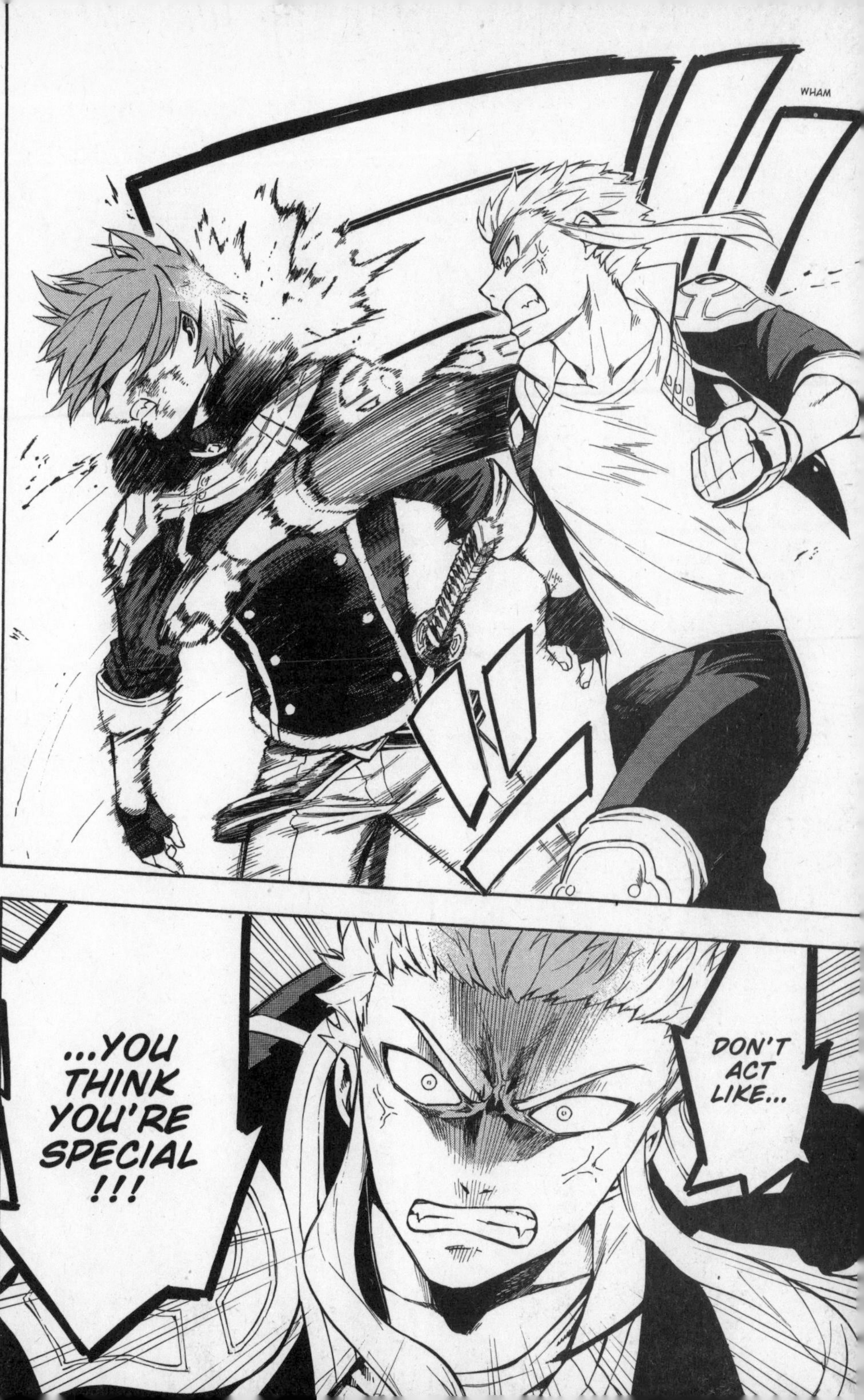
WHAM
DON'T ACT LIKE...
...YOU THINK YOU'RE SPECIAL!!!

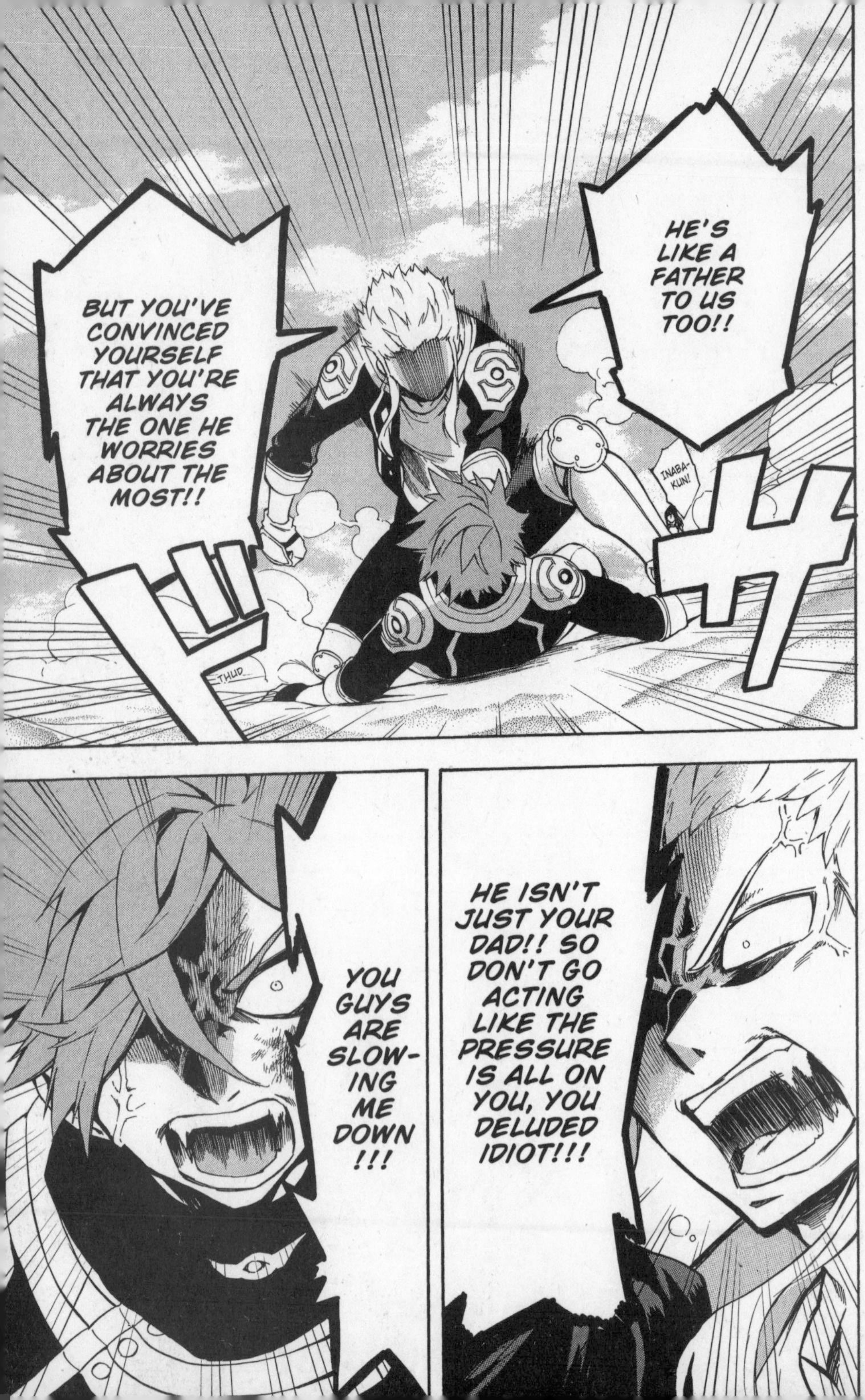
HE'S LIKE A FATHER TO US TOO!!
INABA-KUN!
BUT YOU'VE CONVINCED YOURSELF THAT YOU'RE ALWAYS THE ONE HE WORRIES ABOUT THE MOST!!
THUD
HE ISN'T JUST YOUR DAD!! SO DON'T GO ACTING LIKE THE PRESSURE IS ALL ON YOU, YOU DELUDED IDIOT!!!
YOU GUYS ARE SLOWING ME DOWN!!!

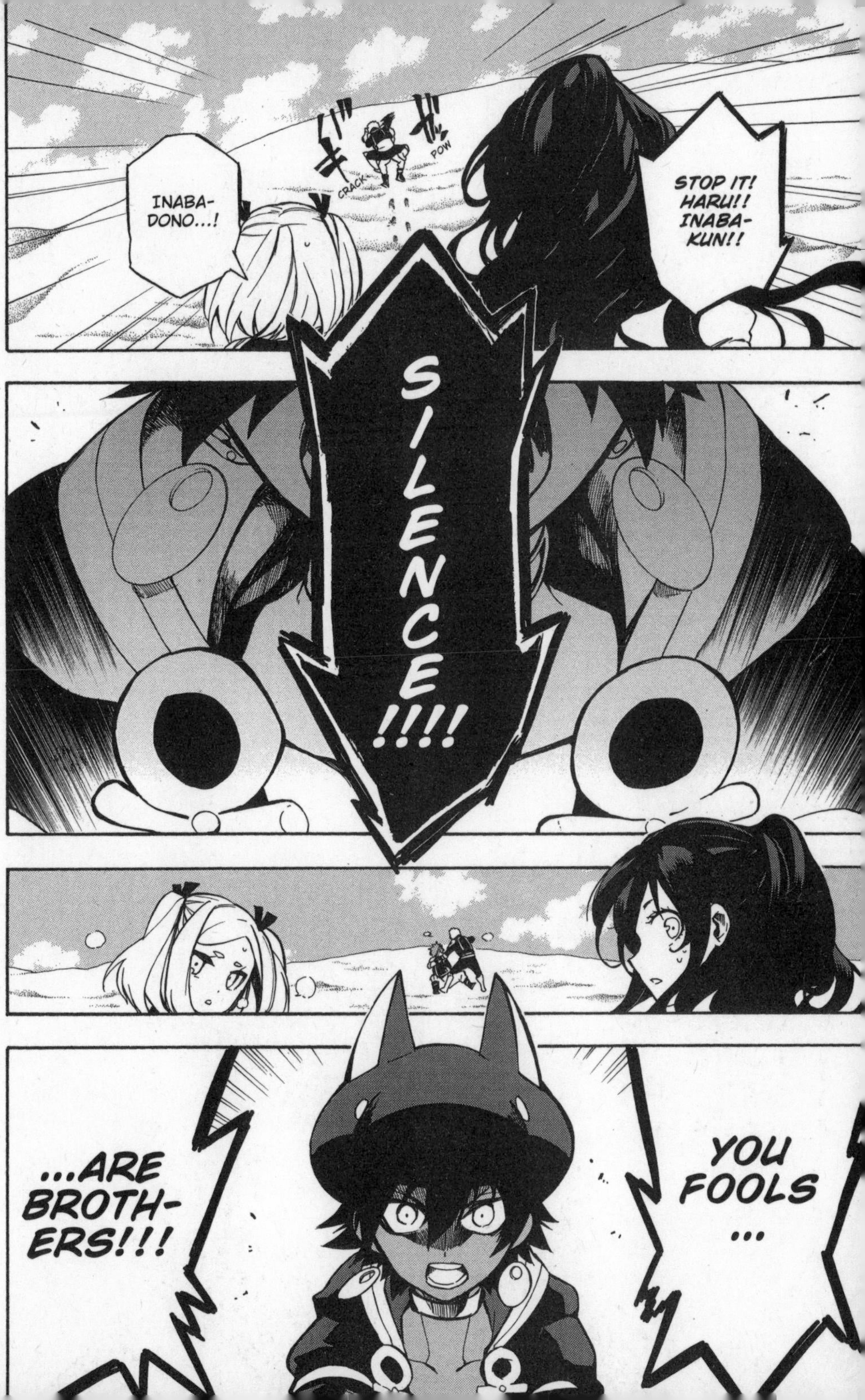
STOP IT! HARU!! INABA-KUN!!
POW
CRACK
INABA-DONO...!
SILENCE!!!!
YOU FOOLS ...
...ARE BROTH-ERS!!!

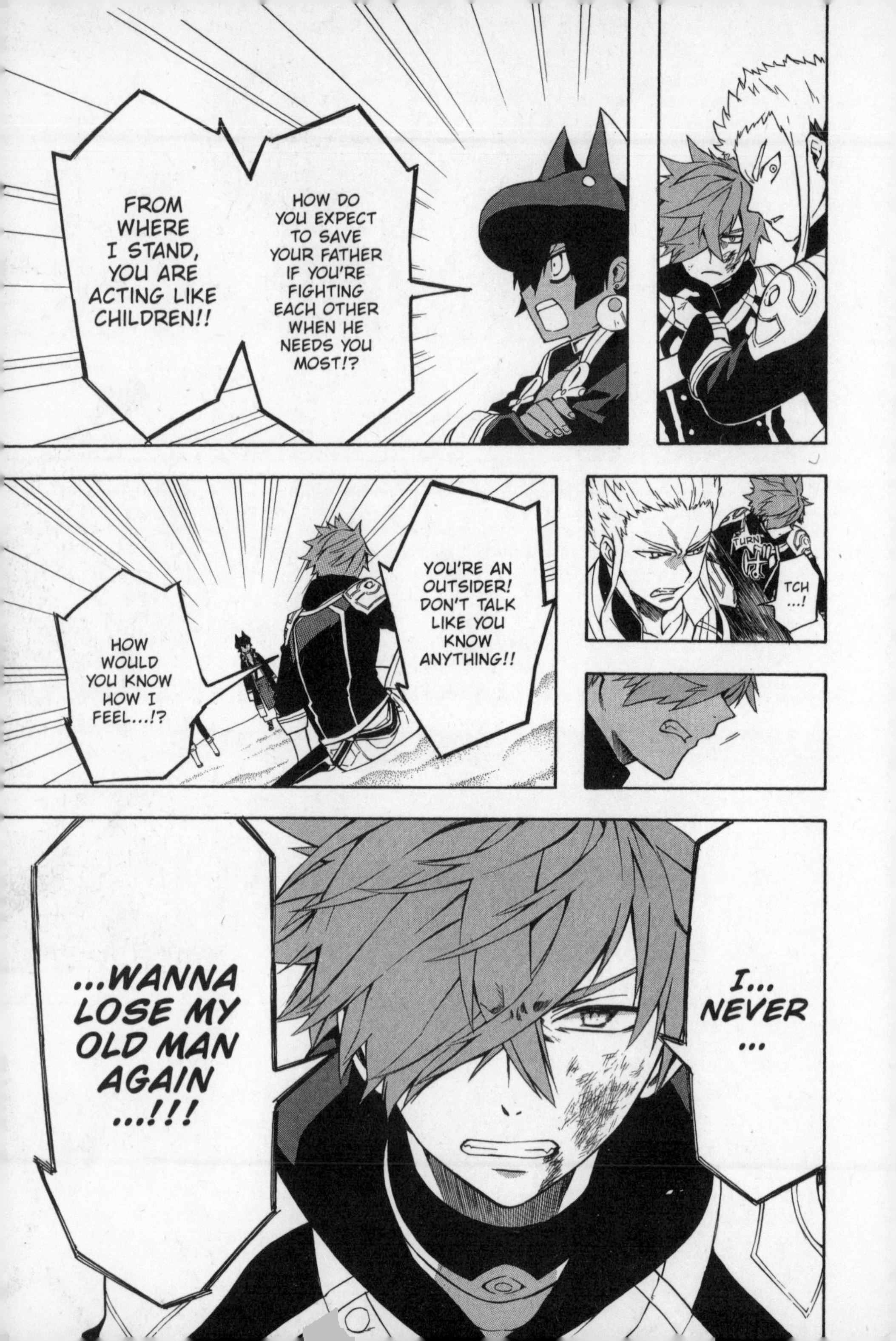
HOW DO YOU EXPECT TO SAVE YOUR FATHER IF YOU'RE FIGHTING EACH OTHER WHEN HE NEEDS YOU MOST!?
FROM WHERE I STAND, YOU ARE ACTING LIKE CHILDREN!!
TURN
TCH ...!
YOU'RE AN OUTSIDER! DON'T TALK LIKE YOU KNOW ANYTHING!!
HOW WOULD YOU KNOW HOW I FEEL...!?
I... NEVER ...
...WANNA LOSE MY OLD MAN AGAIN ...!!!

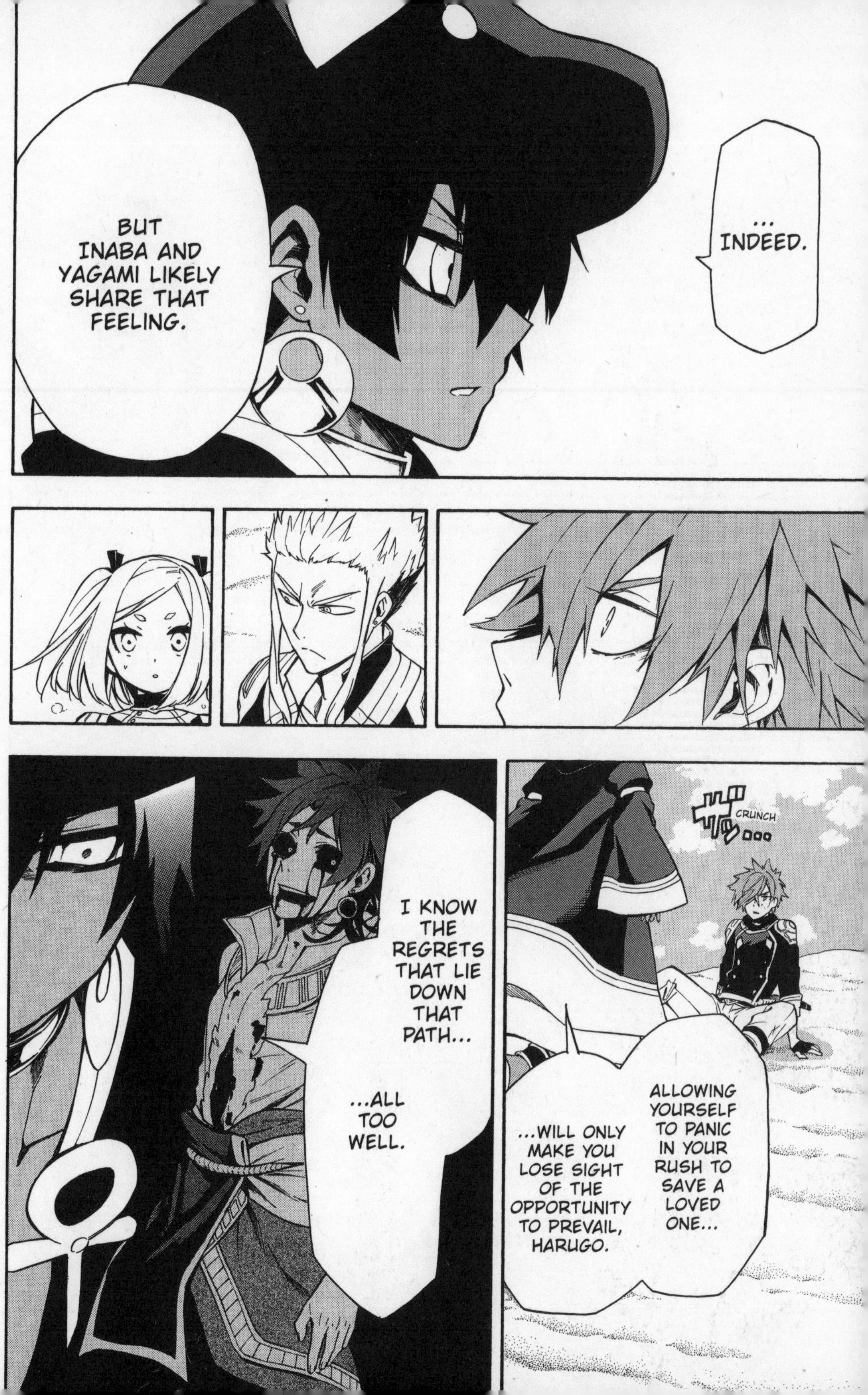
...INDEED.
BUT INABA AND YAGAMI LIKELY SHARE THAT FEELING.
ザッ CRUNCH
ALLOWING YOURSELF TO PANIC IN YOUR RUSH TO SAVE A LOVED ONE...
...WILL ONLY MAKE YOU LOSE SIGHT OF THE OPPORTUNITY TO PREVAIL, HARUGO.
I KNOW THE REGRETS THAT LIE DOWN THAT PATH...
...ALL TOO WELL.

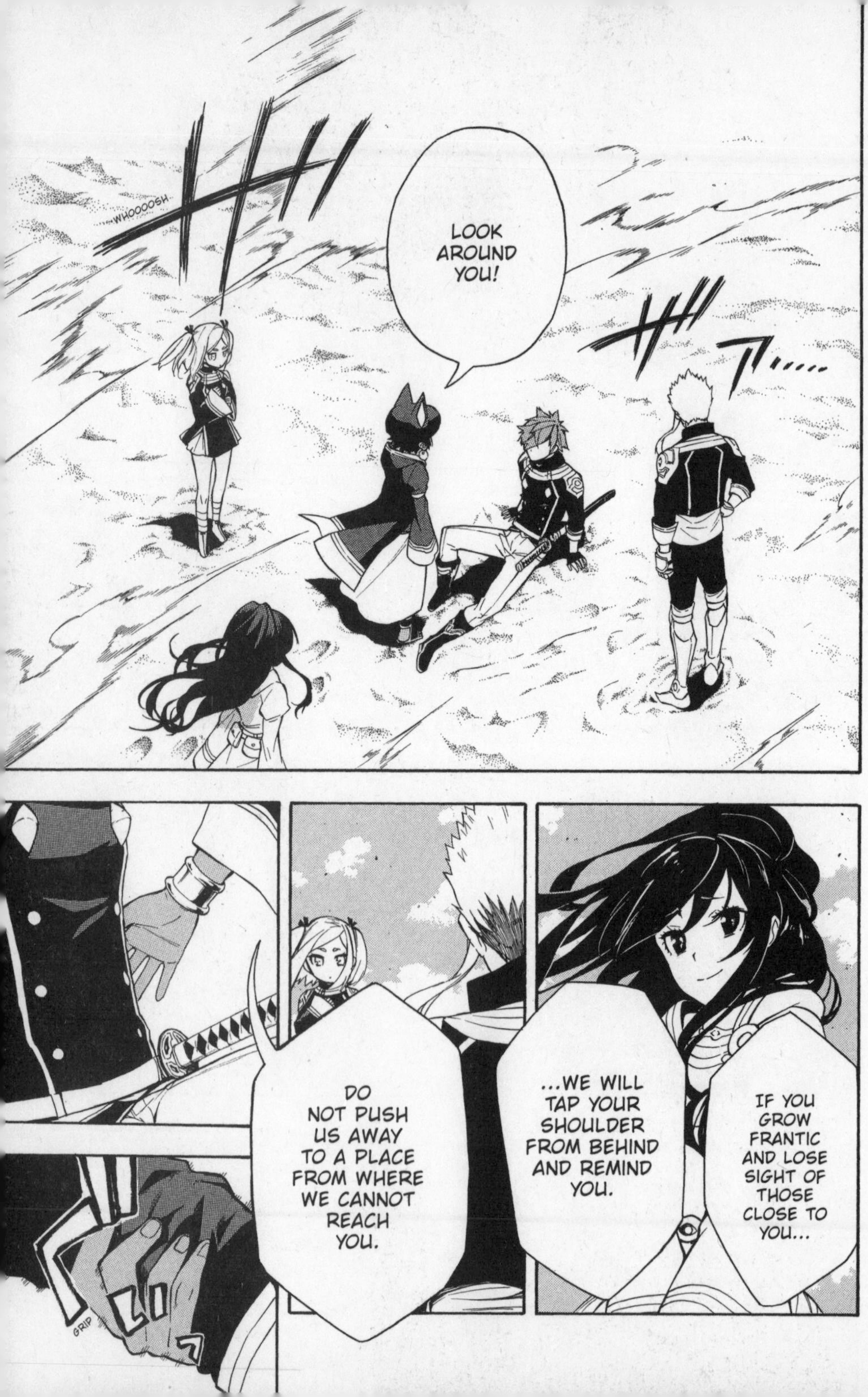
LOOK AROUND YOU!
WHOOOOSH
IF YOU GROW FRANTIC AND LOSE SIGHT OF THOSE CLOSE TO YOU...
...WE WILL TAP YOUR SHOULDER FROM BEHIND AND REMIND YOU.
DO NOT PUSH US AWAY TO A PLACE FROM WHERE WE CANNOT REACH YOU.
GRIP

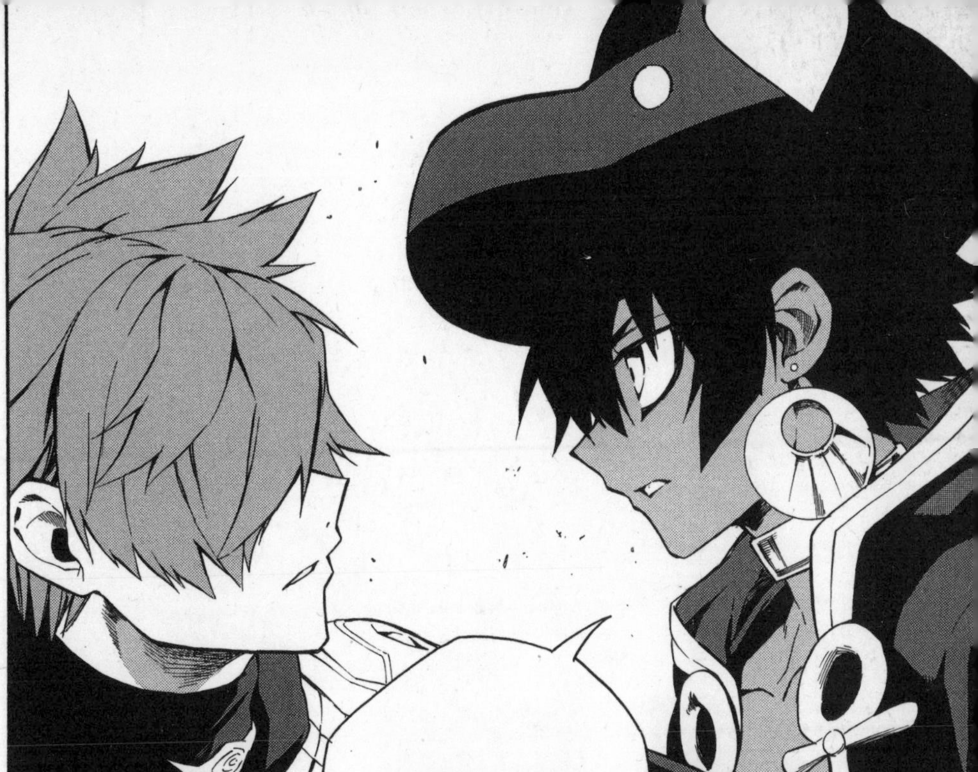
I WILL NOT LET YOUR FAMILY BE SNATCHED FROM ANY OF YOU AGAIN.
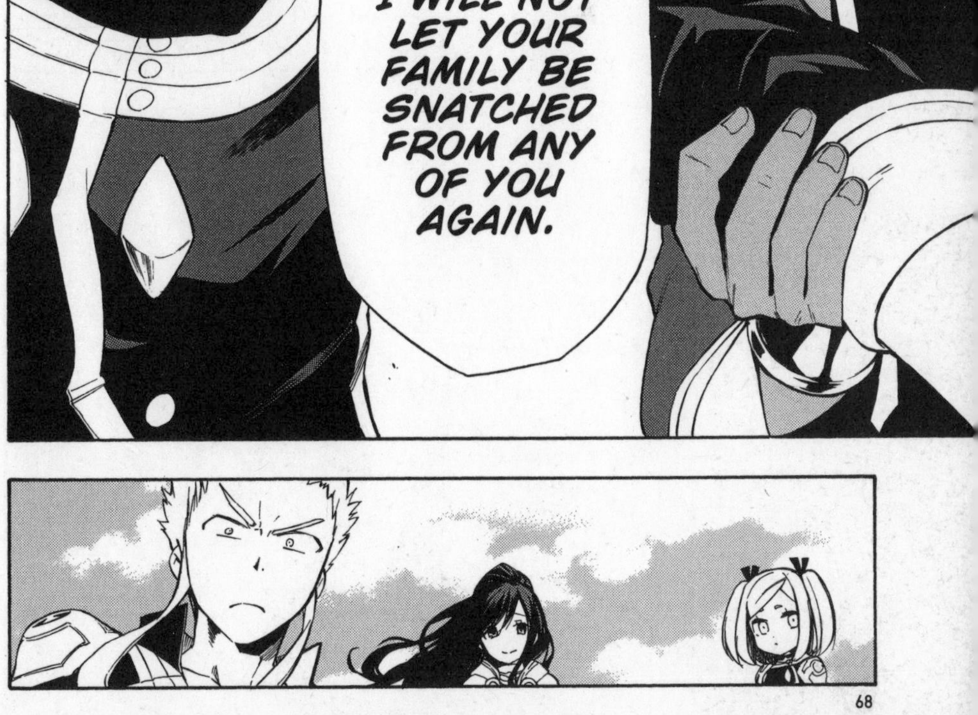

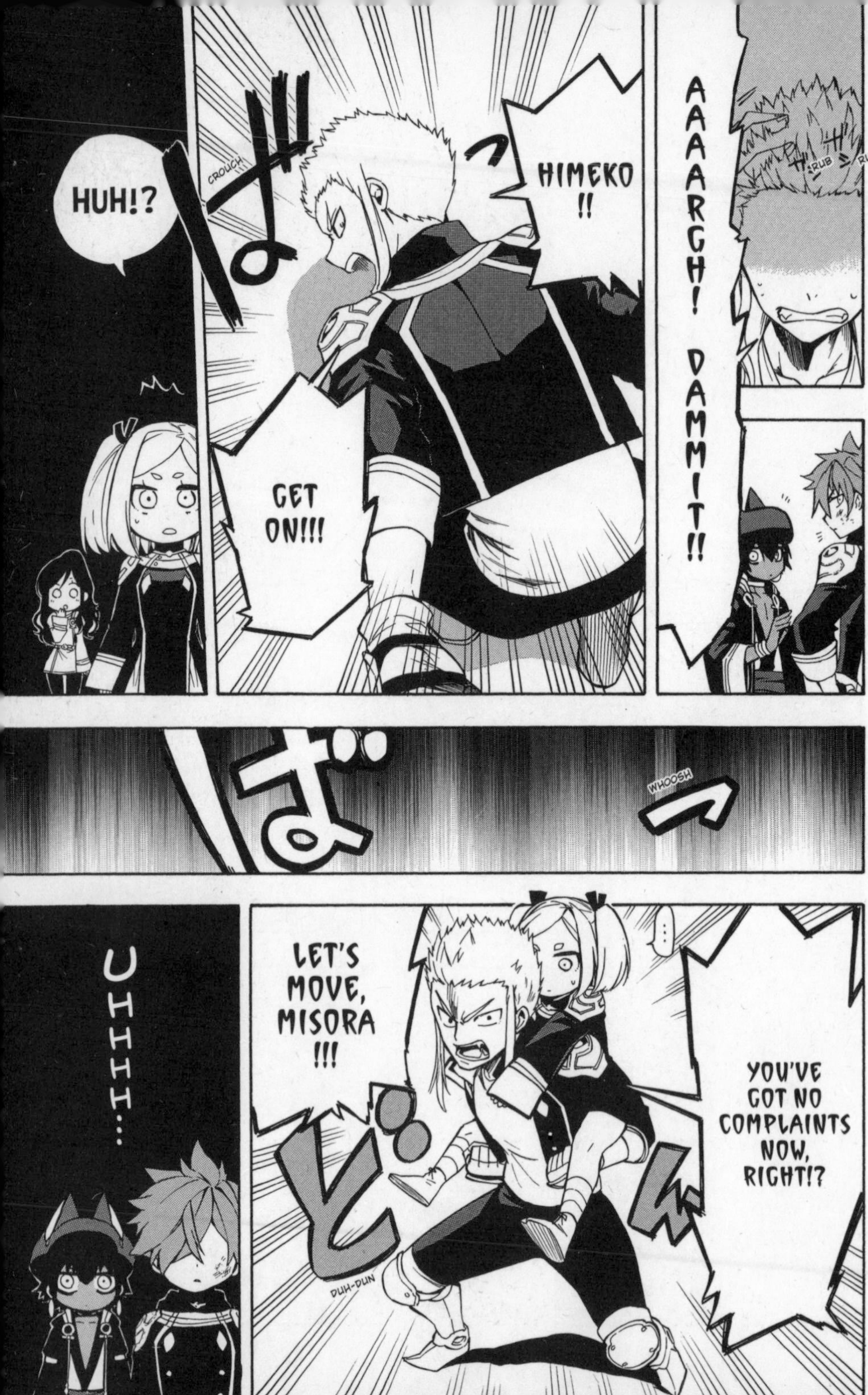
RUB RUB
AAAARGH! DAMMIT!!
HIMEKO!!
CROUCH
GET ON!!!
HUH!?
WHOOSH
...
LET'S MOVE, MISORA!!!
YOU'VE GOT NO COMPLAINTS NOW, RIGHT!?
DUH-DUN
UHHHH...

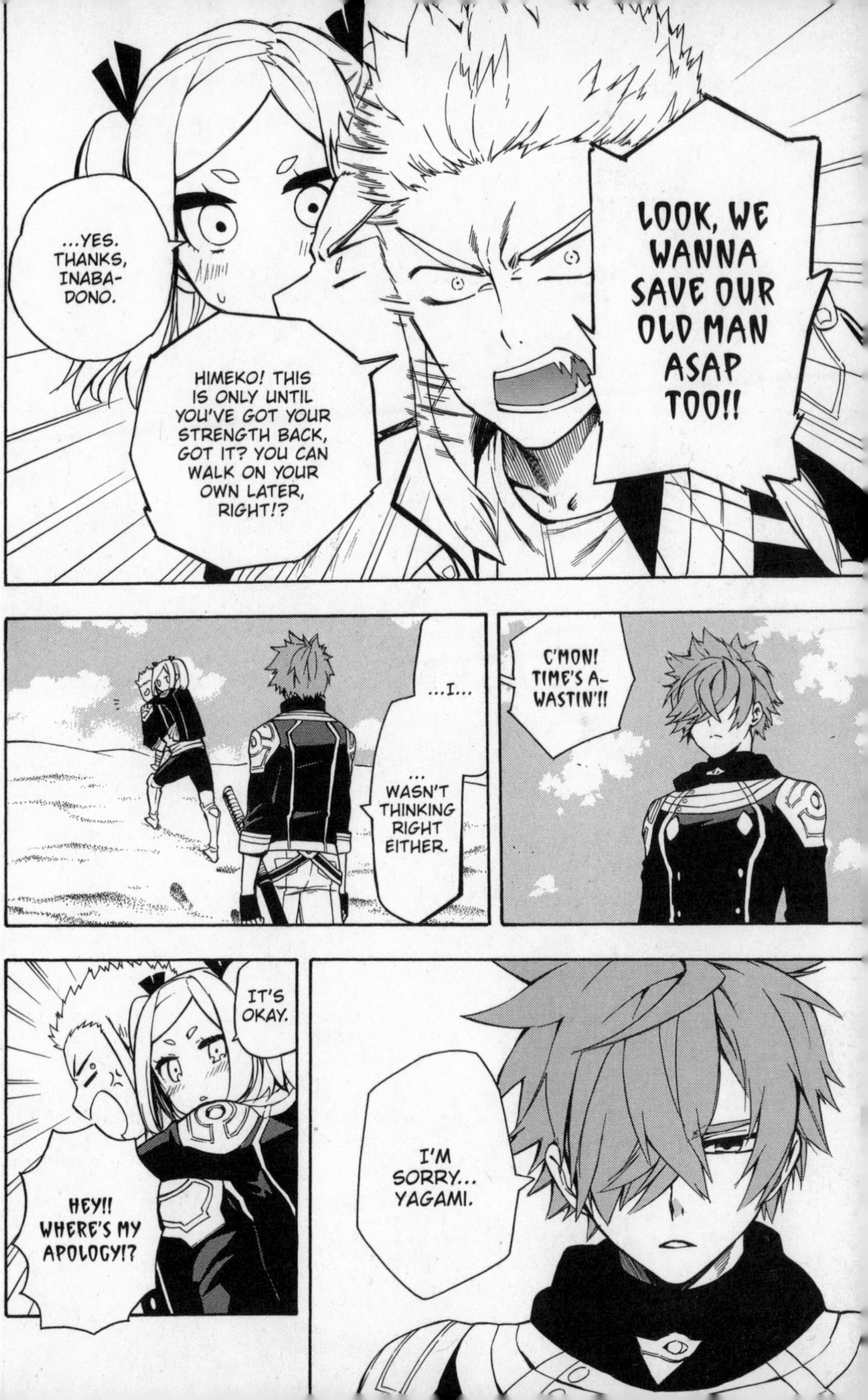
LOOK, WE WANNA SAVE OUR OLD MAN ASAP TOO!!
HIMEKO! THIS IS ONLY UNTIL YOU'VE GOT YOUR STRENGTH BACK, GOT IT? YOU CAN WALK ON YOUR OWN LATER, RIGHT!?
...YES. THANKS, INABA-DONO.
C'MON! TIME'S A-WASTIN'!!
...I...
...WASN'T THINKING RIGHT EITHER.
I'M SORRY... YAGAMI.
IT'S OKAY.
HEY!! WHERE'S MY APOLOGY!?

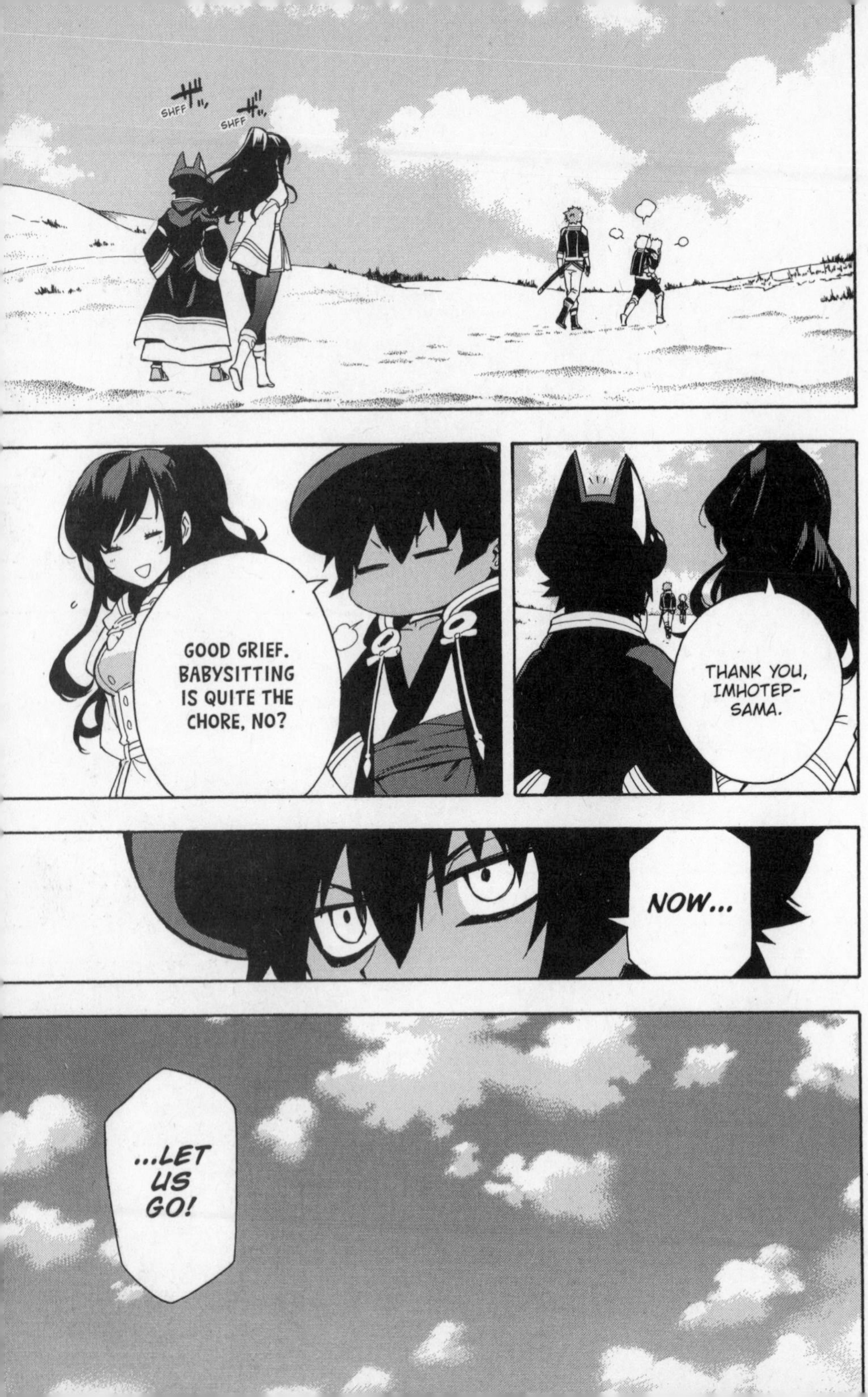
SHFF
SHFF
THANK YOU, IMHOTEP-SAMA.
GOOD GRIEF. BABYSITTING IS QUITE THE CHORE, NO?
NOW...
...LET US GO!

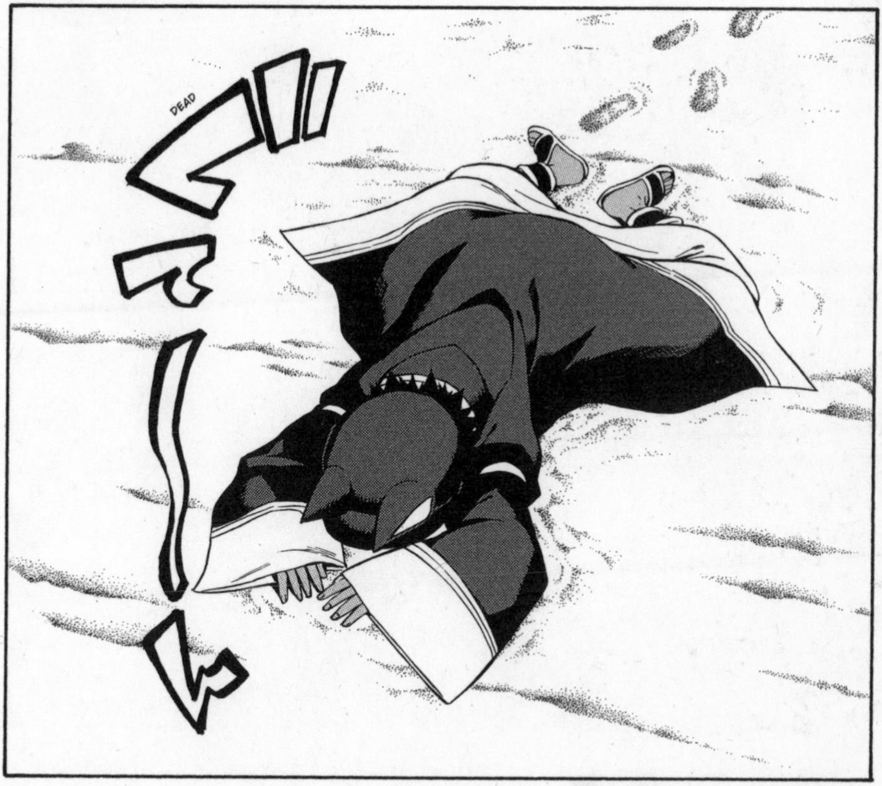
DEAD

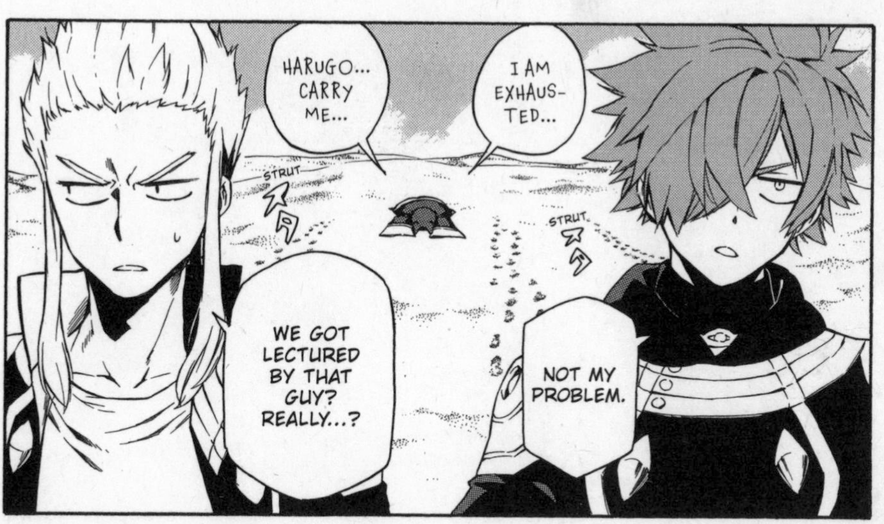
I AM EXHAUS-TED...
HARUGO... CARRY ME...
STRUT
STRUT
NOT MY PROBLEM.
WE GOT LECTURED BY THAT GUY? REALLY...?

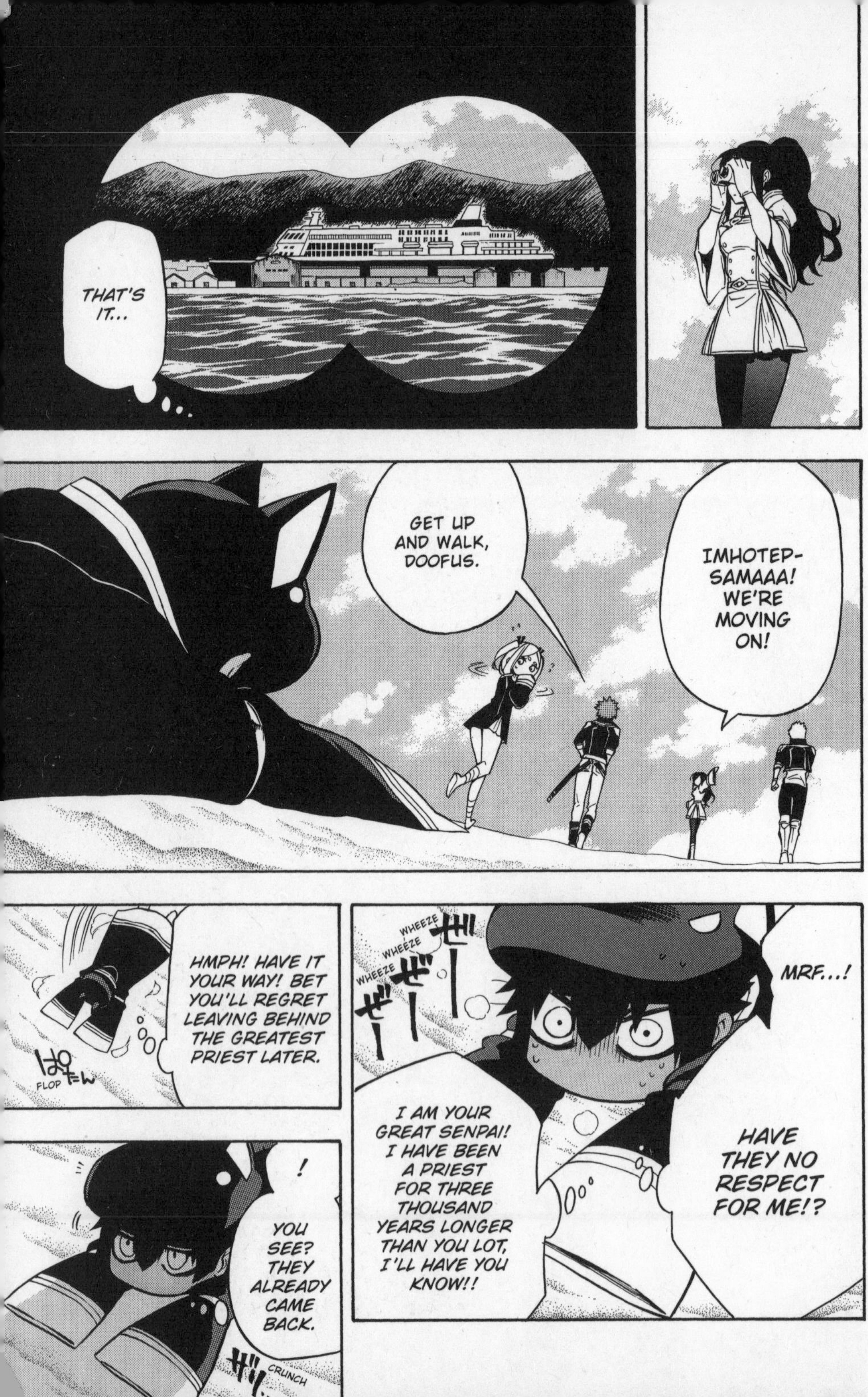
THAT'S IT...
IMHOTEP-SAMAAA! WE'RE MOVING ON!
GET UP AND WALK, DOOFUS.
WHEEZE
WHEEZE
WHEEZE
MRF...!
HAVE THEY NO RESPECT FOR ME!?
I AM YOUR GREAT SENPAI! I HAVE BEEN A PRIEST FOR THREE THOUSAND YEARS LONGER THAN YOU LOT, I'LL HAVE YOU KNOW!!
HMPH! HAVE IT YOUR WAY! BET YOU'LL REGRET LEAVING BEHIND THE GREATEST PRIEST LATER.
FLOP
!
YOU SEE? THEY ALREADY CAME BACK.
CRUNCH

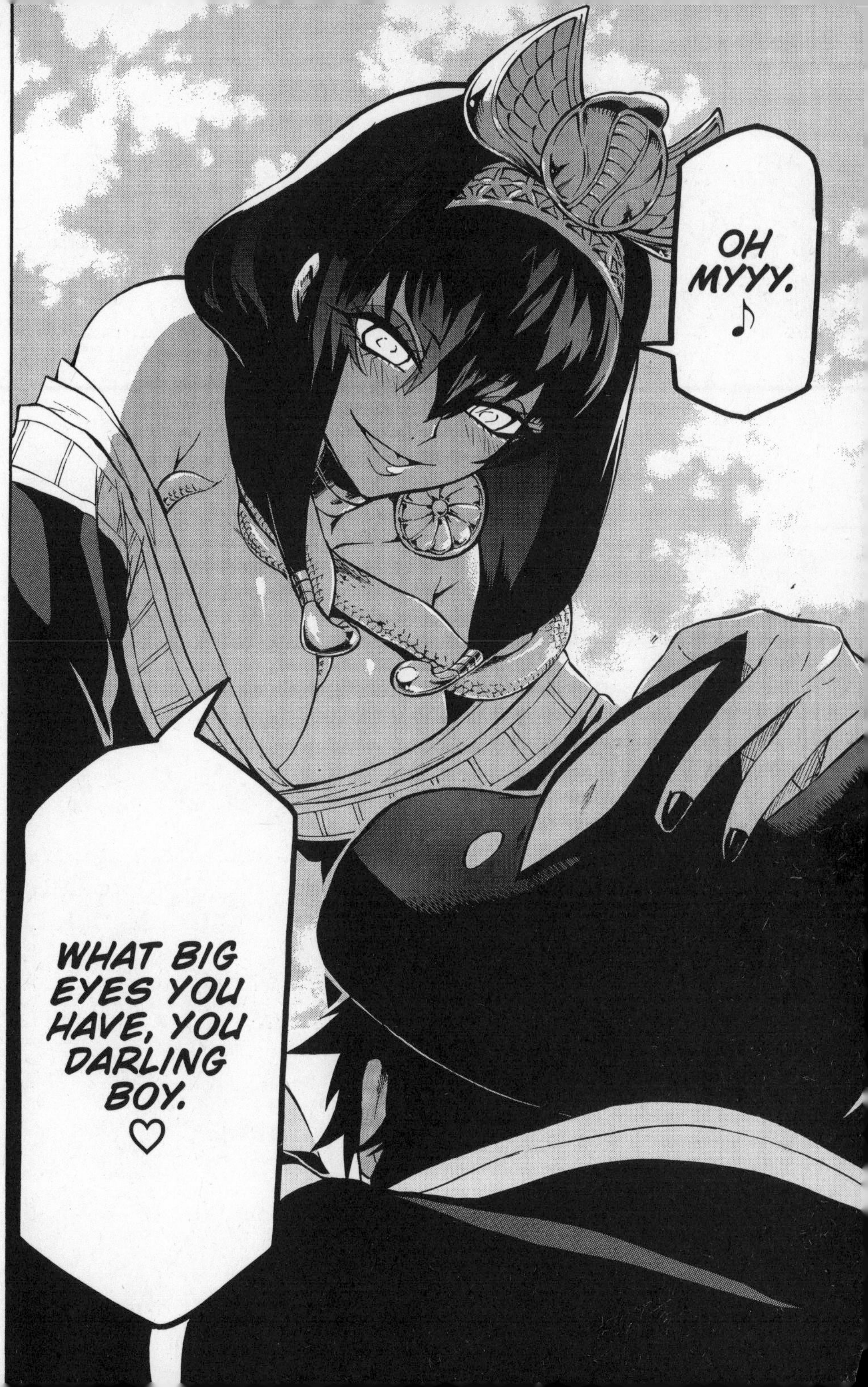
OH MYYY. ♪
WHAT BIG EYES YOU HAVE, YOU DARLING BOY. ♡

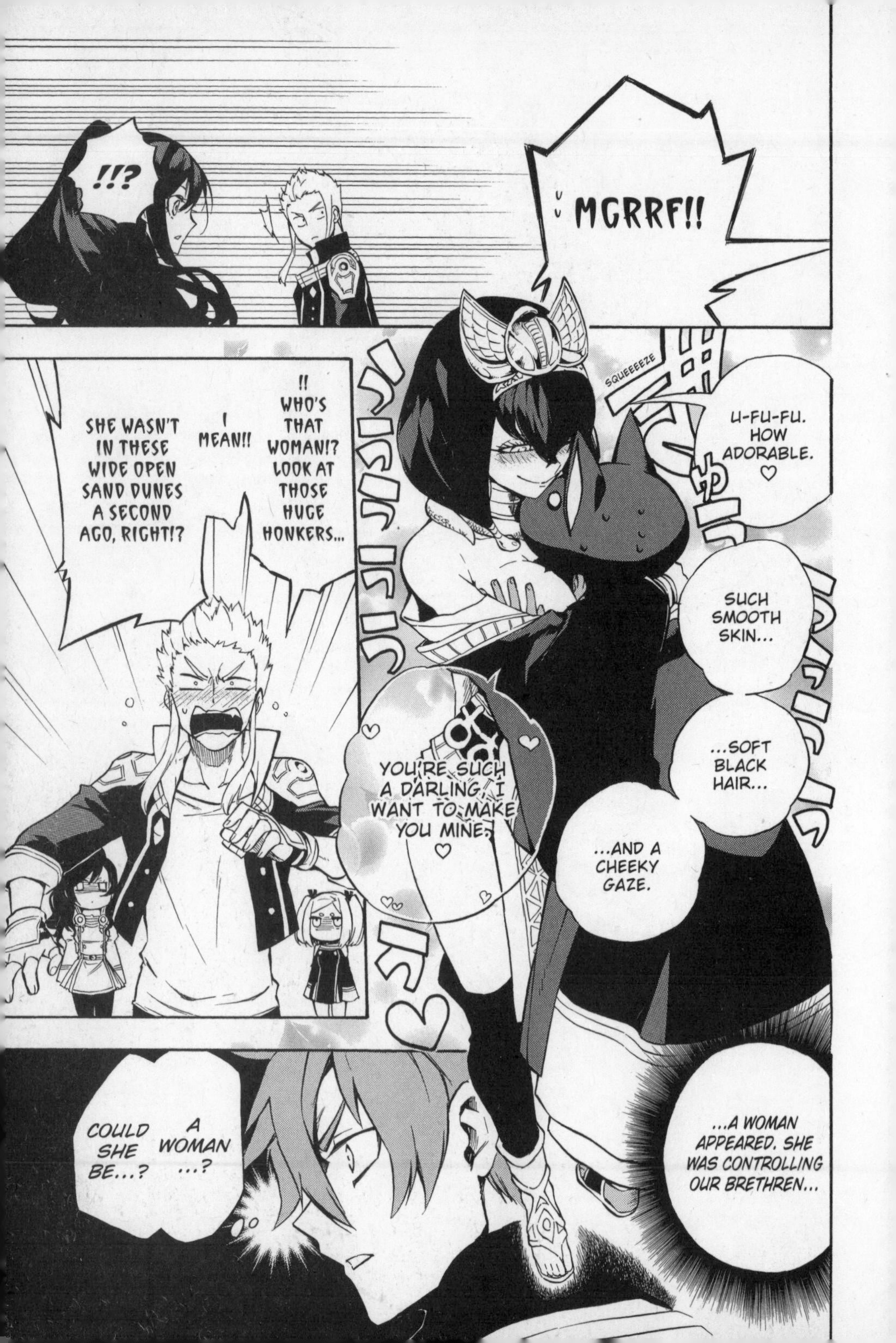
MGRRF!!
!!?
SQUEEEEZE
U-FU-FU. HOW ADORABLE. ♡
SUCH SMOOTH SKIN...
...SOFT BLACK HAIR...
...AND A CHEEKY GAZE.
YOU'RE SUCH A DARLING, I WANT TO MAKE YOU MINE. ♡
!! WHO'S THAT WOMAN!? LOOK AT THOSE HUGE HONKERS...
I MEAN!!
SHE WASN'T IN THESE WIDE OPEN SAND DUNES A SECOND AGO, RIGHT!?
...A WOMAN APPEARED. SHE WAS CONTROLLING OUR BRETHREN...
A WOMAN ...?
COULD SHE BE...?

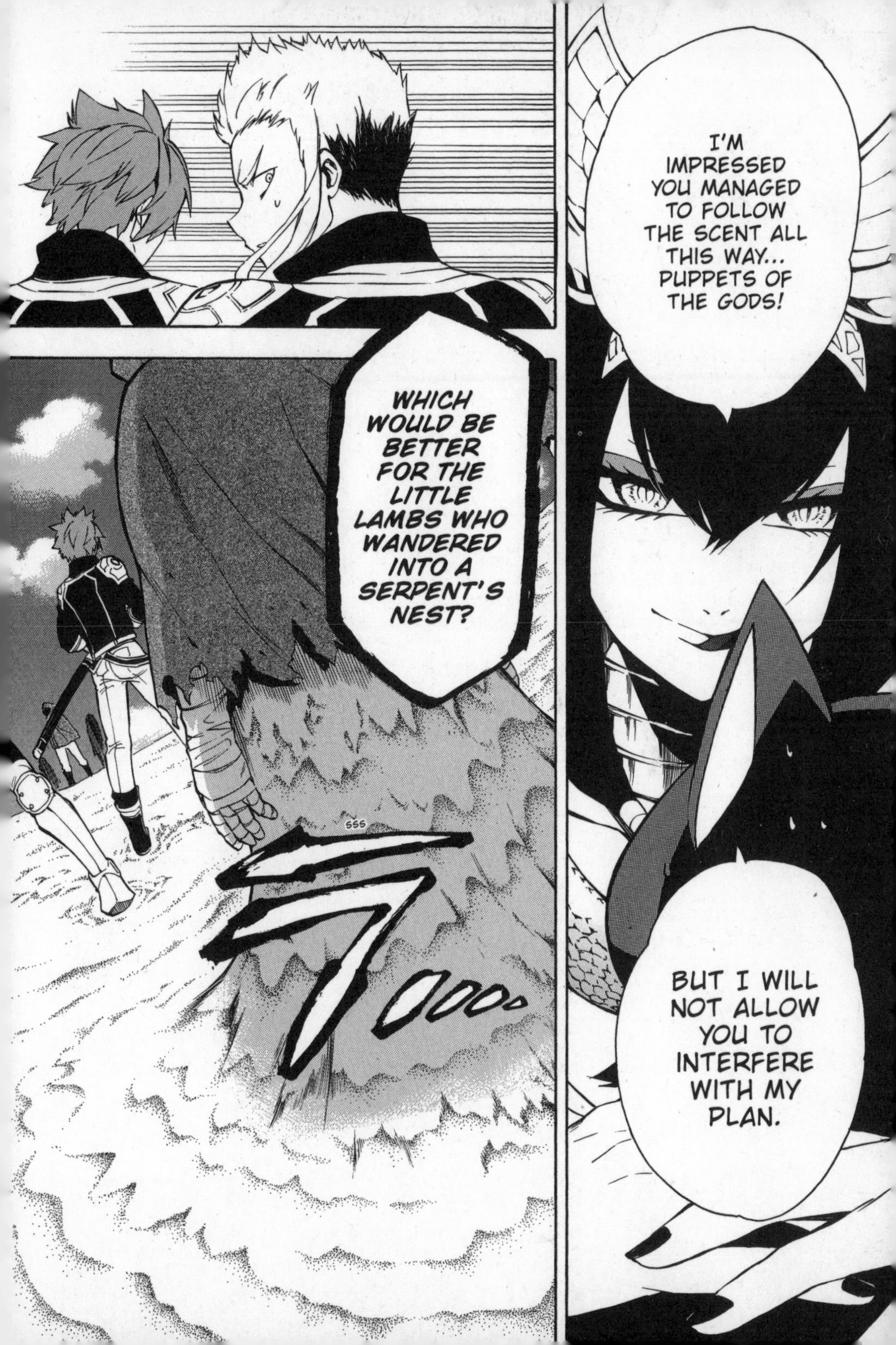
I'M IMPRESSED YOU MANAGED TO FOLLOW THE SCENT ALL THIS WAY... PUPPETS OF THE GODS!
BUT I WILL NOT ALLOW YOU TO INTERFERE WITH MY PLAN.
WHICH WOULD BE BETTER FOR THE LITTLE LAMBS WHO WANDERED INTO A SERPENT'S NEST?
SSS

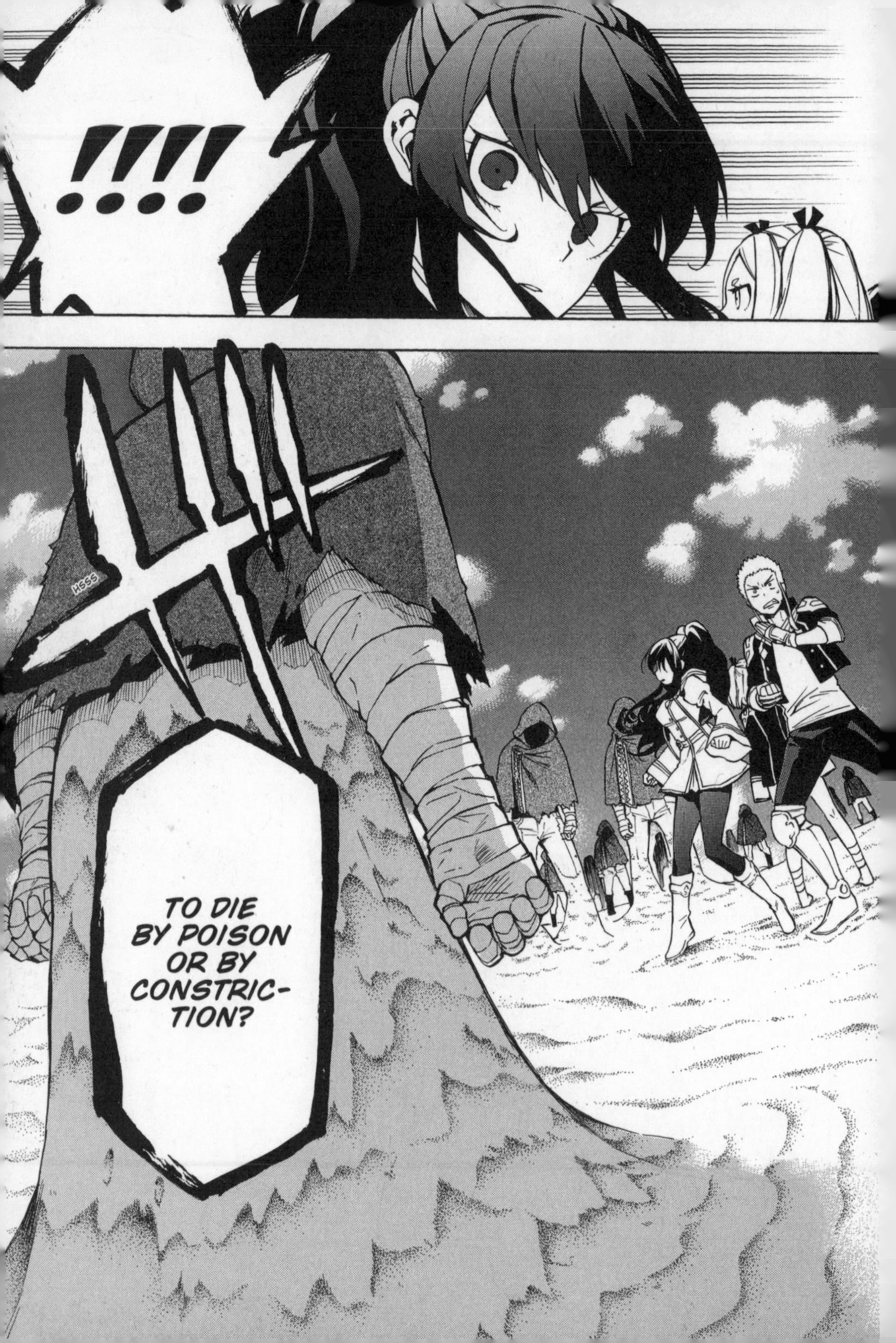
!!!!
HSSS
TO DIE BY POISON OR BY CONSTRIC-TION?

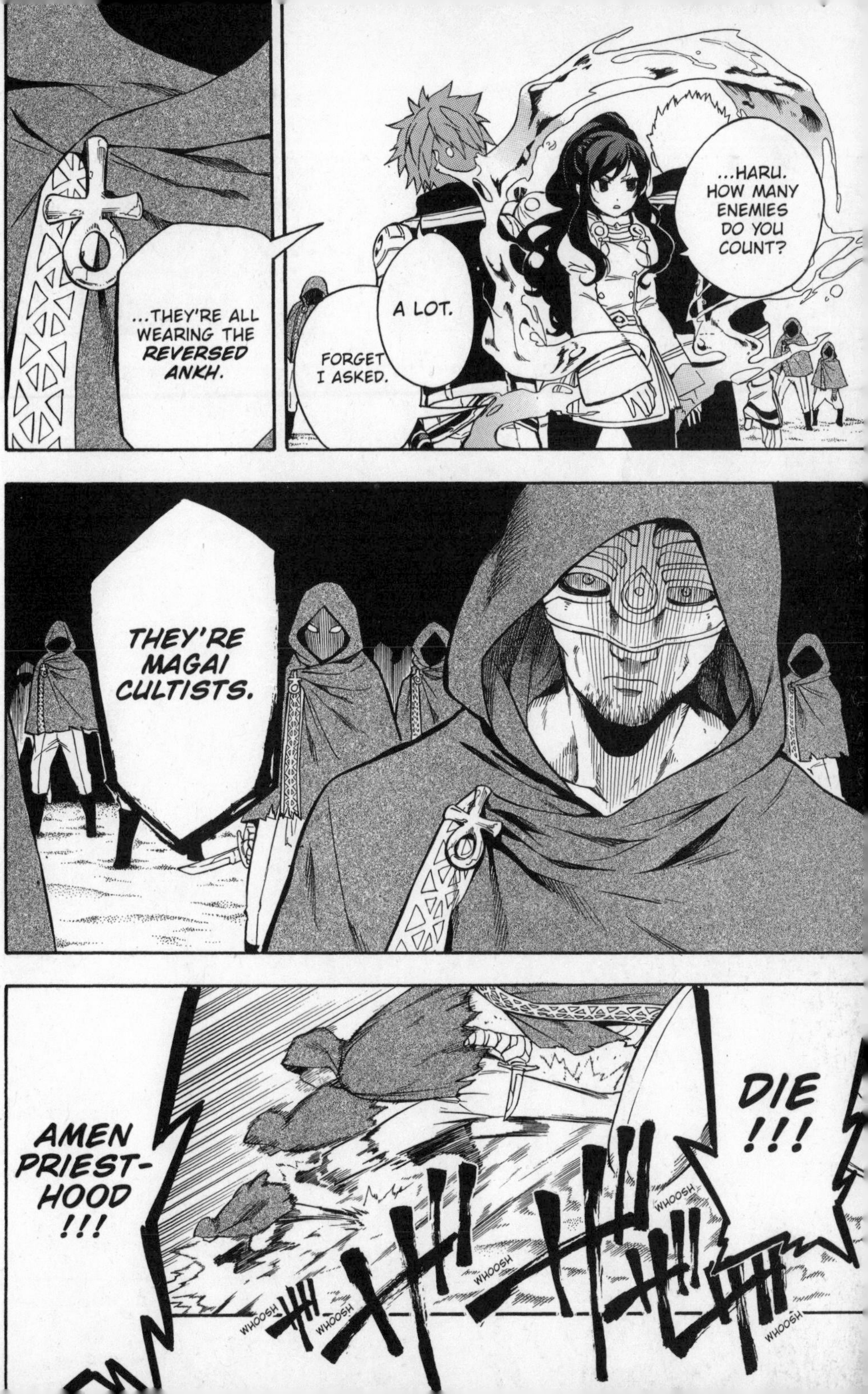
...HARU. HOW MANY ENEMIES DO YOU COUNT?
A LOT.
FORGET I ASKED.
...THEY'RE ALL WEARING THE *REVERSED ANKH.*
THEY'RE MAGAI CULTISTS.
DIE!!!
WHOOSH
WHOOSH
WHOOSH
WHOOSH
WHOOSH
WHOOSH
AMEN PRIEST-HOOD!!!

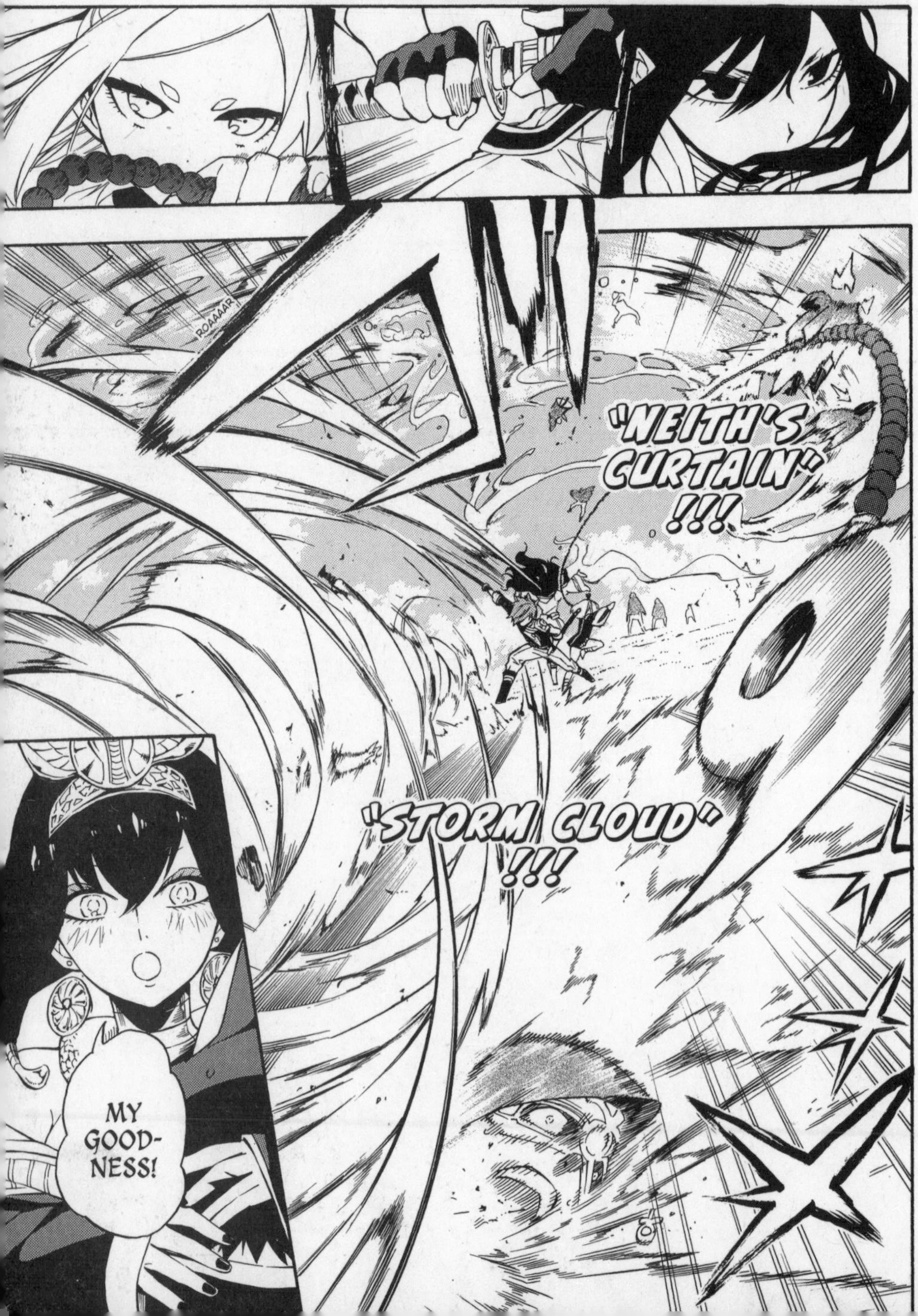
"NEITH'S CURTAIN"!!!
ROAAAAR
"STORM CLOUD"!!!
MY GOOD-NESS!

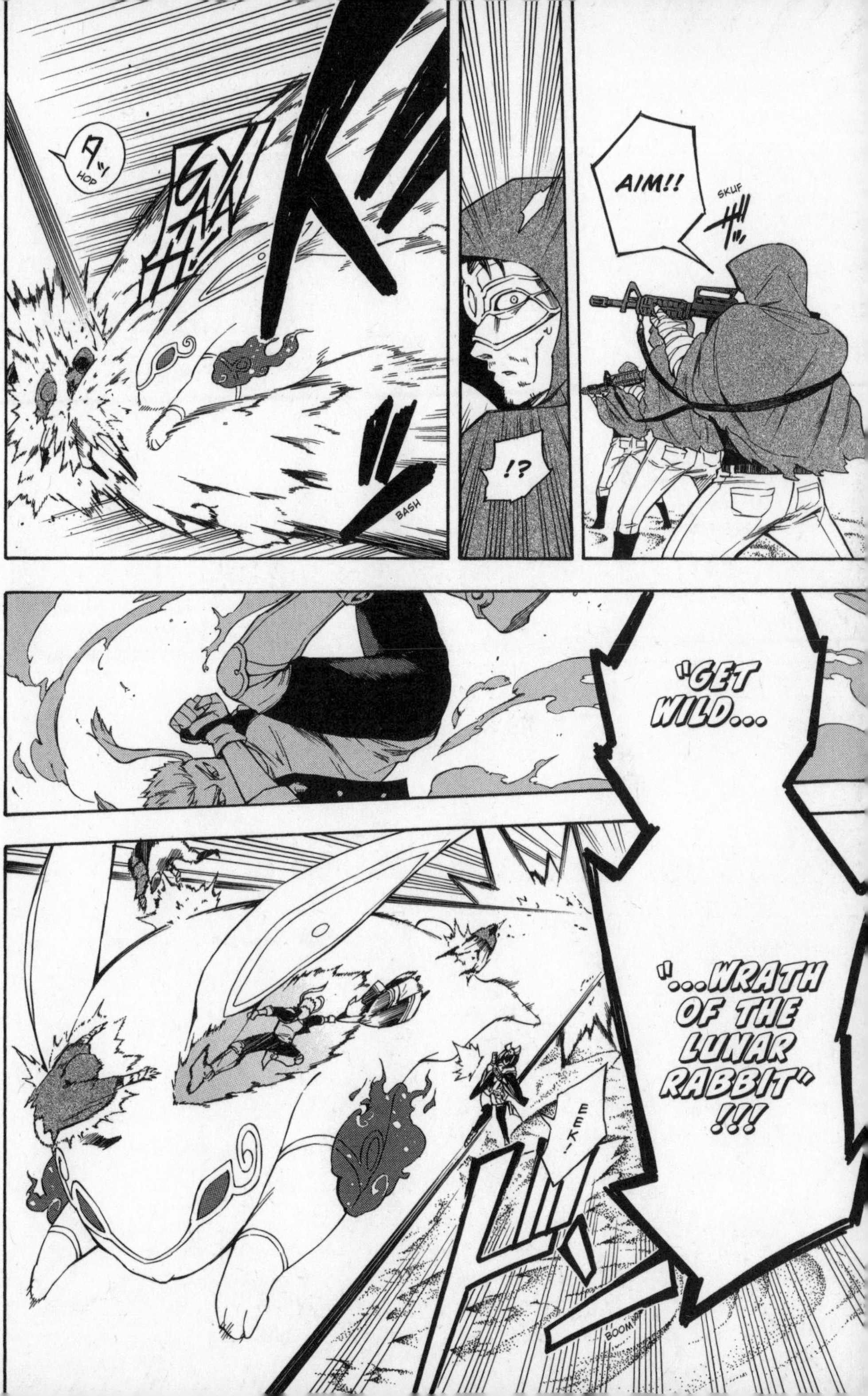
AIM!!
SKUF
!?
タッ
HOP
GYAAH!
BASH
"GET WILD...
"...WRATH OF THE LUNAR RABBIT"!!!
EEK!
BOOM

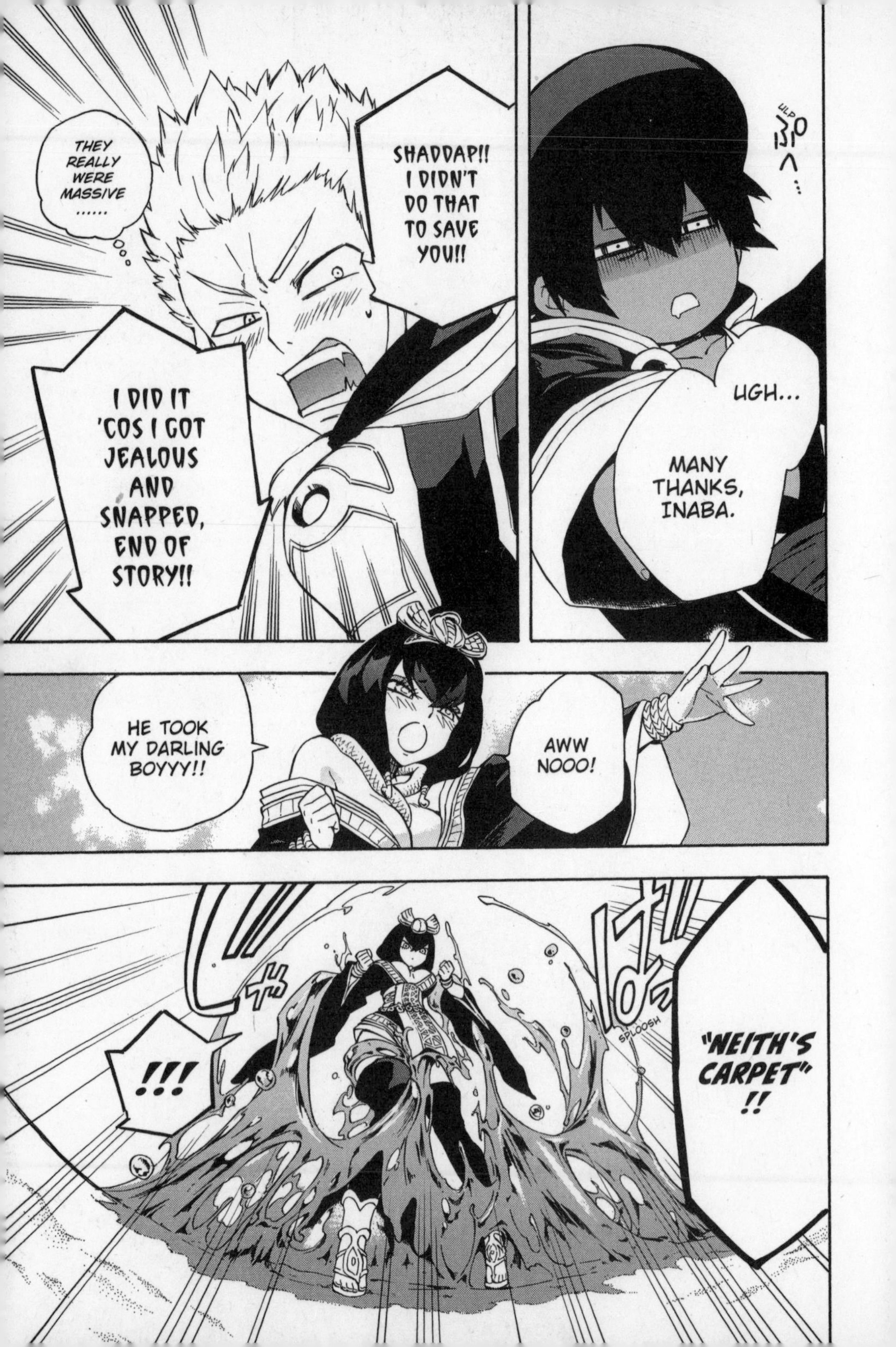
ULP
UGH...
MANY THANKS, INABA.
SHADDAP!! I DIDN'T DO THAT TO SAVE YOU!!
THEY REALLY WERE MASSIVE ......
I DID IT 'COS I GOT JEALOUS AND SNAPPED, END OF STORY!!
AWW NOOO!
HE TOOK MY DARLING BOYYY!!
SPLOOSH
"NEITH'S CARPET"!!
!!!

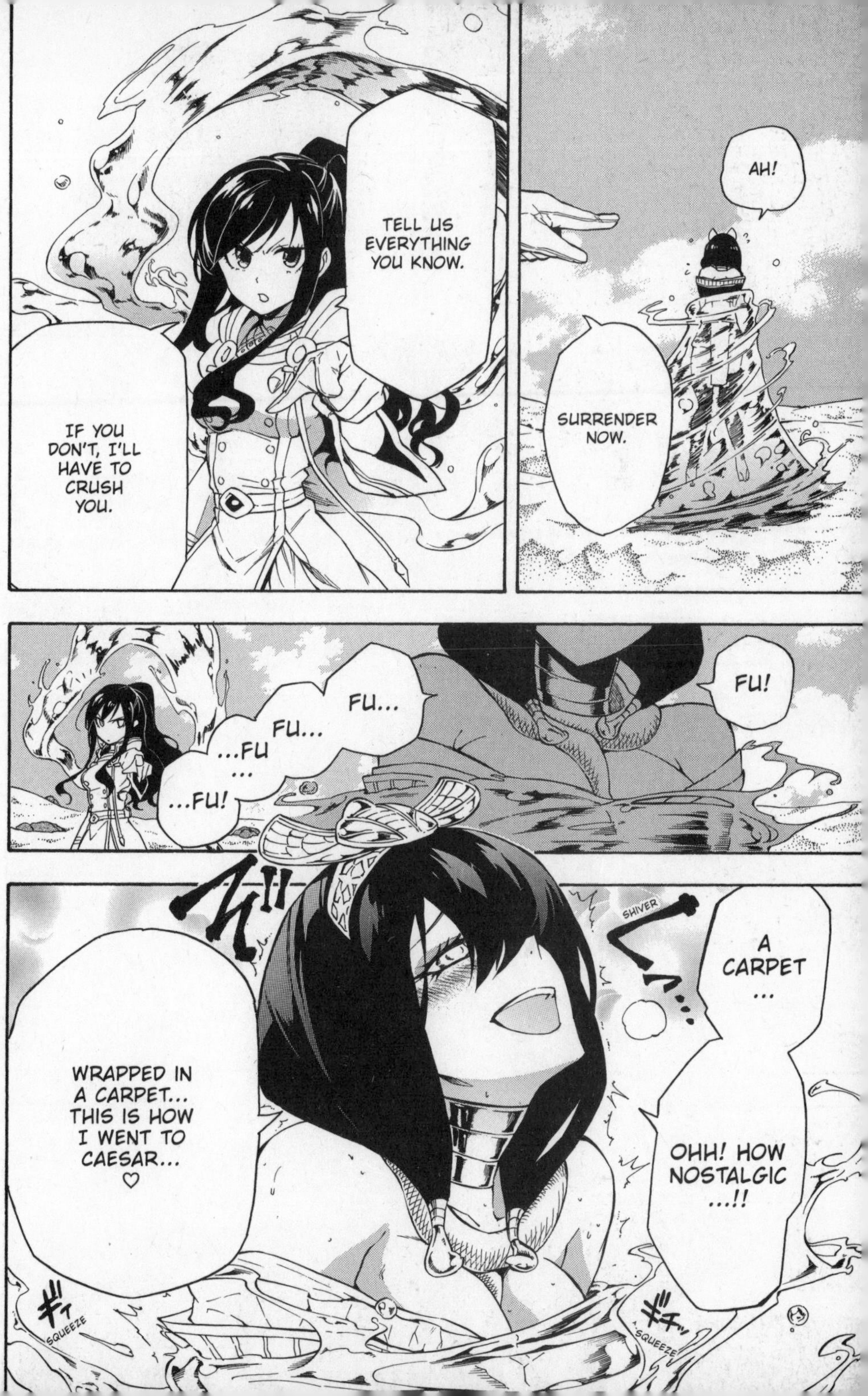
AH!
SURRENDER NOW.
TELL US EVERYTHING YOU KNOW.
IF YOU DON'T, I'LL HAVE TO CRUSH YOU.
FU!
FU...
FU...
...FU ...
...FU!
SHIVER
A CARPET ...
OHH! HOW NOSTALGIC ...!!
WRAPPED IN A CARPET... THIS IS HOW I WENT TO CAESAR... ♡
SQUEEZE
SQUEEZE

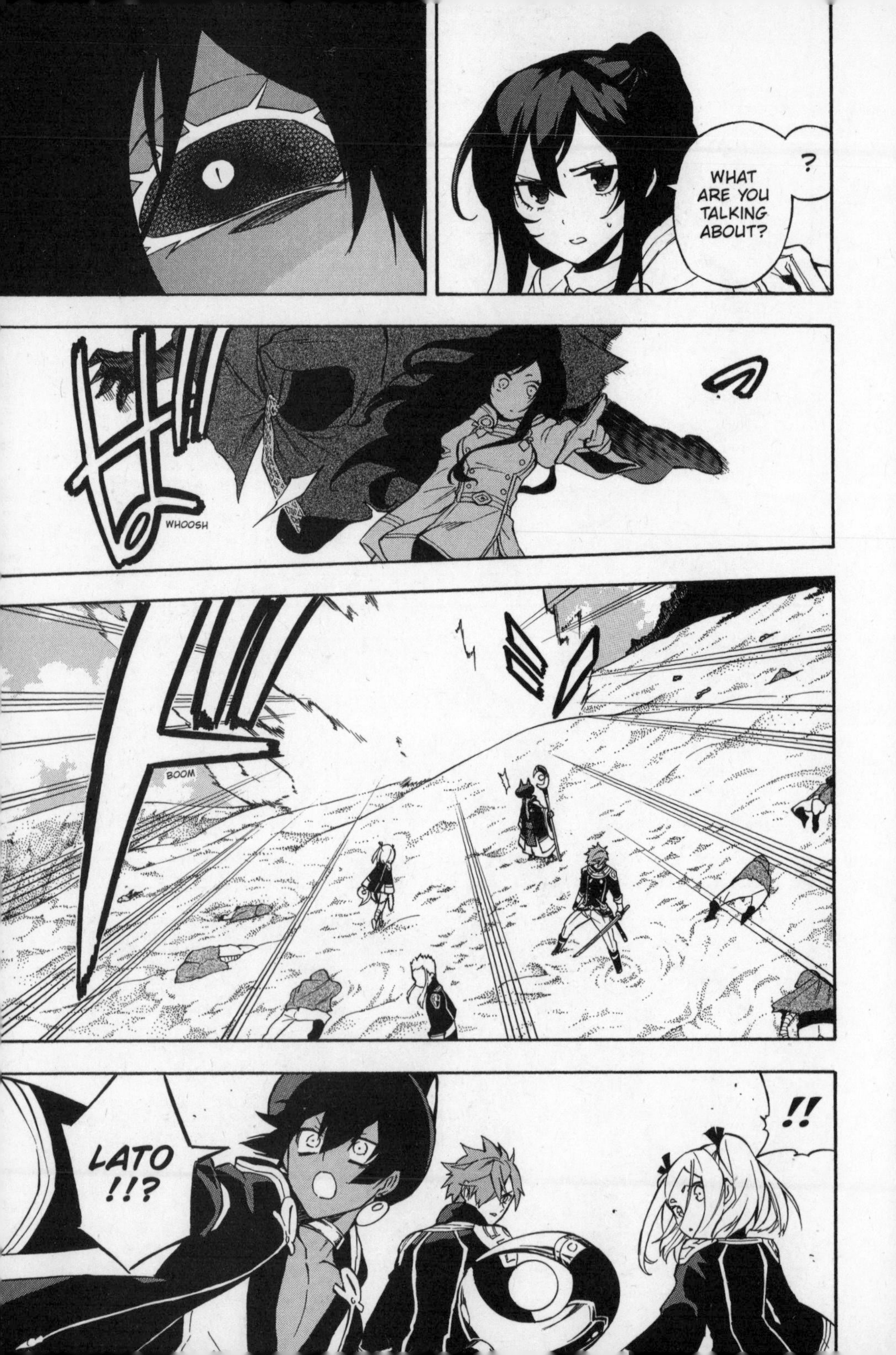
WHAT ARE YOU TALKING ABOUT?
?
?
WHOOSH
BOOM
!!
LATO !!?

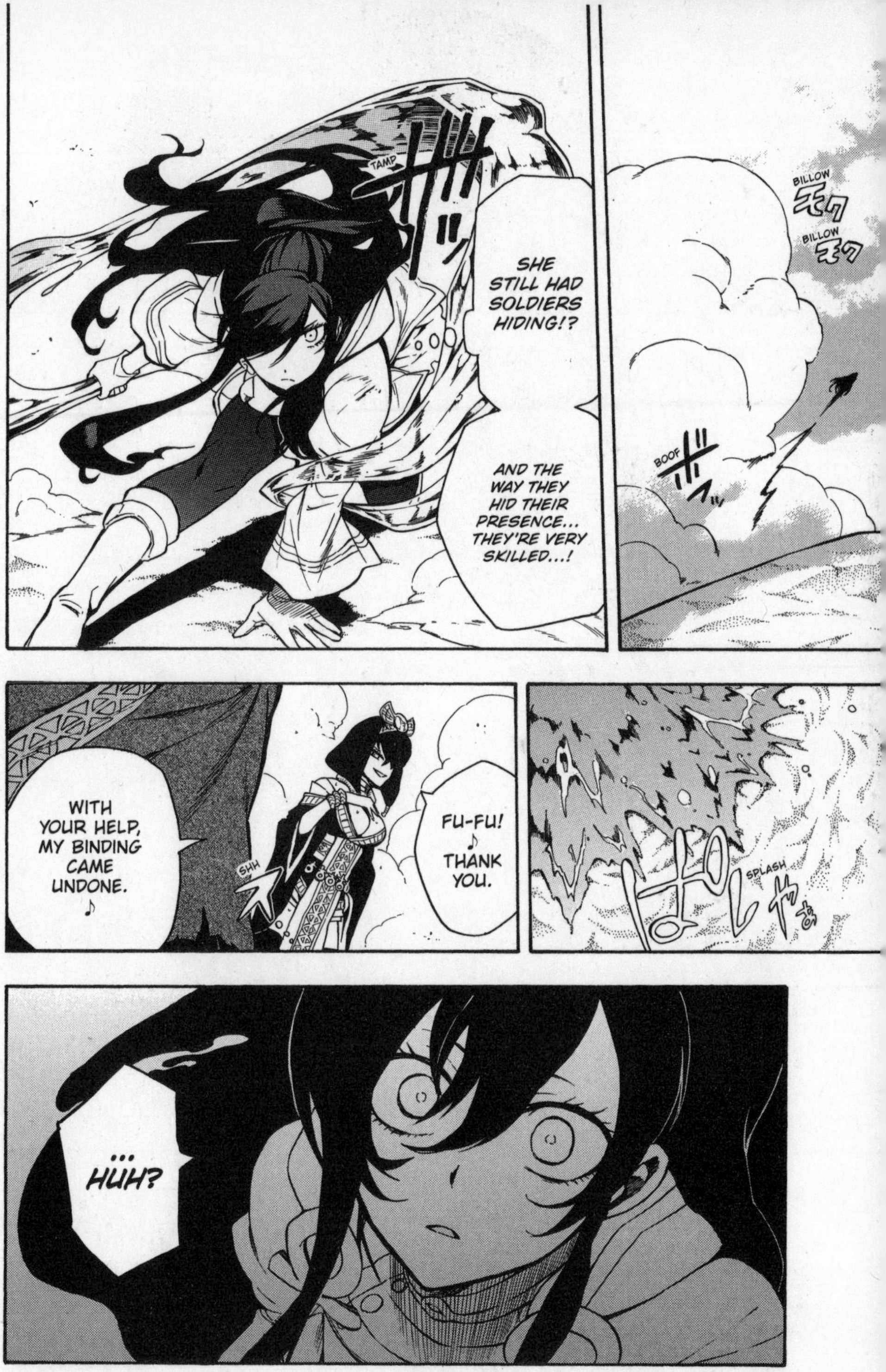
BILLOW
BILLOW
BOOF
TAMP
SHE STILL HAD SOLDIERS HIDING!?
AND THE WAY THEY HID THEIR PRESENCE... THEY'RE VERY SKILLED...!
SPLASH
FU-FU! ♪ THANK YOU.
WITH YOUR HELP, MY BINDING CAME UNDONE. ♪
SHH
...HUH?

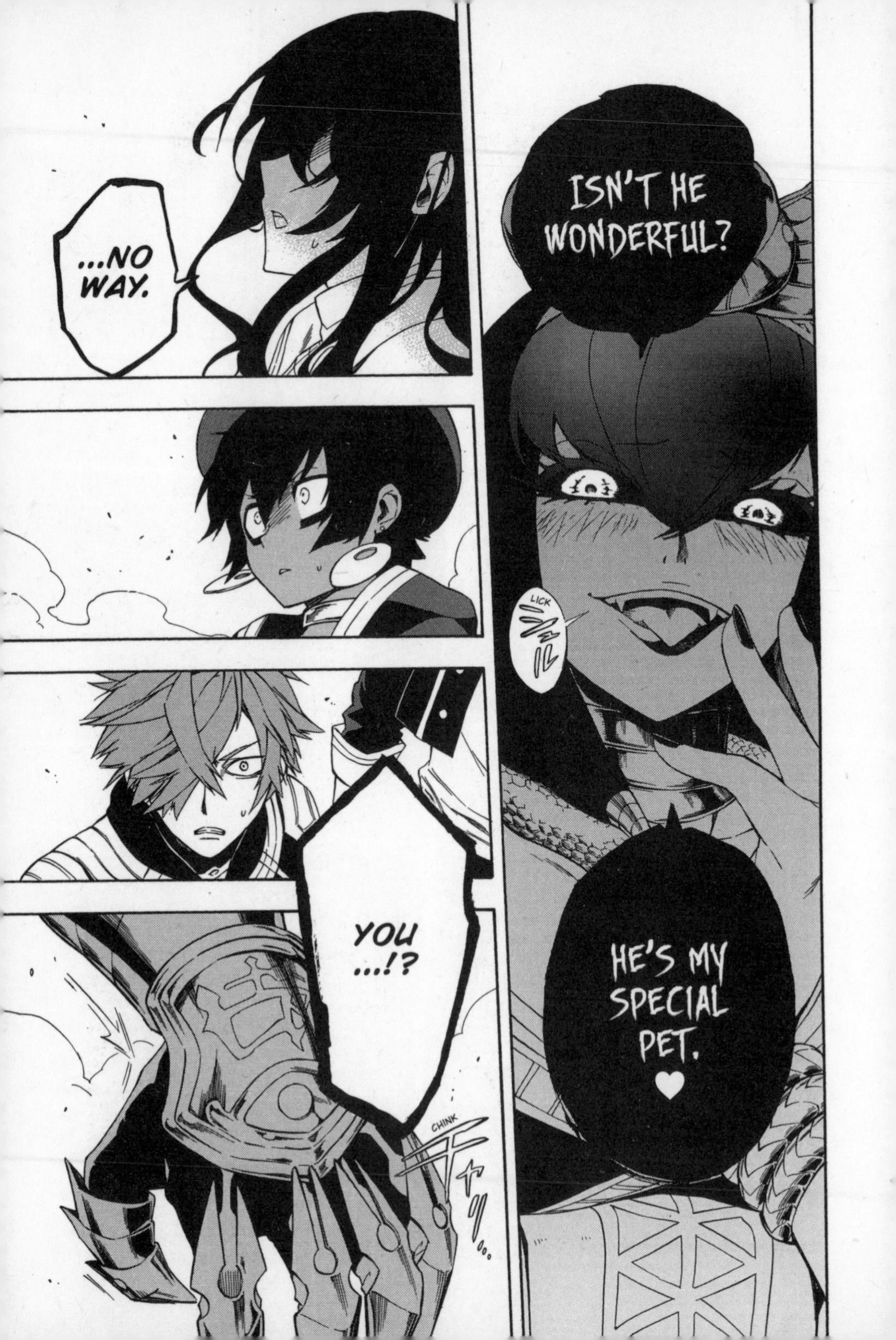
ISN'T HE WONDERFUL?
LICK
HE'S MY SPECIAL PET. ♥
...NO WAY.
YOU ...!?
CHINK

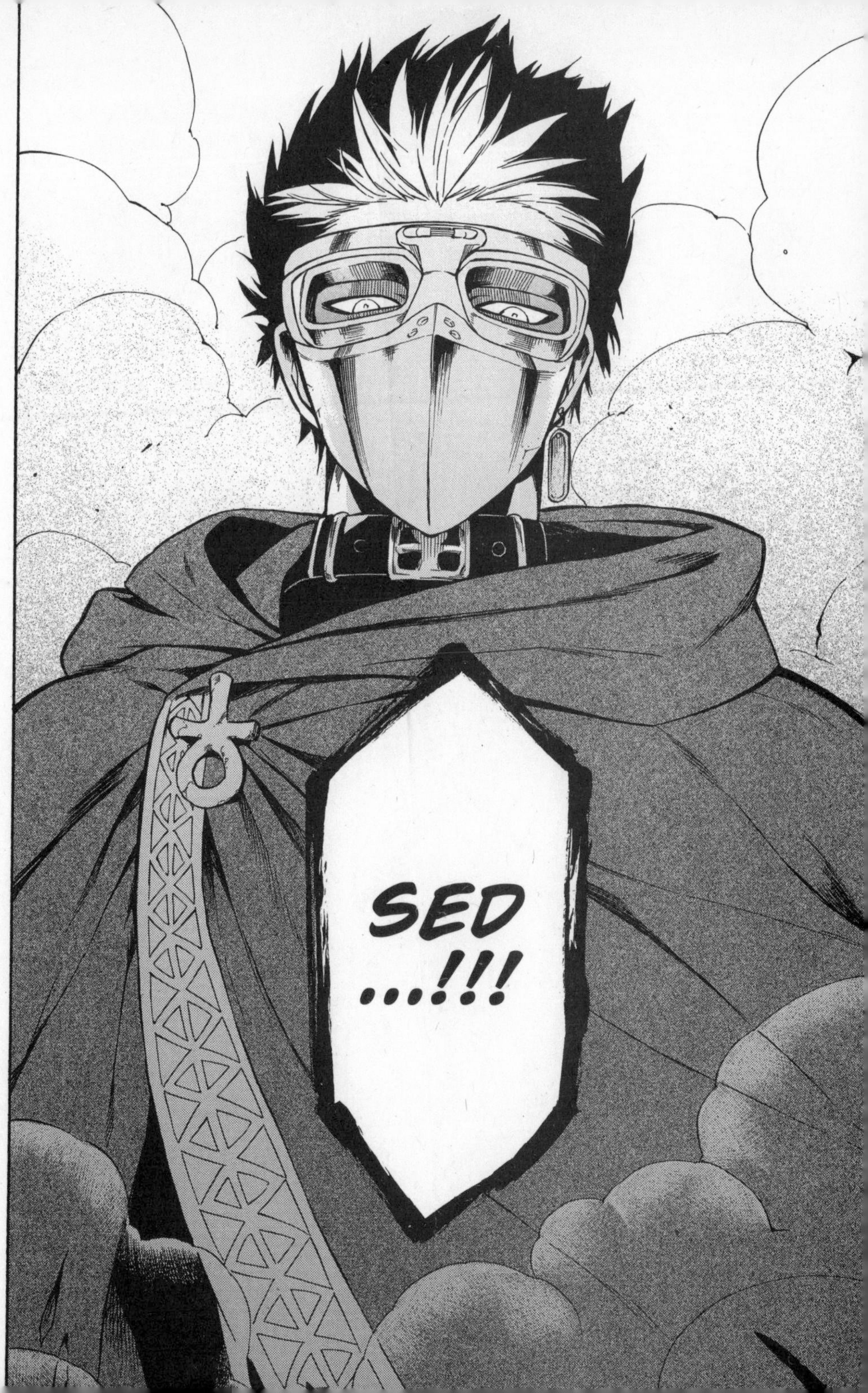
SED ...!!!

Great Priest Imhotep

Great Priest Imhotep

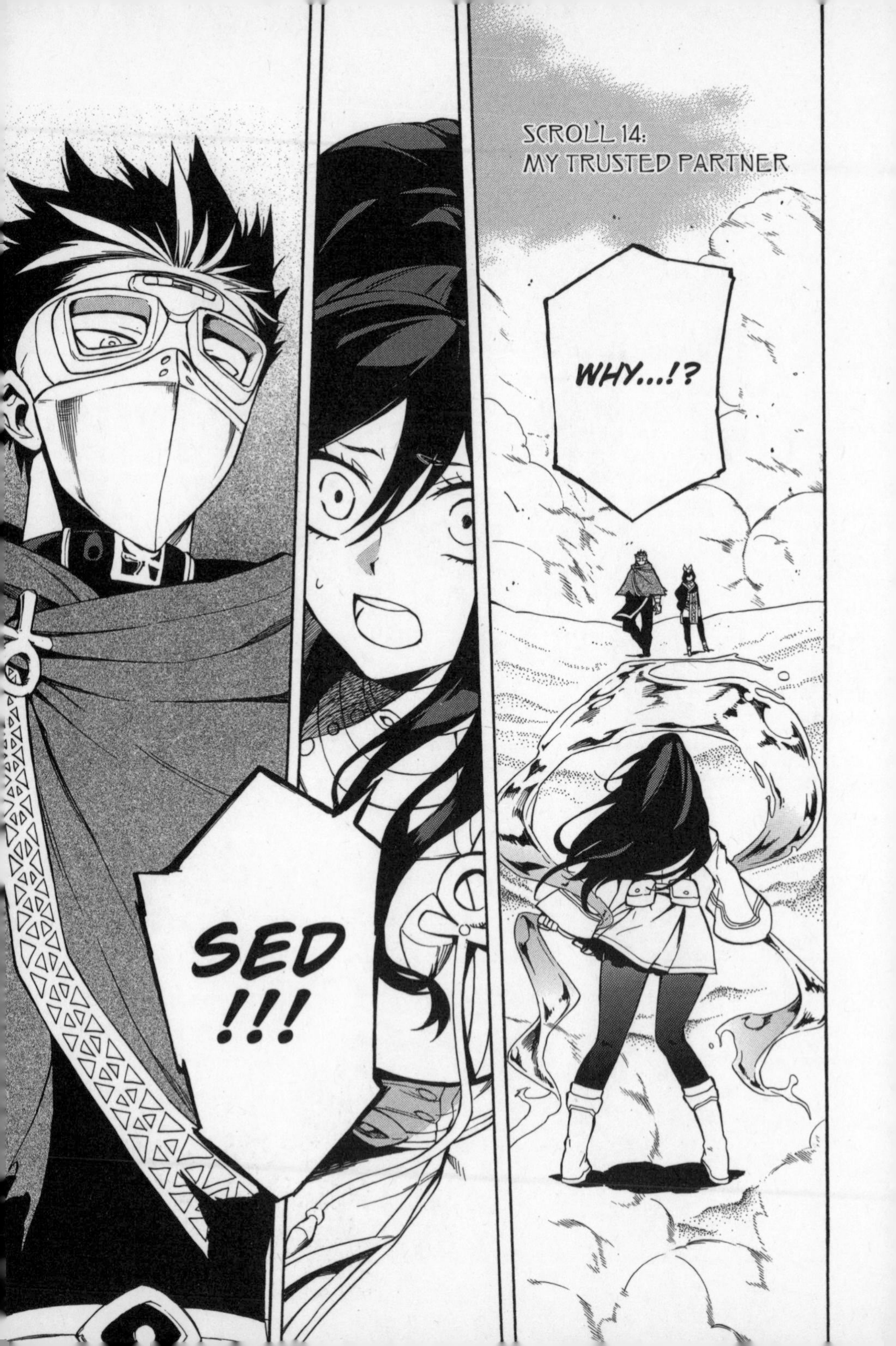
SCROLL 14:
MY TRUSTED PARTNER
WHY...!?
SED !!!

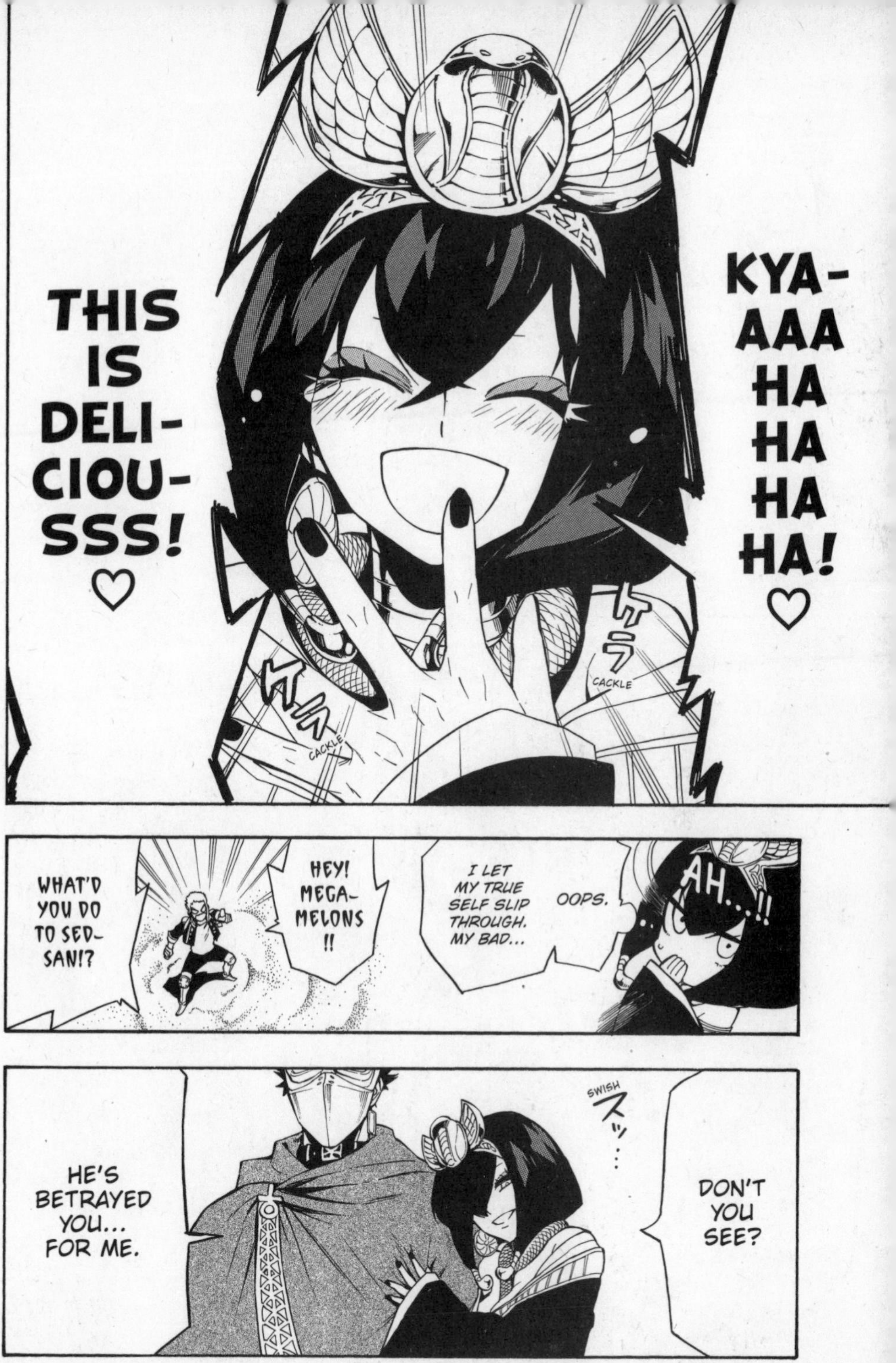
KYA-AAA HA HA HA HA! ♡
THIS IS DELI-CIOU-SSS! ♡
CACKLE
CACKLE
AH...!!
OOPS.
I LET MY TRUE SELF SLIP THROUGH. MY BAD...
HEY! MEGA-MELONS!!
WHAT'D YOU DO TO SED-SAN!?
SWISH
スッ…
DON'T YOU SEE?
HE'S BETRAYED YOU... FOR ME.

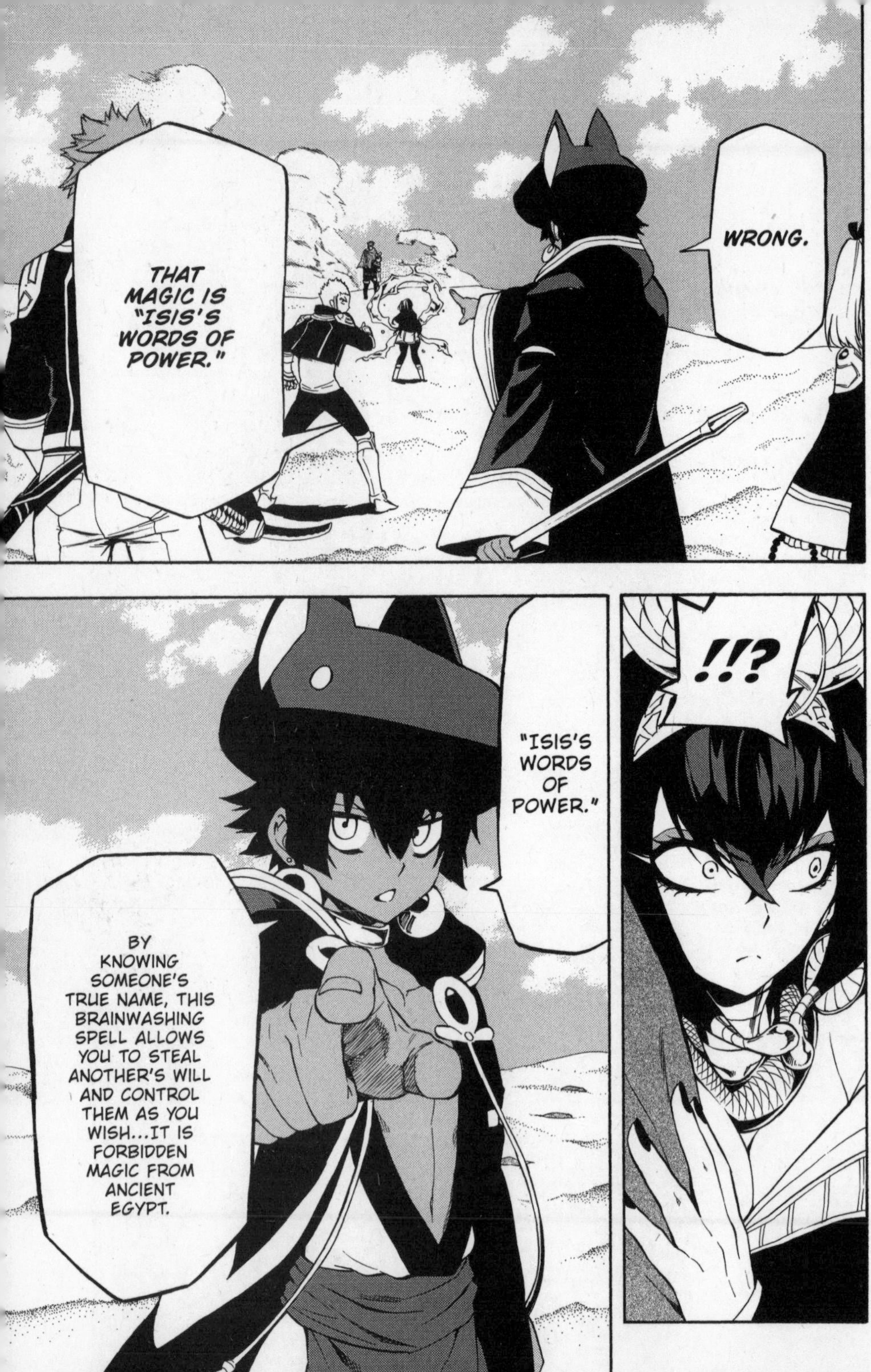
WRONG.
THAT MAGIC IS "ISIS'S WORDS OF POWER."
!!?
"ISIS'S WORDS OF POWER."
BY KNOWING SOMEONE'S TRUE NAME, THIS BRAINWASHING SPELL ALLOWS YOU TO STEAL ANOTHER'S WILL AND CONTROL THEM AS YOU WISH...IT IS FORBIDDEN MAGIC FROM ANCIENT EGYPT.

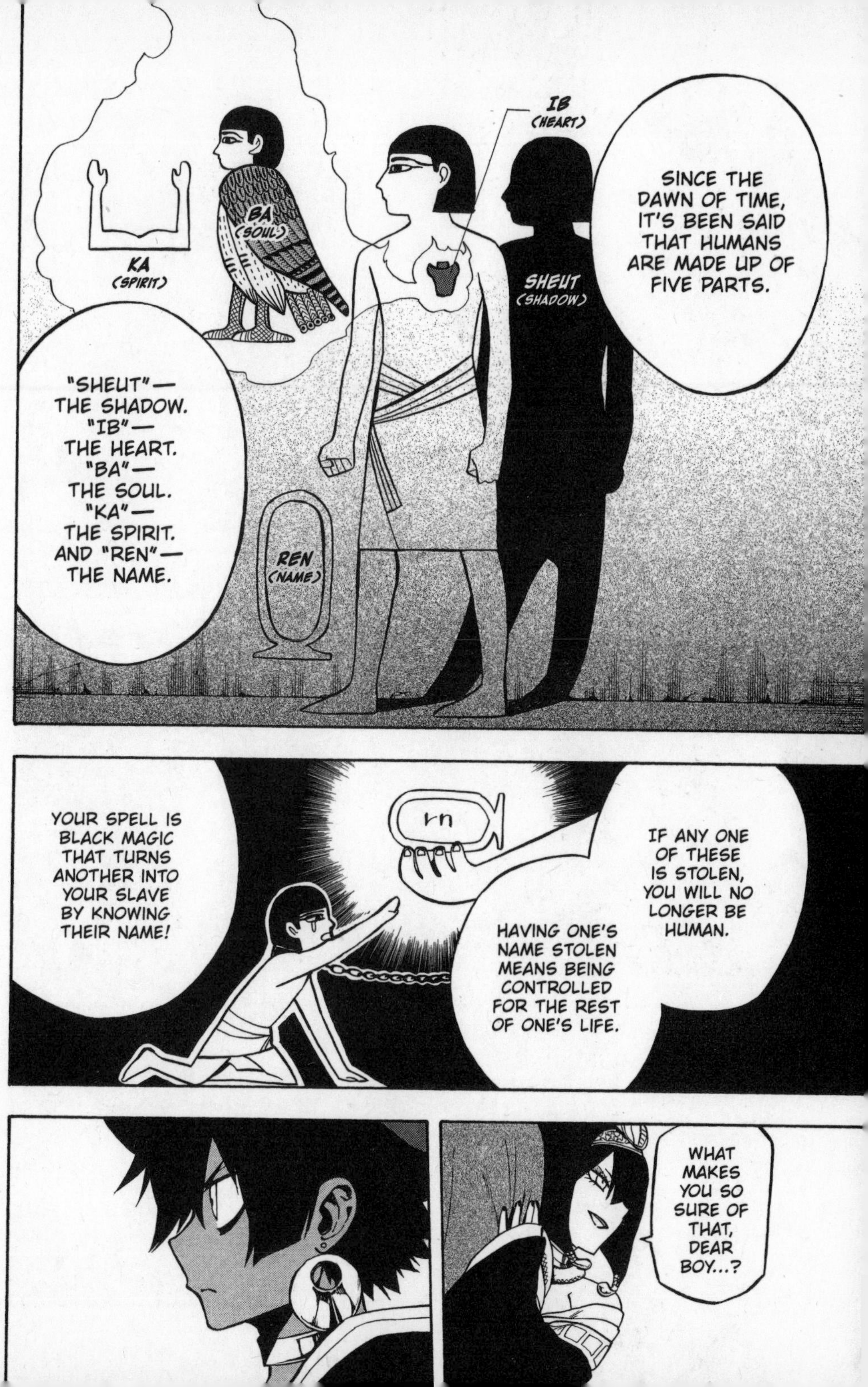
SINCE THE DAWN OF TIME, IT'S BEEN SAID THAT HUMANS ARE MADE UP OF FIVE PARTS.
IB (HEART)
SHEUT (SHADOW)
BA (SOUL)
KA (SPIRIT)
REN (NAME)
"SHEUT"— THE SHADOW. "IB"— THE HEART. "BA"— THE SOUL. "KA"— THE SPIRIT. AND "REN"— THE NAME.
IF ANY ONE OF THESE IS STOLEN, YOU WILL NO LONGER BE HUMAN.
rn
HAVING ONE'S NAME STOLEN MEANS BEING CONTROLLED FOR THE REST OF ONE'S LIFE.
YOUR SPELL IS BLACK MAGIC THAT TURNS ANOTHER INTO YOUR SLAVE BY KNOWING THEIR NAME!
WHAT MAKES YOU SO SURE OF THAT, DEAR BOY...?

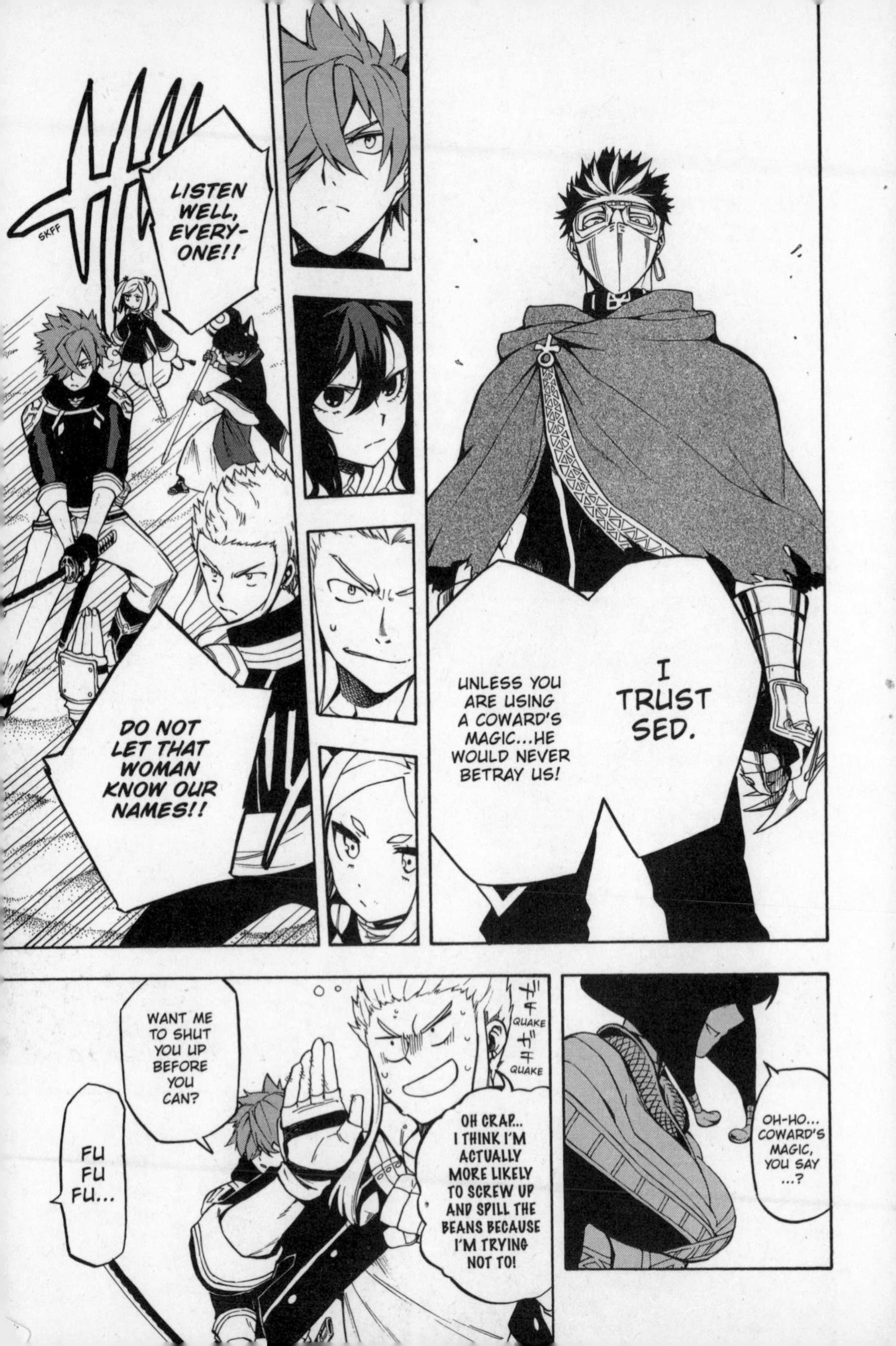
I TRUST SED.
UNLESS YOU ARE USING A COWARD'S MAGIC...HE WOULD NEVER BETRAY US!
SKFF
LISTEN WELL, EVERY-ONE!!
DO NOT LET THAT WOMAN KNOW OUR NAMES!!
OH-HO... COWARD'S MAGIC, YOU SAY ...?
QUAKE
QUAKE
WANT ME TO SHUT YOU UP BEFORE YOU CAN?
FU FU FU...
OH CRAP... I THINK I'M ACTUALLY MORE LIKELY TO SCREW UP AND SPILL THE BEANS BECAUSE I'M TRYING NOT TO!

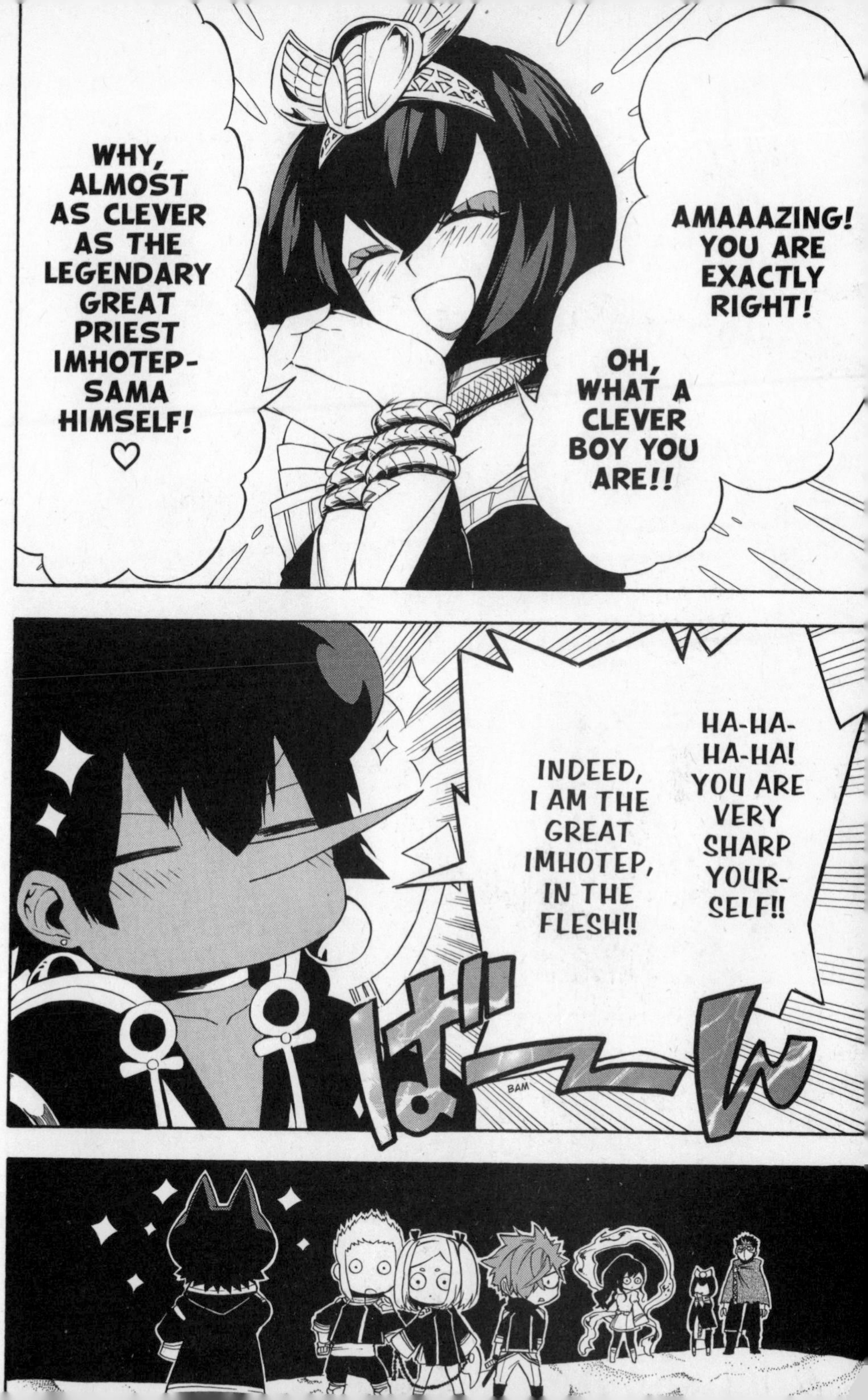
AMAAAZING! YOU ARE EXACTLY RIGHT!
OH, WHAT A CLEVER BOY YOU ARE!!
WHY, ALMOST AS CLEVER AS THE LEGENDARY GREAT PRIEST IMHOTEP-SAMA HIMSELF! ♡
HA-HA-HA-HA! YOU ARE VERY SHARP YOURSELF!!
INDEED, I AM THE GREAT IMHOTEP, IN THE FLESH!!
ばーん
BAM

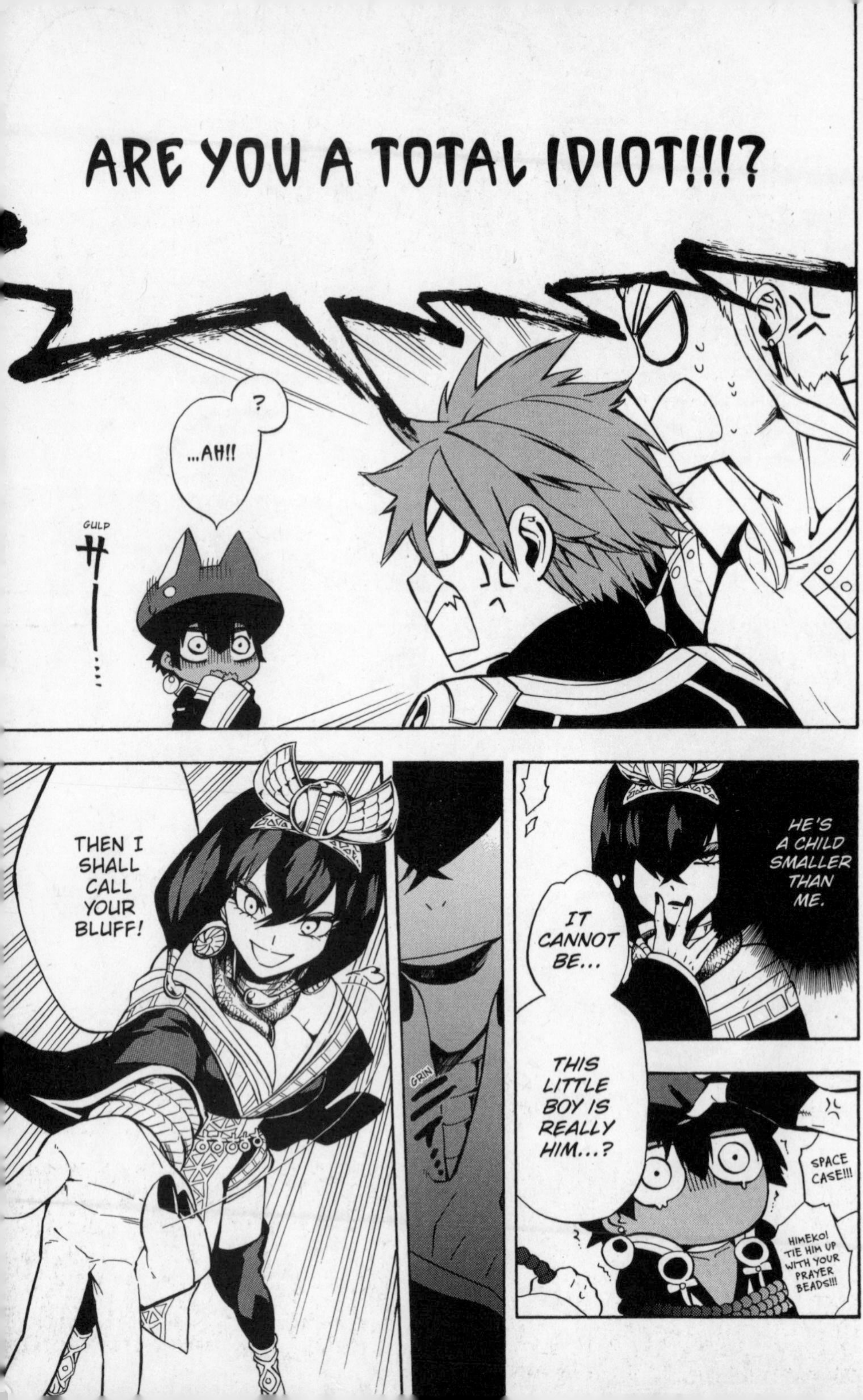
ARE YOU A TOTAL IDIOT!!!?
?
...AH!!
GULP
HE'S A CHILD SMALLER THAN ME.
IT CANNOT BE...
THIS LITTLE BOY IS REALLY HIM...?
SPACE CASE!!!
HIMEKO! TIE HIM UP WITH YOUR PRAYER BEADS!!!
GRIN
THEN I SHALL CALL YOUR BLUFF!

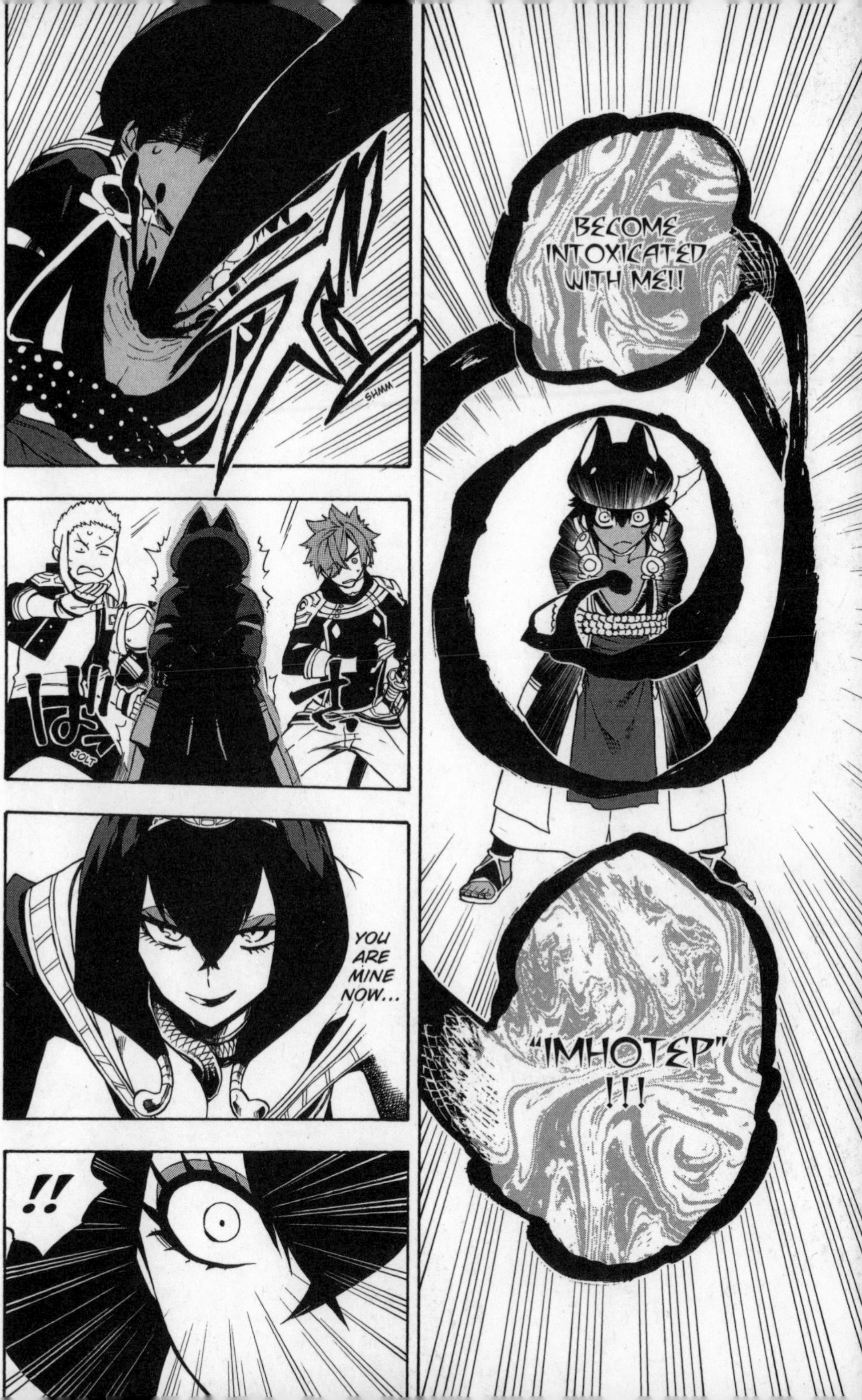
BECOME INTOXICATED WITH ME!!
"IMHOTEP" !!!
SHMM
JOLT
YOU ARE MINE NOW...
!!

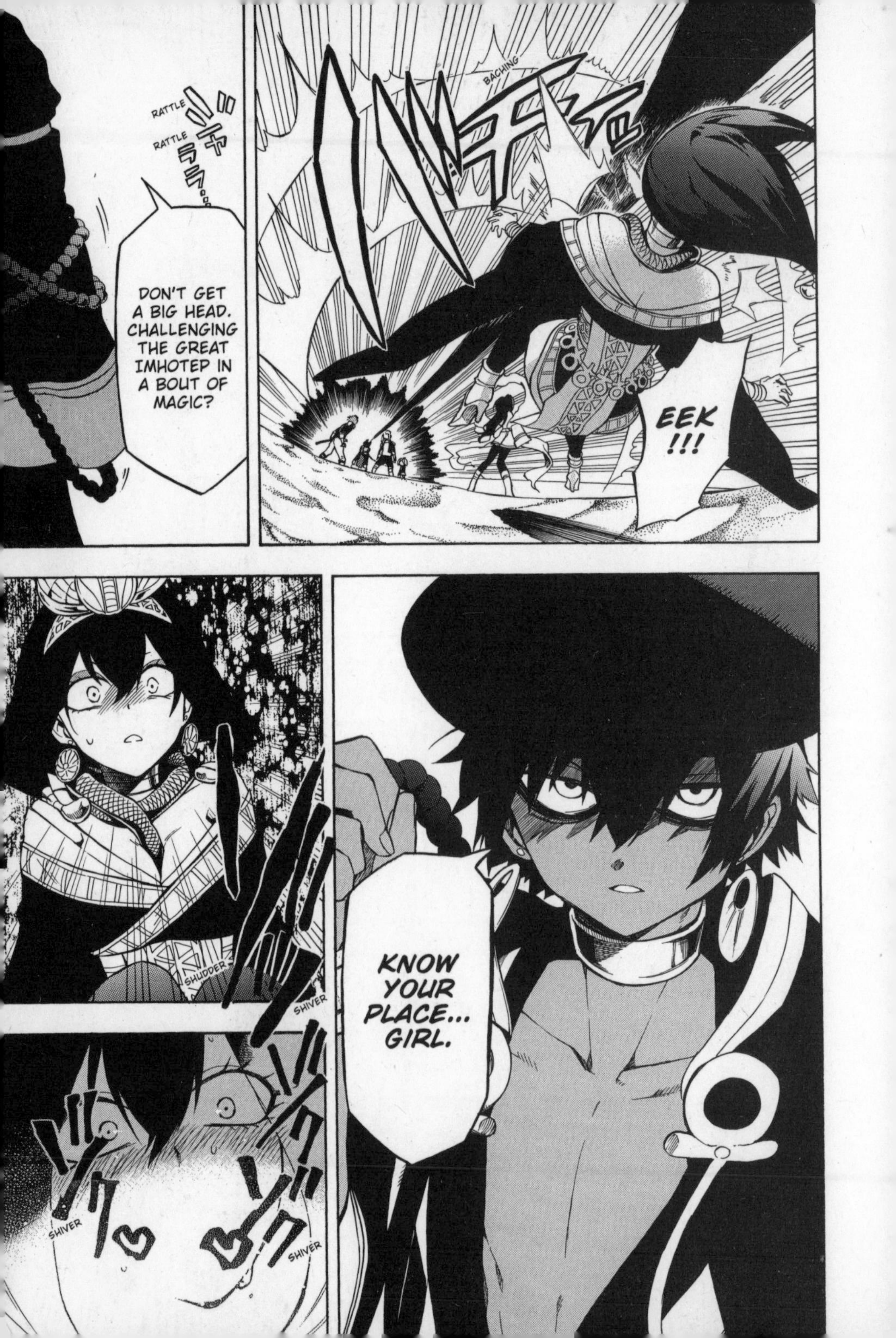
BACHING
EEK!!!
RATTLE
RATTLE
DON'T GET A BIG HEAD. CHALLENGING THE GREAT IMHOTEP IN A BOUT OF MAGIC?
KNOW YOUR PLACE... GIRL.
SHUDDER
SHIVER
SHIVER
SHIVER

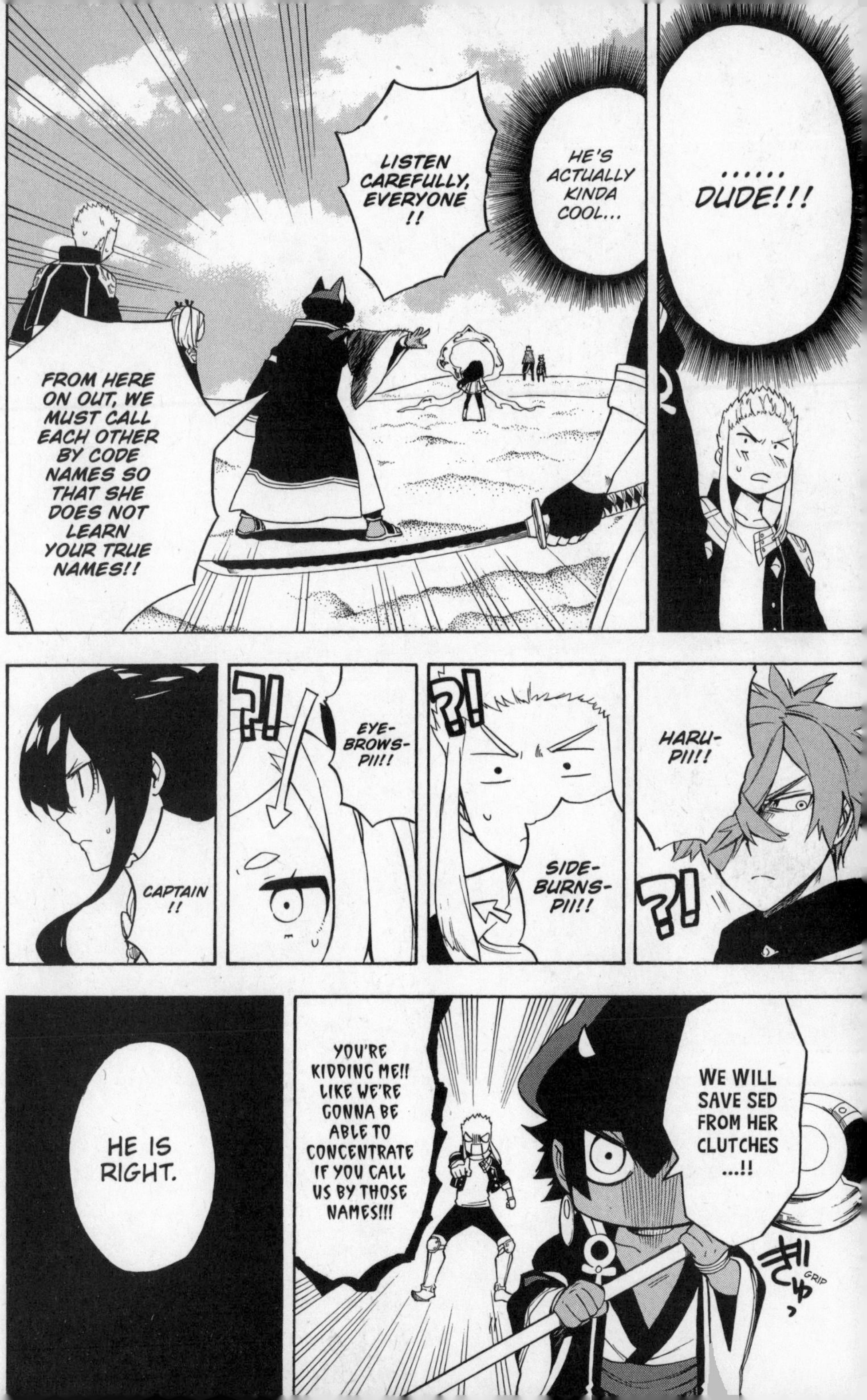
......DUDE!!!
HE'S ACTUALLY KINDA COOL...
LISTEN CAREFULLY, EVERYONE!!
FROM HERE ON OUT, WE MUST CALL EACH OTHER BY CODE NAMES SO THAT SHE DOES NOT LEARN YOUR TRUE NAMES!!
HARU-PII!!
?!
SIDE-BURNS-PII!!
?!
EYE-BROWS-PII!!
?!
CAPTAIN!!
WE WILL SAVE SED FROM HER CLUTCHES...!!
ぎゅっ GRIP
YOU'RE KIDDING ME!! LIKE WE'RE GONNA BE ABLE TO CONCENTRATE IF YOU CALL US BY THOSE NAMES!!!
HE IS RIGHT.

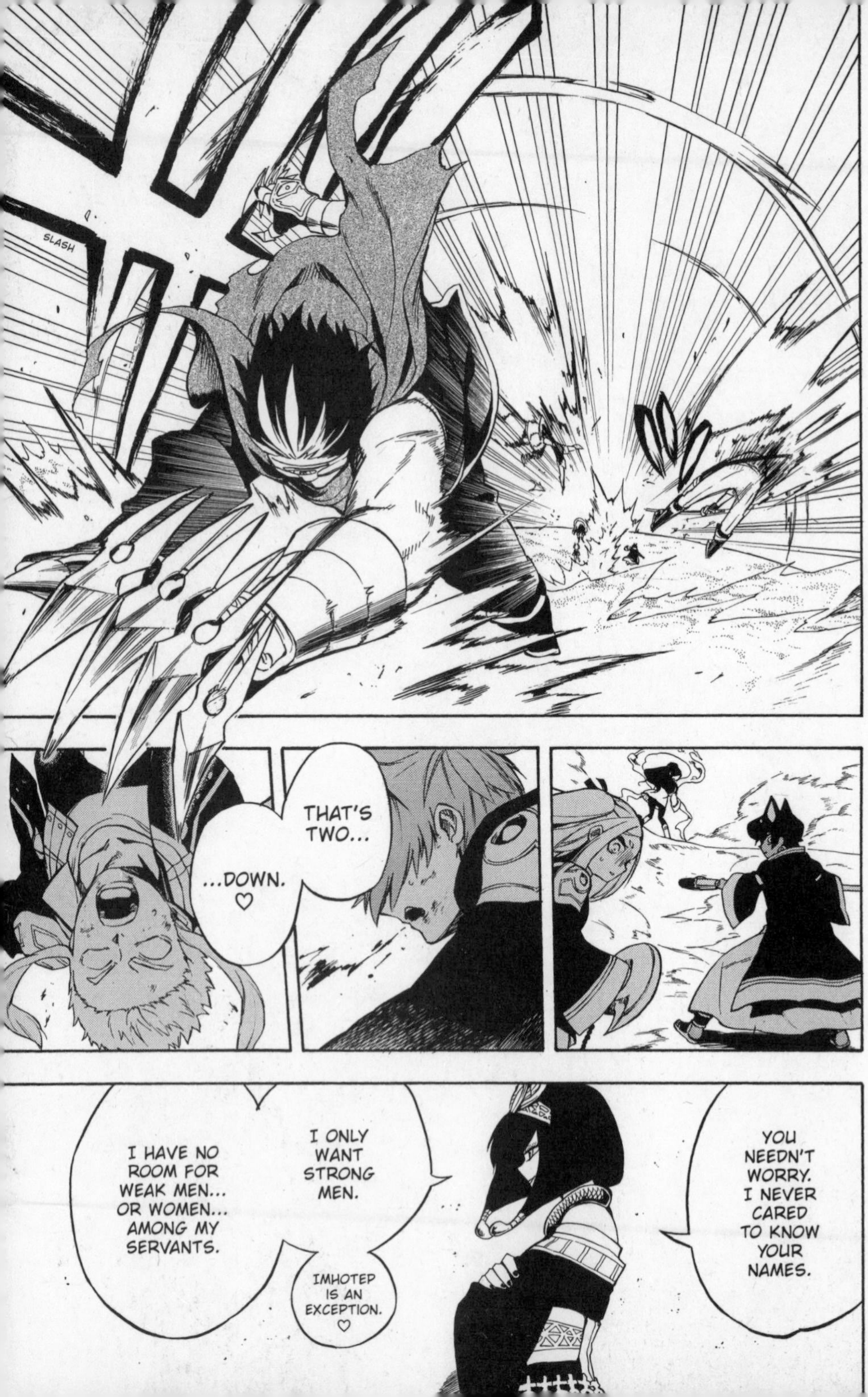
SLASH
THAT'S TWO...
...DOWN. ♡
YOU NEEDN'T WORRY. I NEVER CARED TO KNOW YOUR NAMES.
I ONLY WANT STRONG MEN.
I HAVE NO ROOM FOR WEAK MEN... OR WOMEN... AMONG MY SERVANTS.
IMHOTEP IS AN EXCEPTION. ♡

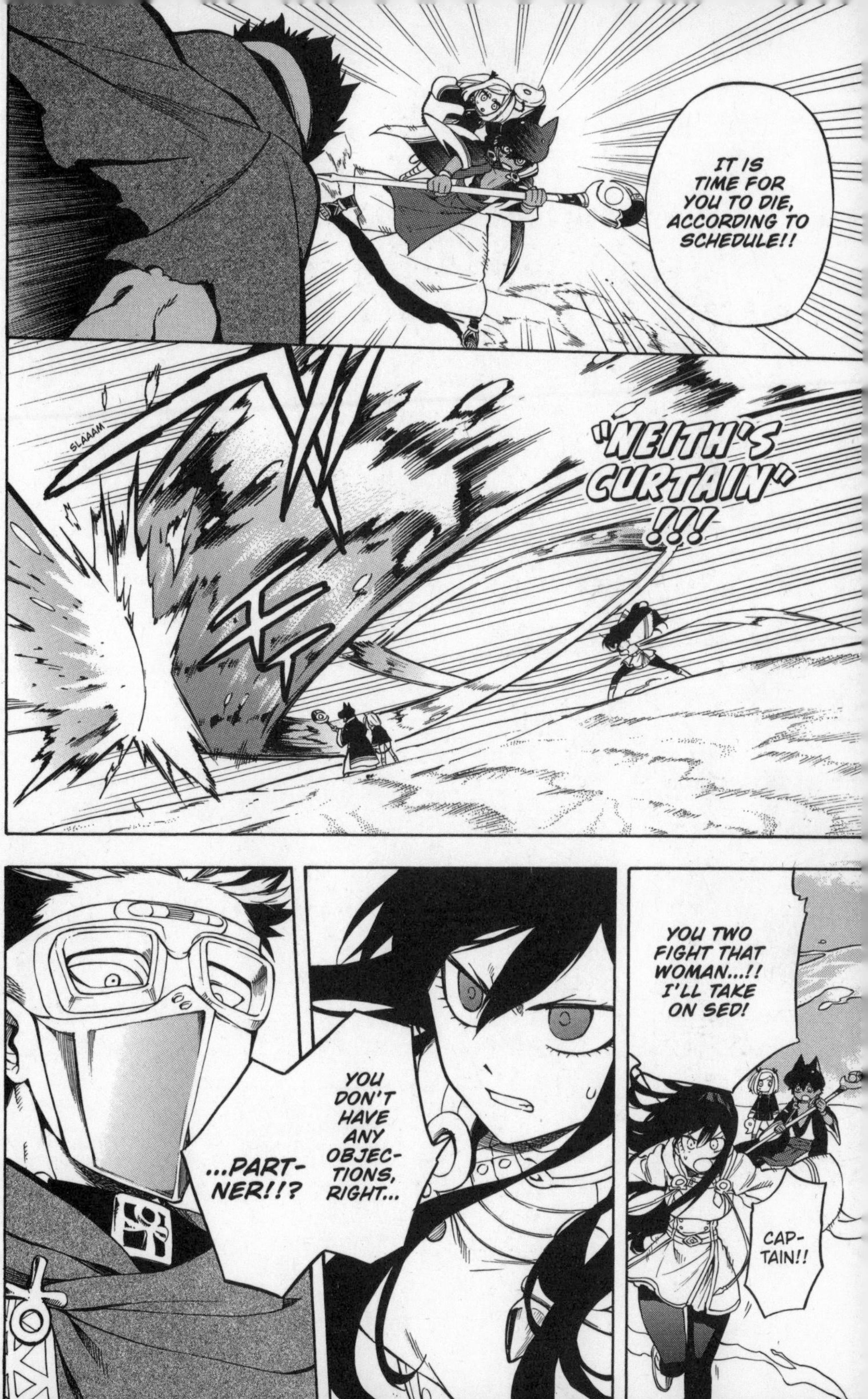
IT IS TIME FOR YOU TO DIE, ACCORDING TO SCHEDULE!!
"NEITH'S CURTAIN" !!!
SLAAAM
YOU TWO FIGHT THAT WOMAN...!! I'LL TAKE ON SED!
CAP-TAIN!!
YOU DON'T HAVE ANY OBJEC-TIONS, RIGHT...
...PART-NER!!?

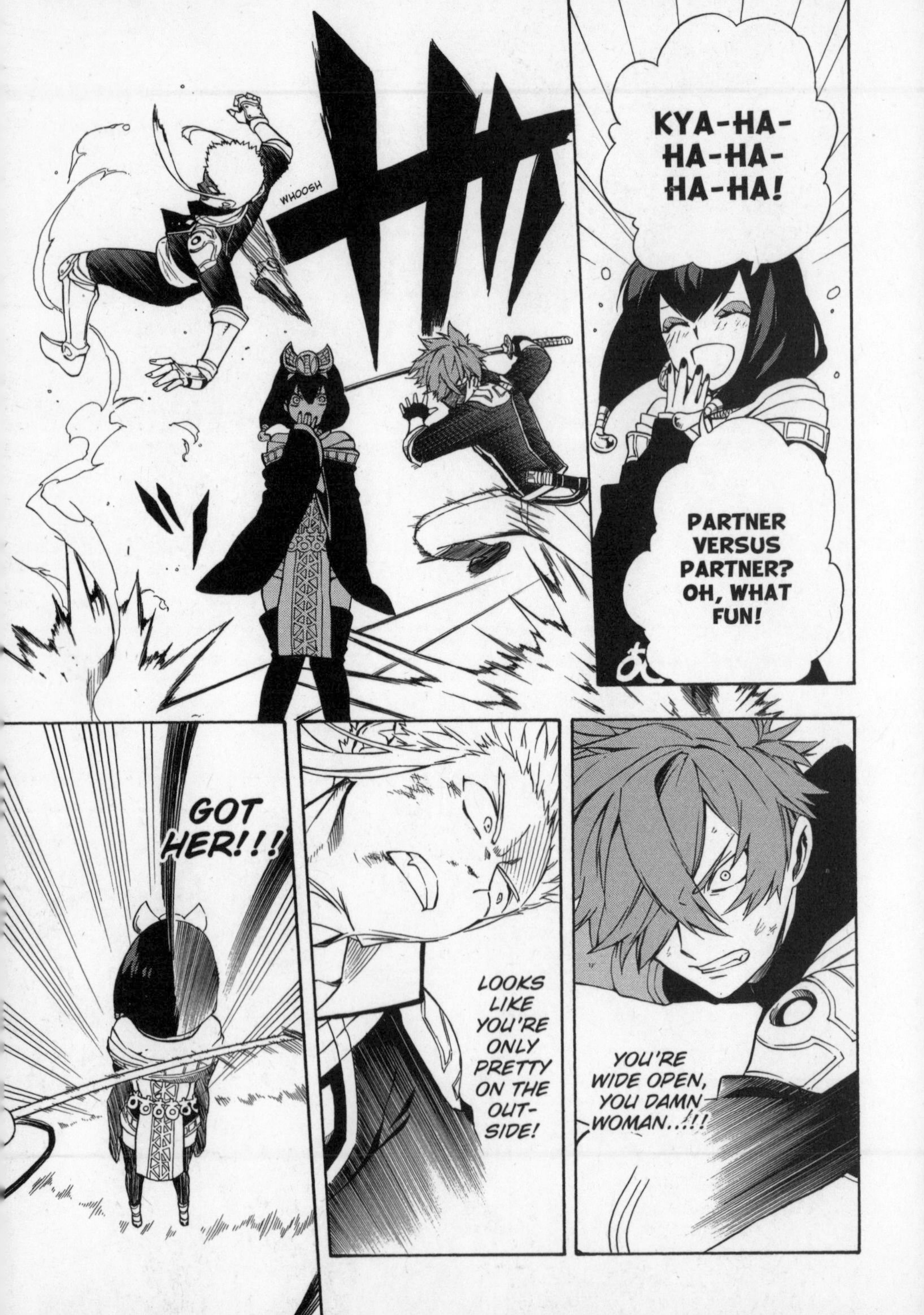
KYA-HA-HA-HA-HA-HA!
PARTNER VERSUS PARTNER? OH, WHAT FUN!
WHOOSH
YOU'RE WIDE OPEN, YOU DAMN WOMAN...!!!
LOOKS LIKE YOU'RE ONLY PRETTY ON THE OUT-SIDE!
GOT HER!!!

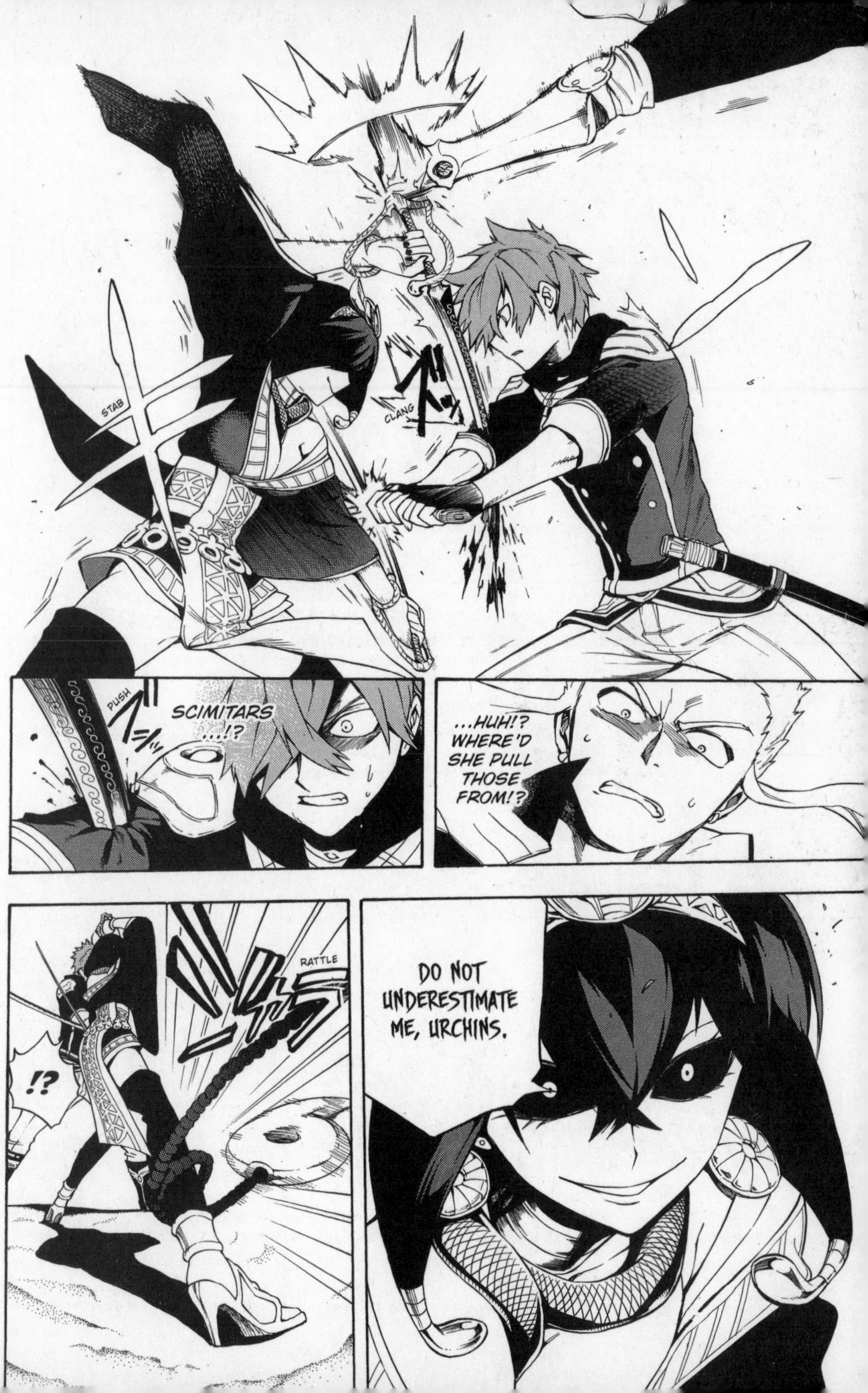
CLANG
STAB
...HUH!? WHERE'D SHE PULL THOSE FROM!?
SCIMITARS ...!?
PUSH
DO NOT UNDERESTIMATE ME, URCHINS.
RATTLE
!?

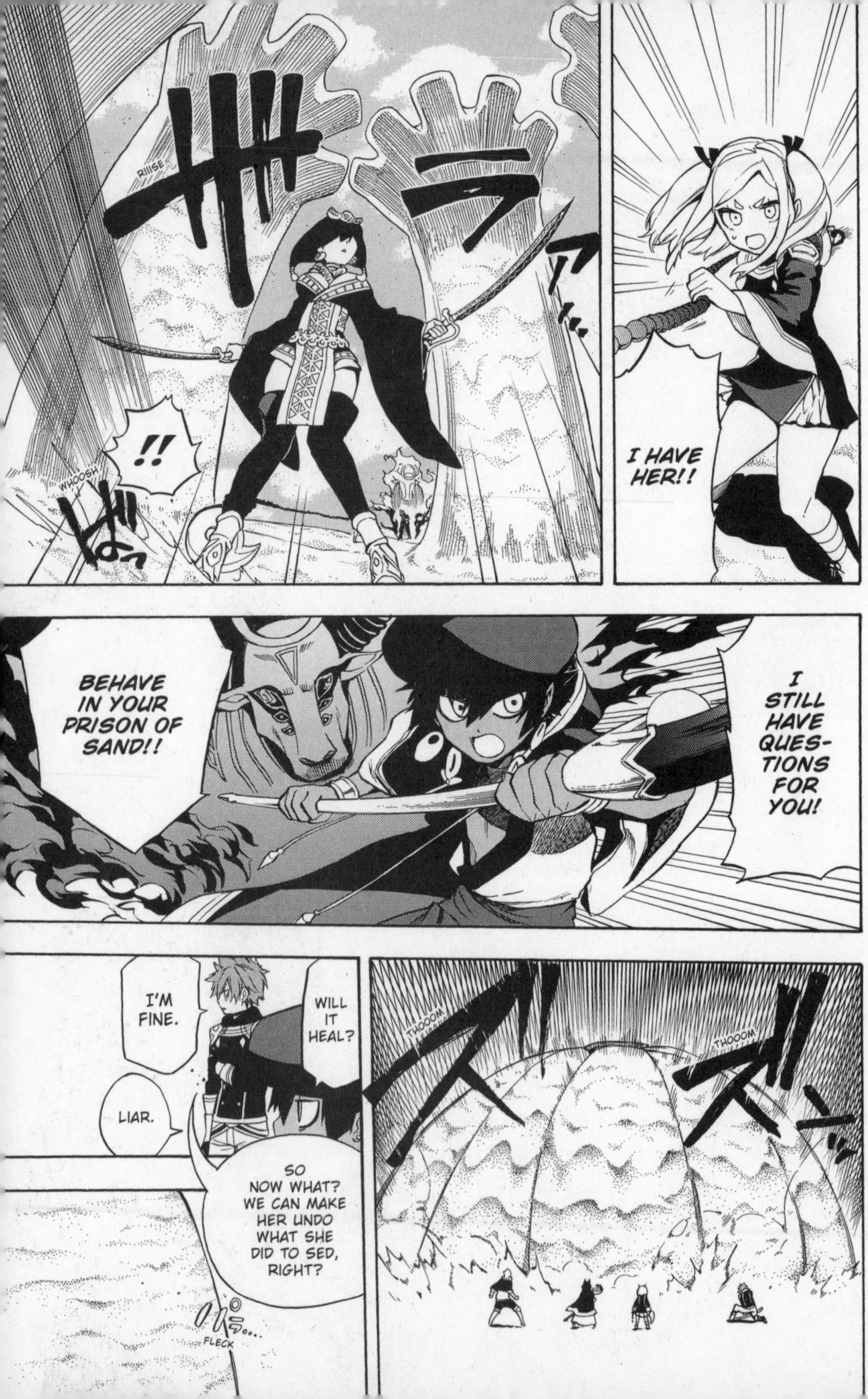
I HAVE HER!!
RIISE
!!
WHOOSH
I STILL HAVE QUES-TIONS FOR YOU!
BEHAVE IN YOUR PRISON OF SAND!!
THOOOM
THOOOM
WILL IT HEAL?
I'M FINE.
LIAR.
SO NOW WHAT? WE CAN MAKE HER UNDO WHAT SHE DID TO SED, RIGHT?
FLECK

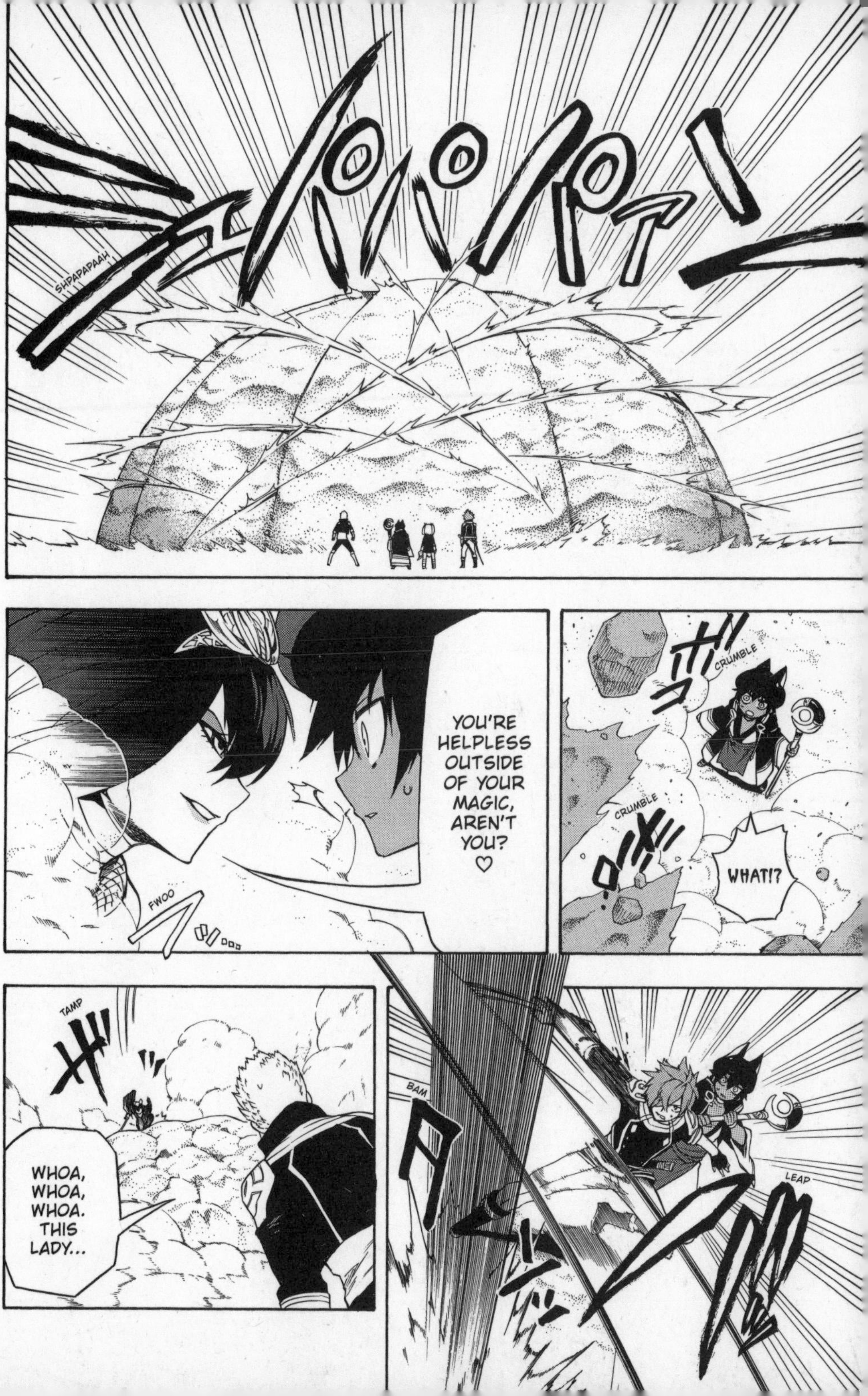
SHPAPAPAAH
CRUMBLE
CRUMBLE
WHAT!?
YOU'RE HELPLESS OUTSIDE OF YOUR MAGIC, AREN'T YOU? ♡
FWOO
BAM
LEAP
TAMP
WHOA, WHOA, WHOA. THIS LADY...

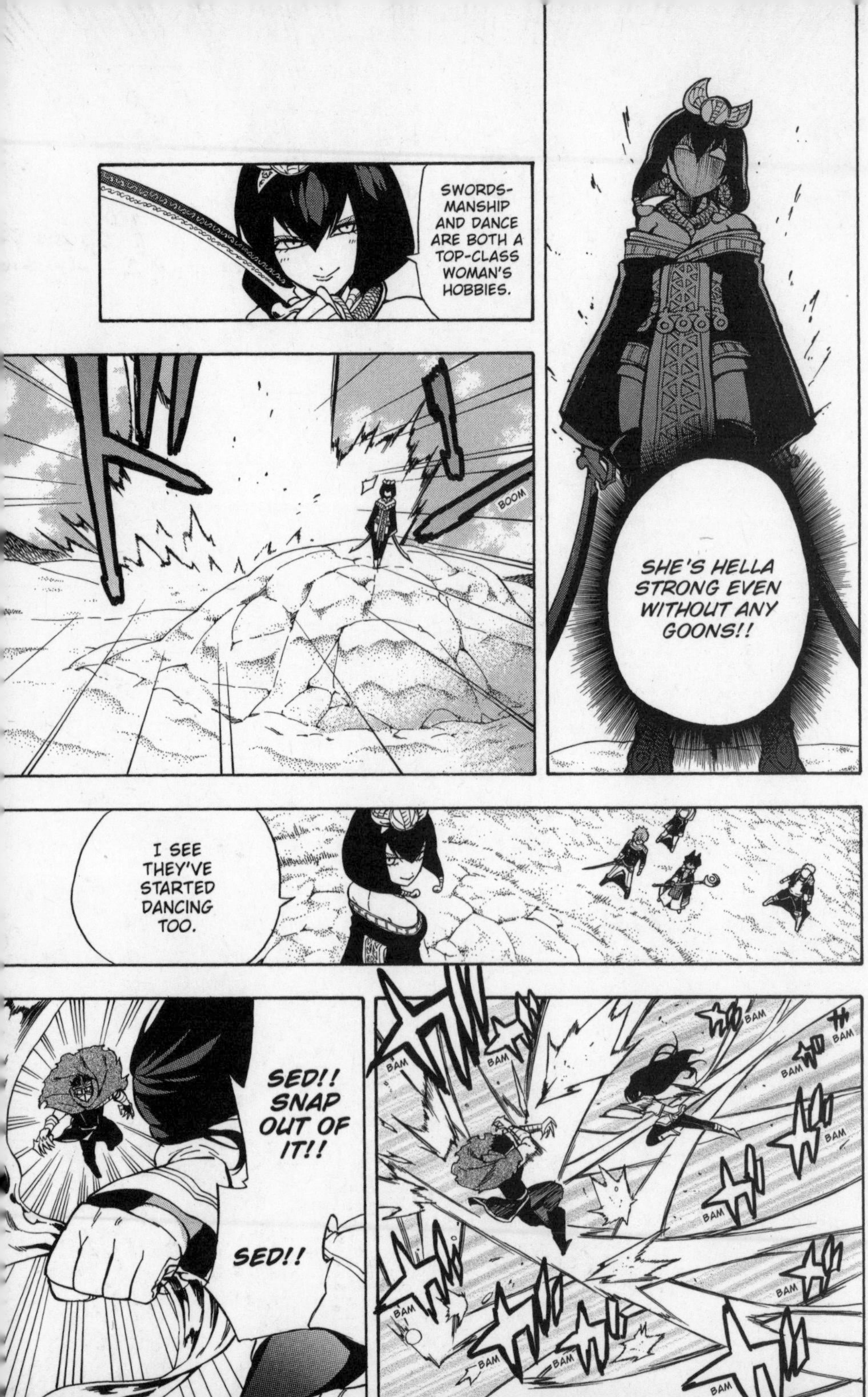
SHE'S HELLA STRONG EVEN WITHOUT ANY GOONS!!
SWORDS-MANSHIP AND DANCE ARE BOTH A TOP-CLASS WOMAN'S HOBBIES.
BOOM
I SEE THEY'VE STARTED DANCING TOO.
BAM
BAM
BAM
BAM
BAM
BAM
BAM
BAM
BAM
BAM
BAM
BAM
SED!! SNAP OUT OF IT!!
SED!!

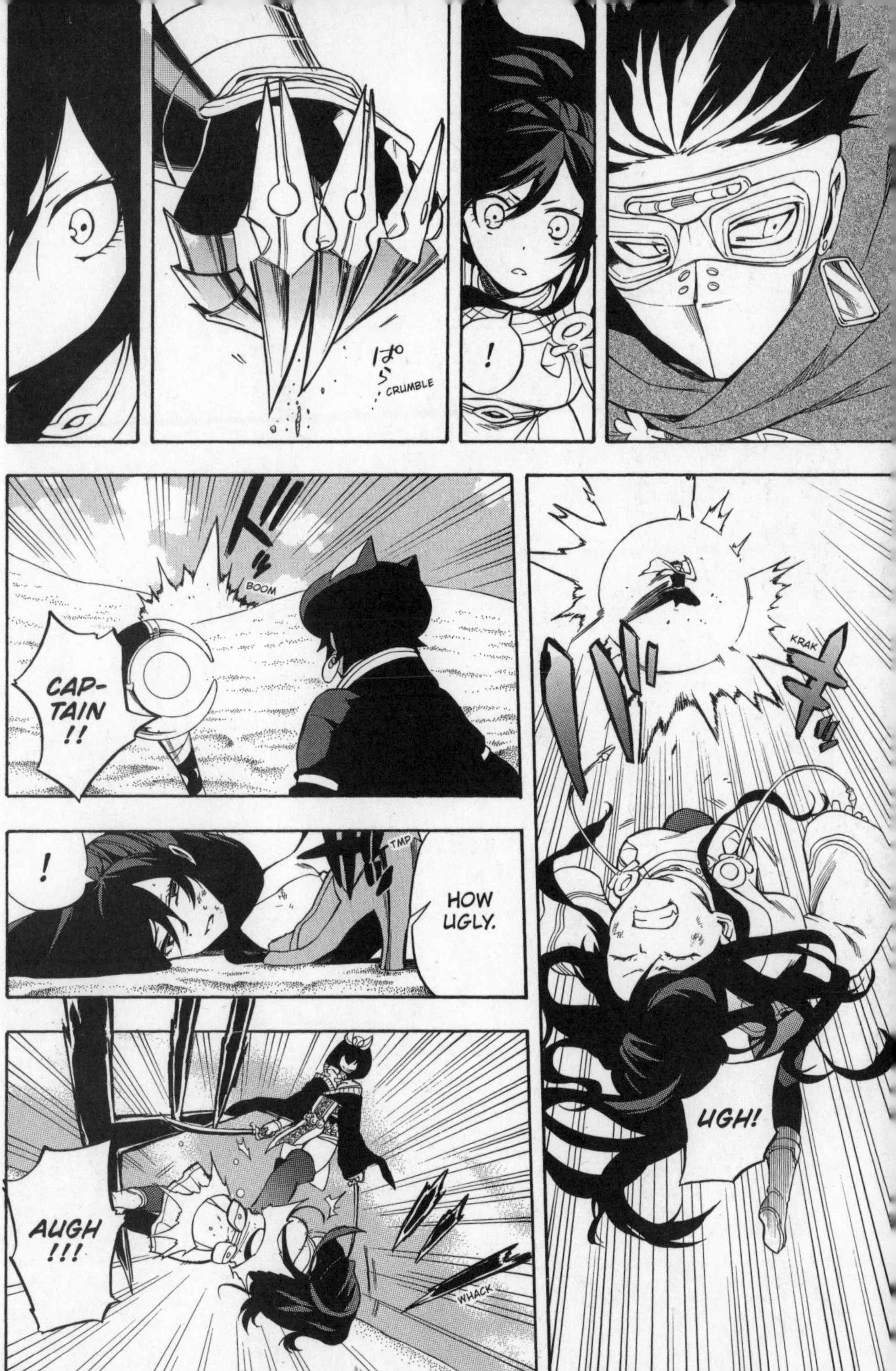
!
ぱら
CRUMBLE
KRAK
UGH!
BOOM
CAP-TAIN!!
HOW UGLY.
TMP
!
WHACK
AUGH!!!

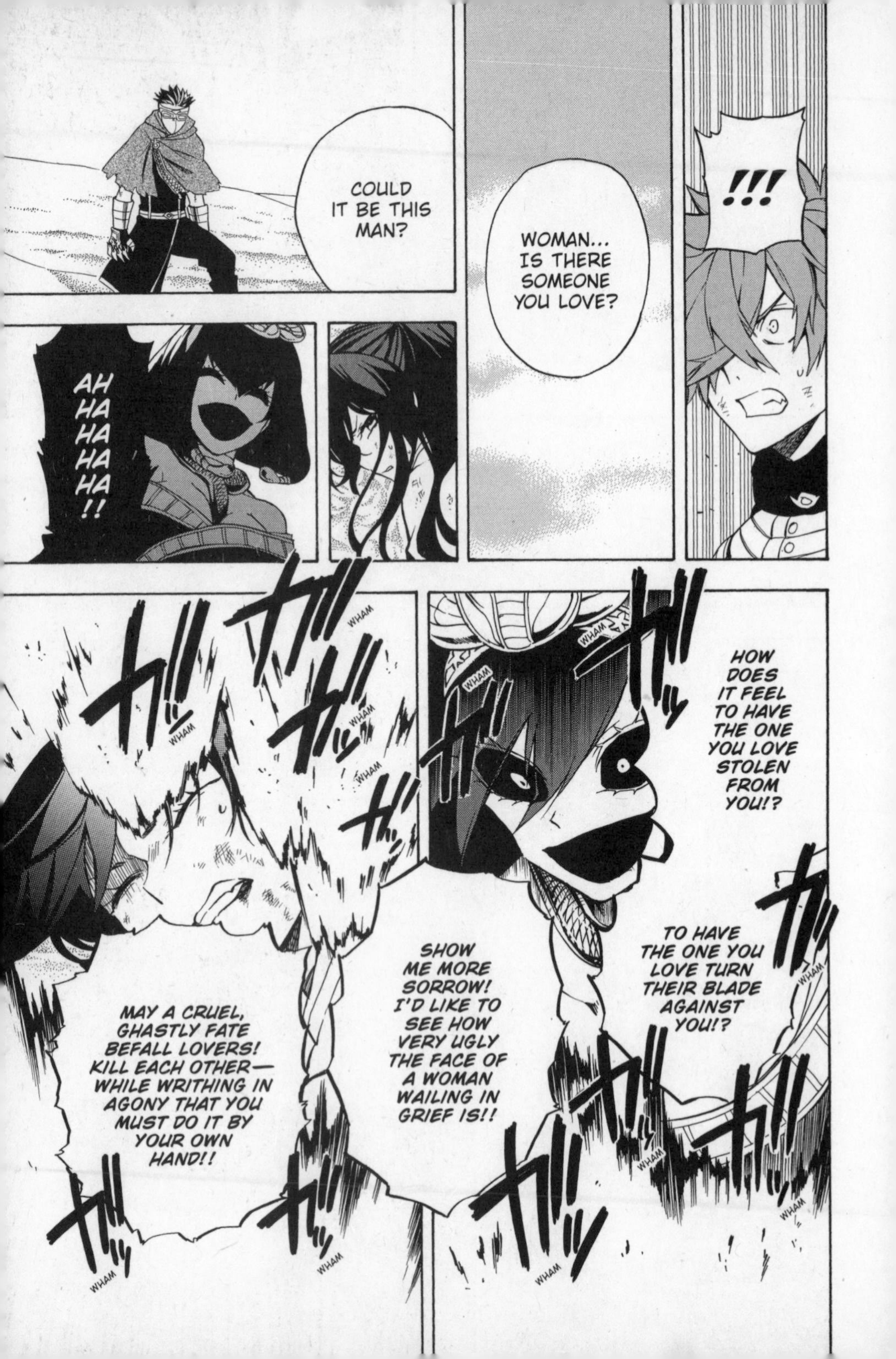
!!!
WOMAN... IS THERE SOMEONE YOU LOVE?
COULD IT BE THIS MAN?
AH HA HA HA HA!!
HOW DOES IT FEEL TO HAVE THE ONE YOU LOVE STOLEN FROM YOU!?
WHAM
TO HAVE THE ONE YOU LOVE TURN THEIR BLADE AGAINST YOU!?
SHOW ME MORE SORROW! I'D LIKE TO SEE HOW VERY UGLY THE FACE OF A WOMAN WAILING IN GRIEF IS!!
WHAM
MAY A CRUEL, GHASTLY FATE BEFALL LOVERS! KILL EACH OTHER—WHILE WRITHING IN AGONY THAT YOU MUST DO IT BY YOUR OWN HAND!!
WHAM

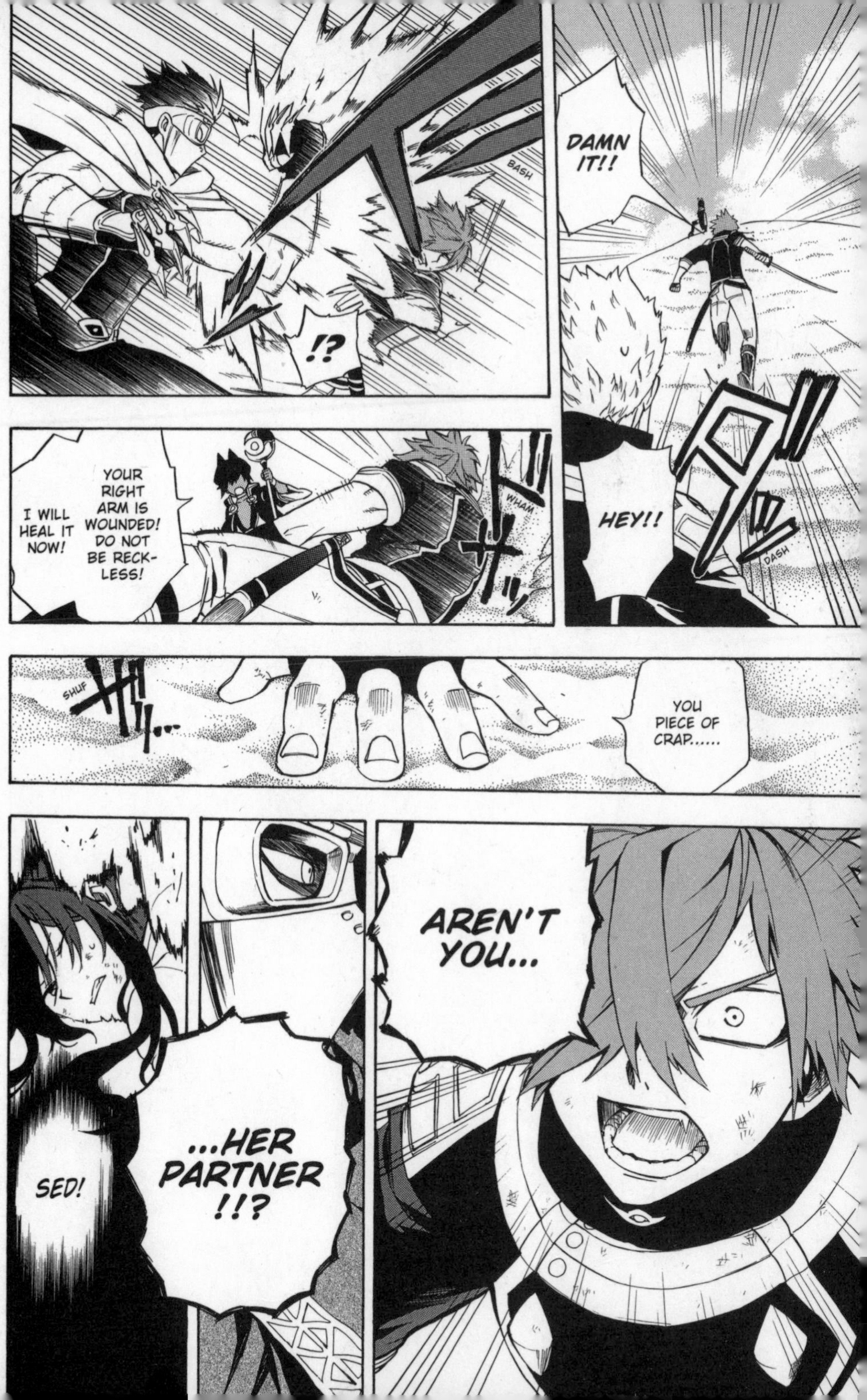
DAMN IT!!
HEY!!
DASH
BASH
!?
WHAM
YOUR RIGHT ARM IS WOUNDED! DO NOT BE RECKLESS!
I WILL HEAL IT NOW!
YOU PIECE OF CRAP......
SHUF
AREN'T YOU...
...HER PARTNER!!?
SED!

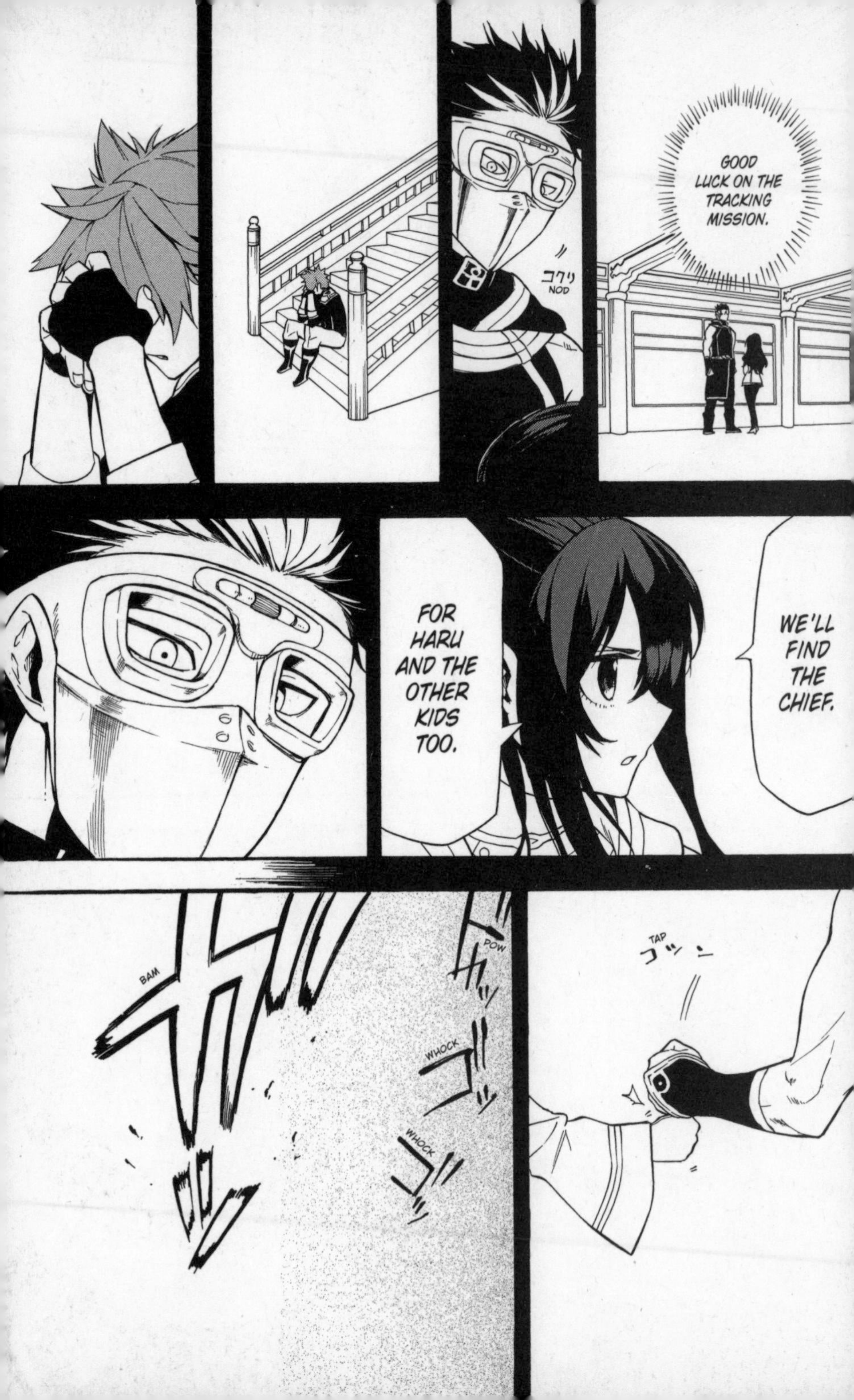
GOOD LUCK ON THE TRACKING MISSION.
コクリ
NOD
WE'LL FIND THE CHIEF.
FOR HARU AND THE OTHER KIDS TOO.
TAP
POW
WHOCK
WHOCK
BAM

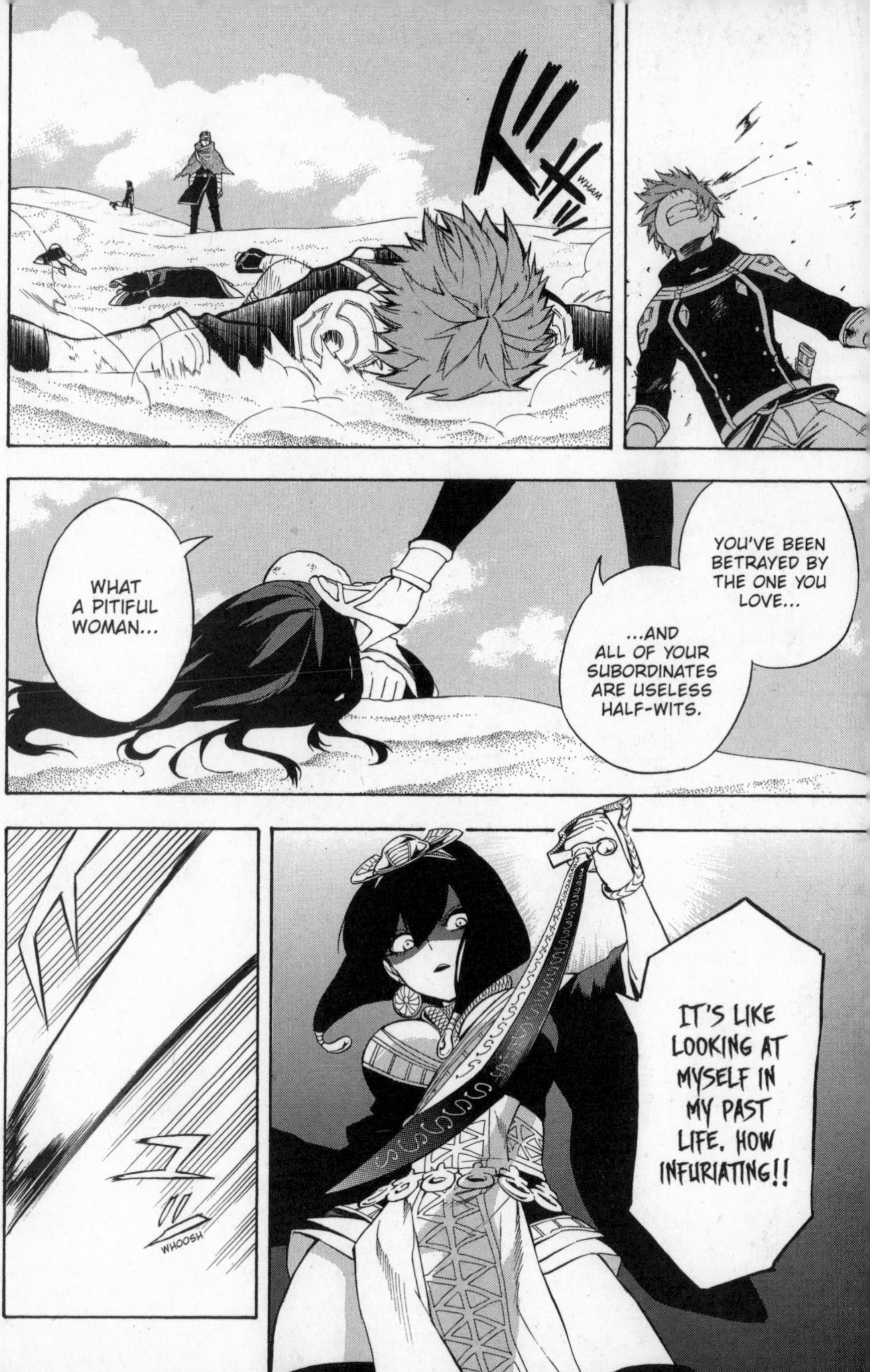
WHAM
YOU'VE BEEN BETRAYED BY THE ONE YOU LOVE...
...AND ALL OF YOUR SUBORDINATES ARE USELESS HALF-WITS.
WHAT A PITIFUL WOMAN...
IT'S LIKE LOOKING AT MYSELF IN MY PAST LIFE. HOW INFURIATING!!
WHOOSH

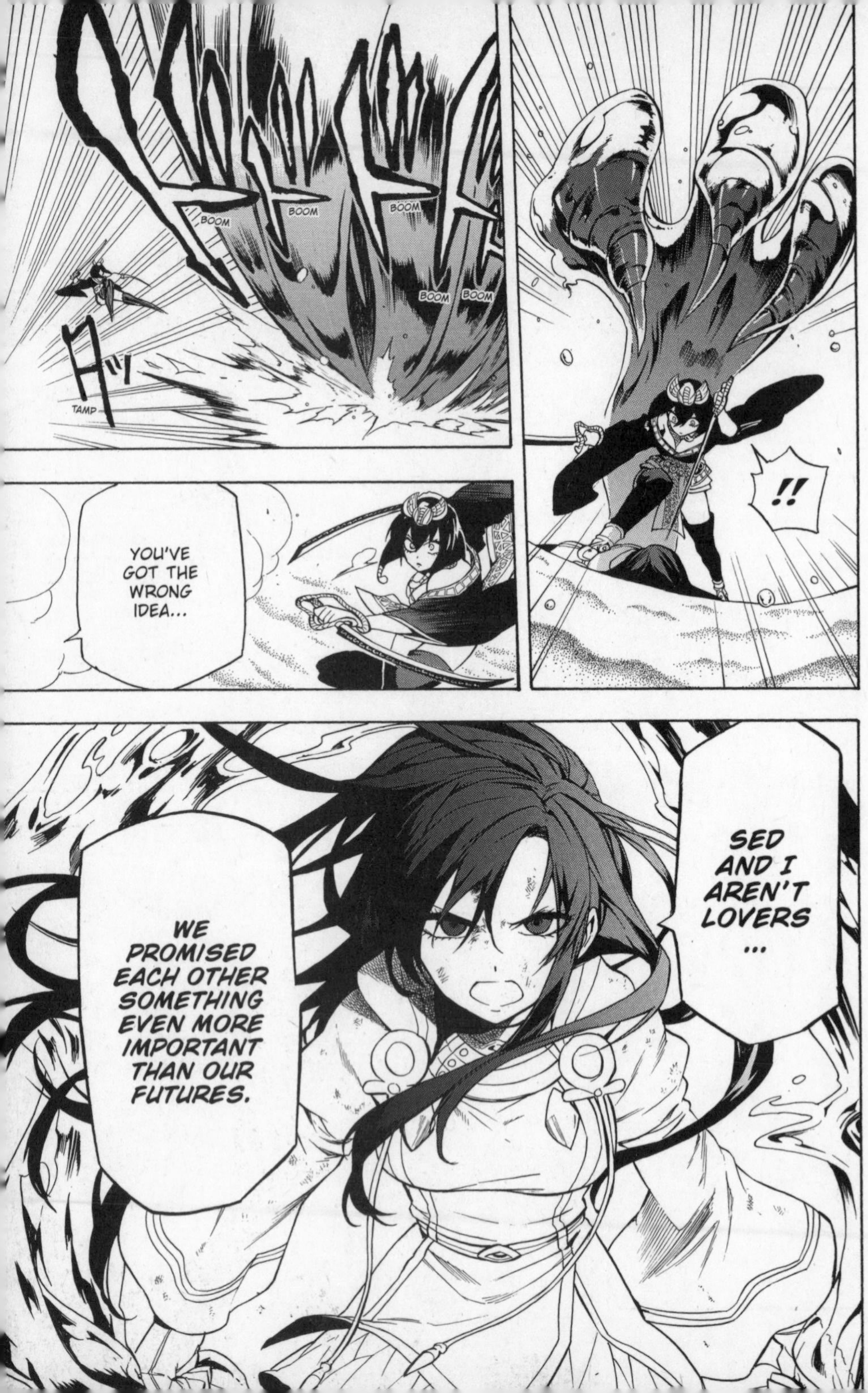
!!
BOOM
BOOM
BOOM
BOOM
BOOM
TAMP
YOU'VE GOT THE WRONG IDEA...
SED AND I AREN'T LOVERS ...
WE PROMISED EACH OTHER SOMETHING EVEN MORE IMPORTANT THAN OUR FUTURES.

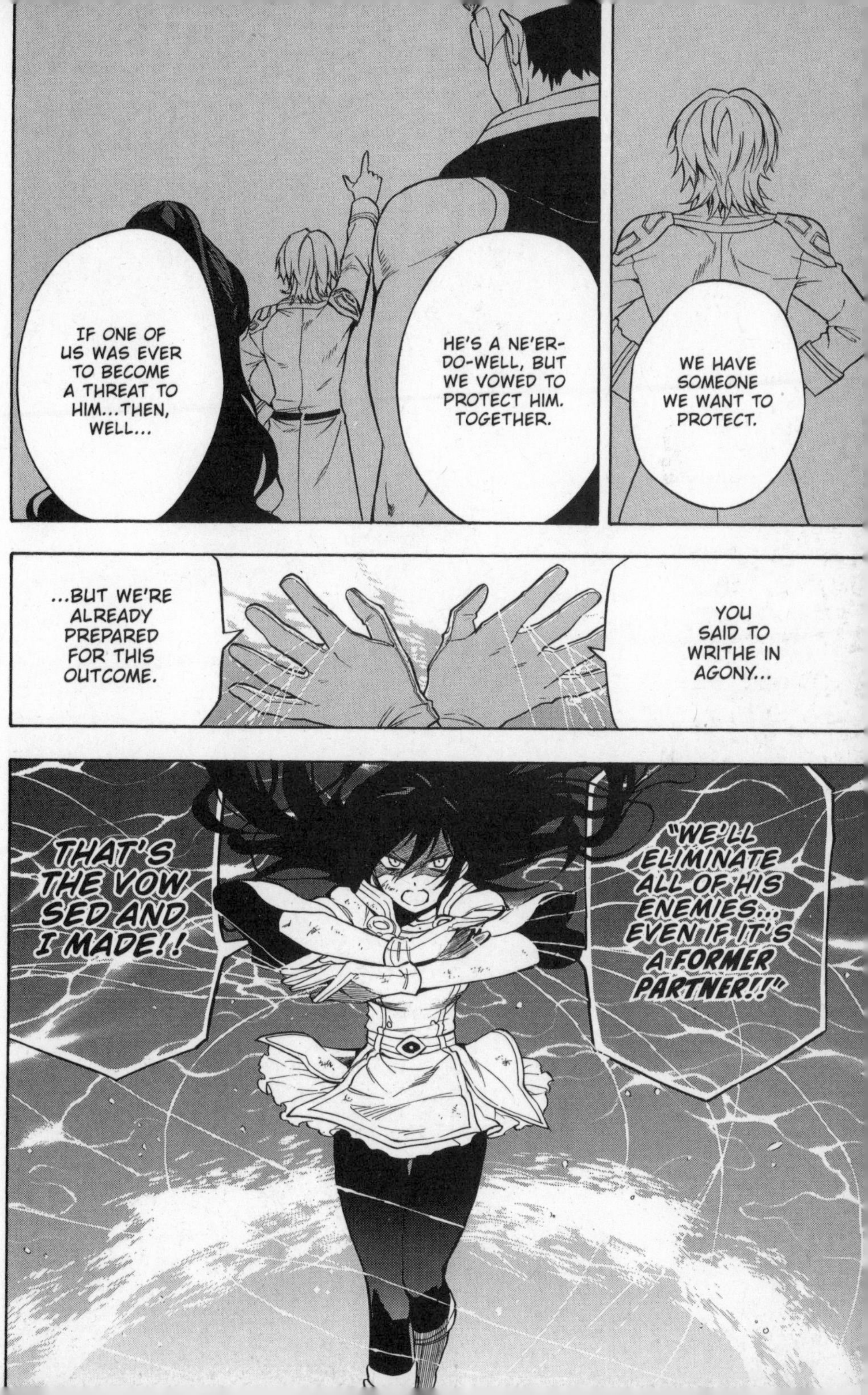
WE HAVE SOMEONE WE WANT TO PROTECT.
HE'S A NE'ER-DO-WELL, BUT WE VOWED TO PROTECT HIM. TOGETHER.
IF ONE OF US WAS EVER TO BECOME A THREAT TO HIM...THEN, WELL...
YOU SAID TO WRITHE IN AGONY...
...BUT WE'RE ALREADY PREPARED FOR THIS OUTCOME.
"WE'LL ELIMINATE ALL OF HIS ENEMIES... EVEN IF IT'S A FORMER PARTNER!!"
THAT'S THE VOW SED AND I MADE!!

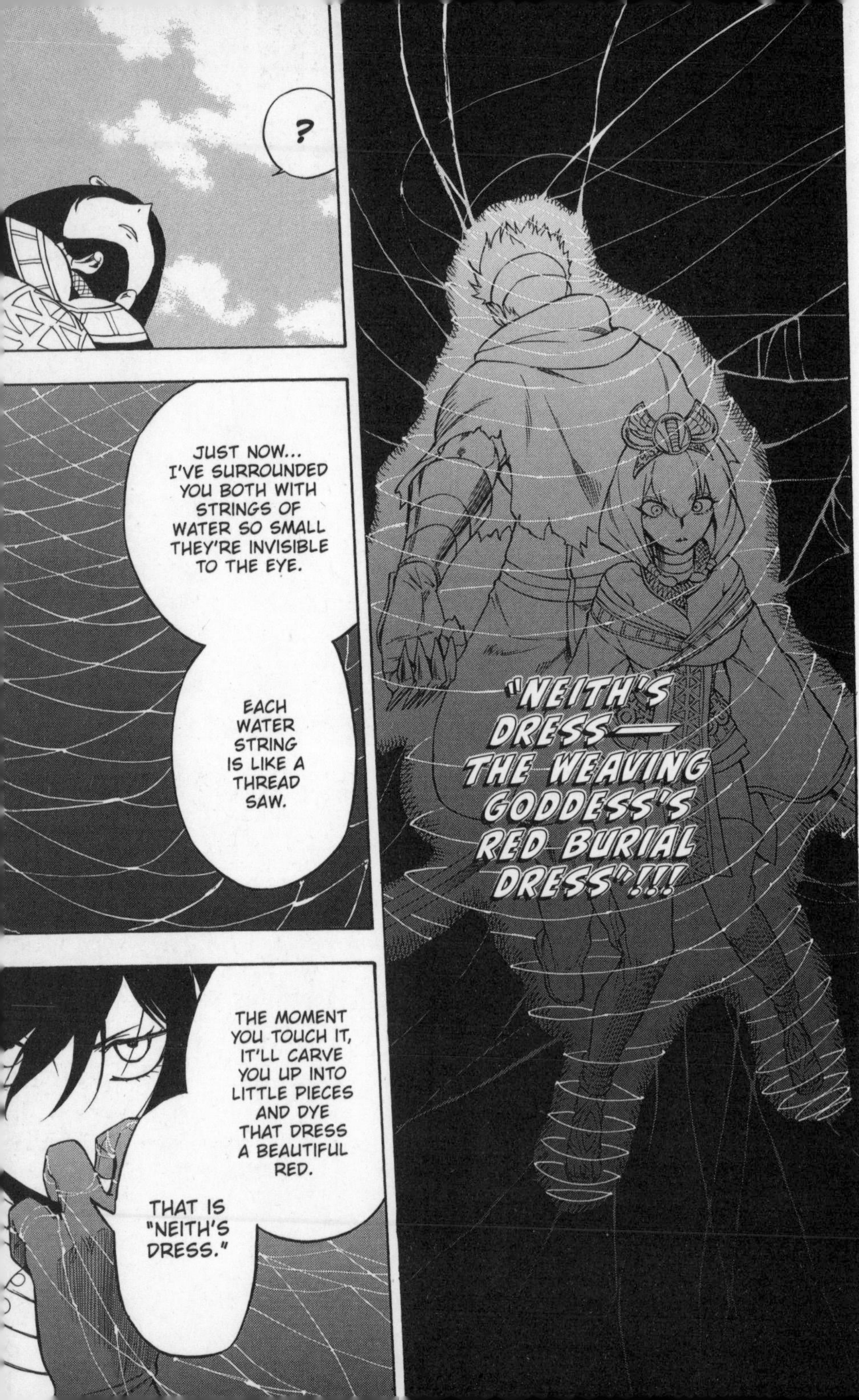
"NEITH'S DRESS— THE WEAVING GODDESS'S RED BURIAL DRESS"!!!
?
JUST NOW... I'VE SURROUNDED YOU BOTH WITH STRINGS OF WATER SO SMALL THEY'RE INVISIBLE TO THE EYE.
EACH WATER STRING IS LIKE A THREAD SAW.
THE MOMENT YOU TOUCH IT, IT'LL CARVE YOU UP INTO LITTLE PIECES AND DYE THAT DRESS A BEAUTIFUL RED.
THAT IS "NEITH'S DRESS."

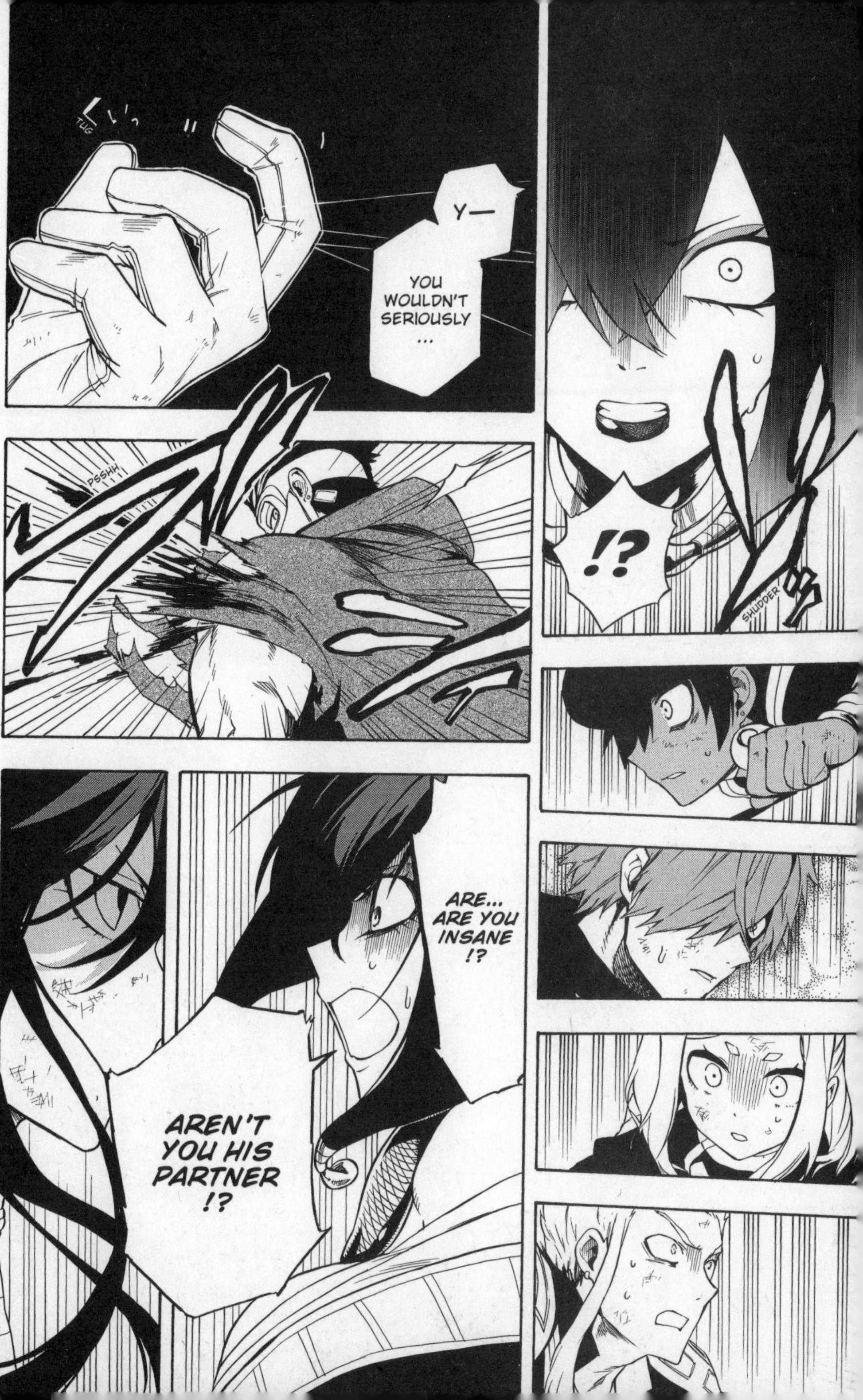
!?
SHUDDER
TUG
Y—
YOU WOULDN'T SERIOUSLY ...
PSSHH
ARE... ARE YOU INSANE !?
AREN'T YOU HIS PARTNER !?

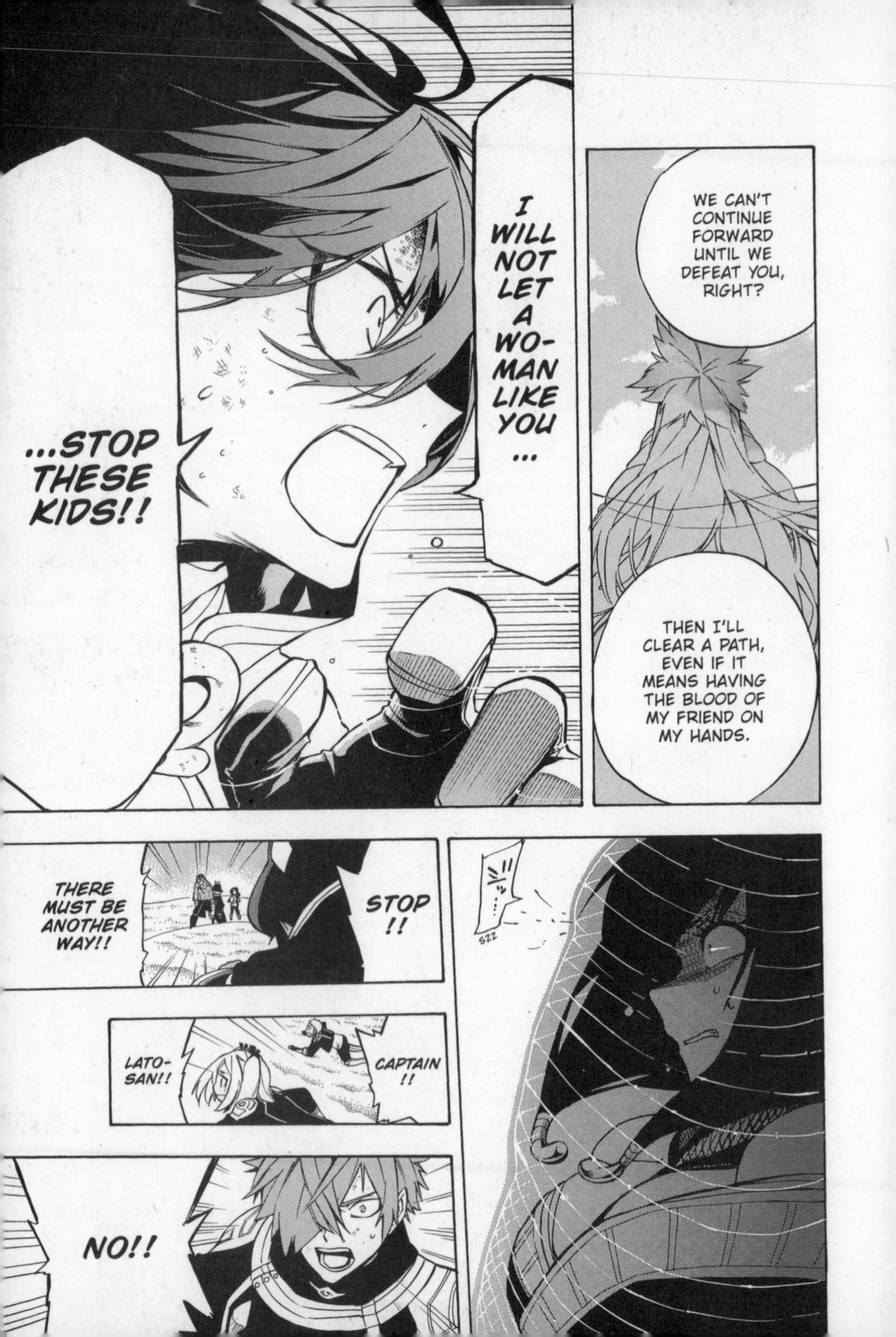
WE CAN'T CONTINUE FORWARD UNTIL WE DEFEAT YOU, RIGHT?
THEN I'LL CLEAR A PATH, EVEN IF IT MEANS HAVING THE BLOOD OF MY FRIEND ON MY HANDS.
I WILL NOT LET A WO-MAN LIKE YOU ...
...STOP THESE KIDS!!
SZZ
STOP !!
THERE MUST BE ANOTHER WAY!!
CAPTAIN !!
LATO-SAN!!
NO!!

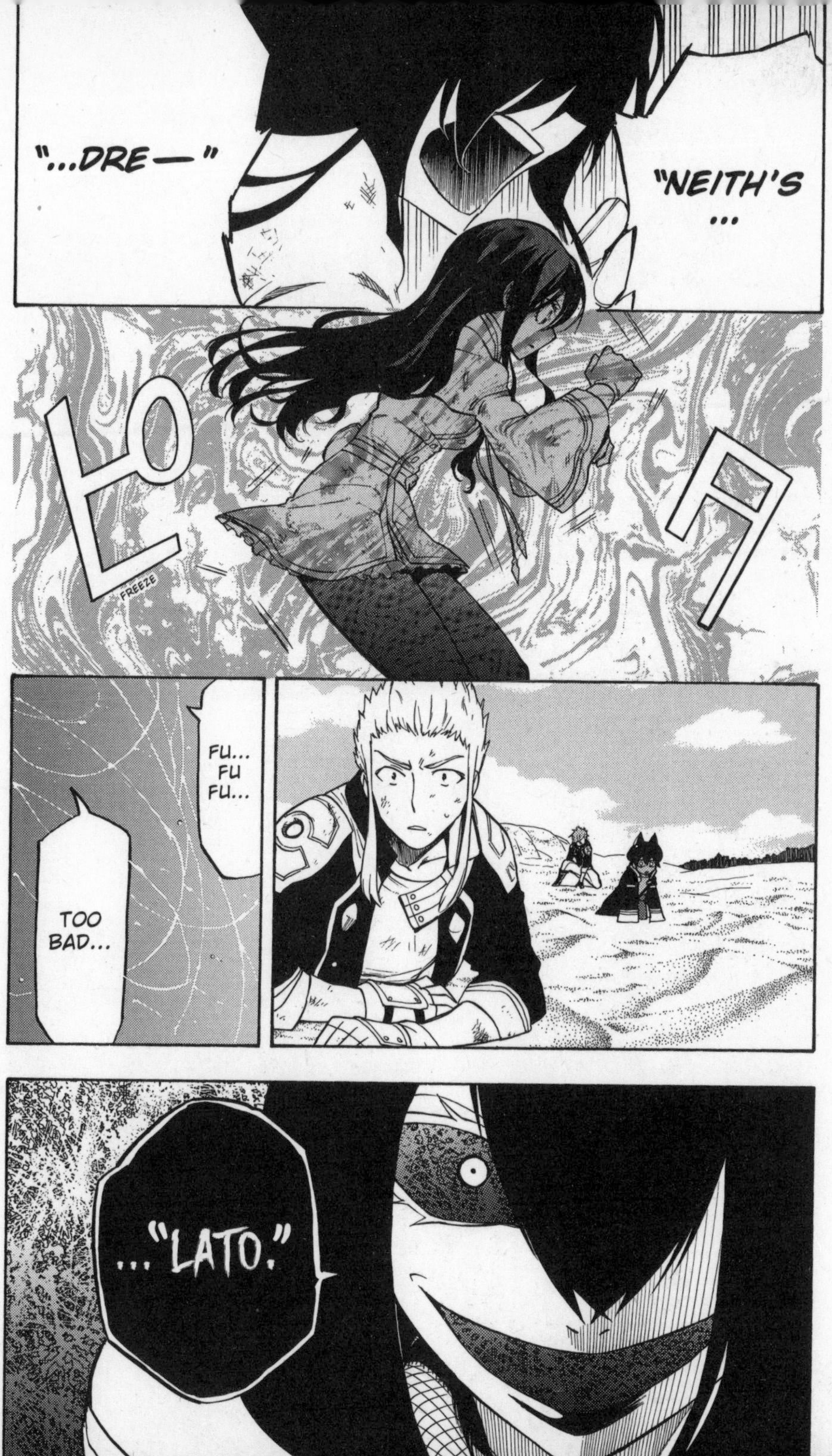
"NEITH'S ...
"...DRE—"
FREEZE
FU... FU FU...
TOO BAD...
..."LATO."

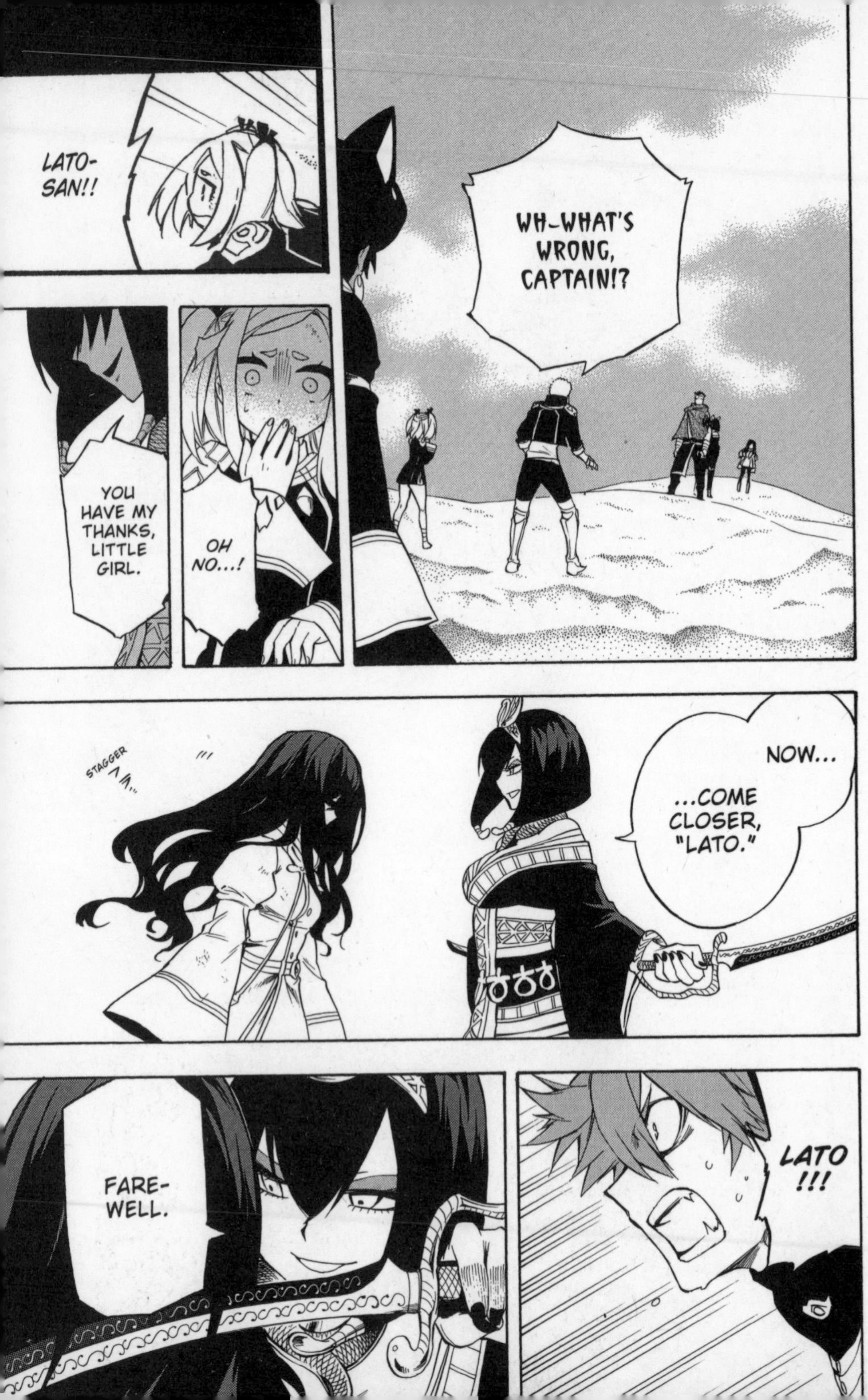
WH-WHAT'S WRONG, CAPTAIN!?
LATO-SAN!!
OH NO...!
YOU HAVE MY THANKS, LITTLE GIRL.
NOW...
...COME CLOSER, "LATO."
STAGGER
LATO!!!
FARE-WELL.

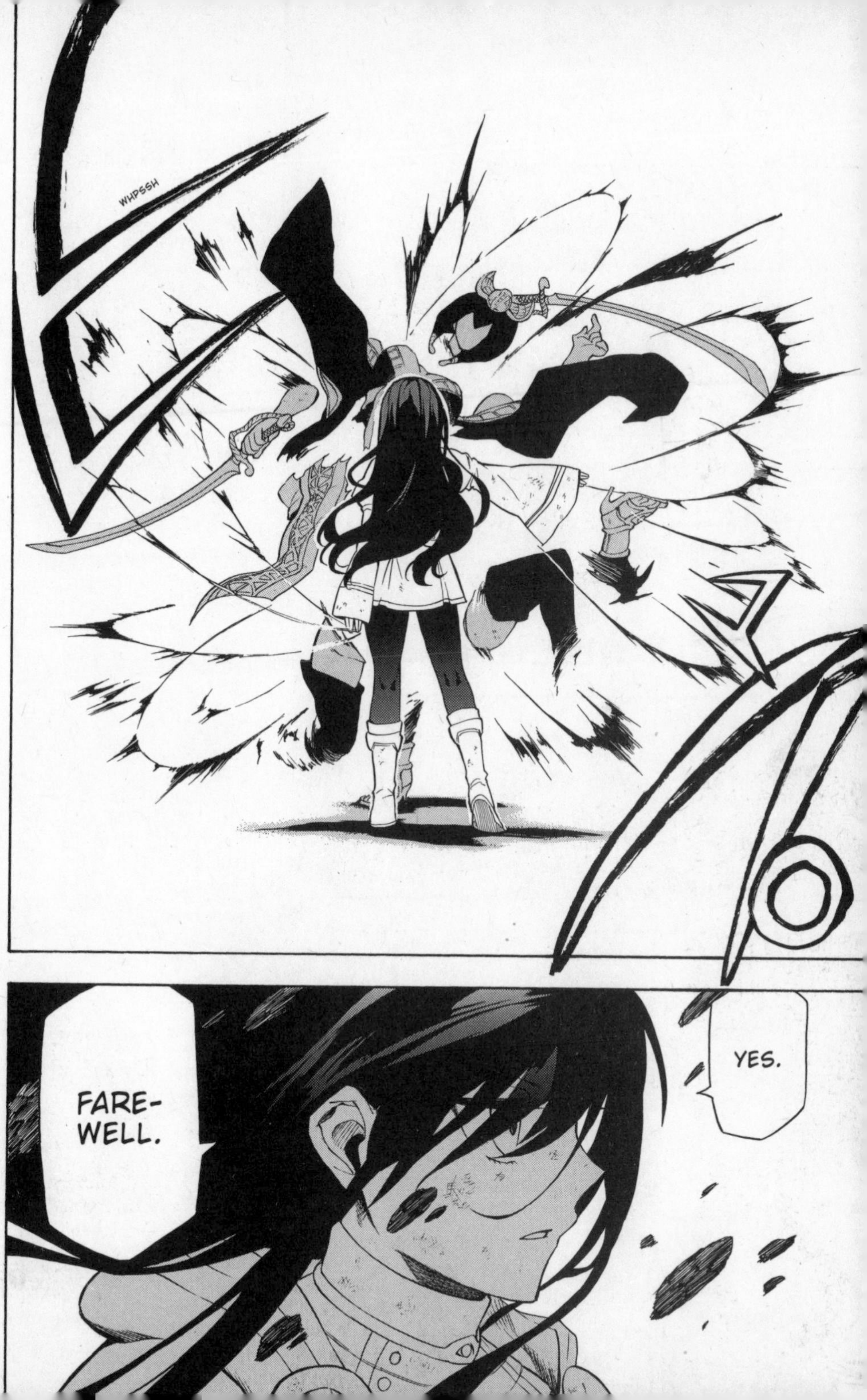
WHPSSH
YES.
FARE-
WELL.

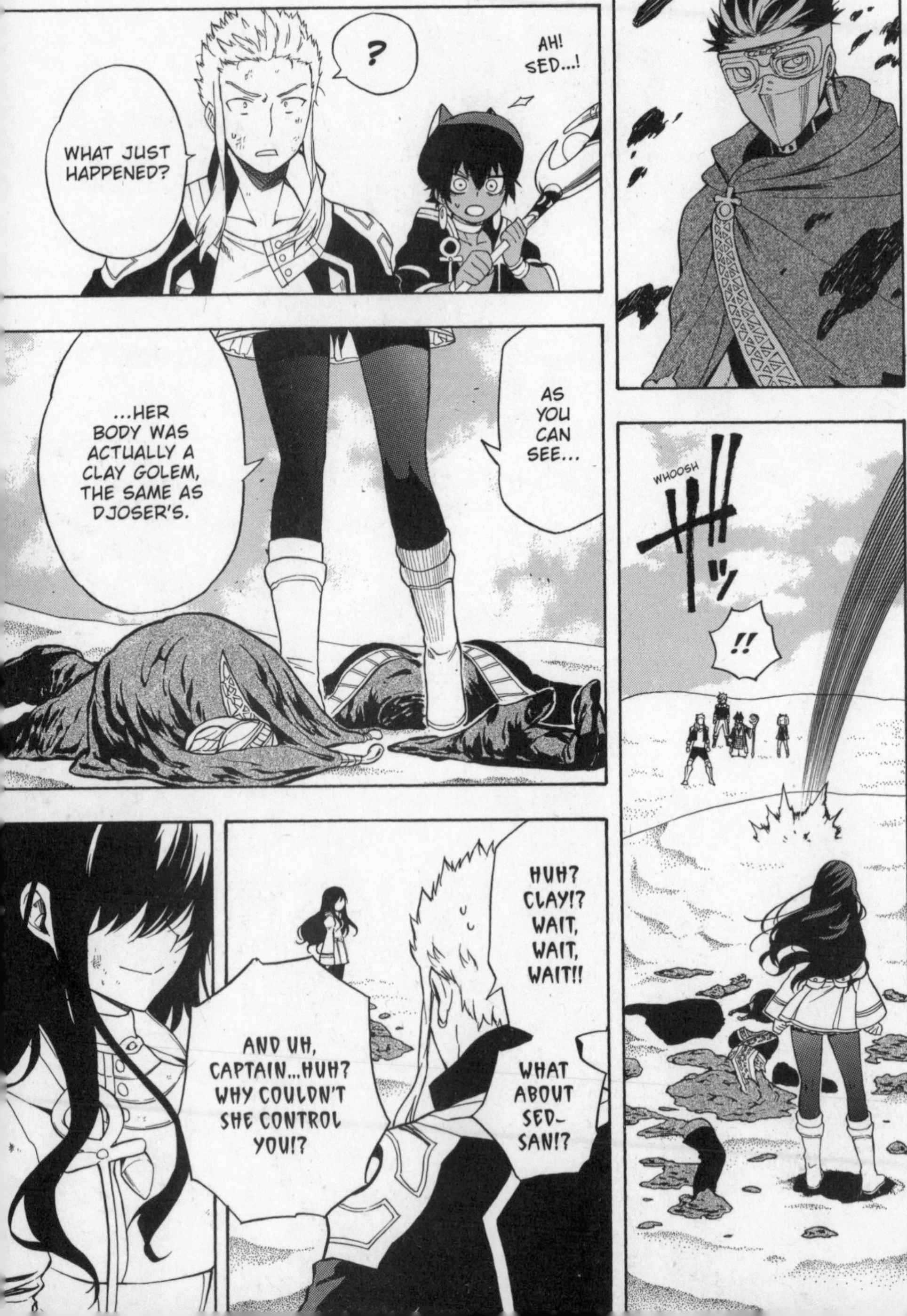
WHOOSH
!!
AH! SED...!
?
WHAT JUST HAPPENED?
AS YOU CAN SEE...
...HER BODY WAS ACTUALLY A CLAY GOLEM, THE SAME AS DJOSER'S.
HUH? CLAY!? WAIT, WAIT, WAIT!!
WHAT ABOUT SED-SAN!?
AND UH, CAPTAIN...HUH? WHY COULDN'T SHE CONTROL YOU!?

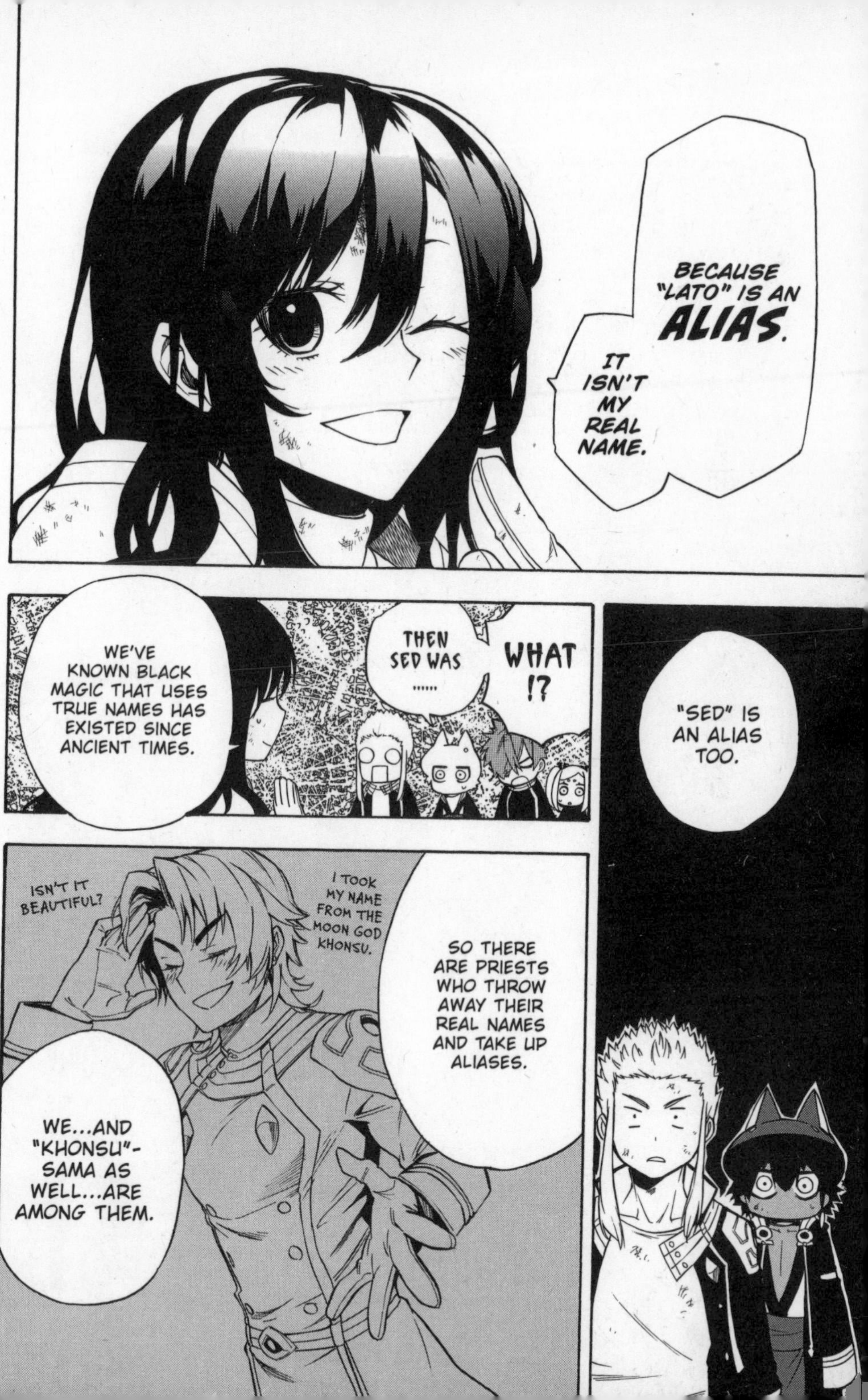
BECAUSE "LATO" IS AN ALIAS.
IT ISN'T MY REAL NAME.
"SED" IS AN ALIAS TOO.
WHAT!?
THEN SED WAS ......
WE'VE KNOWN BLACK MAGIC THAT USES TRUE NAMES HAS EXISTED SINCE ANCIENT TIMES.
SO THERE ARE PRIESTS WHO THROW AWAY THEIR REAL NAMES AND TAKE UP ALIASES.
I TOOK MY NAME FROM THE MOON GOD KHONSU.
ISN'T IT BEAUTIFUL?
WE...AND "KHONSU"-SAMA AS WELL...ARE AMONG THEM.

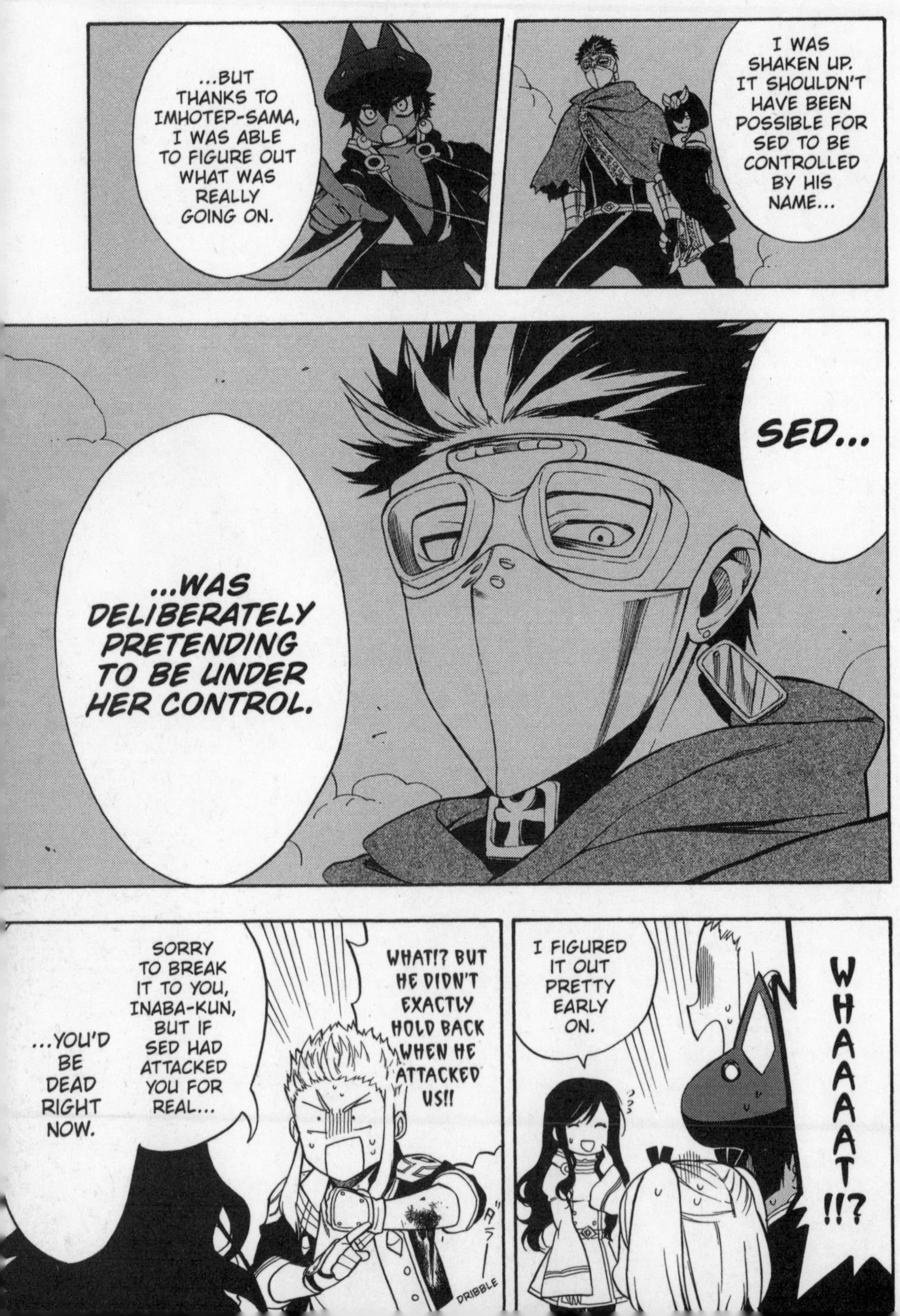
I WAS SHAKEN UP. IT SHOULDN'T HAVE BEEN POSSIBLE FOR SED TO BE CONTROLLED BY HIS NAME...
...BUT THANKS TO IMHOTEP-SAMA, I WAS ABLE TO FIGURE OUT WHAT WAS REALLY GOING ON.
SED...
...WAS DELIBERATELY PRETENDING TO BE UNDER HER CONTROL.
WHAAAAT!!?
I FIGURED IT OUT PRETTY EARLY ON.
WHAT!? BUT HE DIDN'T EXACTLY HOLD BACK WHEN HE ATTACKED US!!
SORRY TO BREAK IT TO YOU, INABA-KUN, BUT IF SED HAD ATTACKED YOU FOR REAL...
...YOU'D BE DEAD RIGHT NOW.
DRIBBLE

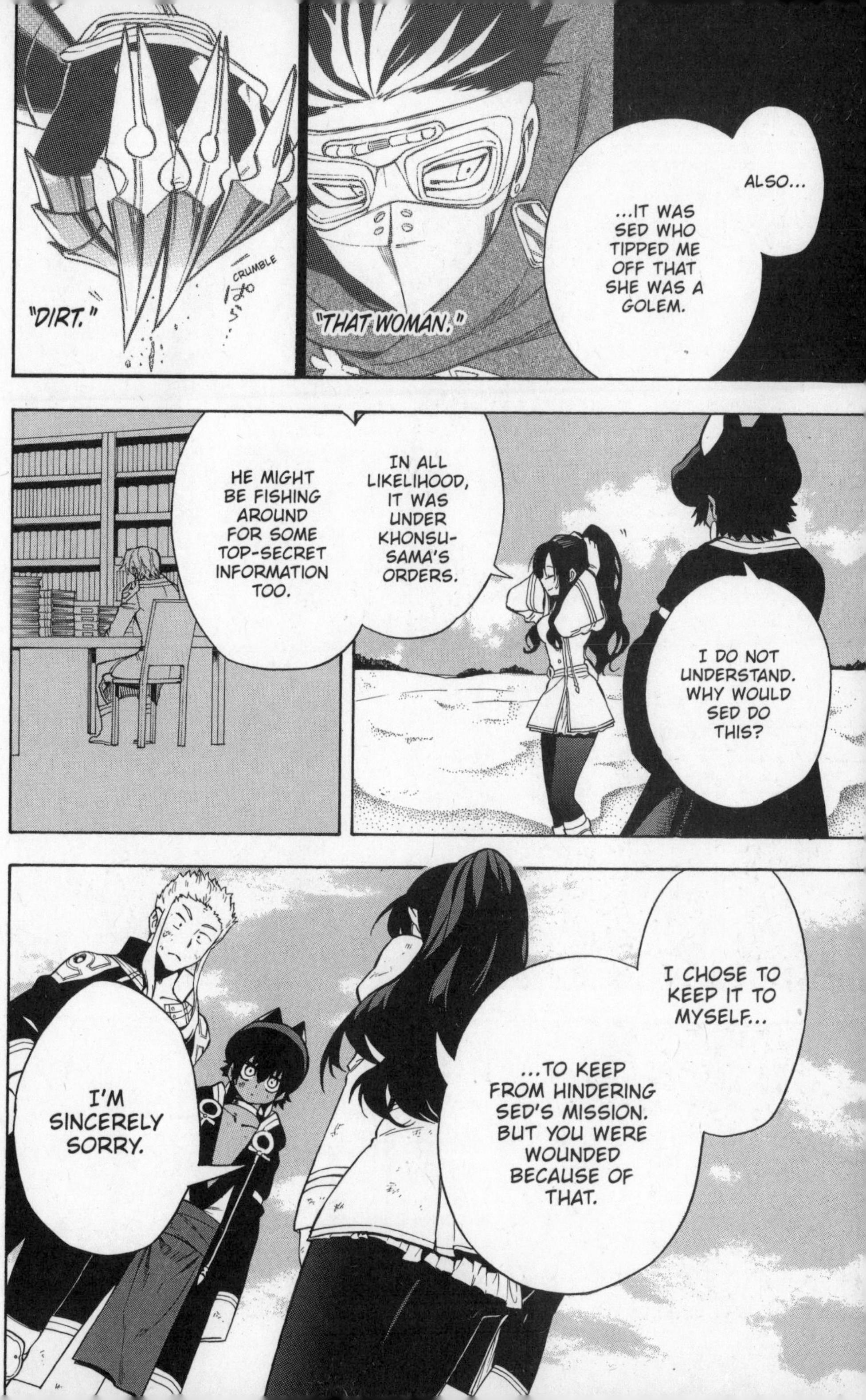
ALSO...
...IT WAS SED WHO TIPPED ME OFF THAT SHE WAS A GOLEM.
"THAT WOMAN."
CRUMBLE
"DIRT."
I DO NOT UNDERSTAND. WHY WOULD SED DO THIS?
IN ALL LIKELIHOOD, IT WAS UNDER KHONSU-SAMA'S ORDERS.
HE MIGHT BE FISHING AROUND FOR SOME TOP-SECRET INFORMATION TOO.
I CHOSE TO KEEP IT TO MYSELF...
...TO KEEP FROM HINDERING SED'S MISSION. BUT YOU WERE WOUNDED BECAUSE OF THAT.
I'M SINCERELY SORRY.

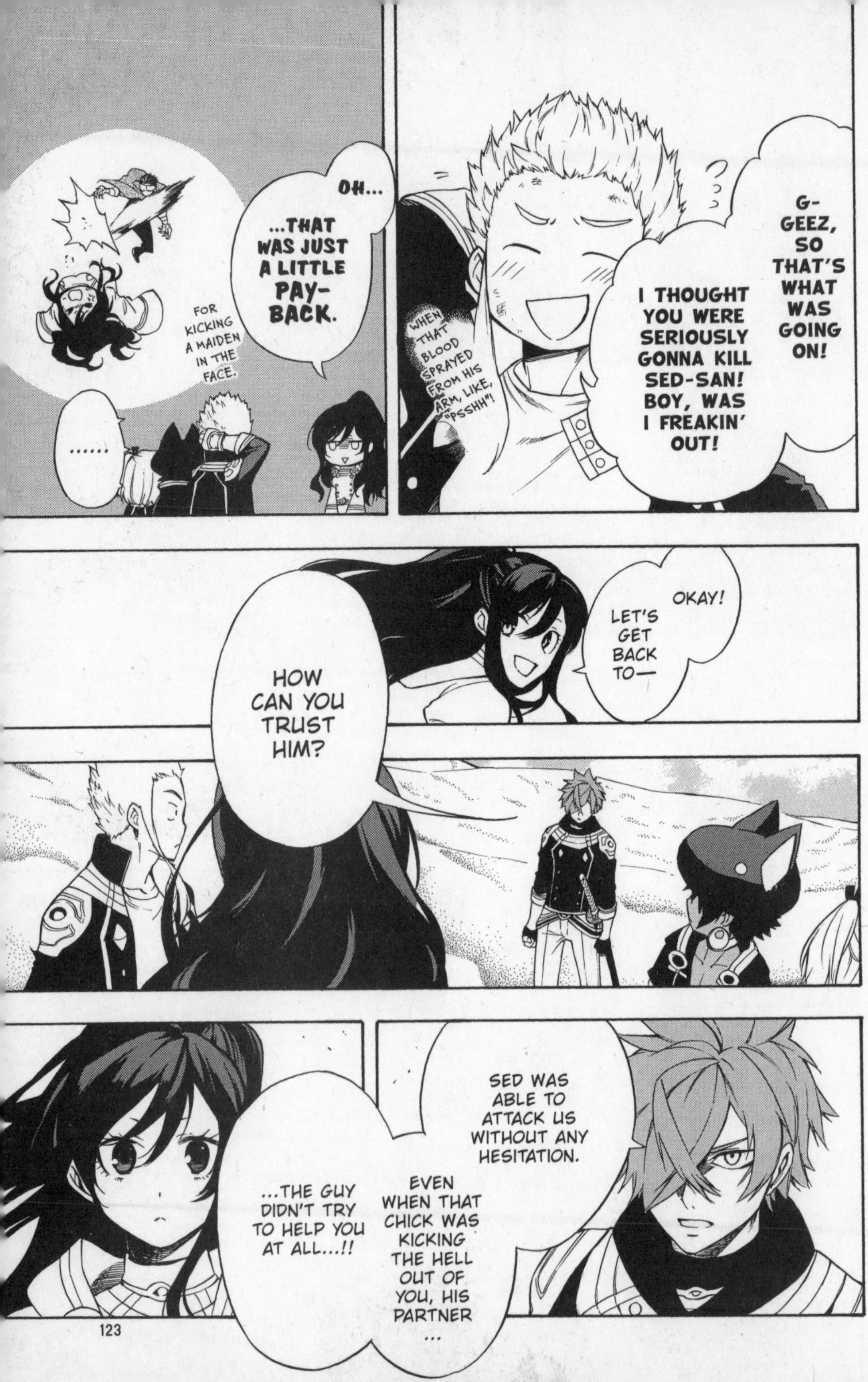
G-GEEZ, SO THAT'S WHAT WAS GOING ON!
I THOUGHT YOU WERE SERIOUSLY GONNA KILL SED-SAN! BOY, WAS I FREAKIN' OUT!
WHEN THAT BLOOD SPRAYED FROM HIS ARM, LIKE, "PSSHH"!
OH...
...THAT WAS JUST A LITTLE PAY-BACK.
FOR KICKING A MAIDEN IN THE FACE.
......
OKAY!
LET'S GET BACK TO—
HOW CAN YOU TRUST HIM?
SED WAS ABLE TO ATTACK US WITHOUT ANY HESITATION.
EVEN WHEN THAT CHICK WAS KICKING THE HELL OUT OF YOU, HIS PARTNER ...
...THE GUY DIDN'T TRY TO HELP YOU AT ALL...!!

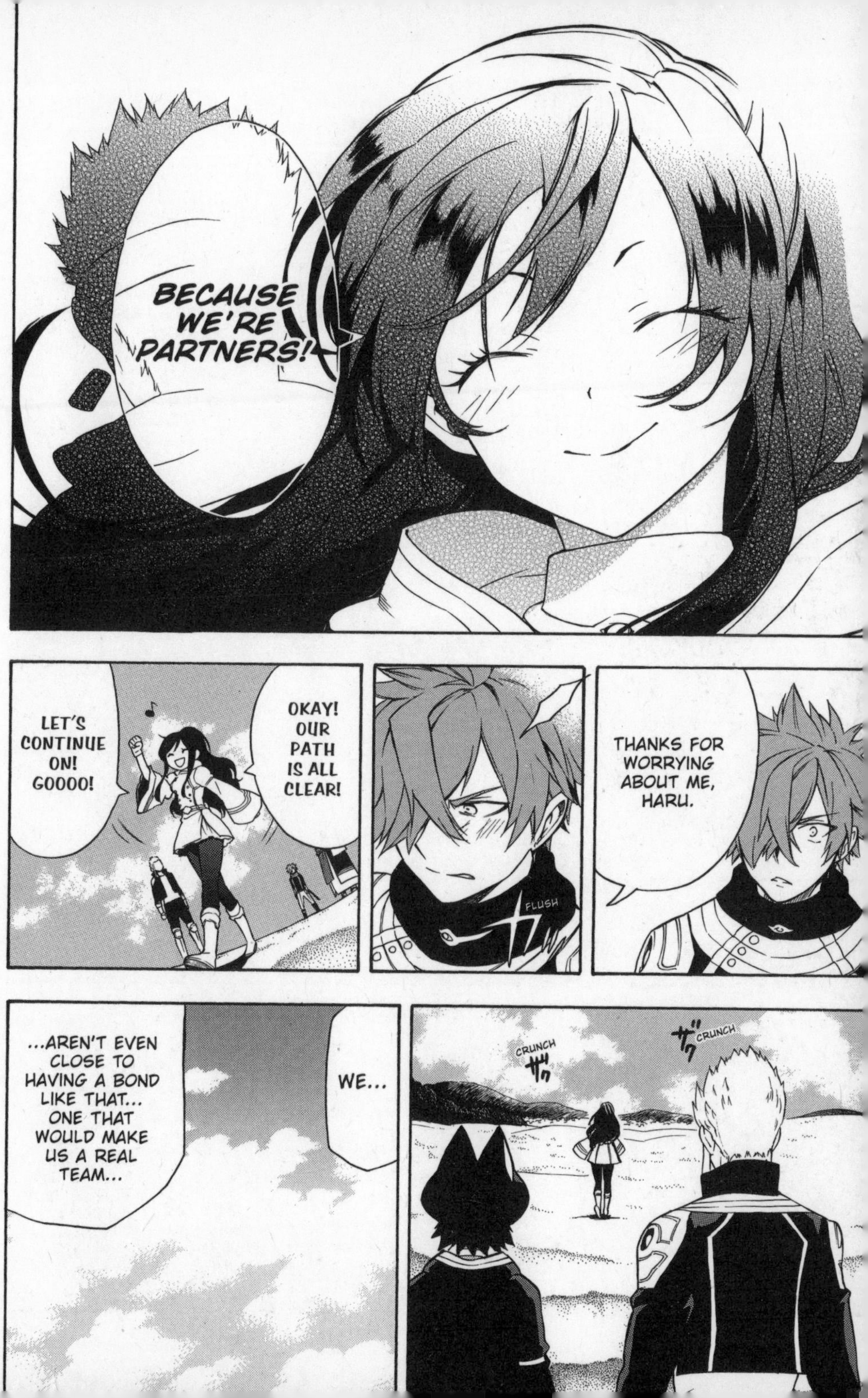
BECAUSE WE'RE PARTNERS!
THANKS FOR WORRYING ABOUT ME, HARU.
FLUSH
OKAY! OUR PATH IS ALL CLEAR!
LET'S CONTINUE ON! GOOOO!
ザク CRUNCH
CRUNCH ザク
WE...
...AREN'T EVEN CLOSE TO HAVING A BOND LIKE THAT... ONE THAT WOULD MAKE US A REAL TEAM...

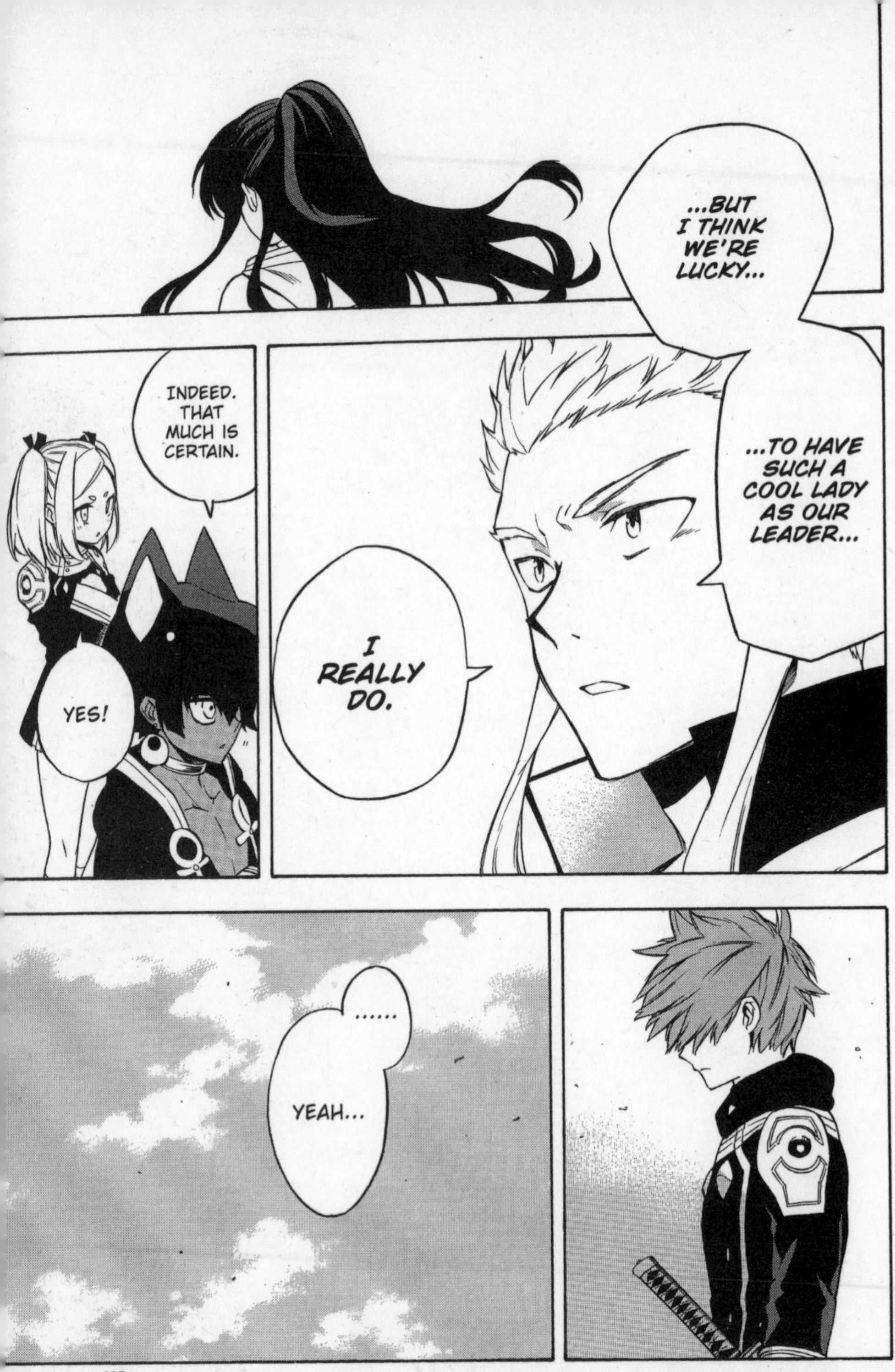
...BUT I THINK WE'RE LUCKY...
...TO HAVE SUCH A COOL LADY AS OUR LEADER...
I REALLY DO.
INDEED. THAT MUCH IS CERTAIN.
YES!
......
YEAH...

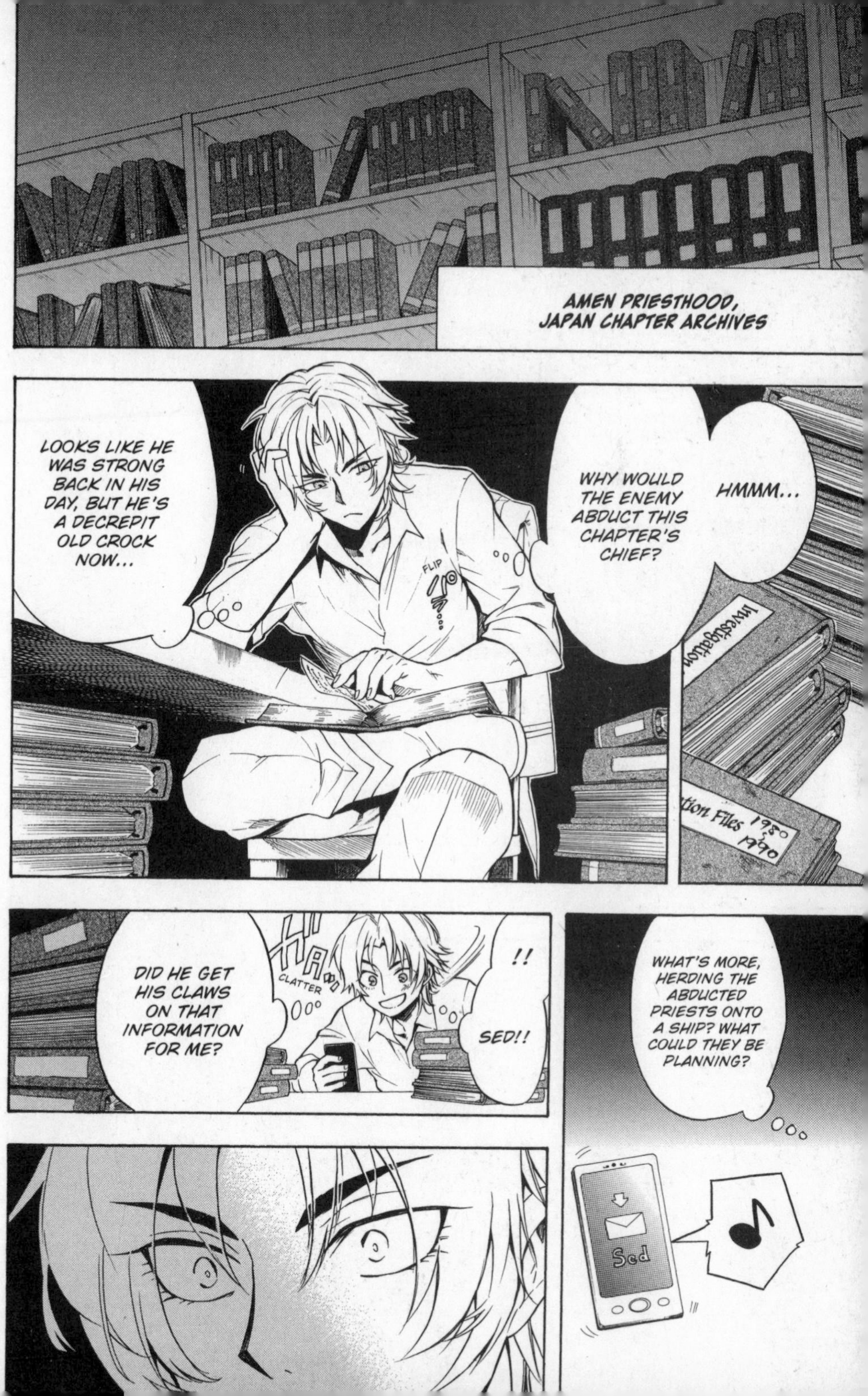
AMEN PRIESTHOOD, JAPAN CHAPTER ARCHIVES
HMMM...
WHY WOULD THE ENEMY ABDUCT THIS CHAPTER'S CHIEF?
FLIP
LOOKS LIKE HE WAS STRONG BACK IN HIS DAY, BUT HE'S A DECREPIT OLD CROCK NOW...
Investigation
tion Files 1950 ~ 1990
WHAT'S MORE, HERDING THE ABDUCTED PRIESTS ONTO A SHIP? WHAT COULD THEY BE PLANNING?
Sed
!!
SED!!
CLATTER
DID HE GET HIS CLAWS ON THAT INFORMATION FOR ME?

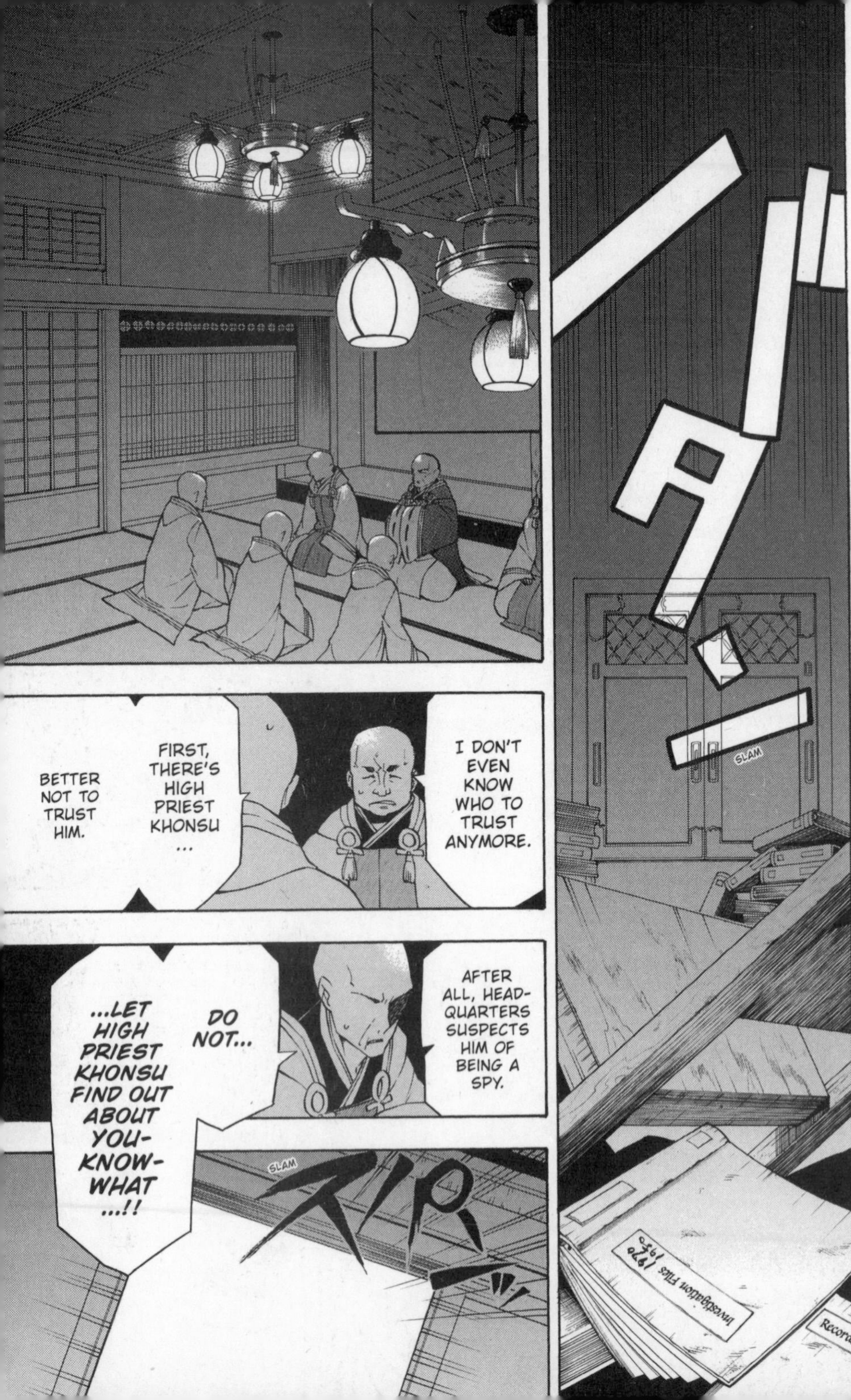
SLAM
Investigation Files
1970
1975
Records
I DON'T EVEN KNOW WHO TO TRUST ANYMORE.
FIRST, THERE'S HIGH PRIEST KHONSU ...
BETTER NOT TO TRUST HIM.
AFTER ALL, HEAD-QUARTERS SUSPECTS HIM OF BEING A SPY.
DO NOT...
...LET HIGH PRIEST KHONSU FIND OUT ABOUT YOU-KNOW-WHAT ...!!
SLAM

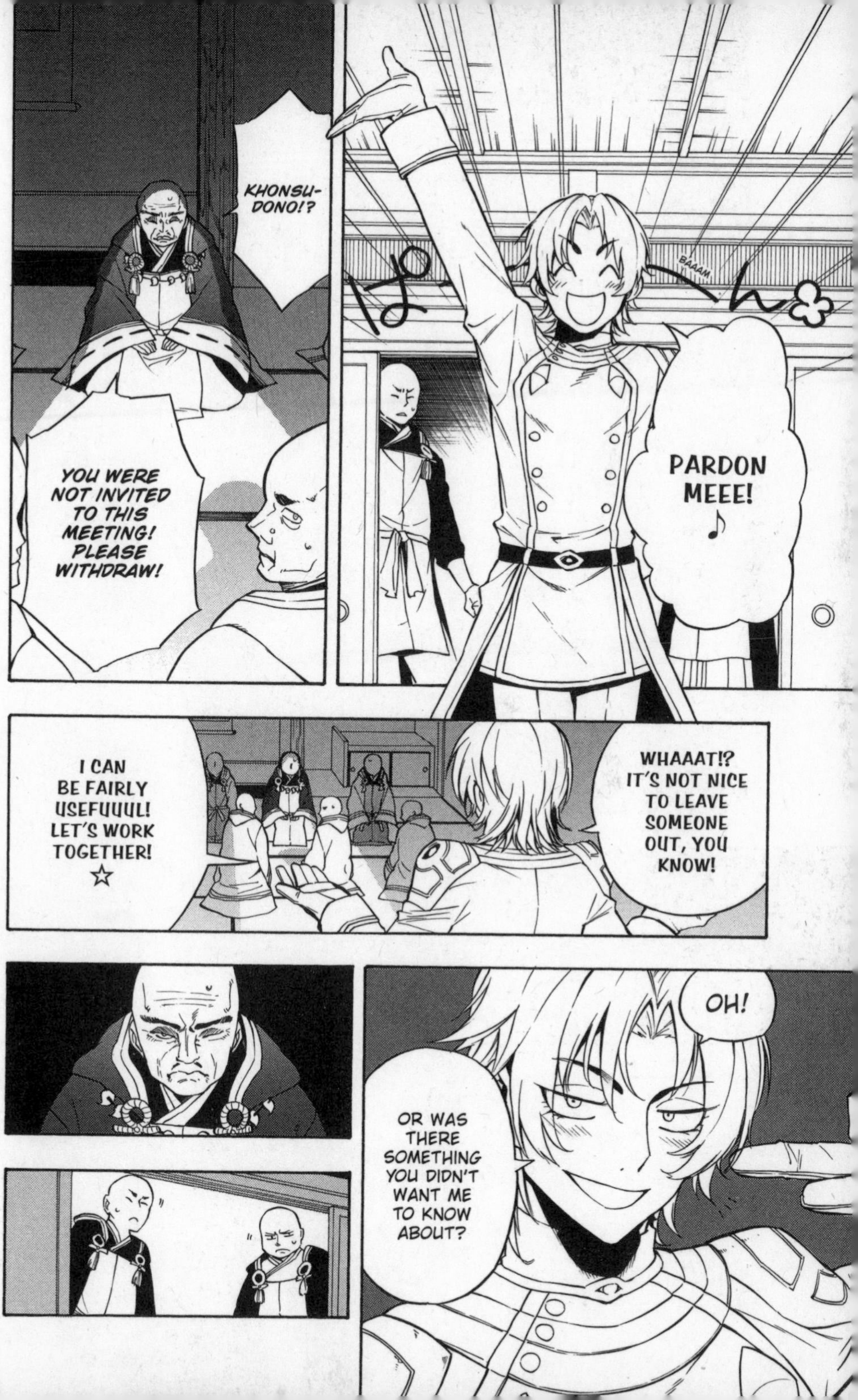
BAAAM
PARDON MEEE! ♪
KHONSU-DONO!?
YOU WERE NOT INVITED TO THIS MEETING! PLEASE WITHDRAW!
WHAAAT!? IT'S NOT NICE TO LEAVE SOMEONE OUT, YOU KNOW!
I CAN BE FAIRLY USEFUUUL! LET'S WORK TOGETHER! ☆
OH!
OR WAS THERE SOMETHING YOU DIDN'T WANT ME TO KNOW ABOUT?

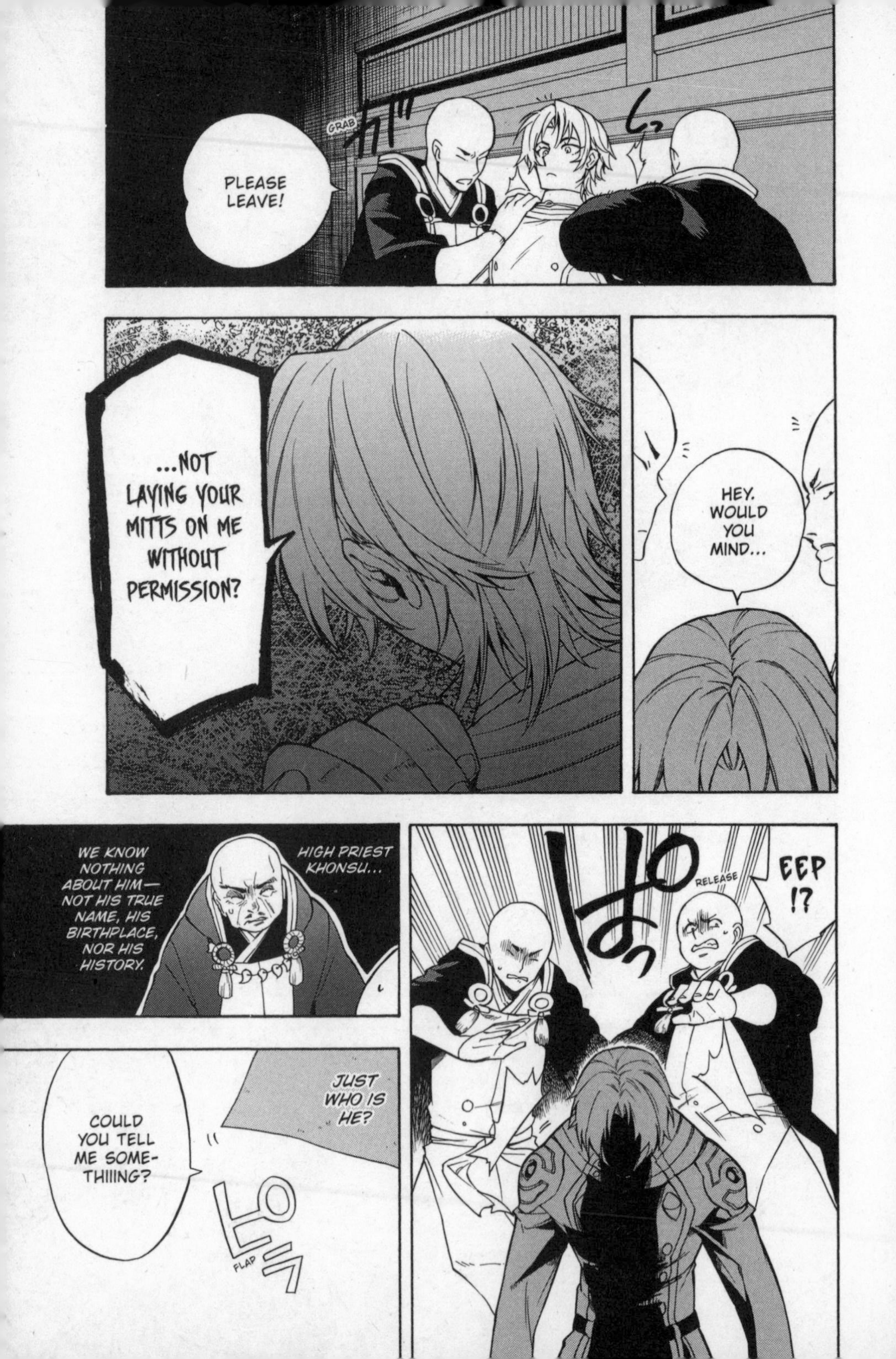
GRAB
PLEASE LEAVE!
HEY. WOULD YOU MIND...
...NOT LAYING YOUR MITTS ON ME WITHOUT PERMISSION?
RELEASE
EEP !?
HIGH PRIEST KHONSU...
WE KNOW NOTHING ABOUT HIM—NOT HIS TRUE NAME, HIS BIRTHPLACE, NOR HIS HISTORY.
JUST WHO IS HE?
COULD YOU TELL ME SOME-THIIING?
FLAP

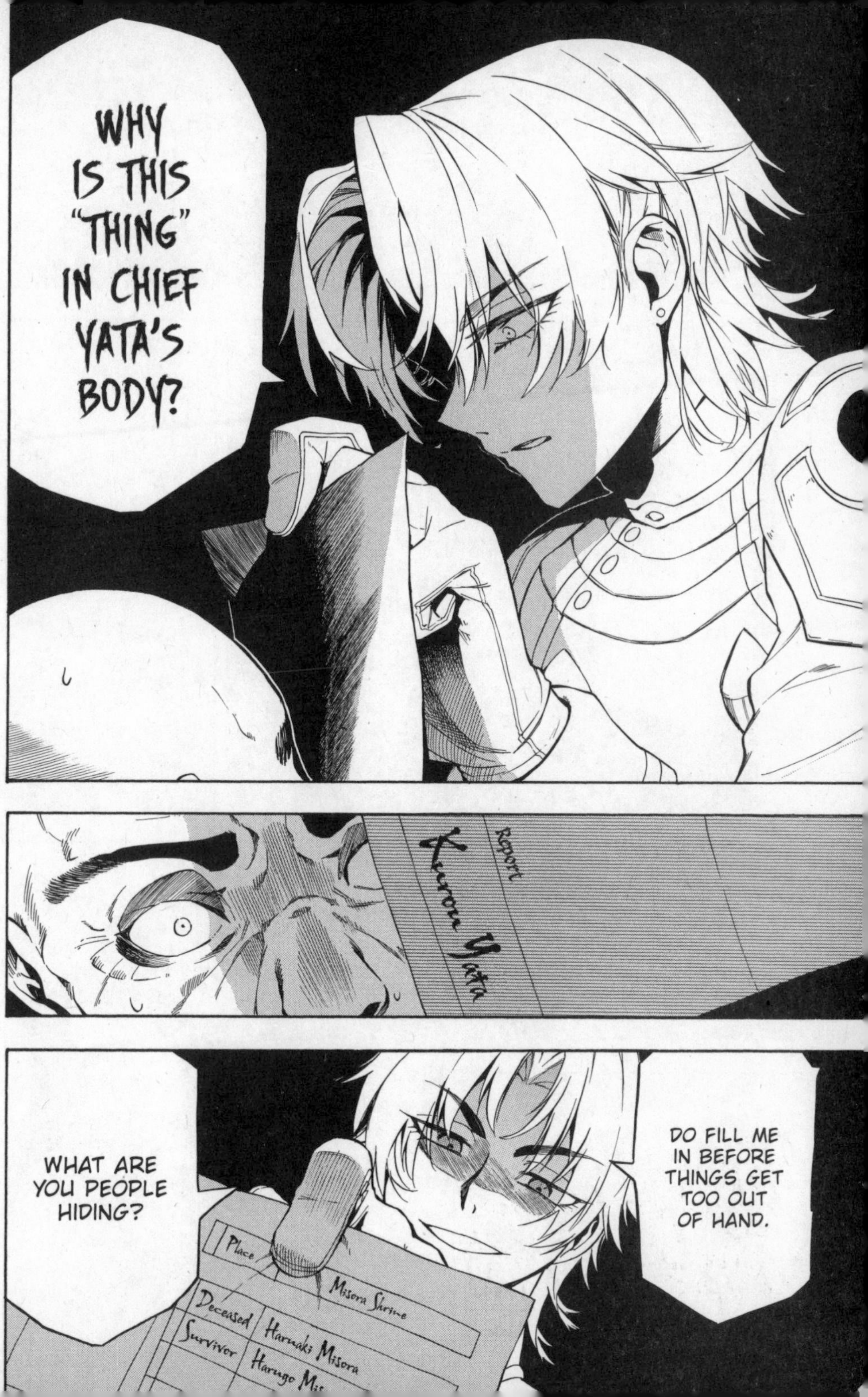
WHY IS THIS "THING" IN CHIEF YATA'S BODY?
Report
DO FILL ME IN BEFORE THINGS GET TOO OUT OF HAND.
WHAT ARE YOU PEOPLE HIDING?
Place
Misora Shrine
Deceased
Haruaki Misora
Survivor

Great Priest Imhotep

Great Priest Imhotep

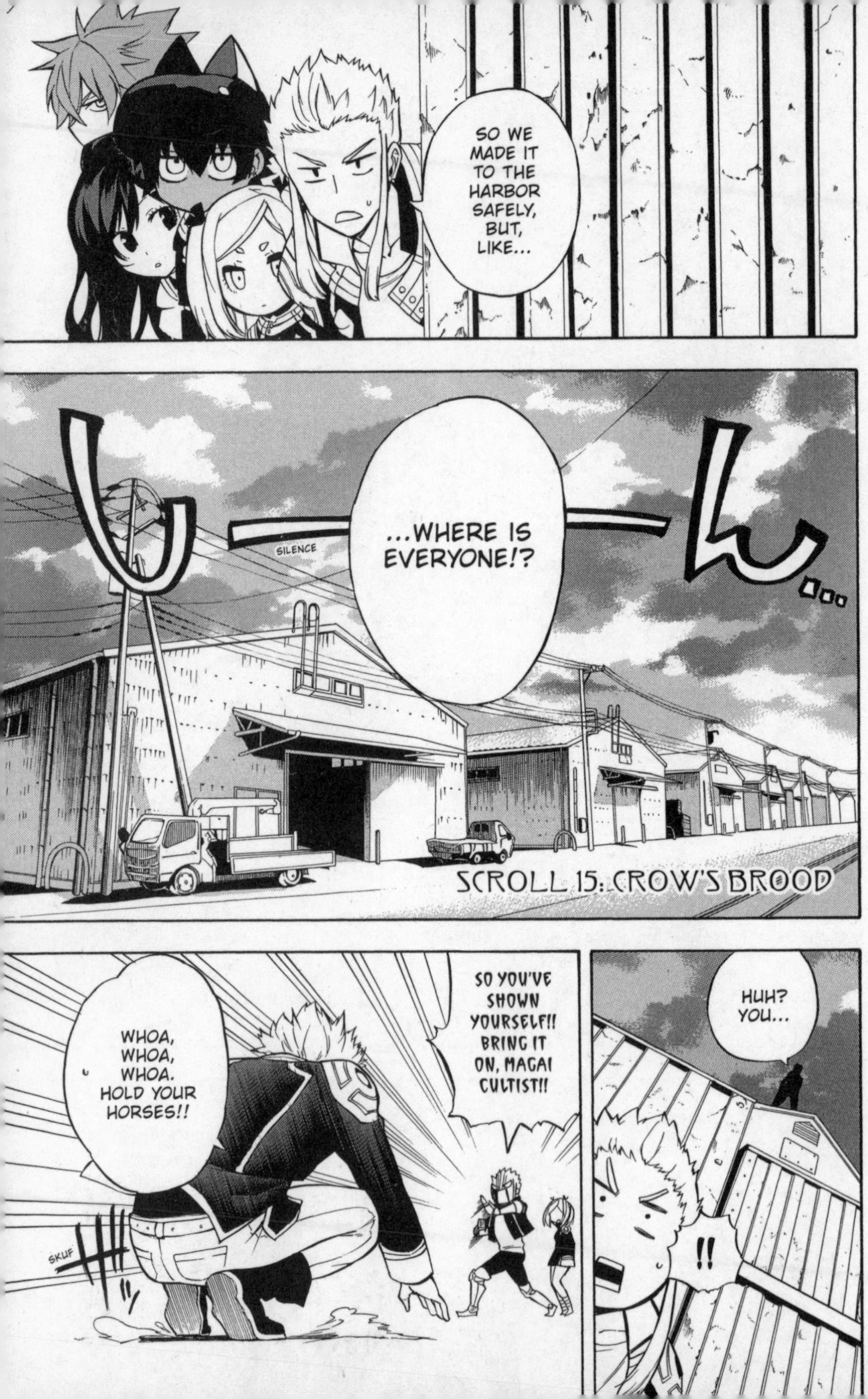
SO WE MADE IT TO THE HARBOR SAFELY, BUT, LIKE...
...WHERE IS EVERYONE!?
SILENCE
SCROLL 15: CROW'S BROOD
HUH? YOU...
!!
SO YOU'VE SHOWN YOURSELF!! BRING IT ON, MAGAI CULTIST!!
WHOA, WHOA, WHOA. HOLD YOUR HORSES!!
SKUF

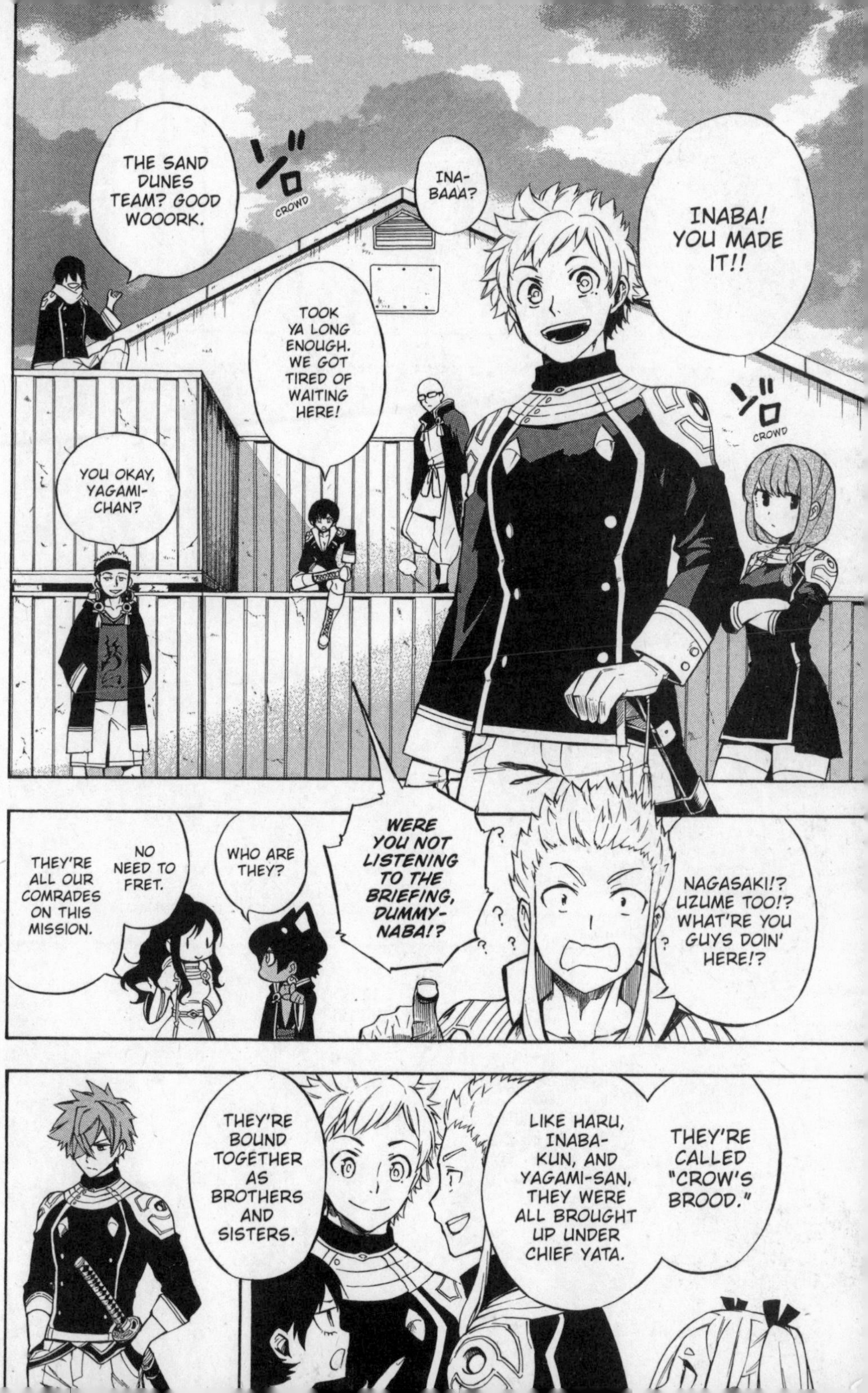
INABA! YOU MADE IT!!
ゾロ
CROWD
INA-BAAA?
TOOK YA LONG ENOUGH. WE GOT TIRED OF WAITING HERE!
ゾロ
CROWD
THE SAND DUNES TEAM? GOOD WOOORK.
YOU OKAY, YAGAMI-CHAN?
NAGASAKI!? UZUME TOO!? WHAT'RE YOU GUYS DOIN' HERE!?
WERE YOU NOT LISTENING TO THE BRIEFING, DUMMY-NABA!?
WHO ARE THEY?
NO NEED TO FRET.
THEY'RE ALL OUR COMRADES ON THIS MISSION.
THEY'RE CALLED "CROW'S BROOD."
LIKE HARU, INABA-KUN, AND YAGAMI-SAN, THEY WERE ALL BROUGHT UP UNDER CHIEF YATA.
THEY'RE BOUND TOGETHER AS BROTHERS AND SISTERS.

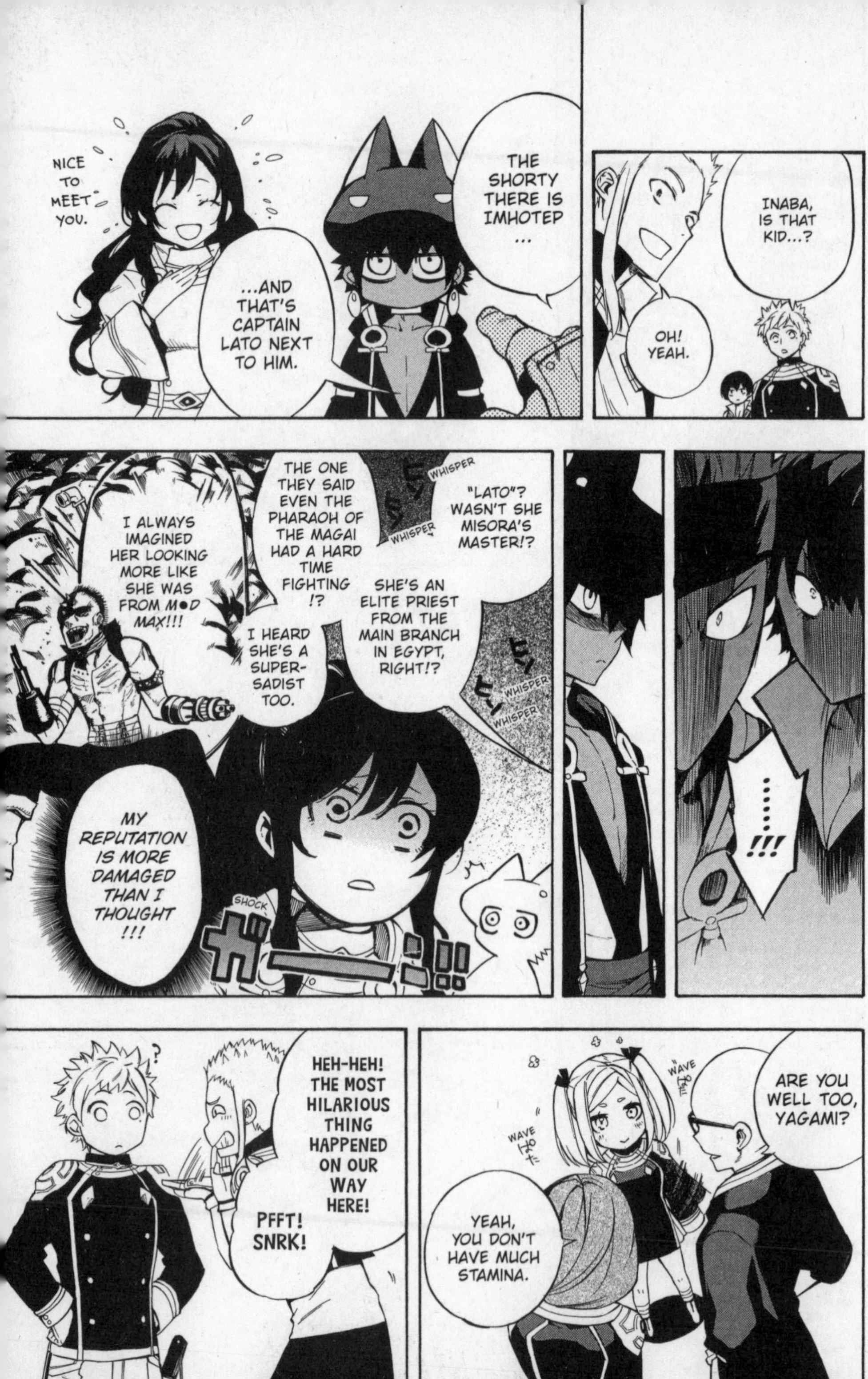
INABA, IS THAT KID...?
OH! YEAH.
THE SHORTY THERE IS IMHOTEP ...
...AND THAT'S CAPTAIN LATO NEXT TO HIM.
NICE TO MEET YOU.
......!!!
"LATO"? WASN'T SHE MISORA'S MASTER!?
WHISPER
WHISPER
THE ONE THEY SAID EVEN THE PHARAOH OF THE MAGAI HAD A HARD TIME FIGHTING!?
SHE'S AN ELITE PRIEST FROM THE MAIN BRANCH IN EGYPT, RIGHT!?
WHISPER
WHISPER
I ALWAYS IMAGINED HER LOOKING MORE LIKE SHE WAS FROM M●D MAX!!!
I HEARD SHE'S A SUPER-SADIST TOO.
MY REPUTATION IS MORE DAMAGED THAN I THOUGHT!!!
SHOCK
ARE YOU WELL TOO, YAGAMI?
WAVE
WAVE
YEAH, YOU DON'T HAVE MUCH STAMINA.
HEH-HEH! THE MOST HILARIOUS THING HAPPENED ON OUR WAY HERE!
PFFT! SNRK!

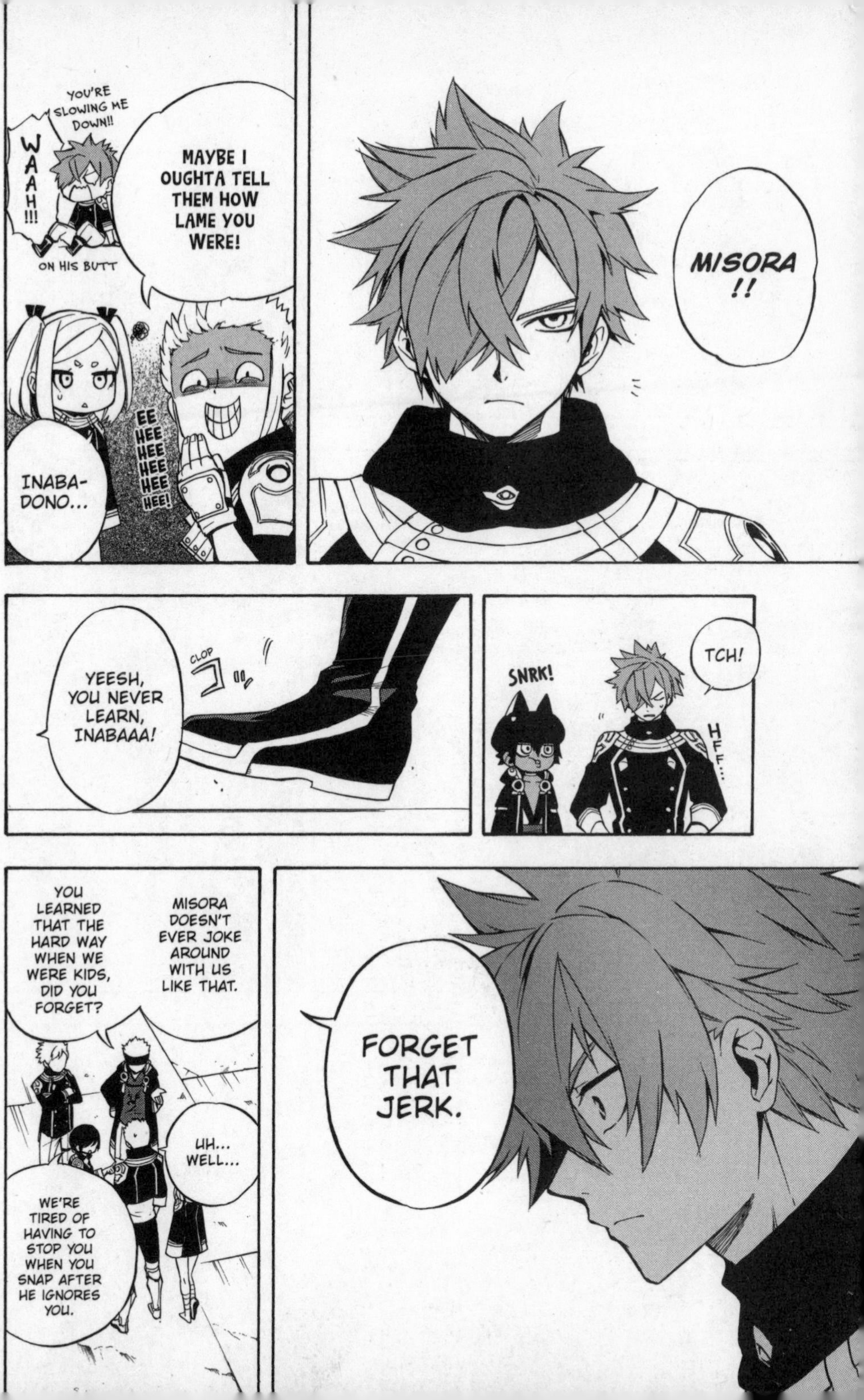
MISORA!!
MAYBE I OUGHTA TELL THEM HOW LAME YOU WERE!
YOU'RE SLOWING ME DOWN!!
WAAAH!!!
ON HIS BUTT
EE HEE HEE HEE HEE HEE!
INABA-DONO...
TCH!
HFF...
SNRK!
CLOP
YEESH, YOU NEVER LEARN, INABAAA!
FORGET THAT JERK.
MISORA DOESN'T EVER JOKE AROUND WITH US LIKE THAT.
YOU LEARNED THAT THE HARD WAY WHEN WE WERE KIDS, DID YOU FORGET?
UH... WELL...
WE'RE TIRED OF HAVING TO STOP YOU WHEN YOU SNAP AFTER HE IGNORES YOU.

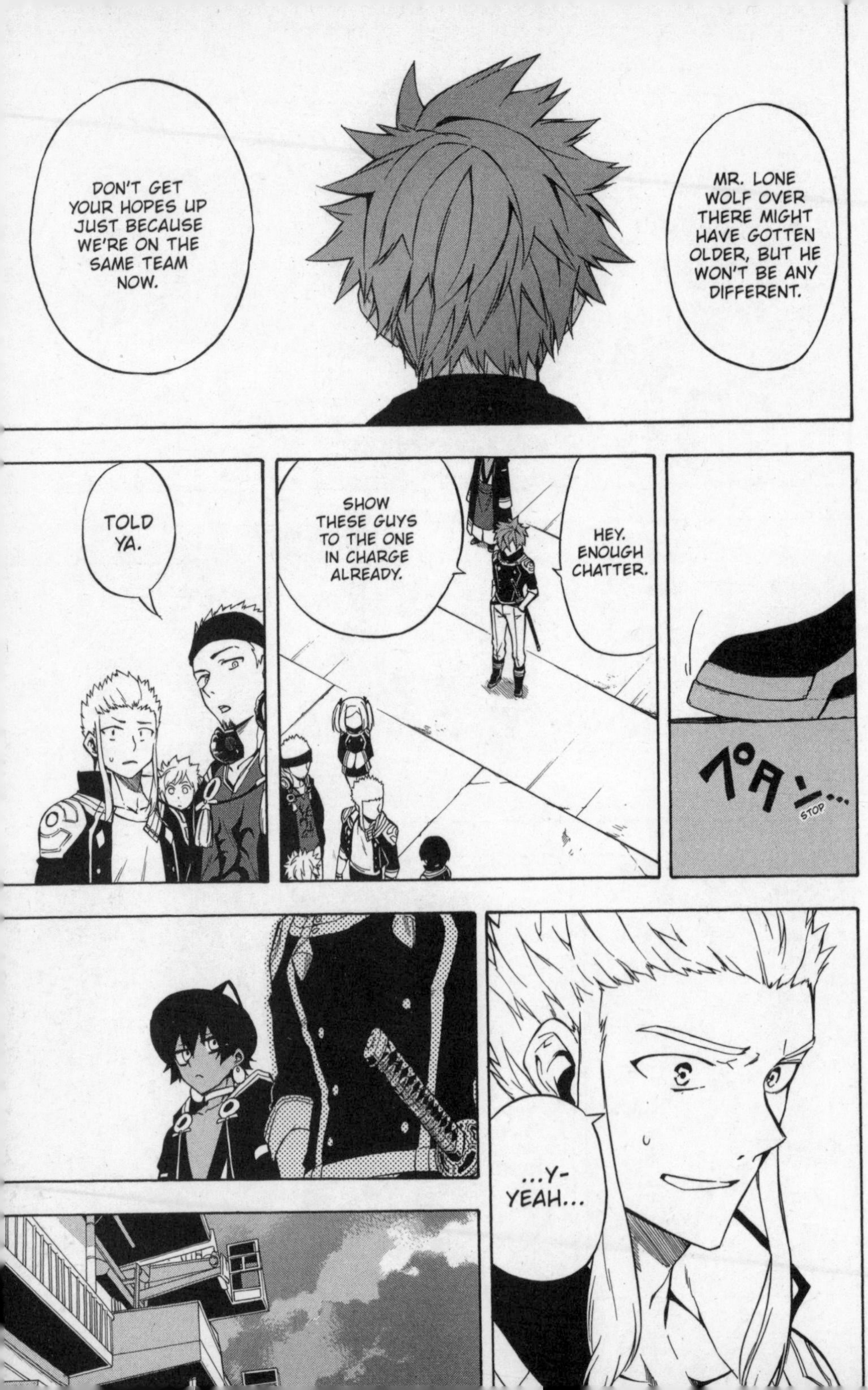
MR. LONE WOLF OVER THERE MIGHT HAVE GOTTEN OLDER, BUT HE WON'T BE ANY DIFFERENT.
DON'T GET YOUR HOPES UP JUST BECAUSE WE'RE ON THE SAME TEAM NOW.
ペタン…
STOP
HEY. ENOUGH CHATTER.
SHOW THESE GUYS TO THE ONE IN CHARGE ALREADY.
TOLD YA.
...Y-YEAH...

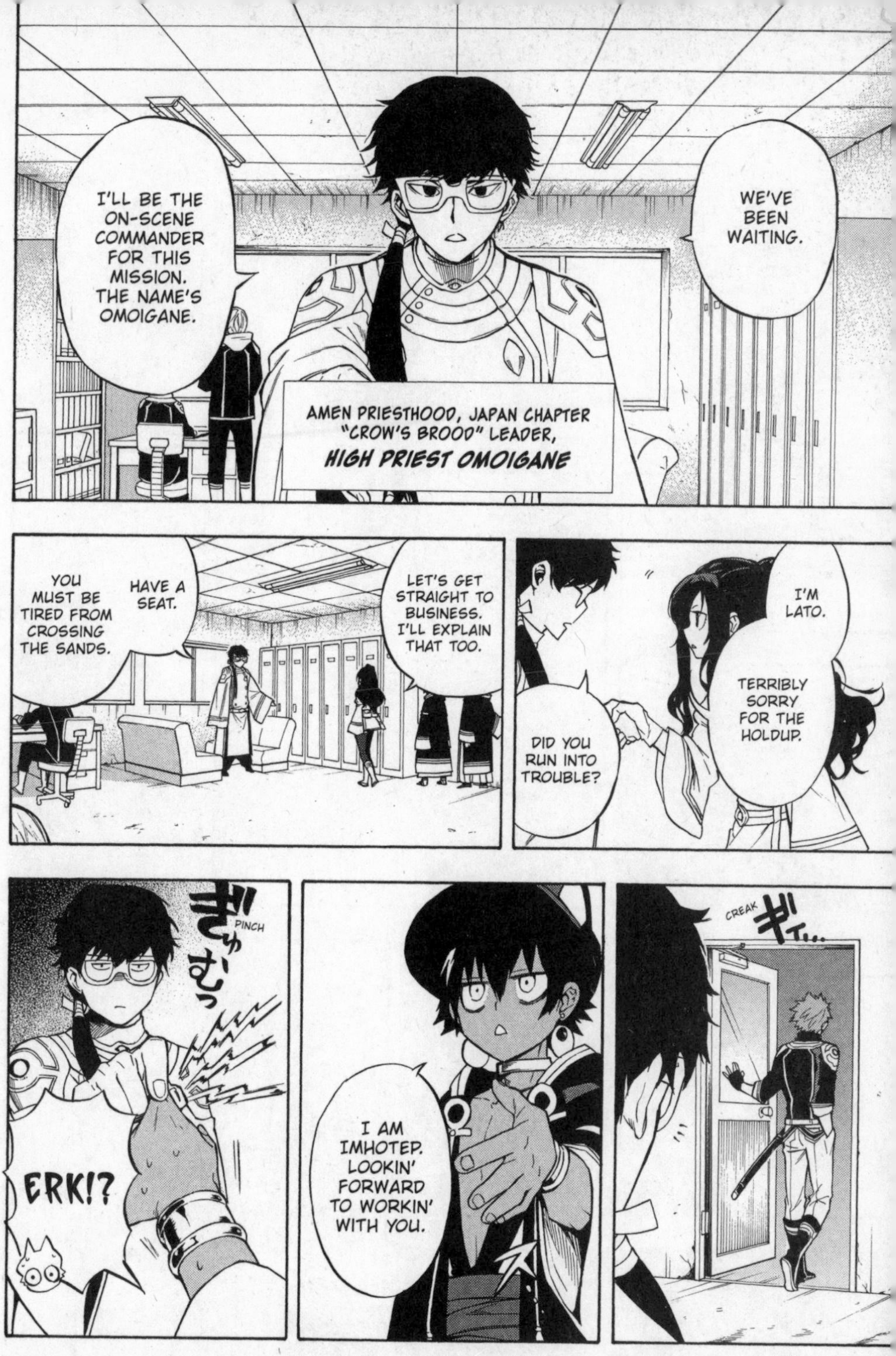
WE'VE BEEN WAITING.
I'LL BE THE ON-SCENE COMMANDER FOR THIS MISSION. THE NAME'S OMOIGANE.
AMEN PRIESTHOOD, JAPAN CHAPTER "CROW'S BROOD" LEADER, HIGH PRIEST OMOIGANE
I'M LATO.
TERRIBLY SORRY FOR THE HOLDUP.
DID YOU RUN INTO TROUBLE?
LET'S GET STRAIGHT TO BUSINESS. I'LL EXPLAIN THAT TOO.
HAVE A SEAT.
YOU MUST BE TIRED FROM CROSSING THE SANDS.
CREAK
I AM IMHOTEP. LOOKIN' FORWARD TO WORKIN' WITH YOU.
PINCH
ERK!?

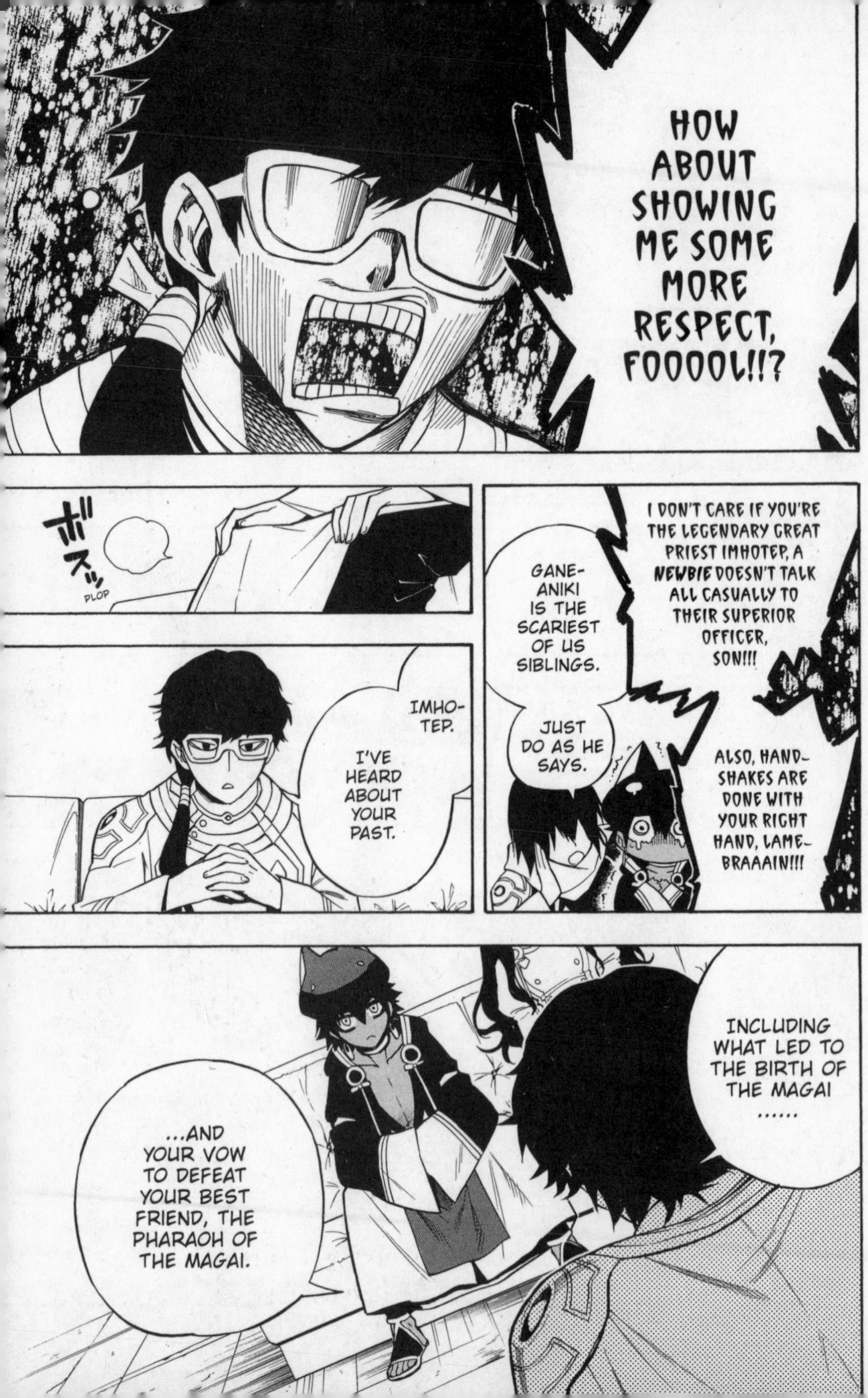
HOW ABOUT SHOWING ME SOME MORE RESPECT, FOOOOL!!?
I DON'T CARE IF YOU'RE THE LEGENDARY GREAT PRIEST IMHOTEP, A NEWBIE DOESN'T TALK ALL CASUALLY TO THEIR SUPERIOR OFFICER, SON!!!
GANE-ANIKI IS THE SCARIEST OF US SIBLINGS.
ALSO, HAND-SHAKES ARE DONE WITH YOUR RIGHT HAND, LAME-BRAAAIN!!!
JUST DO AS HE SAYS.
ボスッ
PLOP
IMHO-TEP.
I'VE HEARD ABOUT YOUR PAST.
INCLUDING WHAT LED TO THE BIRTH OF THE MAGAI ......
...AND YOUR VOW TO DEFEAT YOUR BEST FRIEND, THE PHARAOH OF THE MAGAI.

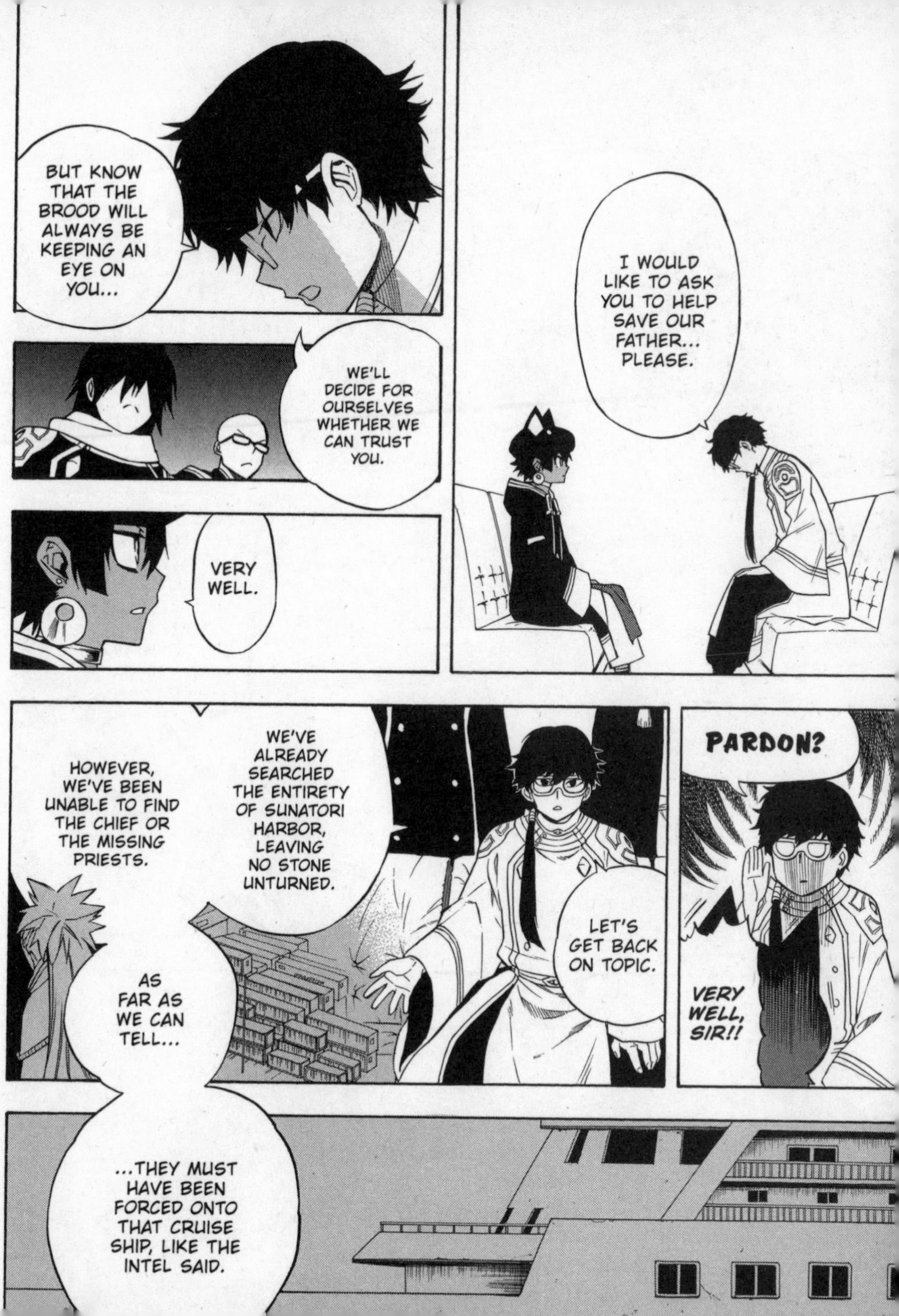
I WOULD LIKE TO ASK YOU TO HELP SAVE OUR FATHER... PLEASE.
BUT KNOW THAT THE BROOD WILL ALWAYS BE KEEPING AN EYE ON YOU...
WE'LL DECIDE FOR OURSELVES WHETHER WE CAN TRUST YOU.
VERY WELL.
PARDON?
VERY WELL, SIR!!
LET'S GET BACK ON TOPIC.
WE'VE ALREADY SEARCHED THE ENTIRETY OF SUNATORI HARBOR, LEAVING NO STONE UNTURNED.
HOWEVER, WE'VE BEEN UNABLE TO FIND THE CHIEF OR THE MISSING PRIESTS.
AS FAR AS WE CAN TELL...
...THEY MUST HAVE BEEN FORCED ONTO THAT CRUISE SHIP, LIKE THE INTEL SAID.

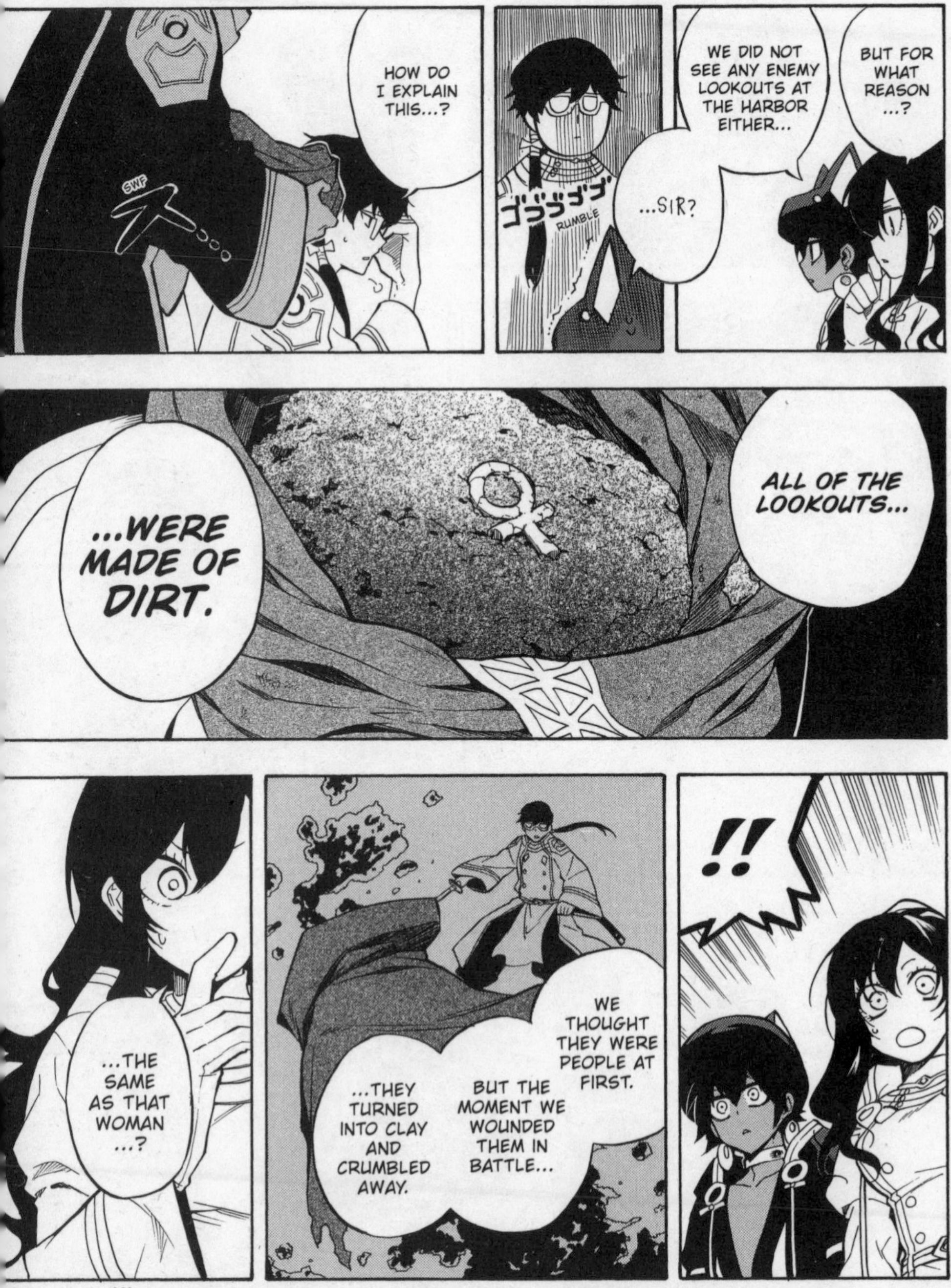
BUT FOR WHAT REASON ...?
WE DID NOT SEE ANY ENEMY LOOKOUTS AT THE HARBOR EITHER...
RUMBLE
...SIR?
HOW DO I EXPLAIN THIS...?
SWF
ALL OF THE LOOKOUTS...
...WERE MADE OF DIRT.
!!
WE THOUGHT THEY WERE PEOPLE AT FIRST.
BUT THE MOMENT WE WOUNDED THEM IN BATTLE...
...THEY TURNED INTO CLAY AND CRUMBLED AWAY.
...THE SAME AS THAT WOMAN ...?

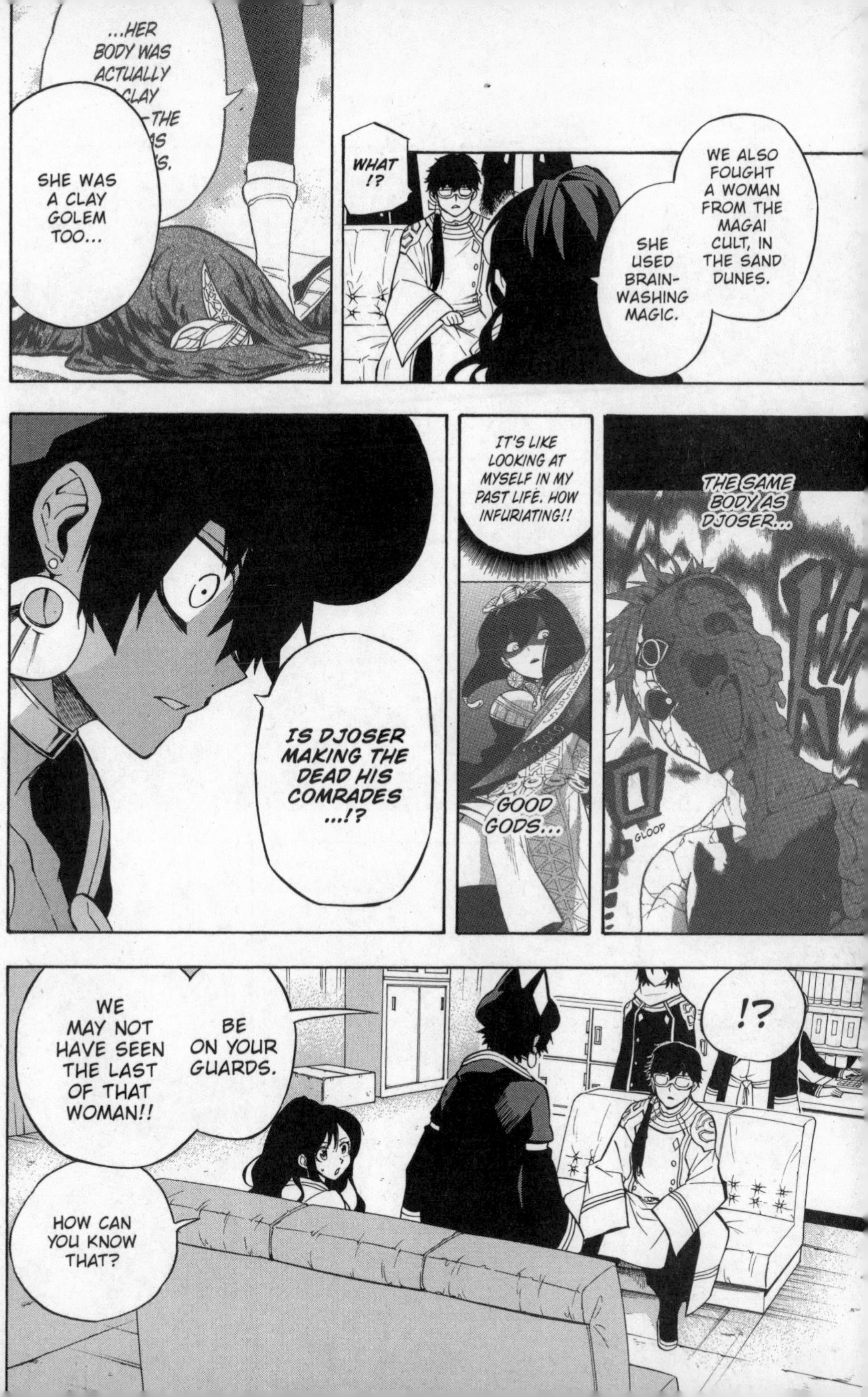
WE ALSO FOUGHT A WOMAN FROM THE MAGAI CULT, IN THE SAND DUNES.
SHE USED BRAIN-WASHING MAGIC.
WHAT!?
...HER BODY WAS ACTUALLY
SHE WAS A CLAY GOLEM TOO...
THE SAME BODY AS DJOSER...
GLOOP
IT'S LIKE LOOKING AT MYSELF IN MY PAST LIFE. HOW INFURIATING!!
GOOD GODS...
IS DJOSER MAKING THE DEAD HIS COMRADES ...!?
!?
BE ON YOUR GUARDS.
WE MAY NOT HAVE SEEN THE LAST OF THAT WOMAN!!
HOW CAN YOU KNOW THAT?

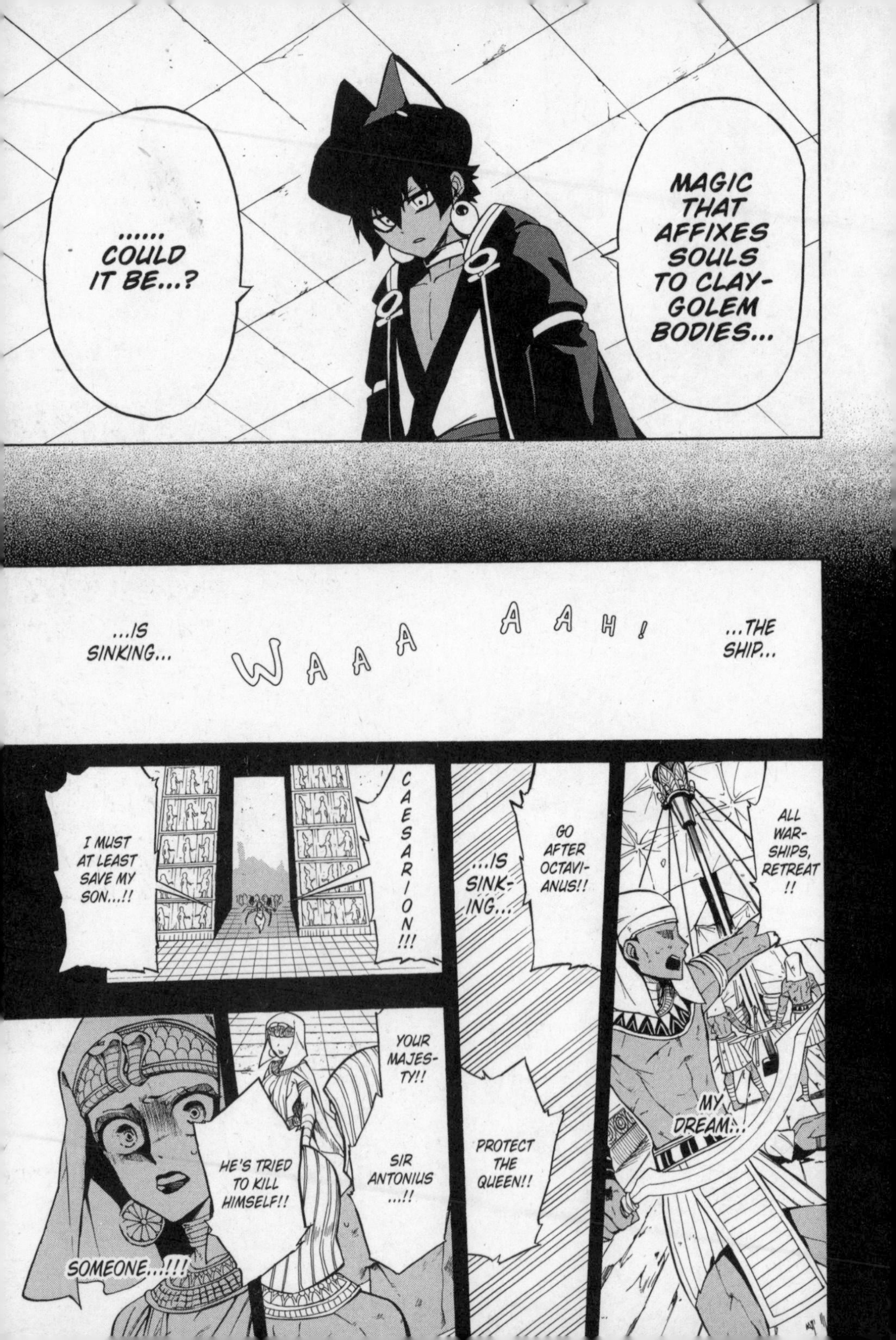
MAGIC THAT AFFIXES SOULS TO CLAY-GOLEM BODIES...
...... COULD IT BE...?
...THE SHIP...
WAAAAAH!
...IS SINKING...
ALL WAR-SHIPS, RETREAT !!
MY DREAM...
GO AFTER OCTAVI-ANUS!!
...IS SINK-ING...
PROTECT THE QUEEN!!
SIR ANTONIUS ...!!
CAESARION!!!
I MUST AT LEAST SAVE MY SON...!!
YOUR MAJES-TY!!
HE'S TRIED TO KILL HIMSELF!!
SOMEONE...!!!!

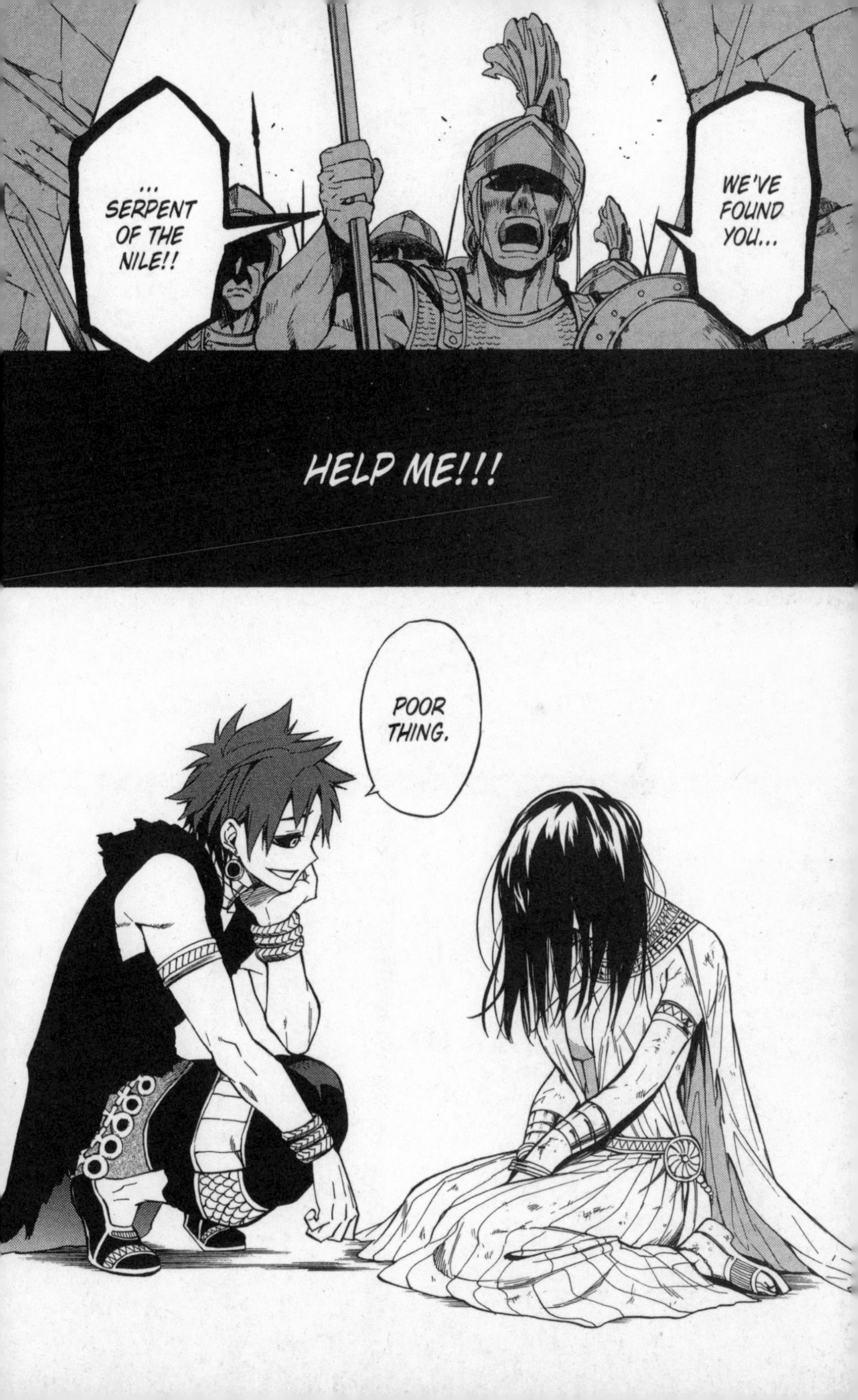
WE'VE FOUND YOU...
...SERPENT OF THE NILE!!
HELP ME!!!
POOR THING.

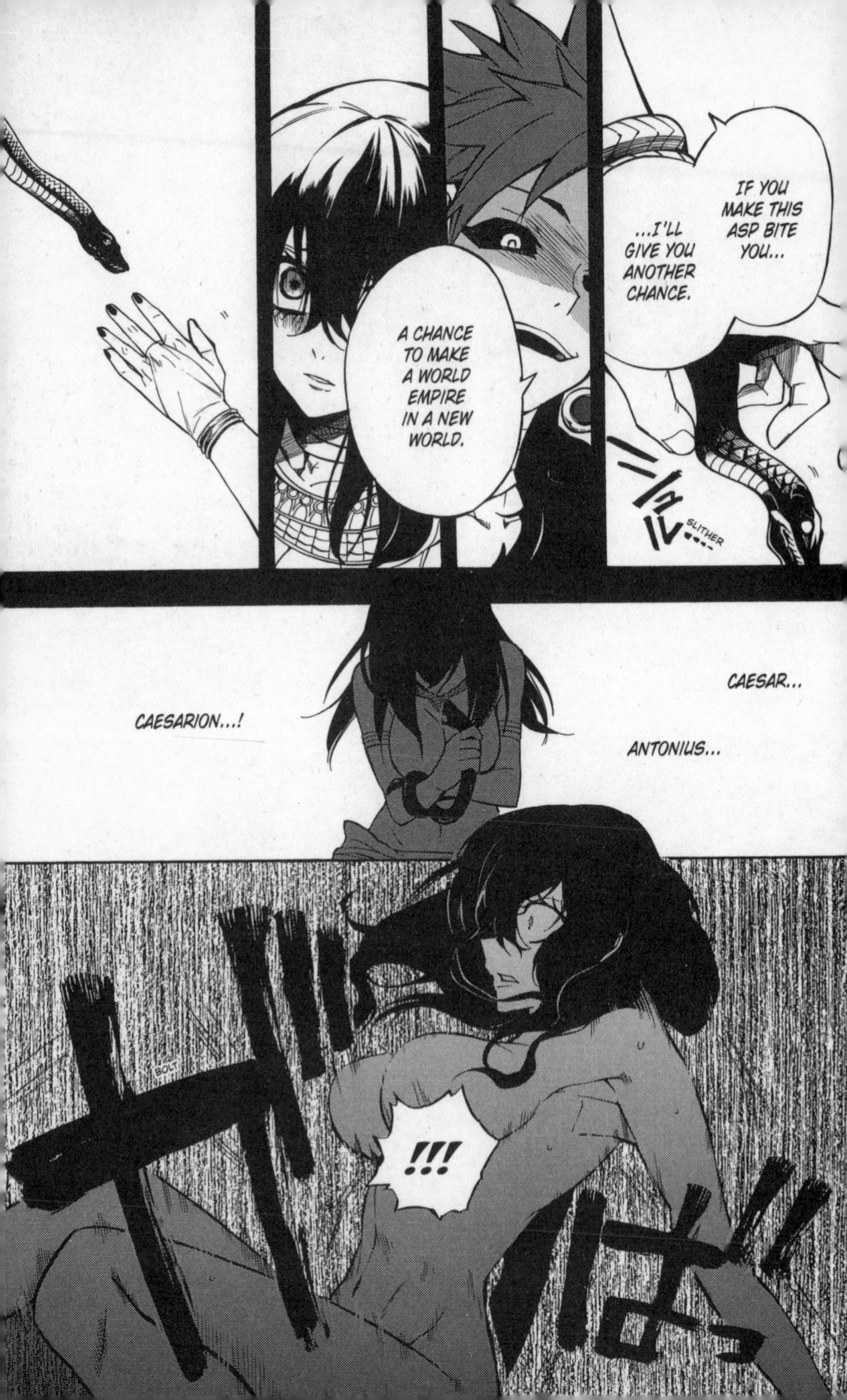
IF YOU MAKE THIS ASP BITE YOU...
...I'LL GIVE YOU ANOTHER CHANCE.
A CHANCE TO MAKE A WORLD EMPIRE IN A NEW WORLD.
SLITHER
CAESAR...
ANTONIUS...
CAESARION...!
BOLT
!!!

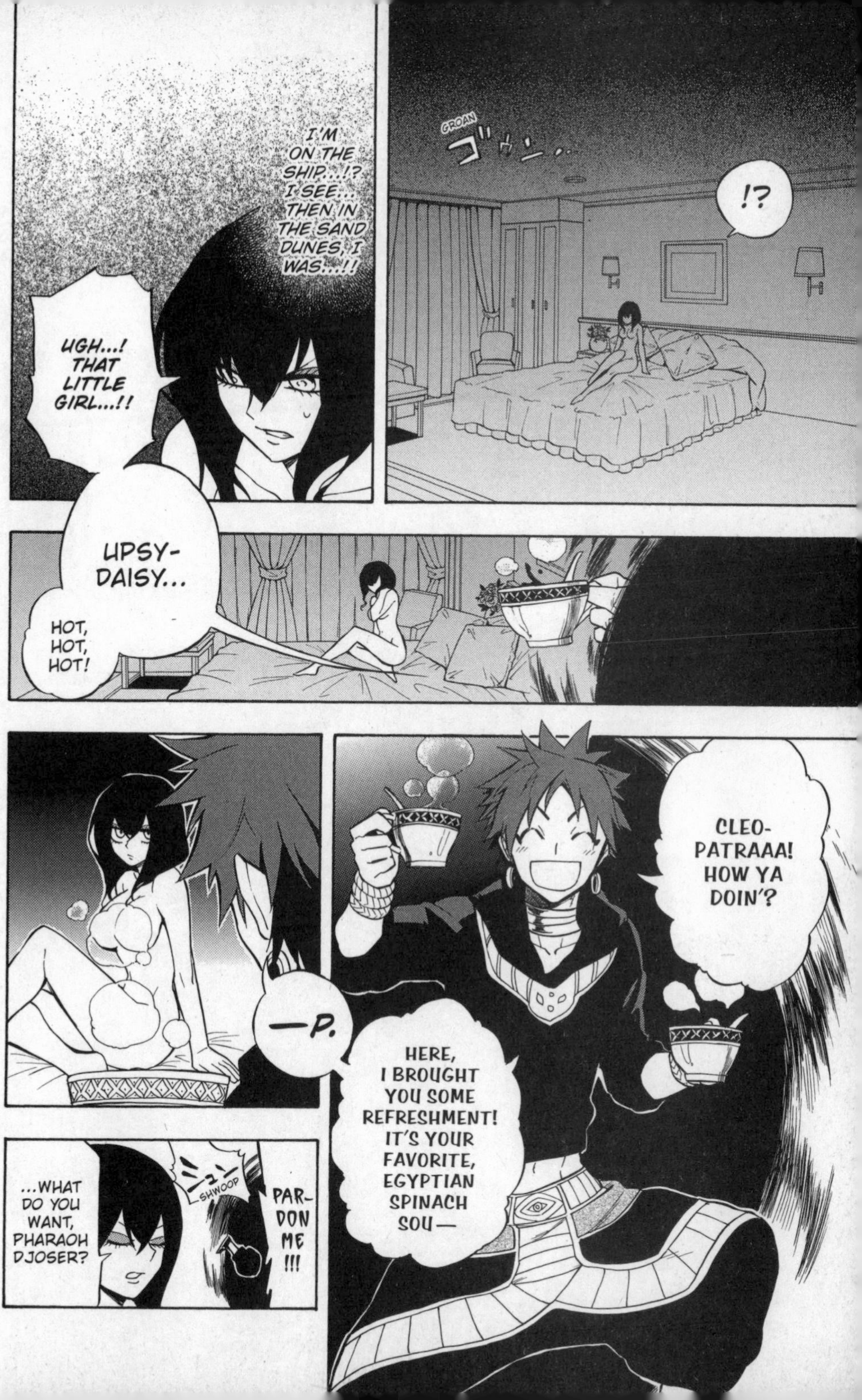
GROAN
!?
I'M ON THE SHIP...!? I SEE... THEN IN THE SAND DUNES, I WAS...!!
UGH...! THAT LITTLE GIRL...!!
UPSY-DAISY...
HOT, HOT, HOT!
CLEO-PATRAAA! HOW YA DOIN'?
HERE, I BROUGHT YOU SOME REFRESHMENT! IT'S YOUR FAVORITE, EGYPTIAN SPINACH SOU—
—P.
PAR-DON ME !!!
SHWOOP
...WHAT DO YOU WANT, PHARAOH DJOSER?

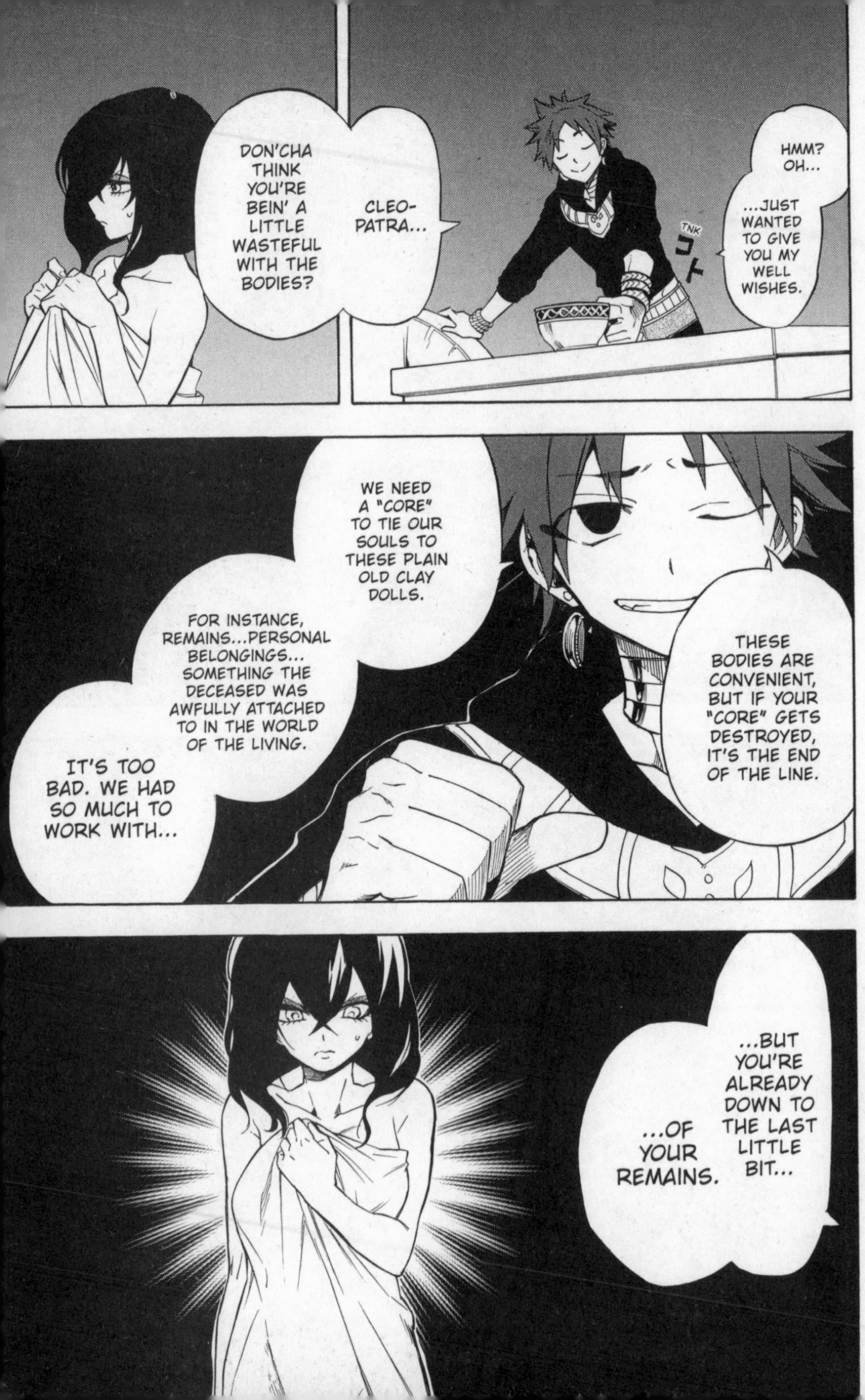
HMM? OH...
...JUST WANTED TO GIVE YOU MY WELL WISHES.
TNK
CLEO-PATRA...
DON'CHA THINK YOU'RE BEIN' A LITTLE WASTEFUL WITH THE BODIES?
THESE BODIES ARE CONVENIENT, BUT IF YOUR "CORE" GETS DESTROYED, IT'S THE END OF THE LINE.
WE NEED A "CORE" TO TIE OUR SOULS TO THESE PLAIN OLD CLAY DOLLS.
FOR INSTANCE, REMAINS...PERSONAL BELONGINGS... SOMETHING THE DECEASED WAS AWFULLY ATTACHED TO IN THE WORLD OF THE LIVING.
IT'S TOO BAD. WE HAD SO MUCH TO WORK WITH...
...BUT YOU'RE ALREADY DOWN TO THE LAST LITTLE BIT...
...OF YOUR REMAINS.

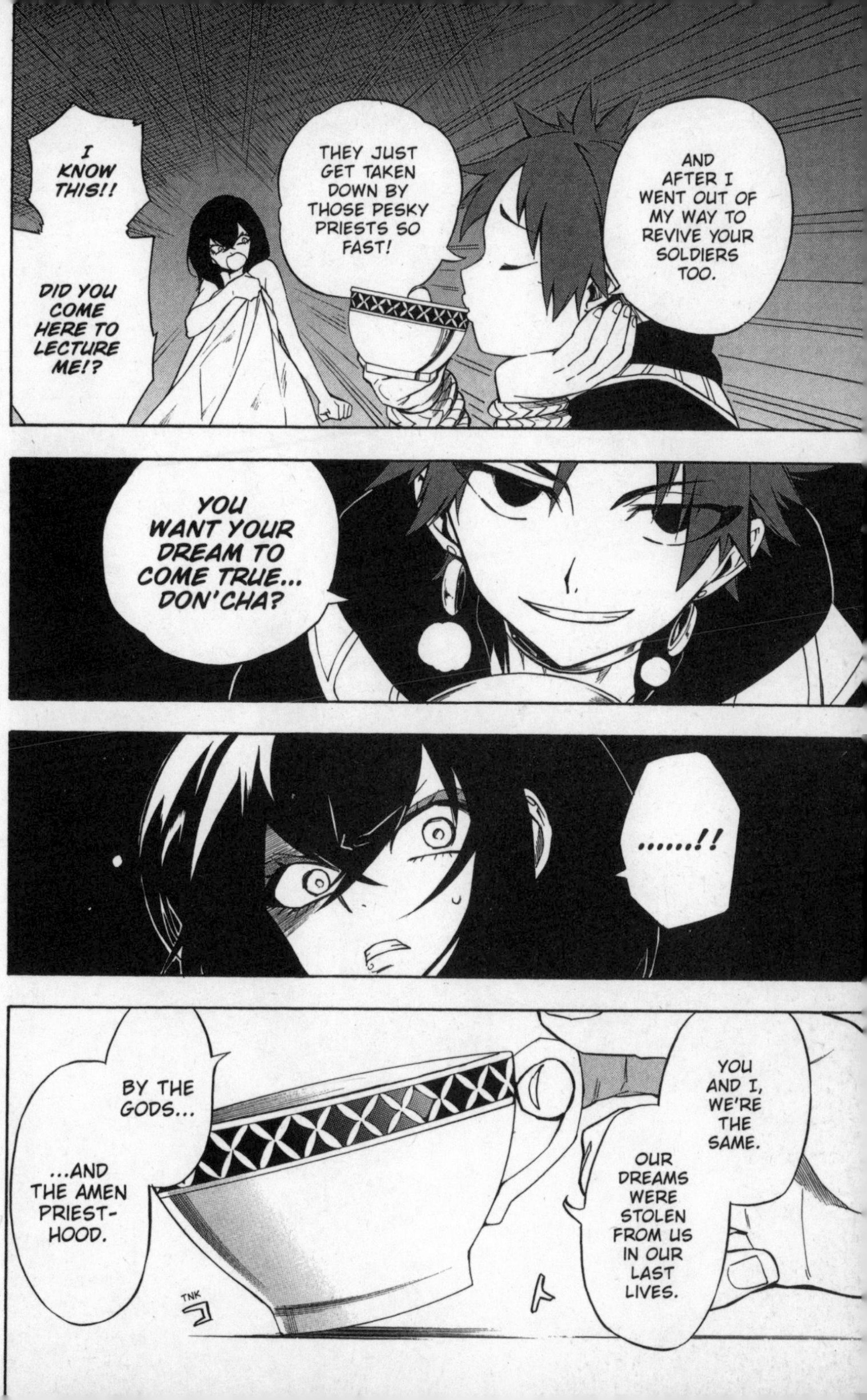
AND AFTER I WENT OUT OF MY WAY TO REVIVE YOUR SOLDIERS TOO.
THEY JUST GET TAKEN DOWN BY THOSE PESKY PRIESTS SO FAST!
I KNOW THIS!!
DID YOU COME HERE TO LECTURE ME!?
YOU WANT YOUR DREAM TO COME TRUE... DON'CHA?
......!!
YOU AND I, WE'RE THE SAME.
OUR DREAMS WERE STOLEN FROM US IN OUR LAST LIVES.
BY THE GODS...
...AND THE AMEN PRIEST-HOOD.
TNK

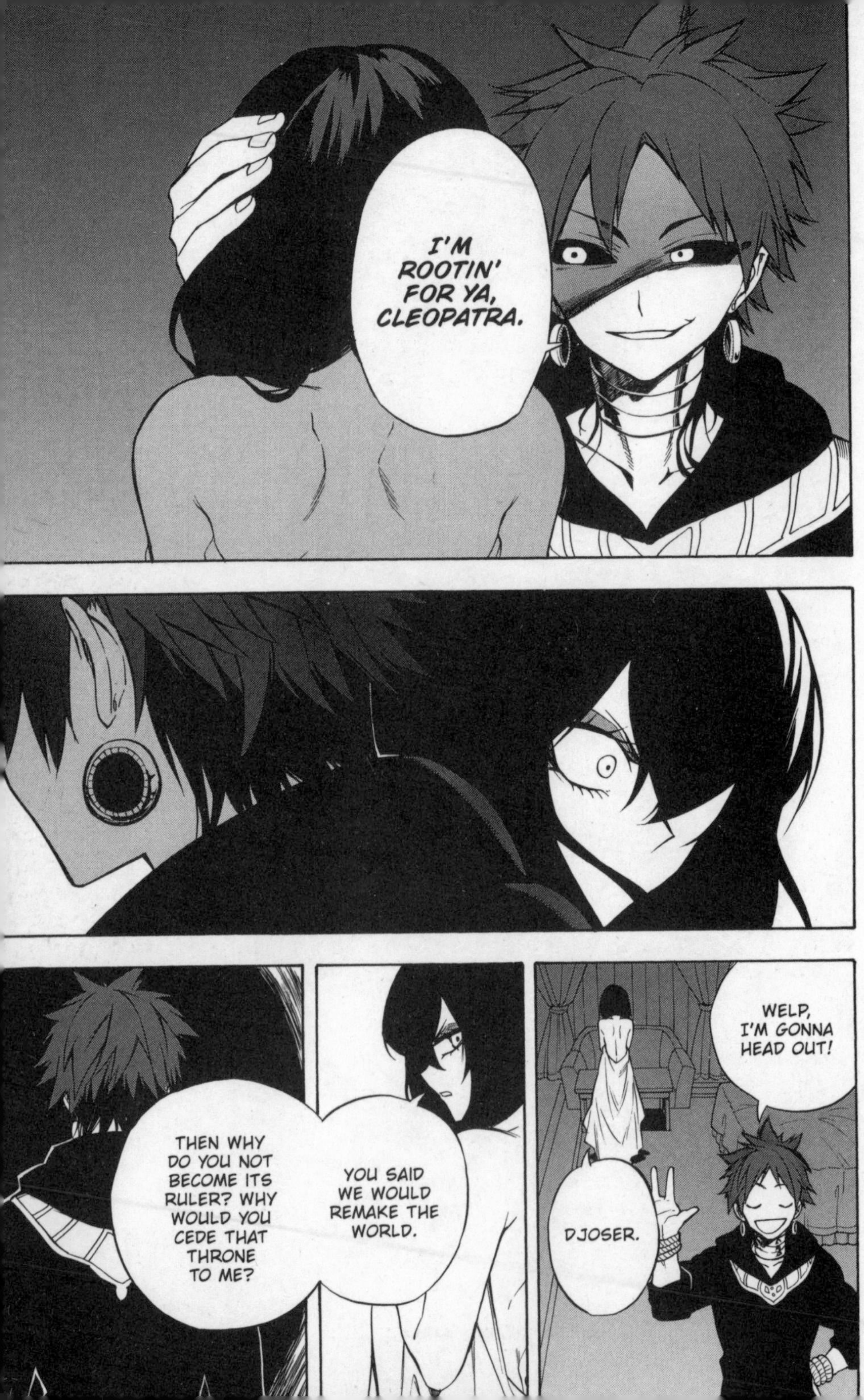
I'M ROOTIN' FOR YA, CLEOPATRA.
WELP, I'M GONNA HEAD OUT!
DJOSER.
YOU SAID WE WOULD REMAKE THE WORLD.
THEN WHY DO YOU NOT BECOME ITS RULER? WHY WOULD YOU CEDE THAT THRONE TO ME?

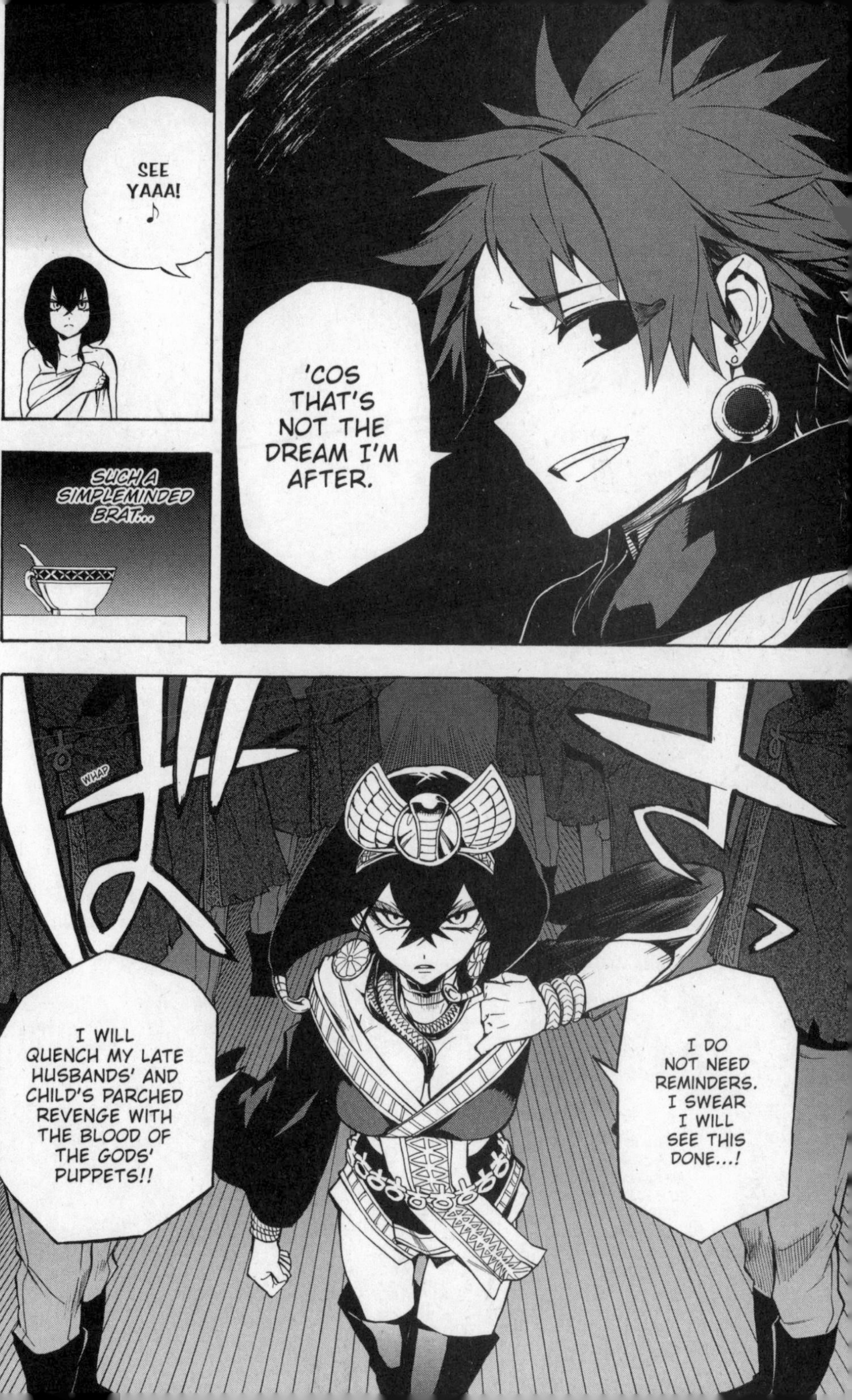
'COS THAT'S NOT THE DREAM I'M AFTER.
SEE YAAA! ♪
SUCH A SIMPLEMINDED BRAT...
WHAP
I DO NOT NEED REMINDERS. I SWEAR I WILL SEE THIS DONE...!
I WILL QUENCH MY LATE HUSBANDS' AND CHILD'S PARCHED REVENGE WITH THE BLOOD OF THE GODS' PUPPETS!!

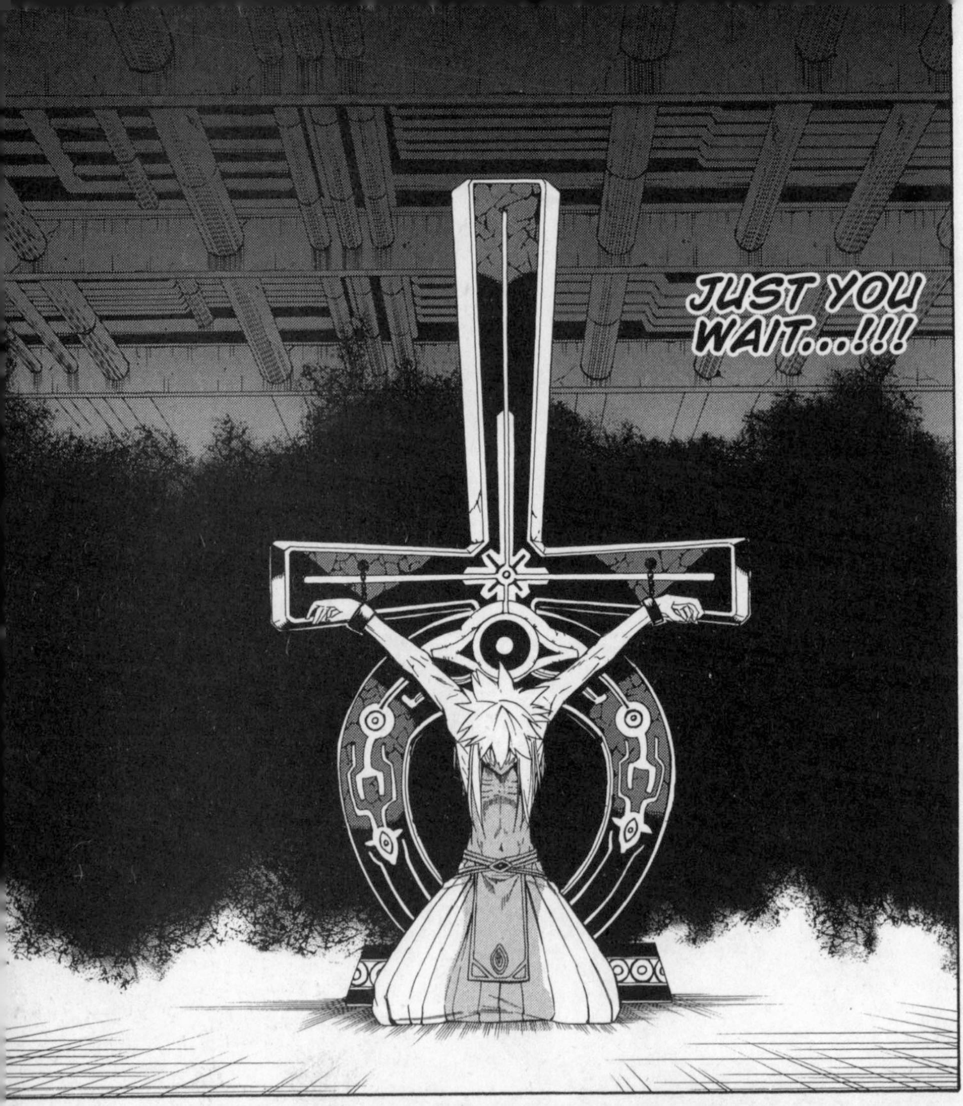
JUST YOU WAIT...!!!
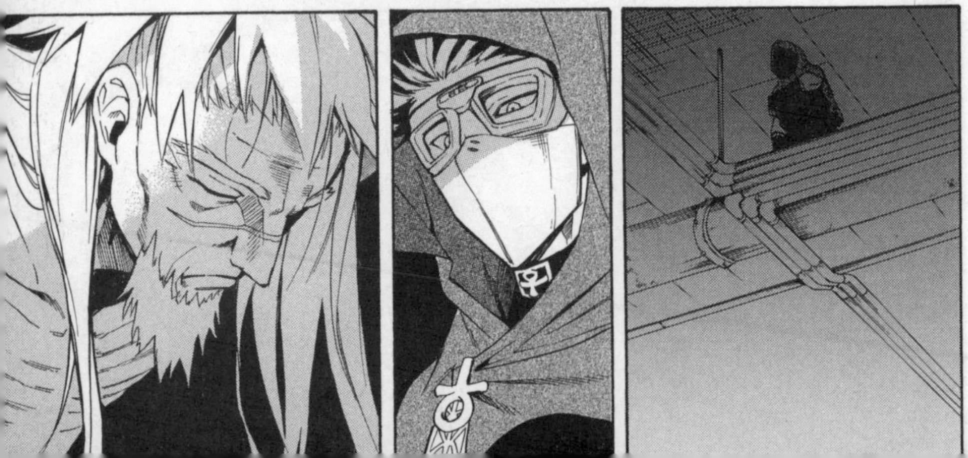

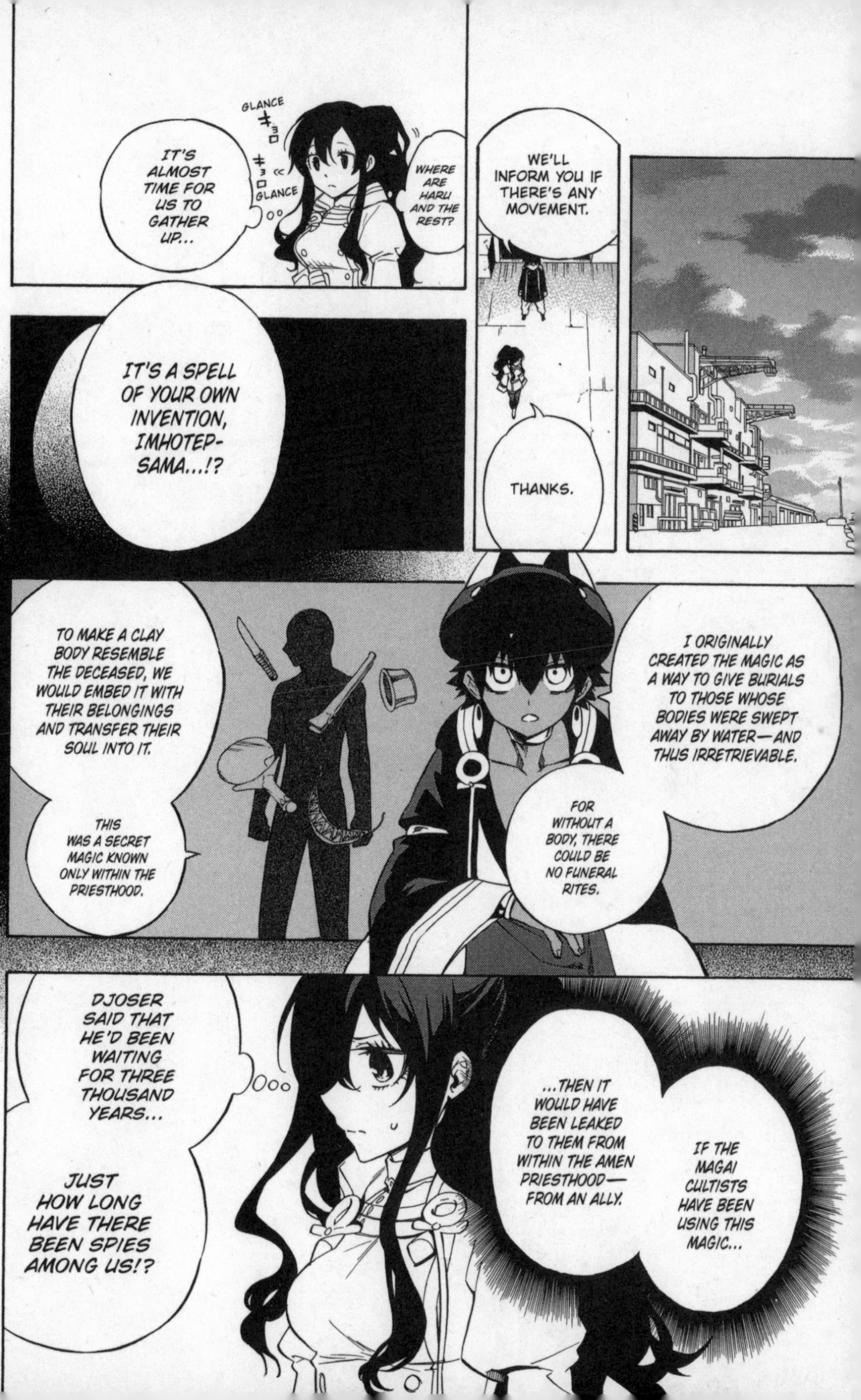

WE'LL INFORM YOU IF THERE'S ANY MOVEMENT.
THANKS.
WHERE ARE HARU AND THE REST?
GLANCE
キョロ
キョロ
GLANCE
IT'S ALMOST TIME FOR US TO GATHER UP...
IT'S A SPELL OF YOUR OWN INVENTION, IMHOTEP-SAMA...!?
I ORIGINALLY CREATED THE MAGIC AS A WAY TO GIVE BURIALS TO THOSE WHOSE BODIES WERE SWEPT AWAY BY WATER—AND THUS IRRETRIEVABLE.
FOR WITHOUT A BODY, THERE COULD BE NO FUNERAL RITES.
TO MAKE A CLAY BODY RESEMBLE THE DECEASED, WE WOULD EMBED IT WITH THEIR BELONGINGS AND TRANSFER THEIR SOUL INTO IT.
THIS WAS A SECRET MAGIC KNOWN ONLY WITHIN THE PRIESTHOOD.
IF THE MAGAI CULTISTS HAVE BEEN USING THIS MAGIC...
...THEN IT WOULD HAVE BEEN LEAKED TO THEM FROM WITHIN THE AMEN PRIESTHOOD—FROM AN ALLY.
DJOSER SAID THAT HE'D BEEN WAITING FOR THREE THOUSAND YEARS...
JUST HOW LONG HAVE THERE BEEN SPIES AMONG US!?

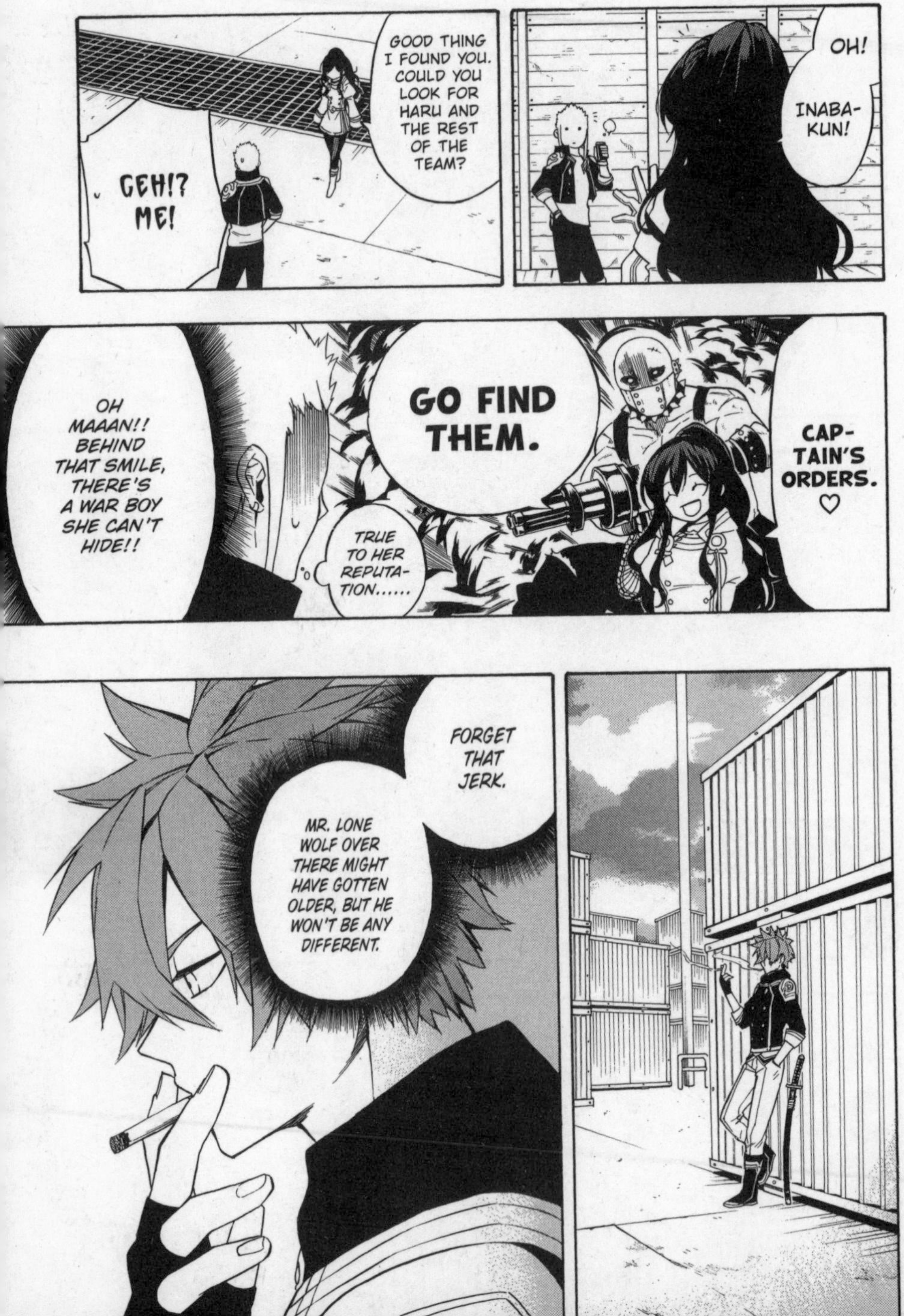
OH!
INABA-KUN!
GOOD THING I FOUND YOU. COULD YOU LOOK FOR HARU AND THE REST OF THE TEAM?
GEH!? ME!
CAP-TAIN'S ORDERS. ♡
GO FIND THEM.
TRUE TO HER REPUTA-TION......
OH MAAAN!! BEHIND THAT SMILE, THERE'S A WAR BOY SHE CAN'T HIDE!!
FORGET THAT JERK.
MR. LONE WOLF OVER THERE MIGHT HAVE GOTTEN OLDER, BUT HE WON'T BE ANY DIFFERENT.

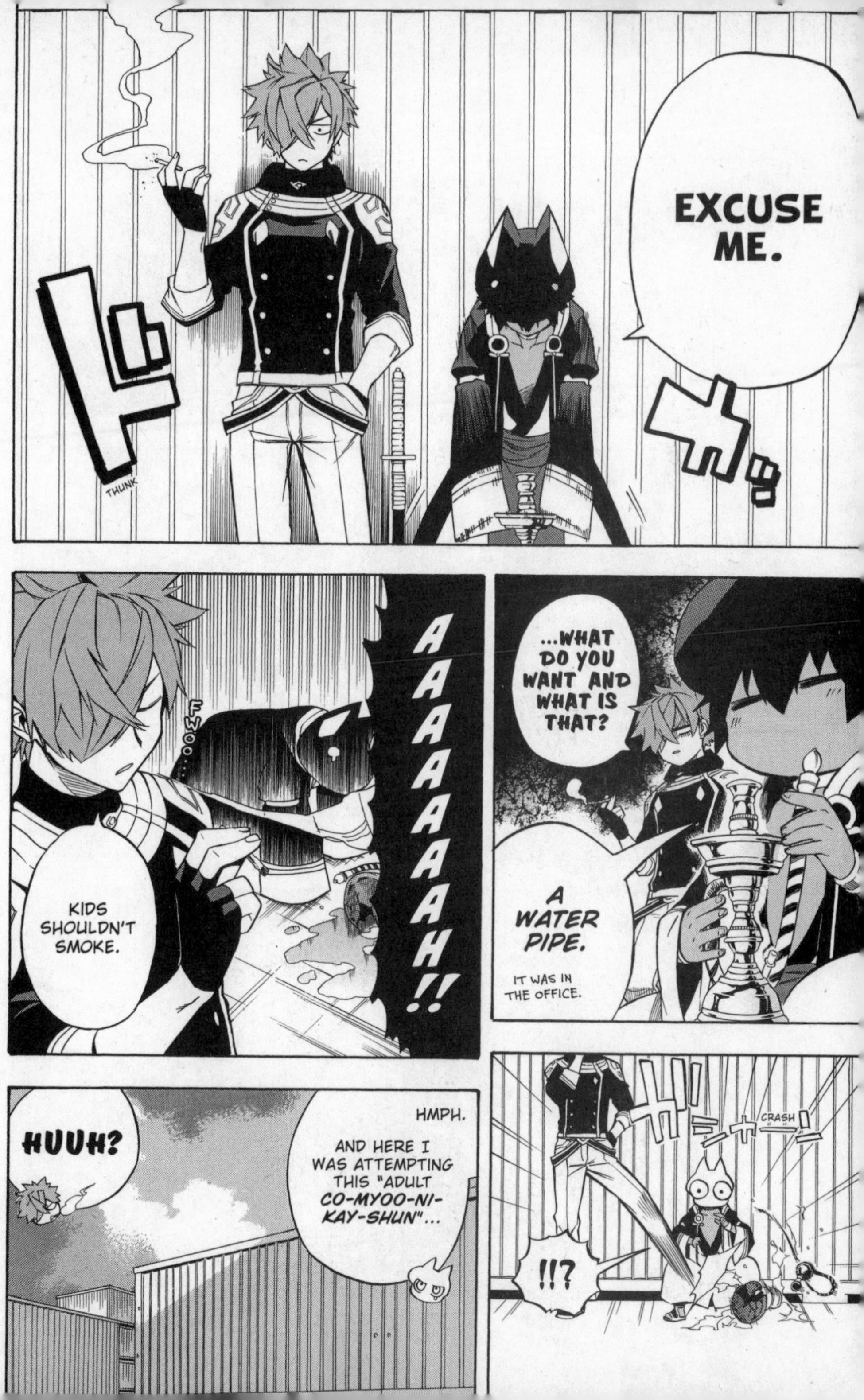
EXCUSE ME.
THUNK
...WHAT DO YOU WANT AND WHAT IS THAT?
A WATER PIPE.
IT WAS IN THE OFFICE.
AAAAAAAAAH!!
FWOO...
KIDS SHOULDN'T SMOKE.
CRASH
!!?
HMPH.
AND HERE I WAS ATTEMPTING THIS "ADULT CO-MYOO-NI-KAY-SHUN"...
HUUH?

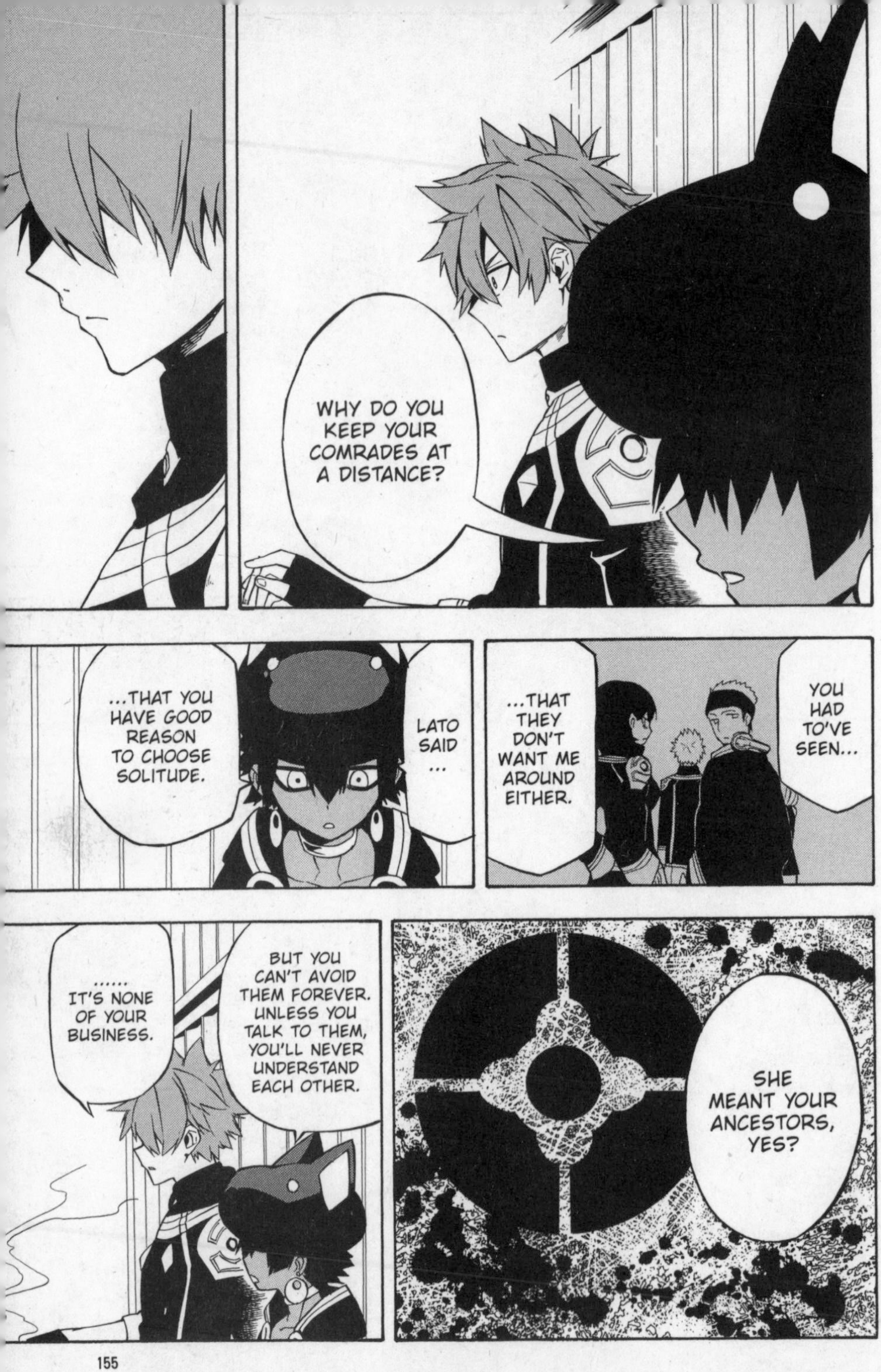
WHY DO YOU KEEP YOUR COMRADES AT A DISTANCE?
YOU HAD TO'VE SEEN...
...THAT THEY DON'T WANT ME AROUND EITHER.
LATO SAID ...
...THAT YOU HAVE GOOD REASON TO CHOOSE SOLITUDE.
SHE MEANT YOUR ANCESTORS, YES?
BUT YOU CAN'T AVOID THEM FOREVER. UNLESS YOU TALK TO THEM, YOU'LL NEVER UNDERSTAND EACH OTHER.
...... IT'S NONE OF YOUR BUSINESS.

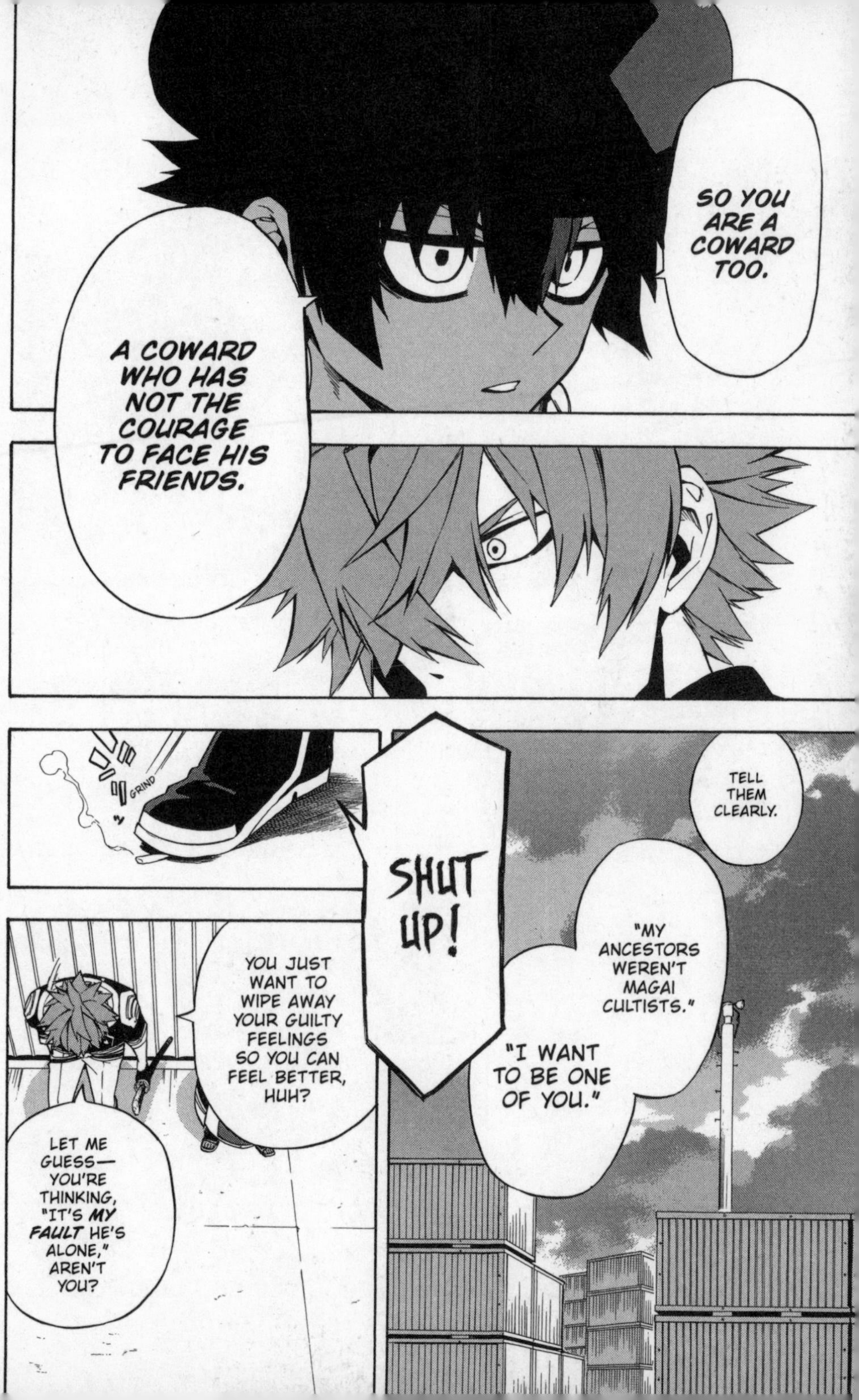
SO YOU ARE A COWARD TOO.
A COWARD WHO HAS NOT THE COURAGE TO FACE HIS FRIENDS.
TELL THEM CLEARLY.
"MY ANCESTORS WEREN'T MAGAI CULTISTS."
"I WANT TO BE ONE OF YOU."
SHUT UP!
GRIND
YOU JUST WANT TO WIPE AWAY YOUR GUILTY FEELINGS SO YOU CAN FEEL BETTER, HUH?
LET ME GUESS—YOU'RE THINKING, "IT'S *MY FAULT* HE'S ALONE," AREN'T YOU?

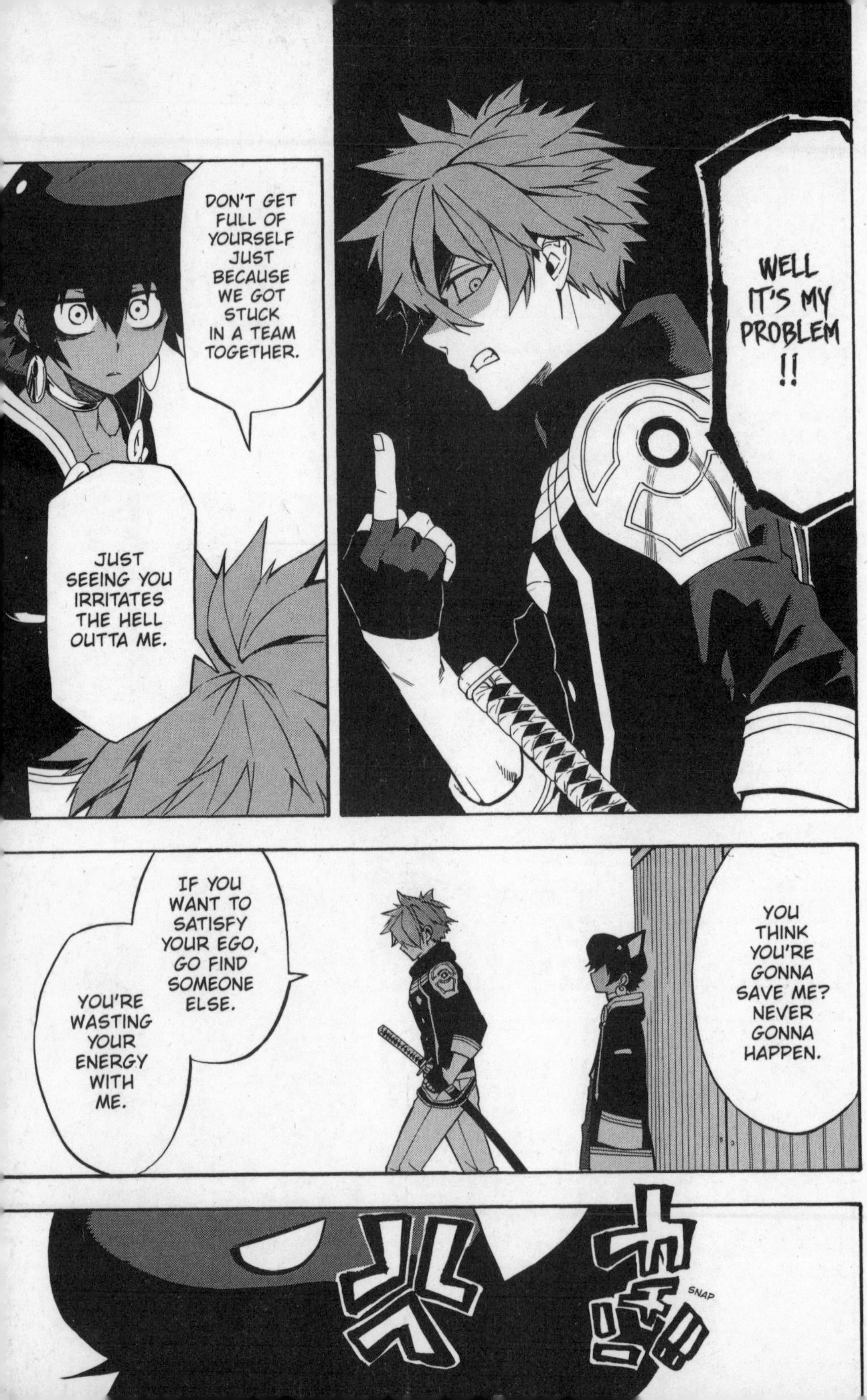
WELL IT'S MY PROBLEM !!
DON'T GET FULL OF YOURSELF JUST BECAUSE WE GOT STUCK IN A TEAM TOGETHER.
JUST SEEING YOU IRRITATES THE HELL OUTTA ME.
YOU THINK YOU'RE GONNA SAVE ME? NEVER GONNA HAPPEN.
IF YOU WANT TO SATISFY YOUR EGO, GO FIND SOMEONE ELSE.
YOU'RE WASTING YOUR ENERGY WITH ME.
SNAP

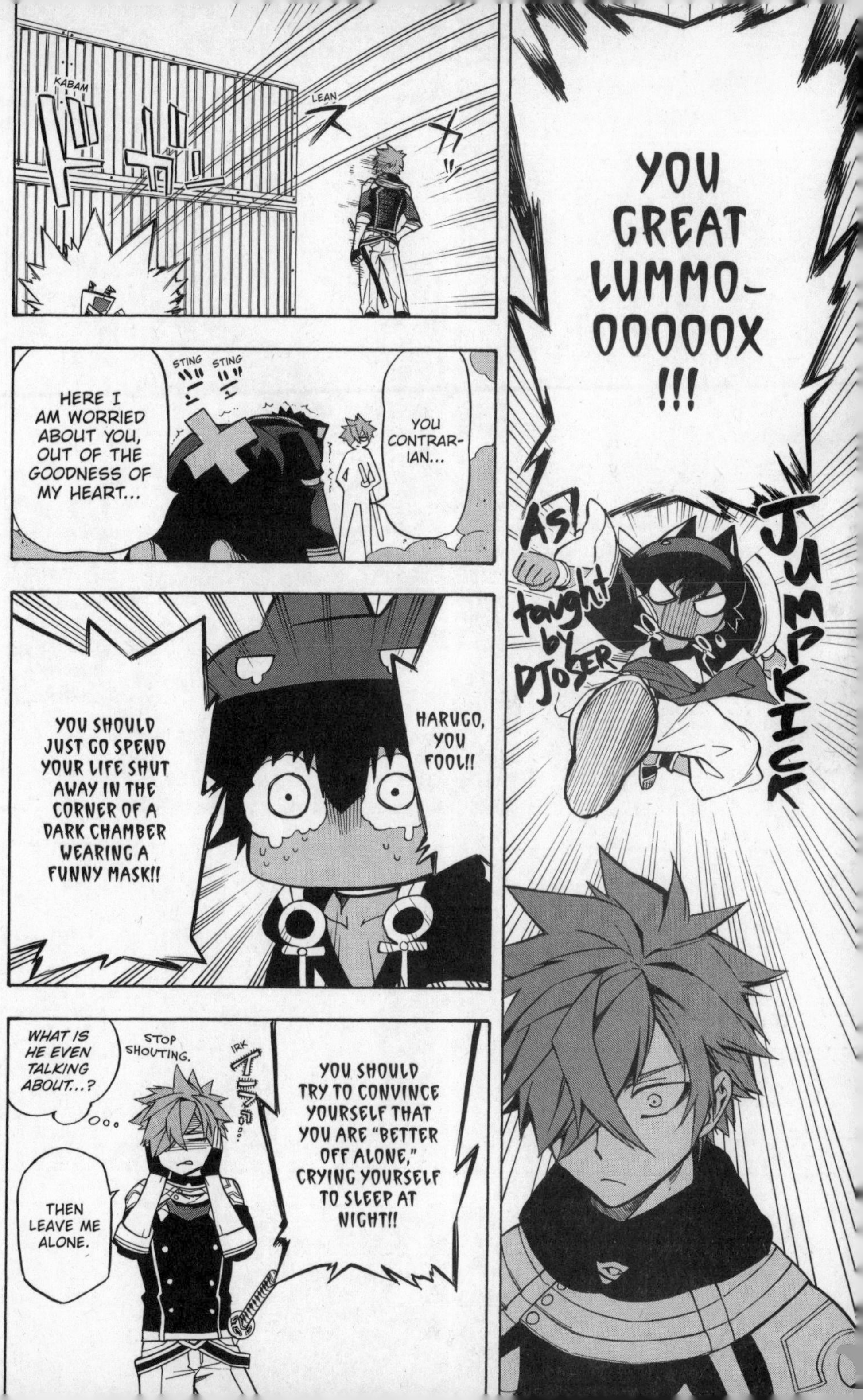
YOU GREAT LUMMO-OOOOOX!!!
JUMPKICK
As taught by DJOSER
LEAN
KABAM
YOU CONTRARIAN...
STING STING
HERE I AM WORRIED ABOUT YOU, OUT OF THE GOODNESS OF MY HEART...
HARUGO, YOU FOOL!!
YOU SHOULD JUST GO SPEND YOUR LIFE SHUT AWAY IN THE CORNER OF A DARK CHAMBER WEARING A FUNNY MASK!!
YOU SHOULD TRY TO CONVINCE YOURSELF THAT YOU ARE "BETTER OFF ALONE," CRYING YOURSELF TO SLEEP AT NIGHT!!
IRK
STOP SHOUTING.
WHAT IS HE EVEN TALKING ABOUT...?
THEN LEAVE ME ALONE.

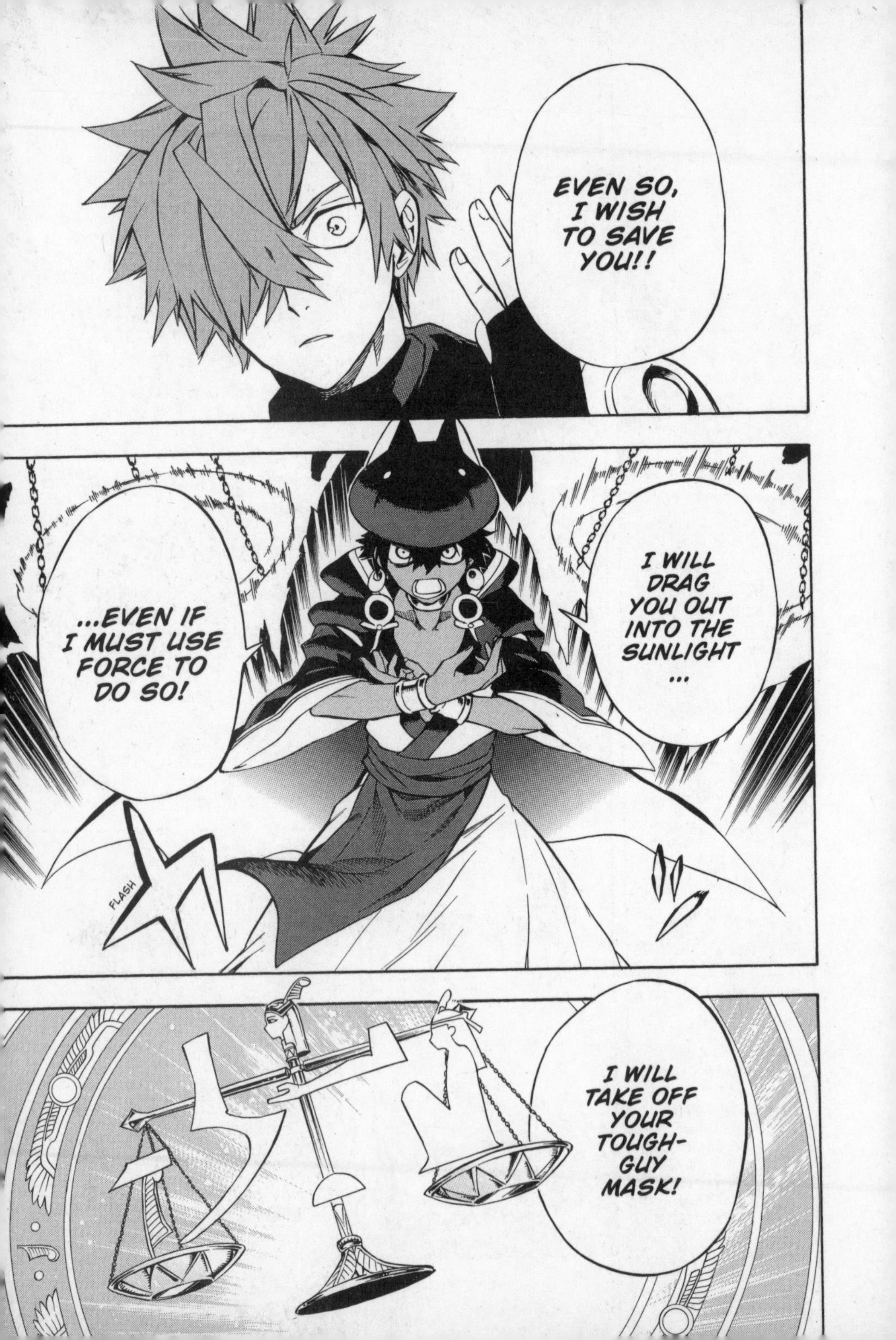
EVEN SO, I WISH TO SAVE YOU!!
I WILL DRAG YOU OUT INTO THE SUNLIGHT ...
...EVEN IF I MUST USE FORCE TO DO SO!
FLASH
I WILL TAKE OFF YOUR TOUGH-GUY MASK!

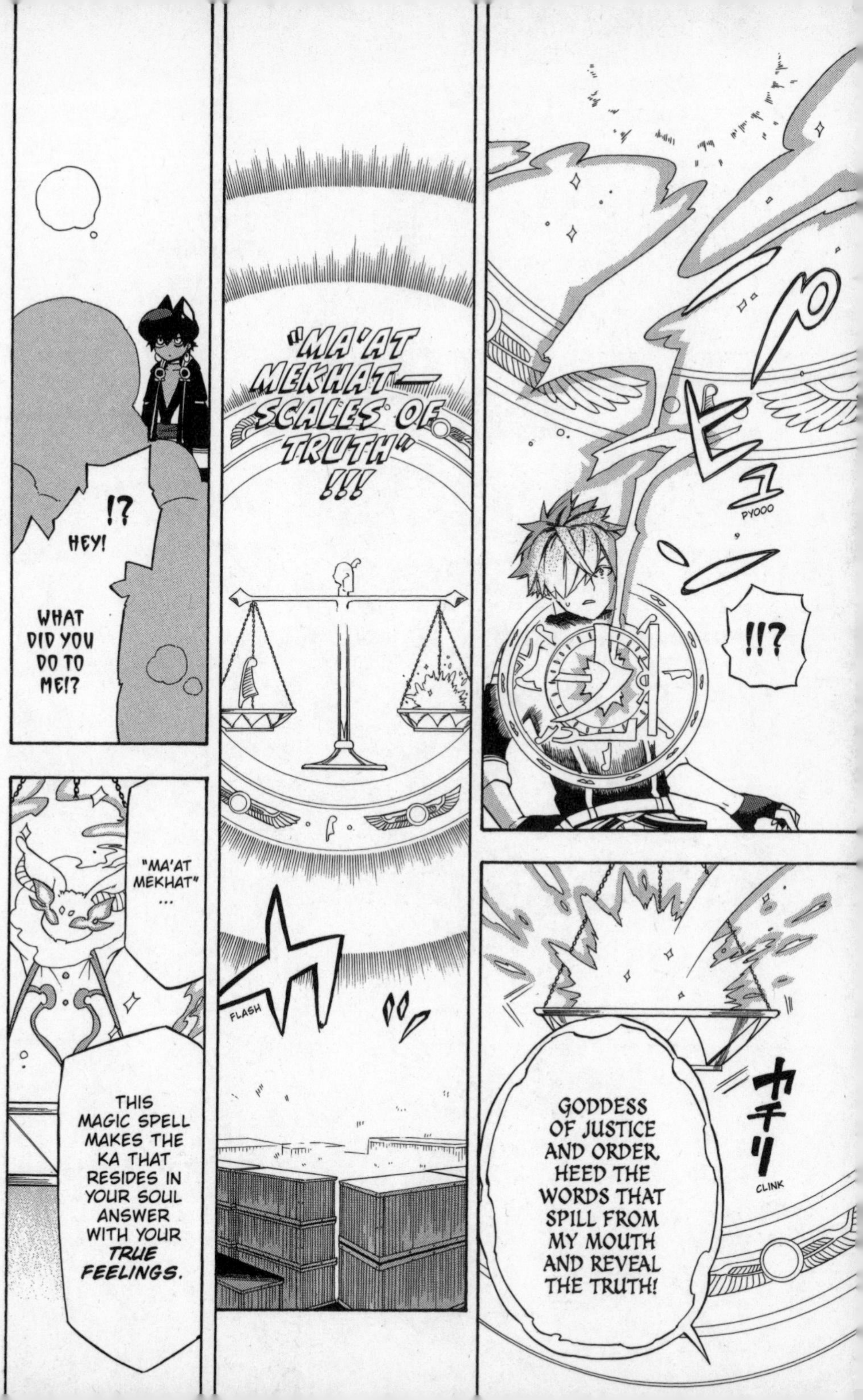
PYOOO
!!?
CLINK
GODDESS OF JUSTICE AND ORDER, HEED THE WORDS THAT SPILL FROM MY MOUTH AND REVEAL THE TRUTH!
"MA'AT MEKHAT—SCALES OF TRUTH"!!!
FLASH
!?
HEY!
WHAT DID YOU DO TO ME!?
"MA'AT MEKHAT"...
THIS MAGIC SPELL MAKES THE KA THAT RESIDES IN YOUR SOUL ANSWER WITH YOUR TRUE FEELINGS.

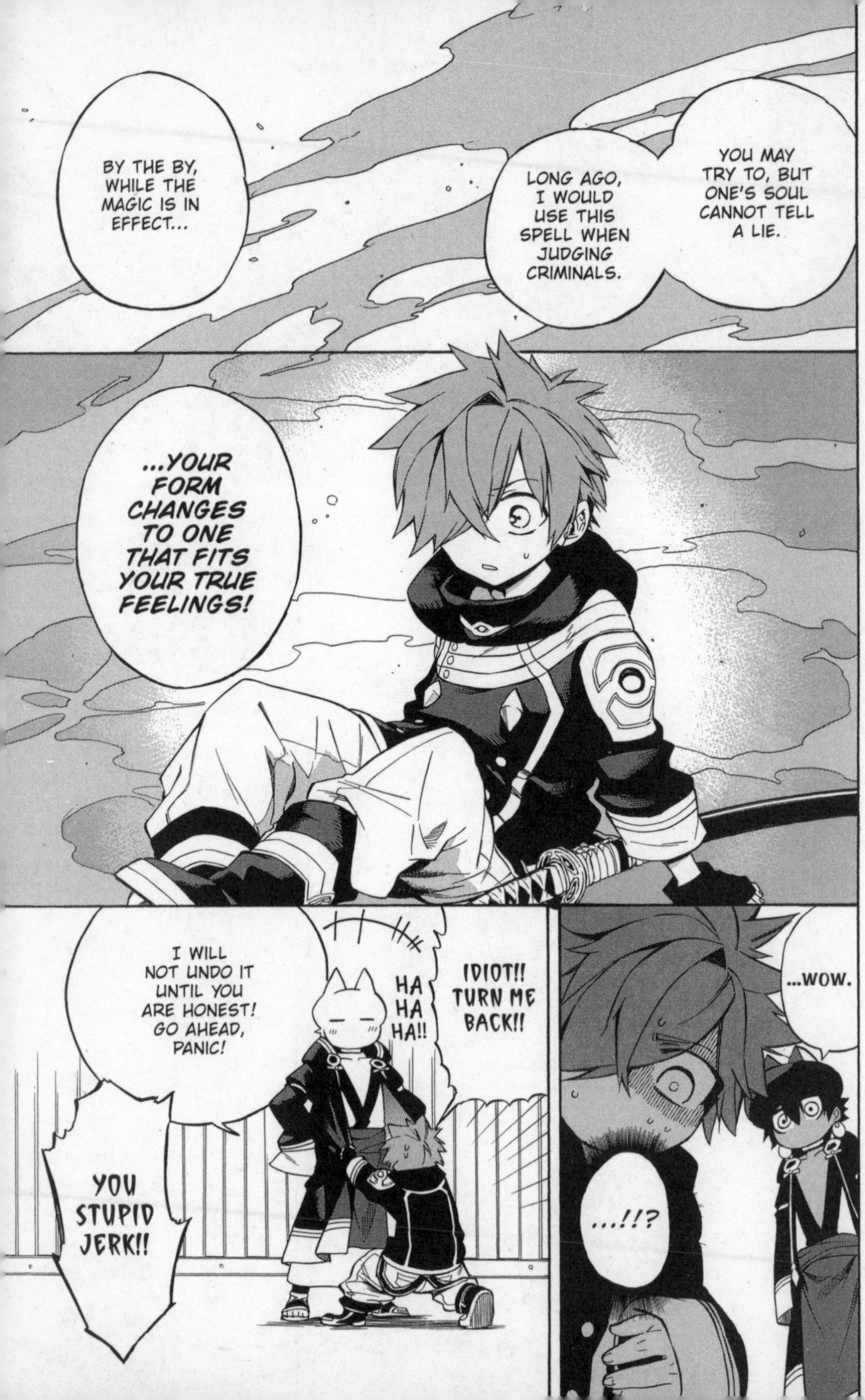
YOU MAY TRY TO, BUT ONE'S SOUL CANNOT TELL A LIE.
LONG AGO, I WOULD USE THIS SPELL WHEN JUDGING CRIMINALS.
BY THE BY, WHILE THE MAGIC IS IN EFFECT...
...YOUR FORM CHANGES TO ONE THAT FITS YOUR TRUE FEELINGS!
...WOW.
...!!?
IDIOT!! TURN ME BACK!!
HA HA HA!!
I WILL NOT UNDO IT UNTIL YOU ARE HONEST! GO AHEAD, PANIC!
YOU STUPID JERK!!

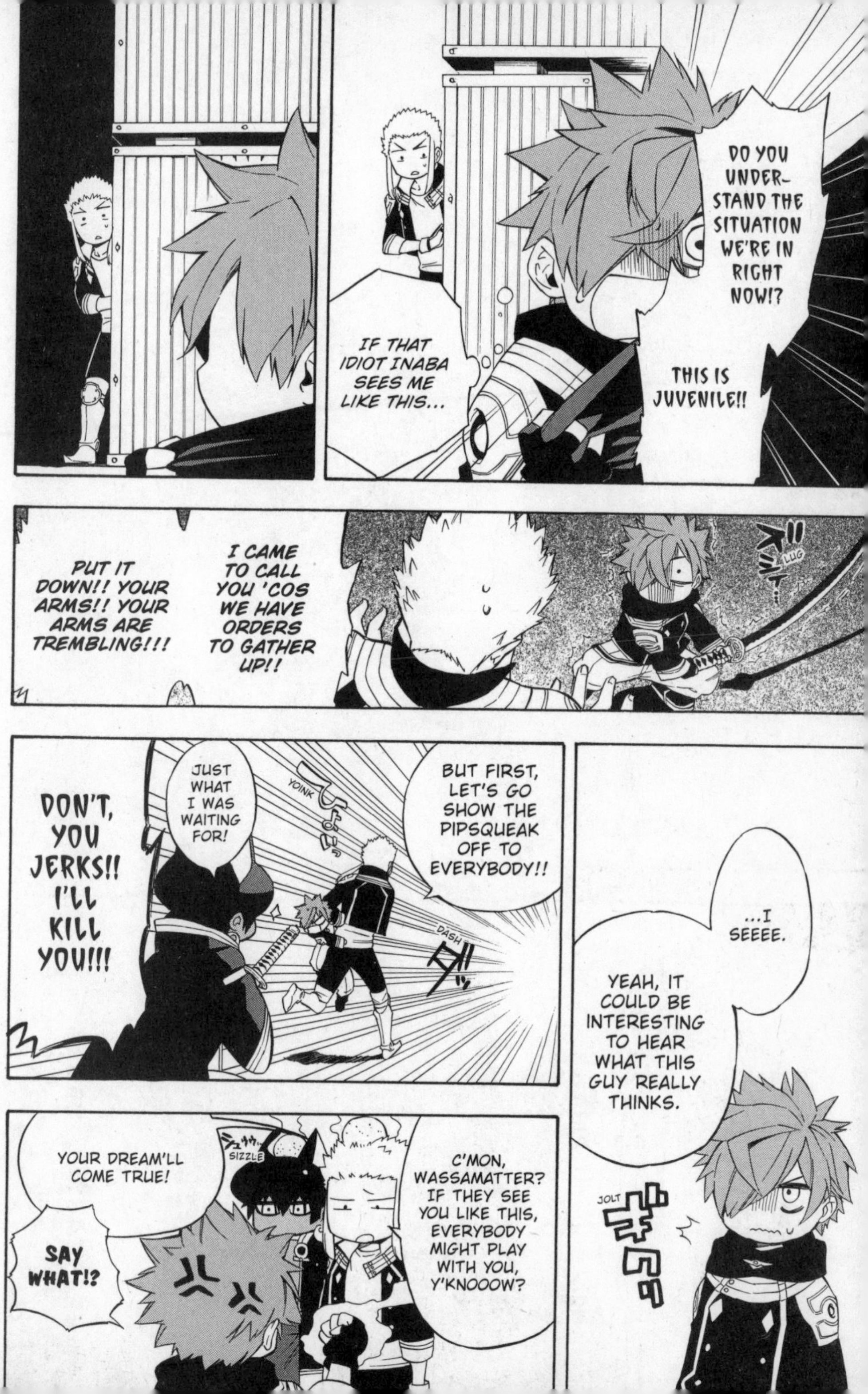
DO YOU UNDER-STAND THE SITUATION WE'RE IN RIGHT NOW!?
THIS IS JUVENILE!!
IF THAT IDIOT INABA SEES ME LIKE THIS...
LUG
I CAME TO CALL YOU 'COS WE HAVE ORDERS TO GATHER UP!!
PUT IT DOWN!! YOUR ARMS!! YOUR ARMS ARE TREMBLING!!!
...I SEEEE.
YEAH, IT COULD BE INTERESTING TO HEAR WHAT THIS GUY REALLY THINKS.
JOLT
BUT FIRST, LET'S GO SHOW THE PIPSQUEAK OFF TO EVERYBODY!!
YOINK
JUST WHAT I WAS WAITING FOR!
DASH
DON'T, YOU JERKS!! I'LL KILL YOU!!!
C'MON, WASSAMATTER? IF THEY SEE YOU LIKE THIS, EVERYBODY MIGHT PLAY WITH YOU, Y'KNOOOW?
SIZZLE
YOUR DREAM'LL COME TRUE!
SAY WHAT!?

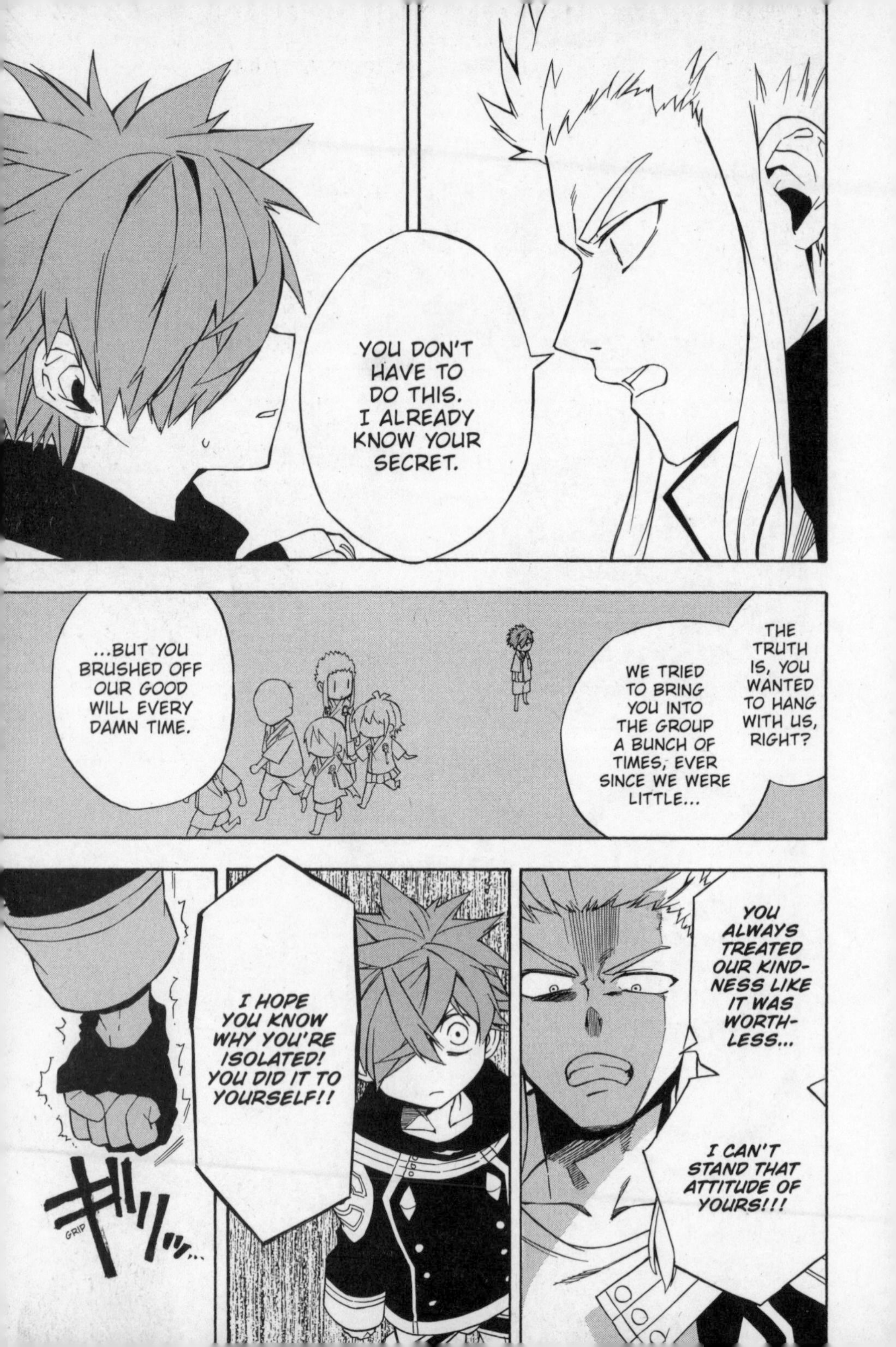
YOU DON'T HAVE TO DO THIS. I ALREADY KNOW YOUR SECRET.
THE TRUTH IS, YOU WANTED TO HANG WITH US, RIGHT?
WE TRIED TO BRING YOU INTO THE GROUP A BUNCH OF TIMES, EVER SINCE WE WERE LITTLE...
...BUT YOU BRUSHED OFF OUR GOOD WILL EVERY DAMN TIME.
YOU ALWAYS TREATED OUR KINDNESS LIKE IT WAS WORTHLESS...
I CAN'T STAND THAT ATTITUDE OF YOURS!!!
I HOPE YOU KNOW WHY YOU'RE ISOLATED! YOU DID IT TO YOURSELF!!
ギリッ...
GRIP

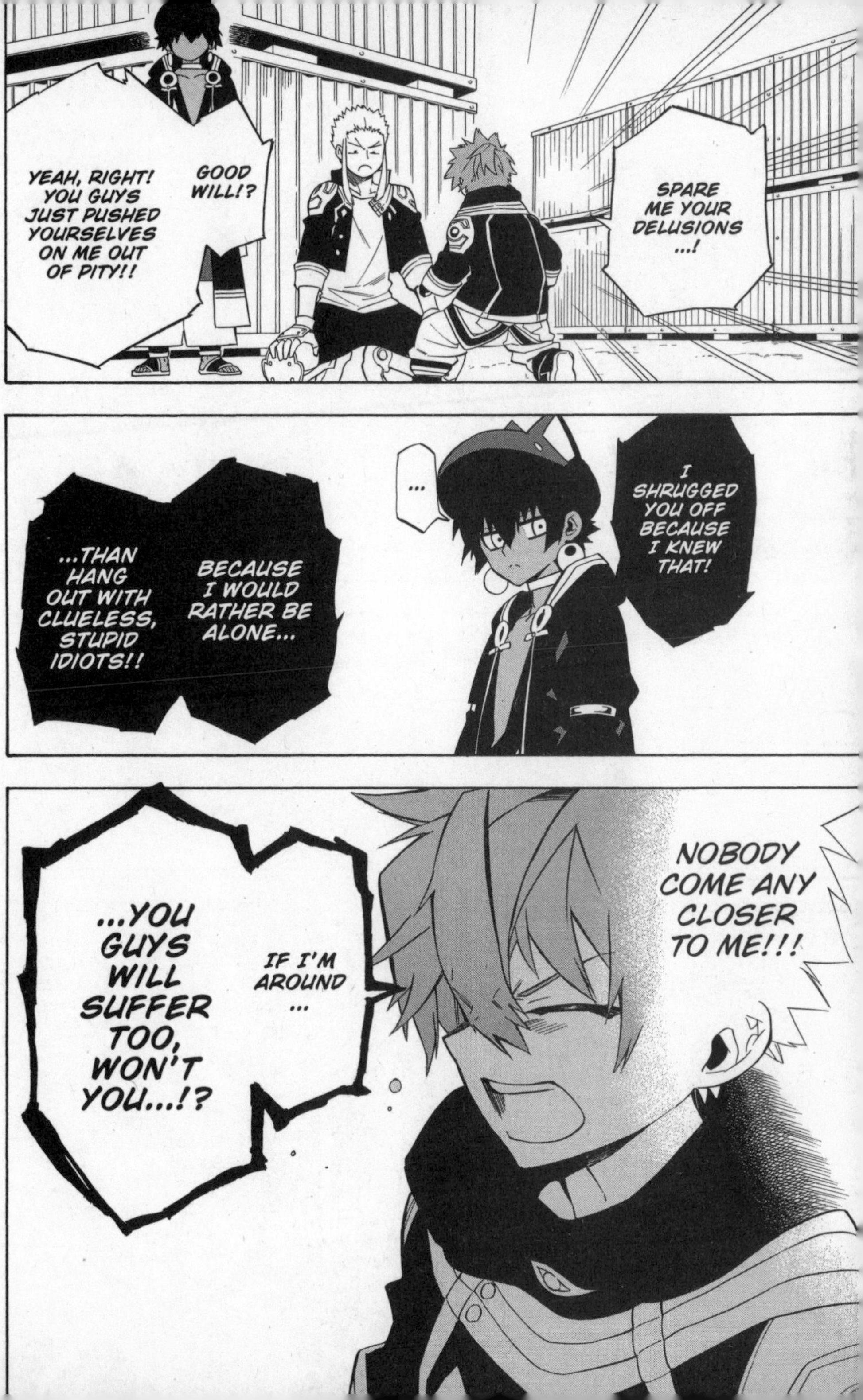
SPARE ME YOUR DELUSIONS ...!
GOOD WILL!?
YEAH, RIGHT! YOU GUYS JUST PUSHED YOURSELVES ON ME OUT OF PITY!!
I SHRUGGED YOU OFF BECAUSE I KNEW THAT!
...
BECAUSE I WOULD RATHER BE ALONE...
...THAN HANG OUT WITH CLUELESS, STUPID IDIOTS!!
NOBODY COME ANY CLOSER TO ME!!!
IF I'M AROUND ...
...YOU GUYS WILL SUFFER TOO, WON'T YOU...!?

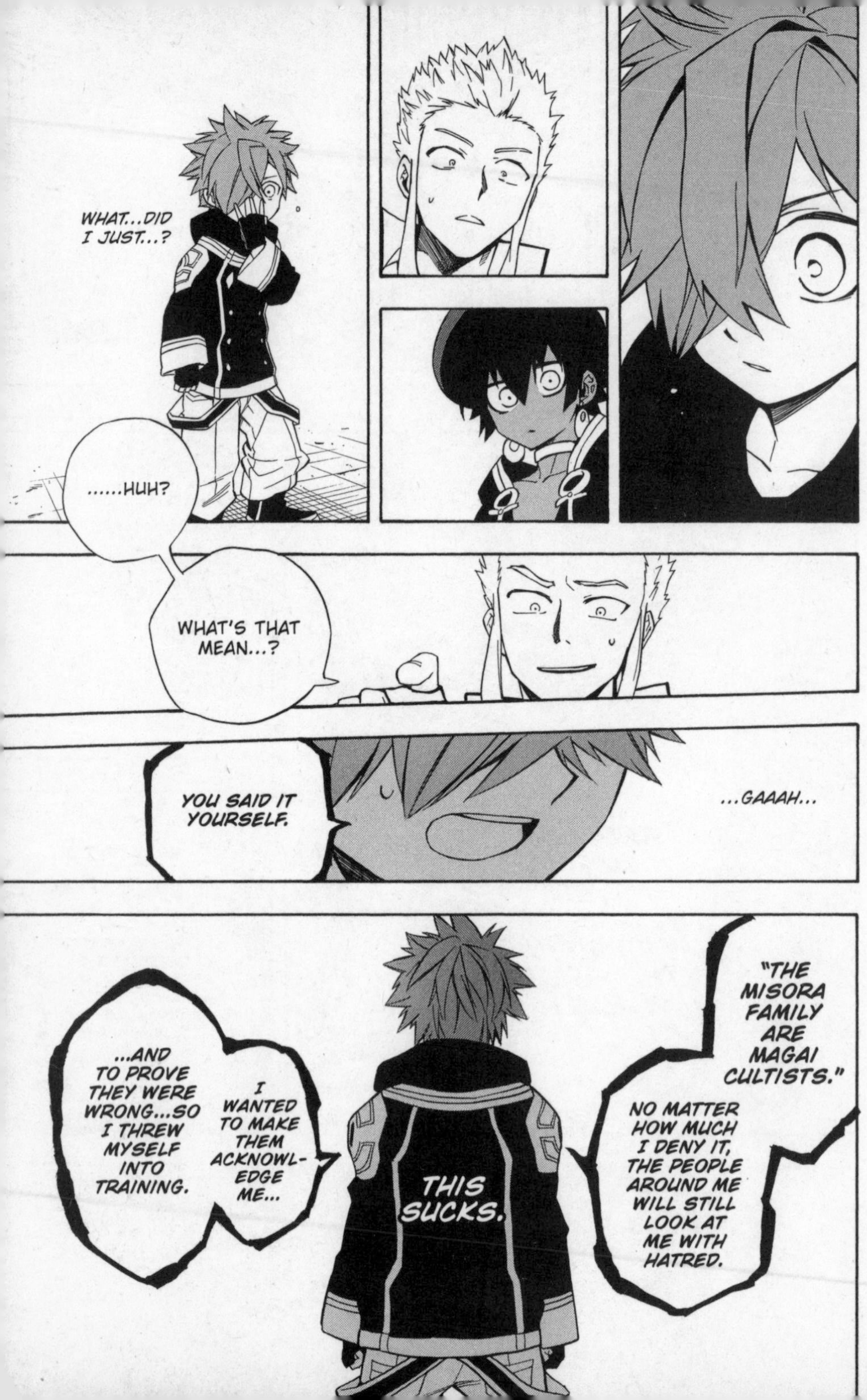
WHAT...DID I JUST...?
......HUH?
WHAT'S THAT MEAN...?
...GAAAH...
YOU SAID IT YOURSELF.
"THE MISORA FAMILY ARE MAGAI CULTISTS."
NO MATTER HOW MUCH I DENY IT, THE PEOPLE AROUND ME WILL STILL LOOK AT ME WITH HATRED.
THIS SUCKS.
I WANTED TO MAKE THEM ACKNOWL-EDGE ME...
...AND TO PROVE THEY WERE WRONG...SO I THREW MYSELF INTO TRAINING.

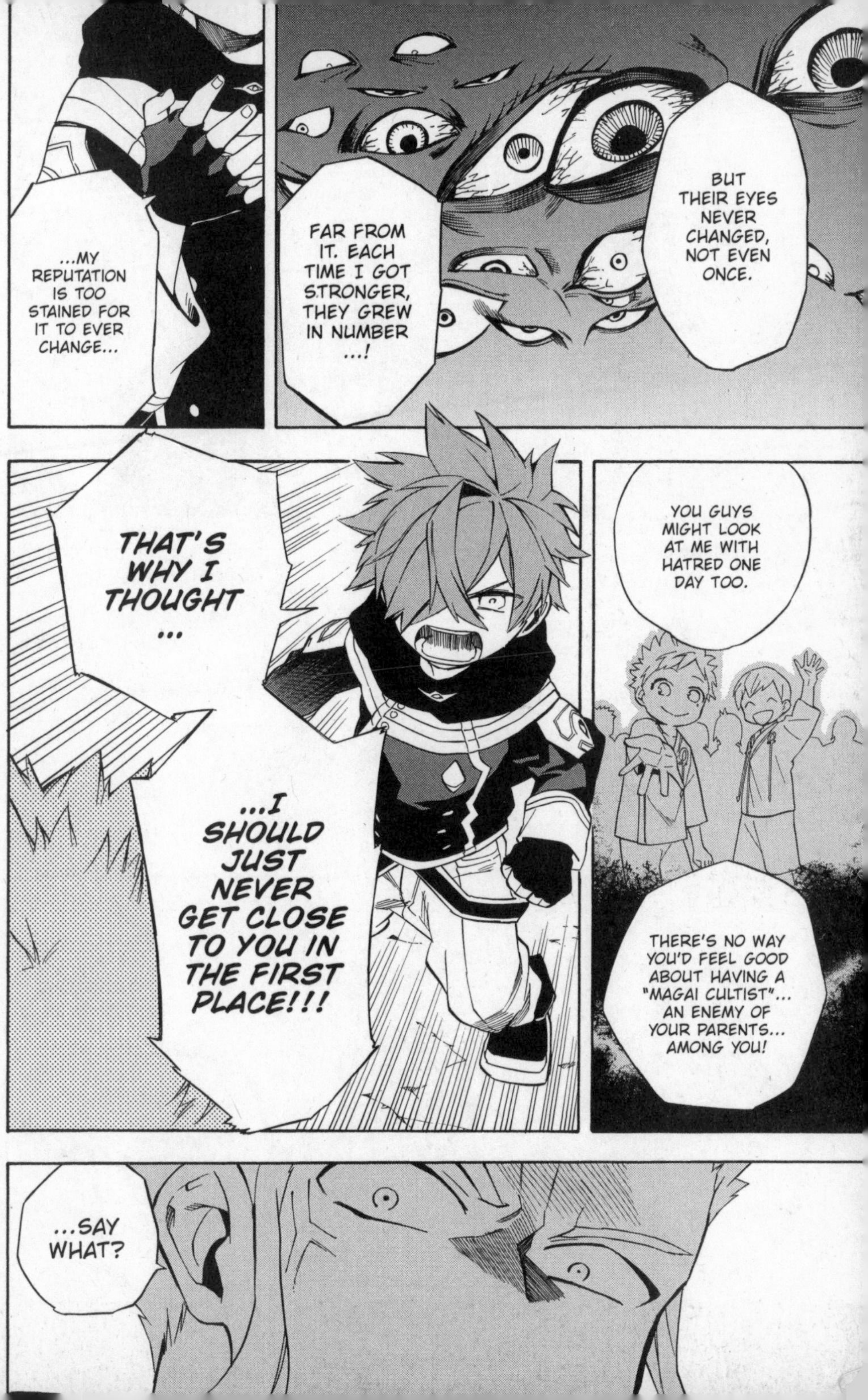
BUT THEIR EYES NEVER CHANGED, NOT EVEN ONCE.
FAR FROM IT. EACH TIME I GOT STRONGER, THEY GREW IN NUMBER ...!
...MY REPUTATION IS TOO STAINED FOR IT TO EVER CHANGE...
YOU GUYS MIGHT LOOK AT ME WITH HATRED ONE DAY TOO.
THERE'S NO WAY YOU'D FEEL GOOD ABOUT HAVING A "MAGAI CULTIST"... AN ENEMY OF YOUR PARENTS... AMONG YOU!
THAT'S WHY I THOUGHT ...
...I SHOULD JUST NEVER GET CLOSE TO YOU IN THE FIRST PLACE!!!
...SAY WHAT?

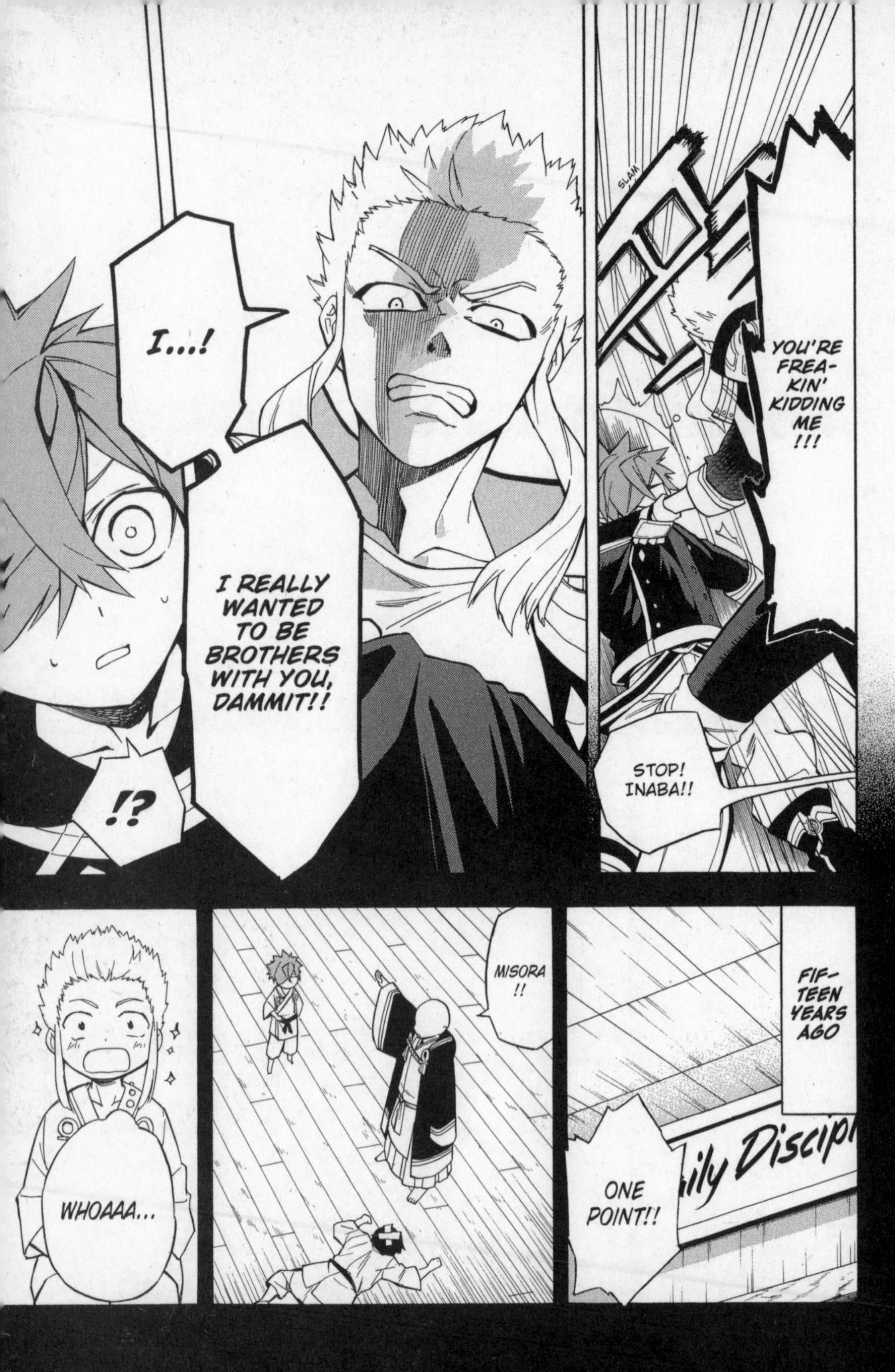
SLAM
YOU'RE FREAKIN' KIDDING ME!!!
STOP! INABA!!
I...!
I REALLY WANTED TO BE BROTHERS WITH YOU, DAMMIT!!
!?
FIFTEEN YEARS AGO
ONE POINT!!
MISORA!!
WHOAAA...

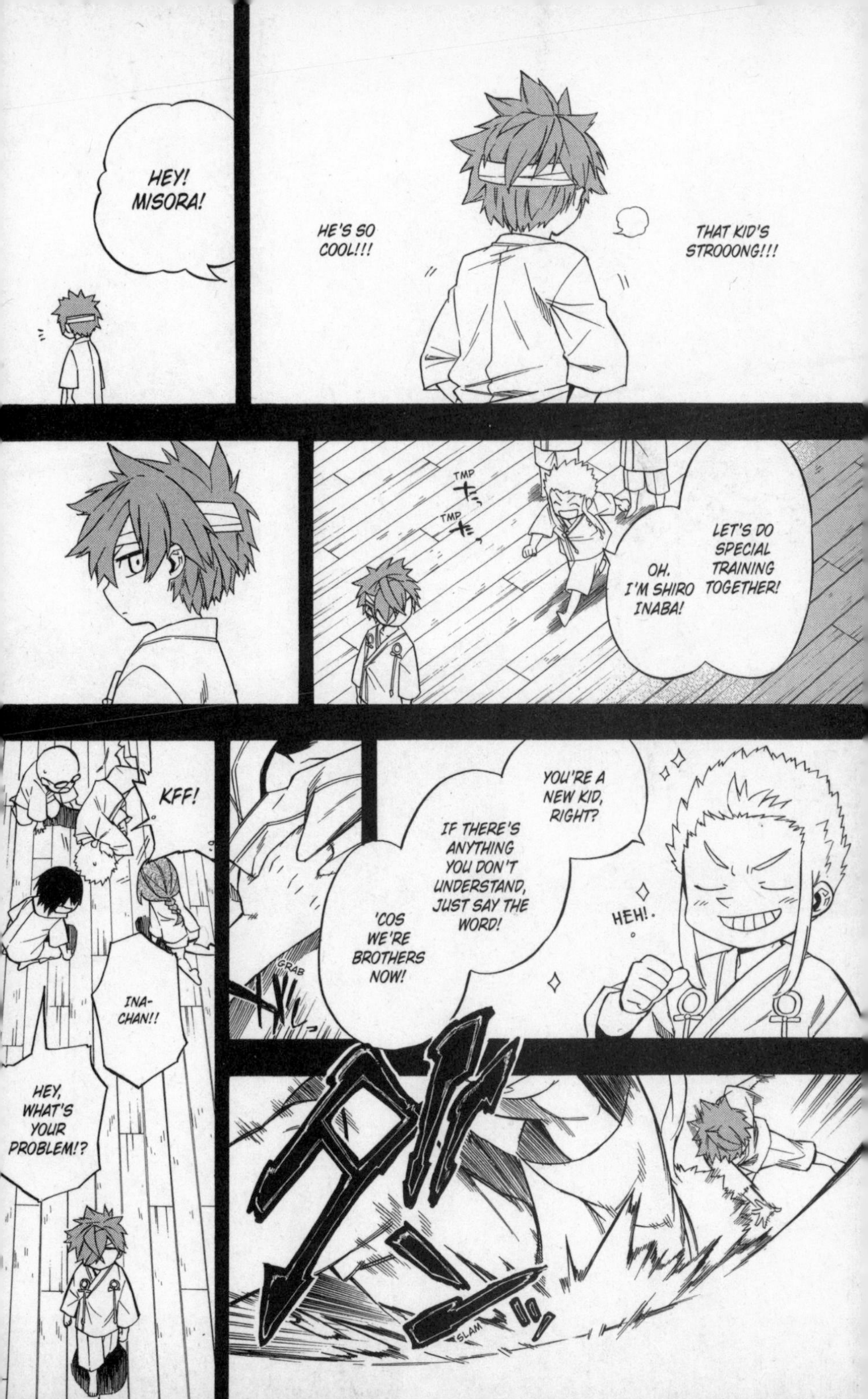
THAT KID'S STROOONG!!!
HE'S SO COOL!!!
HEY! MISORA!
TMP TMP
OH. I'M SHIRO INABA!
LET'S DO SPECIAL TRAINING TOGETHER!
YOU'RE A NEW KID, RIGHT?
HEH!
IF THERE'S ANYTHING YOU DON'T UNDERSTAND, JUST SAY THE WORD!
'COS WE'RE BROTHERS NOW!
GRAB
SLAM
KFF!
INA-CHAN!!
HEY, WHAT'S YOUR PROBLEM!?

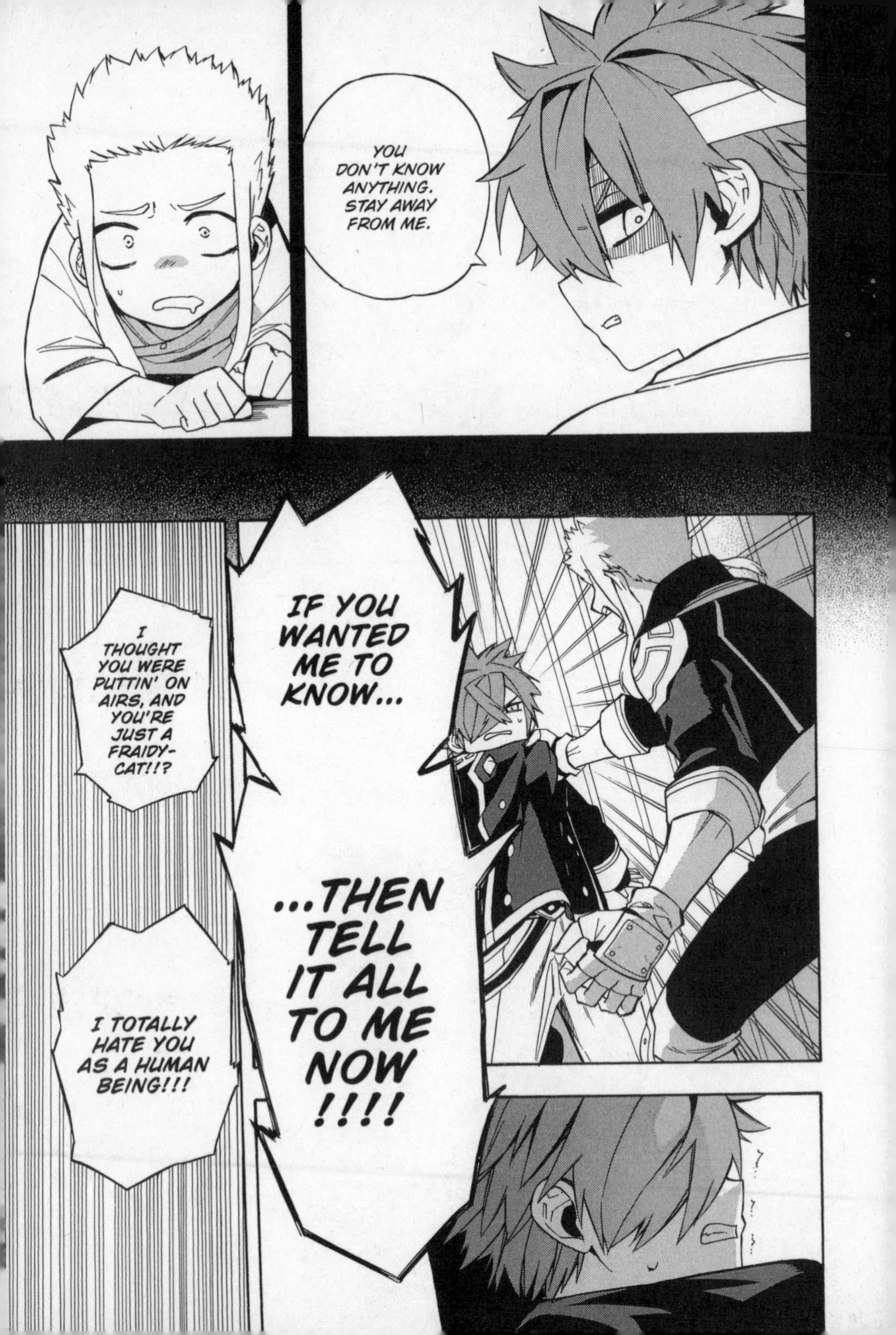
YOU DON'T KNOW ANYTHING. STAY AWAY FROM ME.
IF YOU WANTED ME TO KNOW...
...THEN TELL IT ALL TO ME NOW!!!!
I THOUGHT YOU WERE PUTTIN' ON AIRS, AND YOU'RE JUST A FRAIDY-CAT!!?
I TOTALLY HATE YOU AS A HUMAN BEING!!!

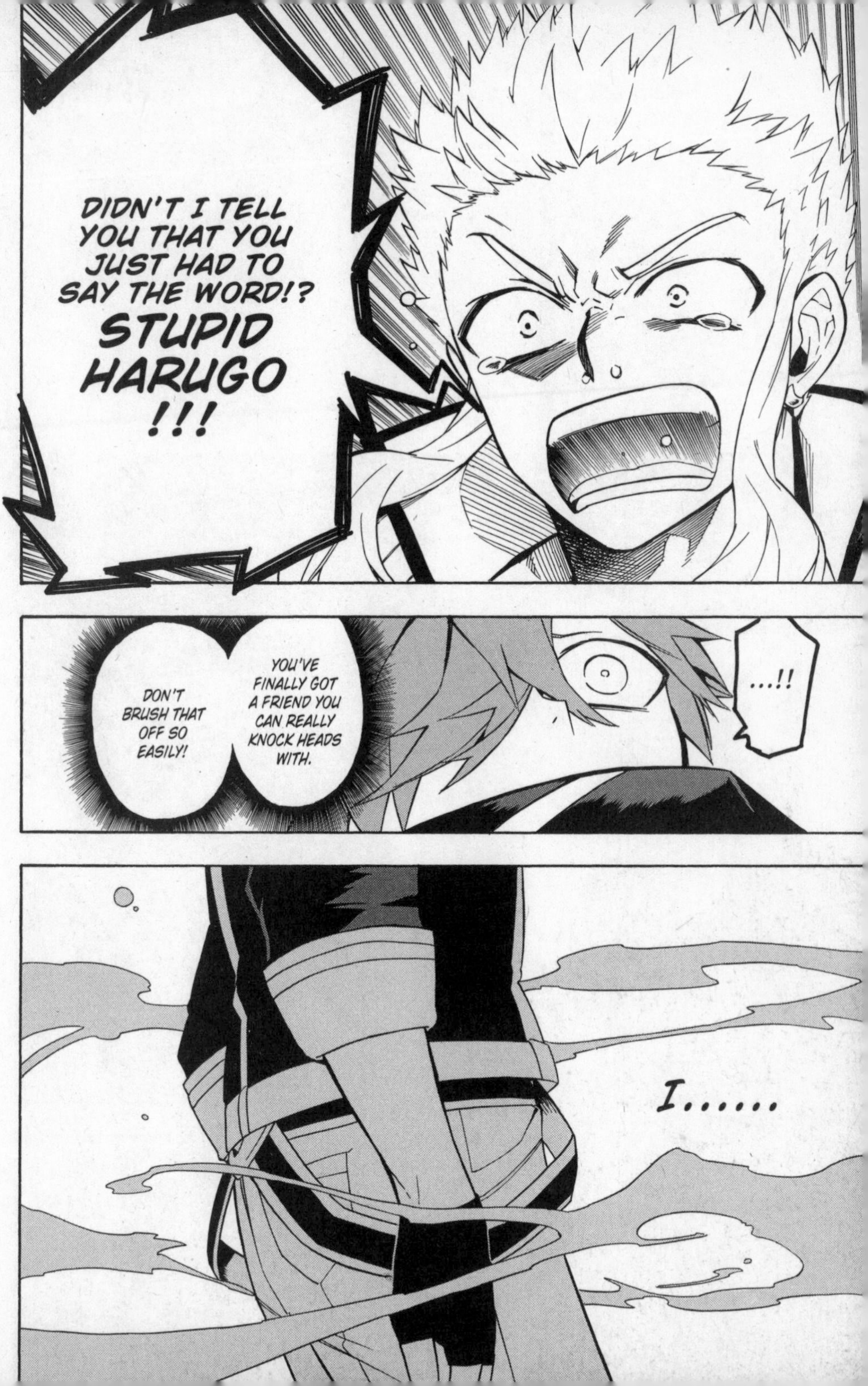
DIDN'T I TELL YOU THAT YOU JUST HAD TO SAY THE WORD!? STUPID HARUGO !!!
...!!
YOU'VE FINALLY GOT A FRIEND YOU CAN REALLY KNOCK HEADS WITH.
DON'T BRUSH THAT OFF SO EASILY!
I......

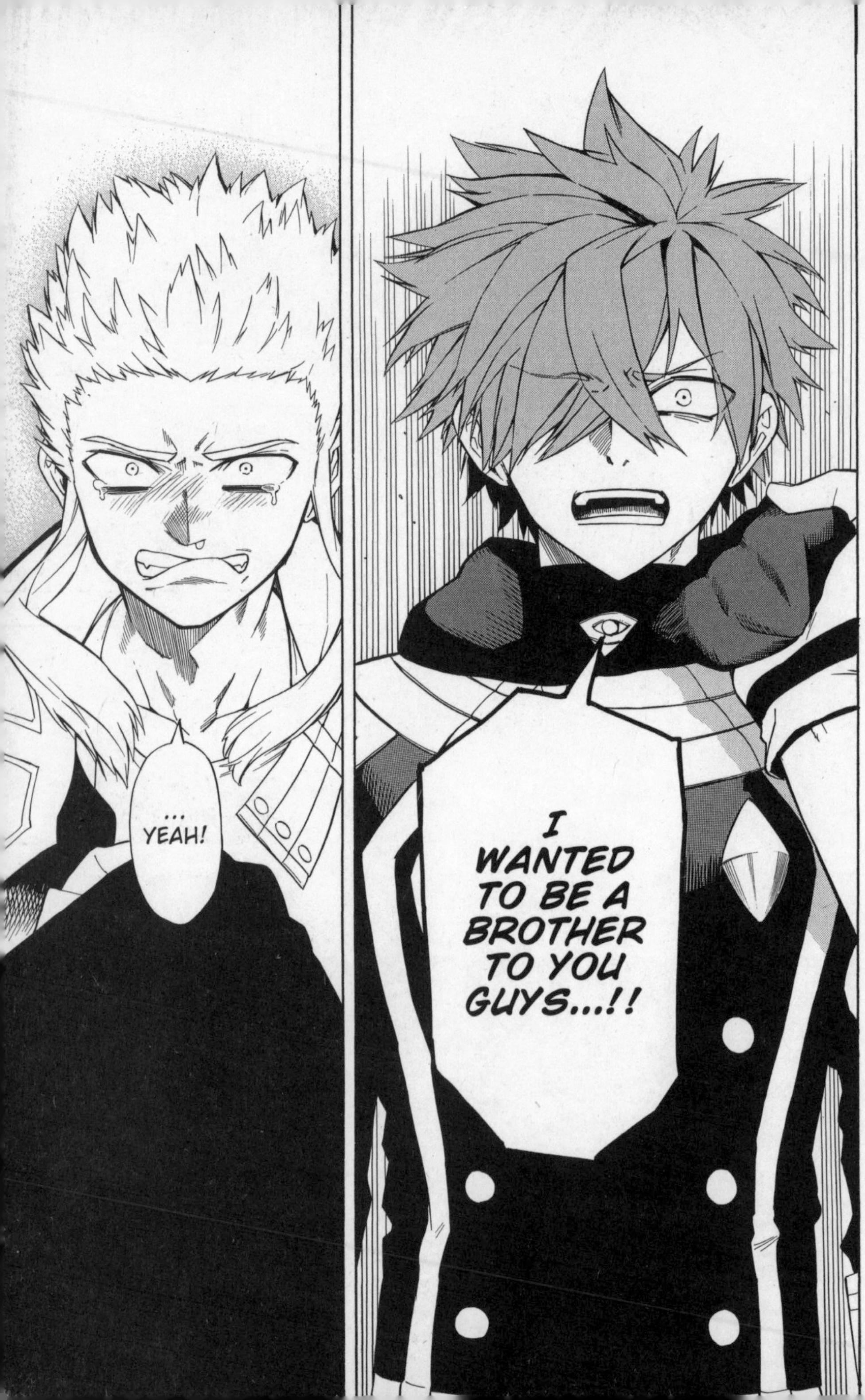
I WANTED TO BE A BROTHER TO YOU GUYS...!!
... YEAH!

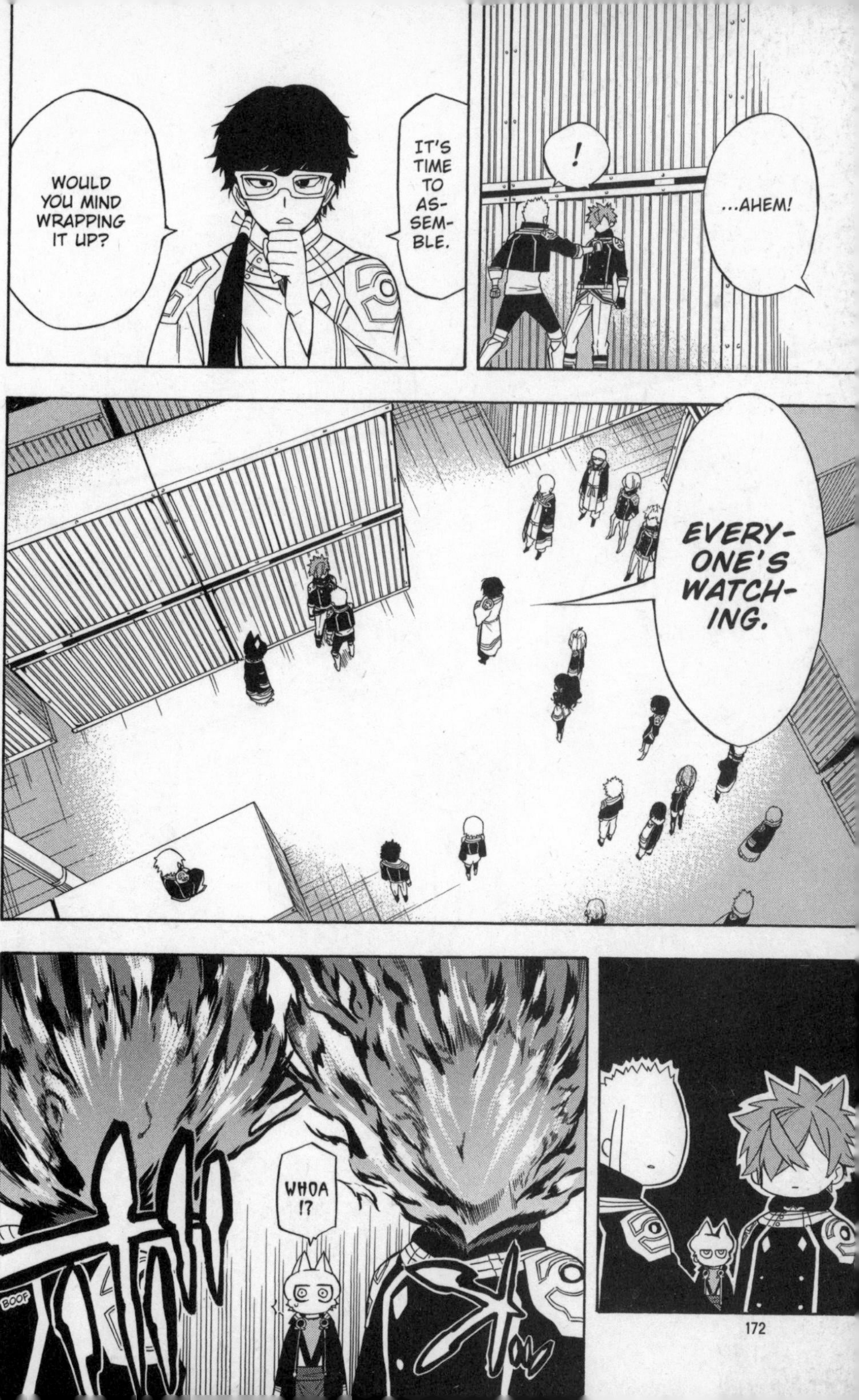
...AHEM!
!
IT'S TIME TO AS-SEM-BLE.
WOULD YOU MIND WRAPPING IT UP?
EVERY-ONE'S WATCH-ING.
WHOA !?
BOOP

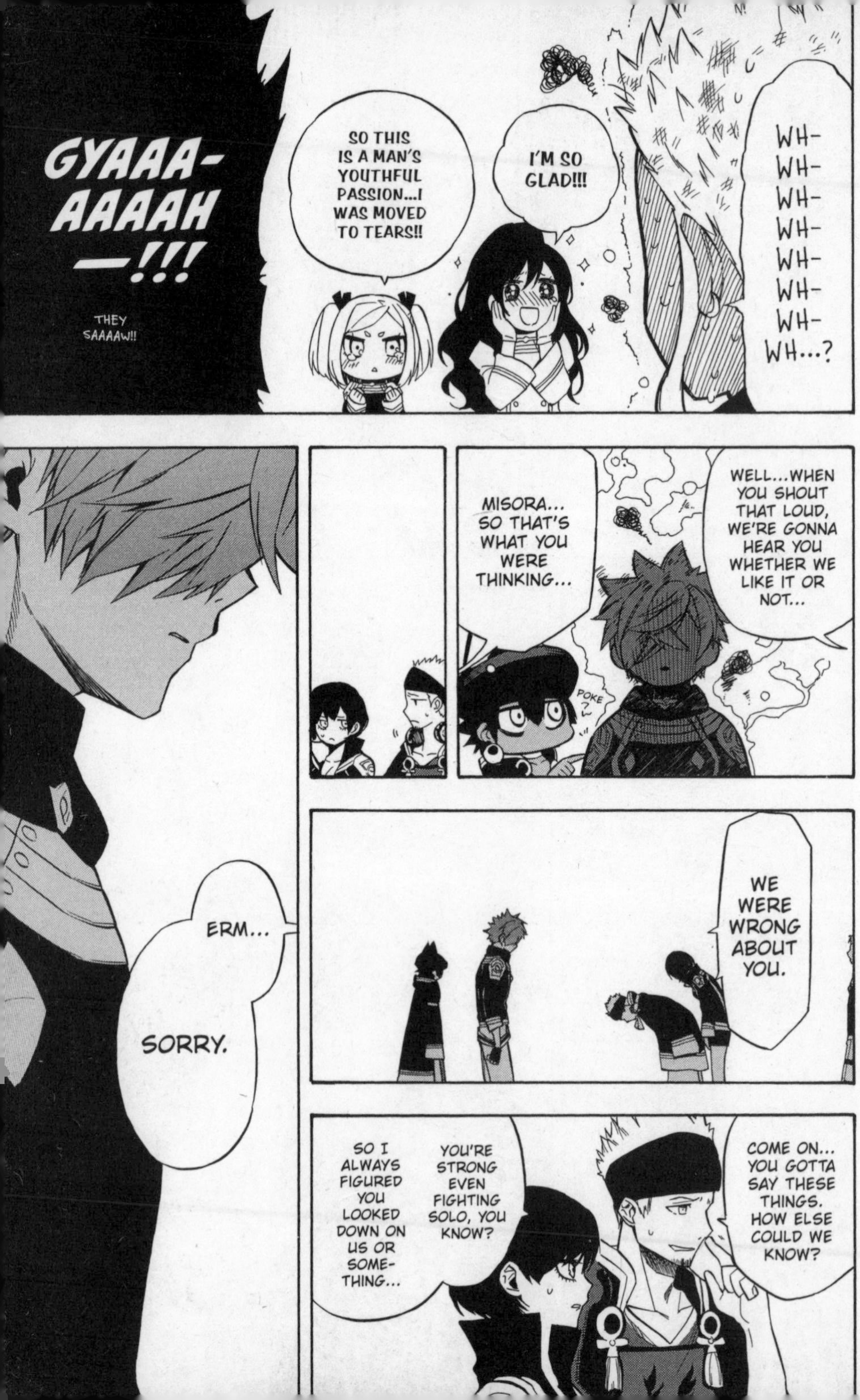
WH-WH-WH-WH-WH-WH-WH-WH...?
I'M SO GLAD!!!
SO THIS IS A MAN'S YOUTHFUL PASSION...I WAS MOVED TO TEARS!!
GYAAA-AAAAH—!!!
THEY SAAAAW!!
WELL...WHEN YOU SHOUT THAT LOUD, WE'RE GONNA HEAR YOU WHETHER WE LIKE IT OR NOT...
MISORA... SO THAT'S WHAT YOU WERE THINKING...
POKE
WE WERE WRONG ABOUT YOU.
COME ON... YOU GOTTA SAY THESE THINGS. HOW ELSE COULD WE KNOW?
YOU'RE STRONG EVEN FIGHTING SOLO, YOU KNOW?
SO I ALWAYS FIGURED YOU LOOKED DOWN ON US OR SOME-THING...
ERM...
SORRY.

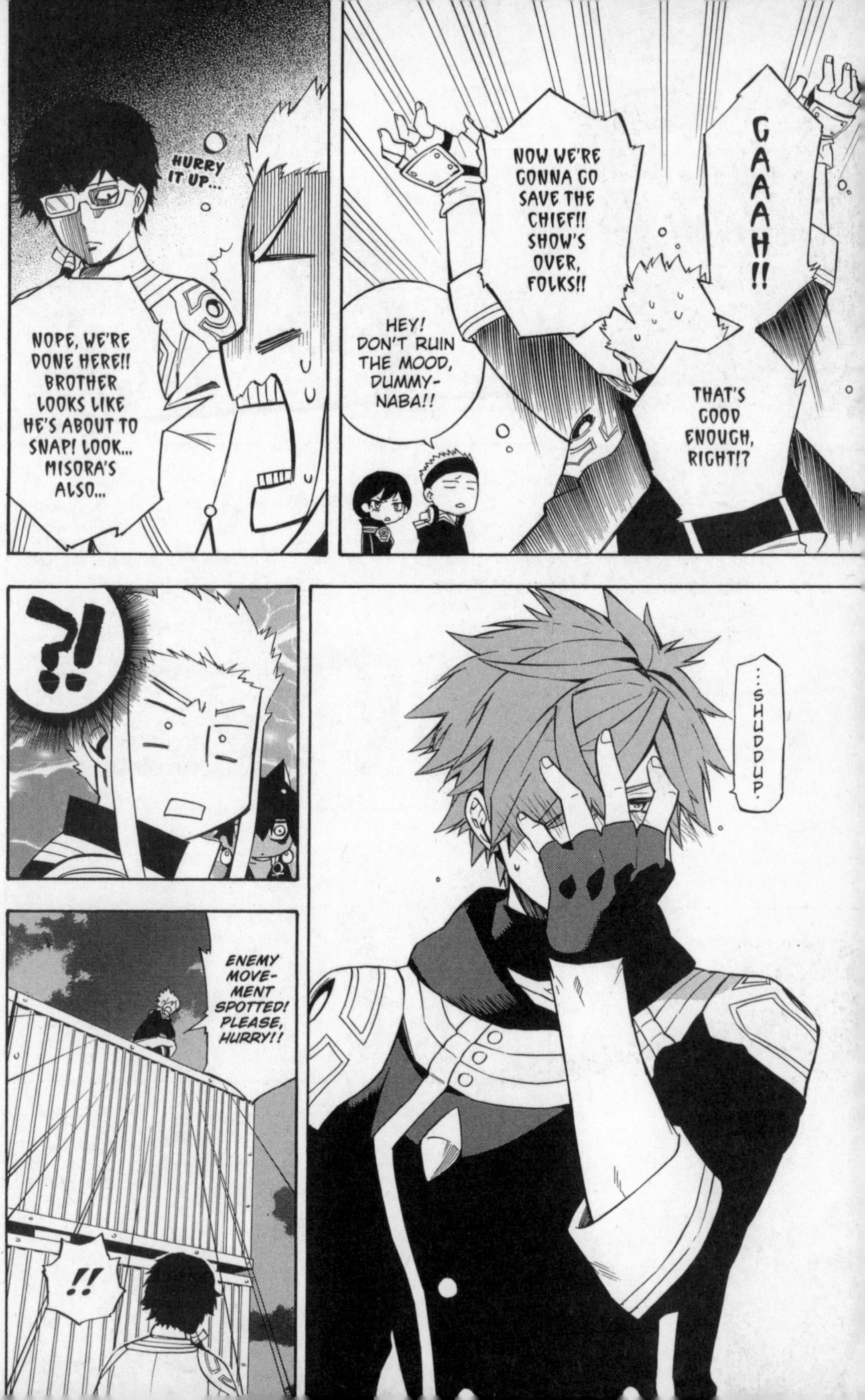
GAAAH!!
THAT'S GOOD ENOUGH, RIGHT!?
NOW WE'RE GONNA GO SAVE THE CHIEF!! SHOW'S OVER, FOLKS!!
HEY! DON'T RUIN THE MOOD, DUMMY-NABA!!
HURRY IT UP...
NOPE, WE'RE DONE HERE!! BROTHER LOOKS LIKE HE'S ABOUT TO SNAP! LOOK... MISORA'S ALSO...
...SHUDDUP.
?!
ENEMY MOVE-MENT SPOTTED! PLEASE, HURRY!!
!!

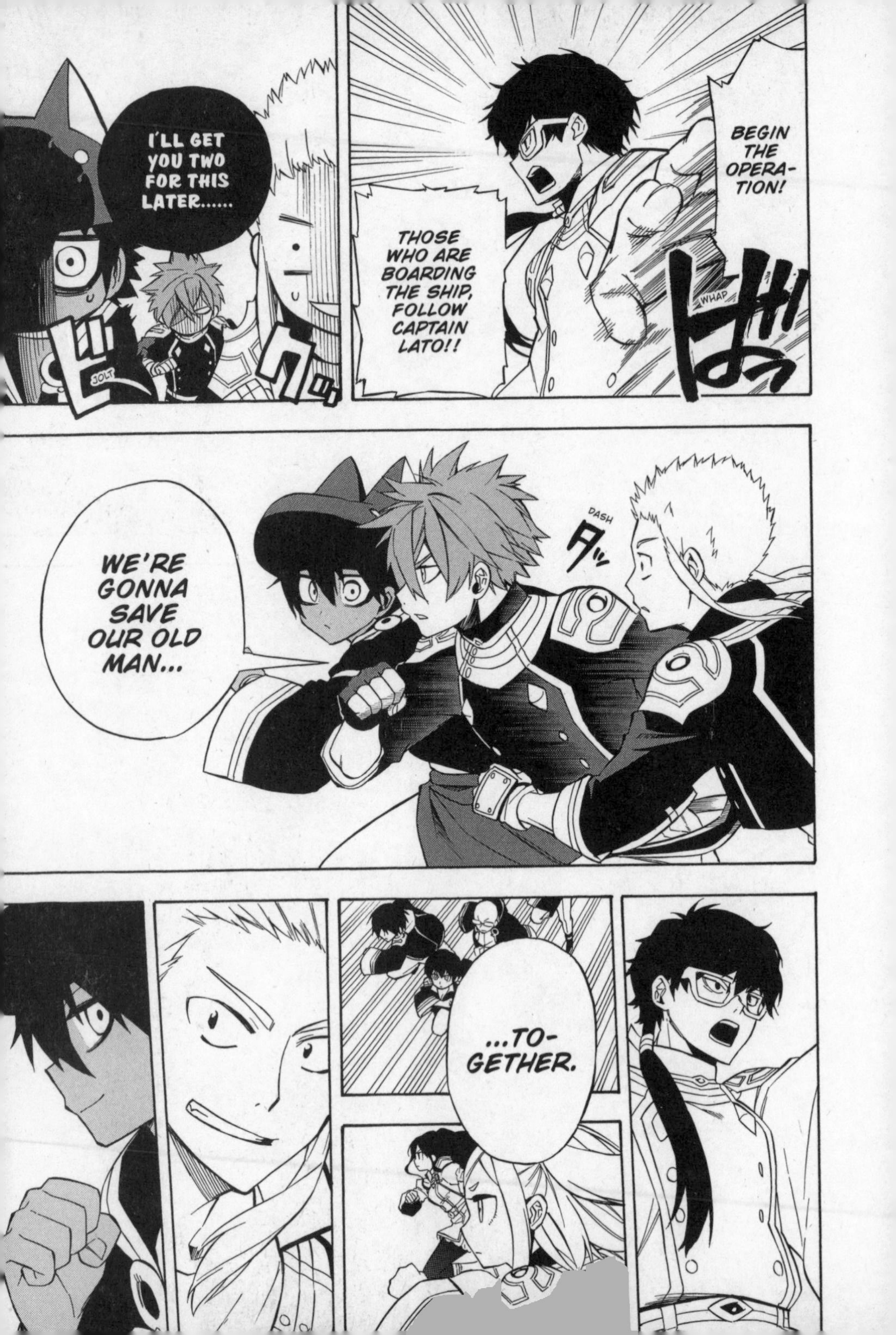
BEGIN THE OPERA-TION!
THOSE WHO ARE BOARDING THE SHIP, FOLLOW CAPTAIN LATO!!
WHAP
I'LL GET YOU TWO FOR THIS LATER......
JOLT
DASH
WE'RE GONNA SAVE OUR OLD MAN...
...TO-GETHER.

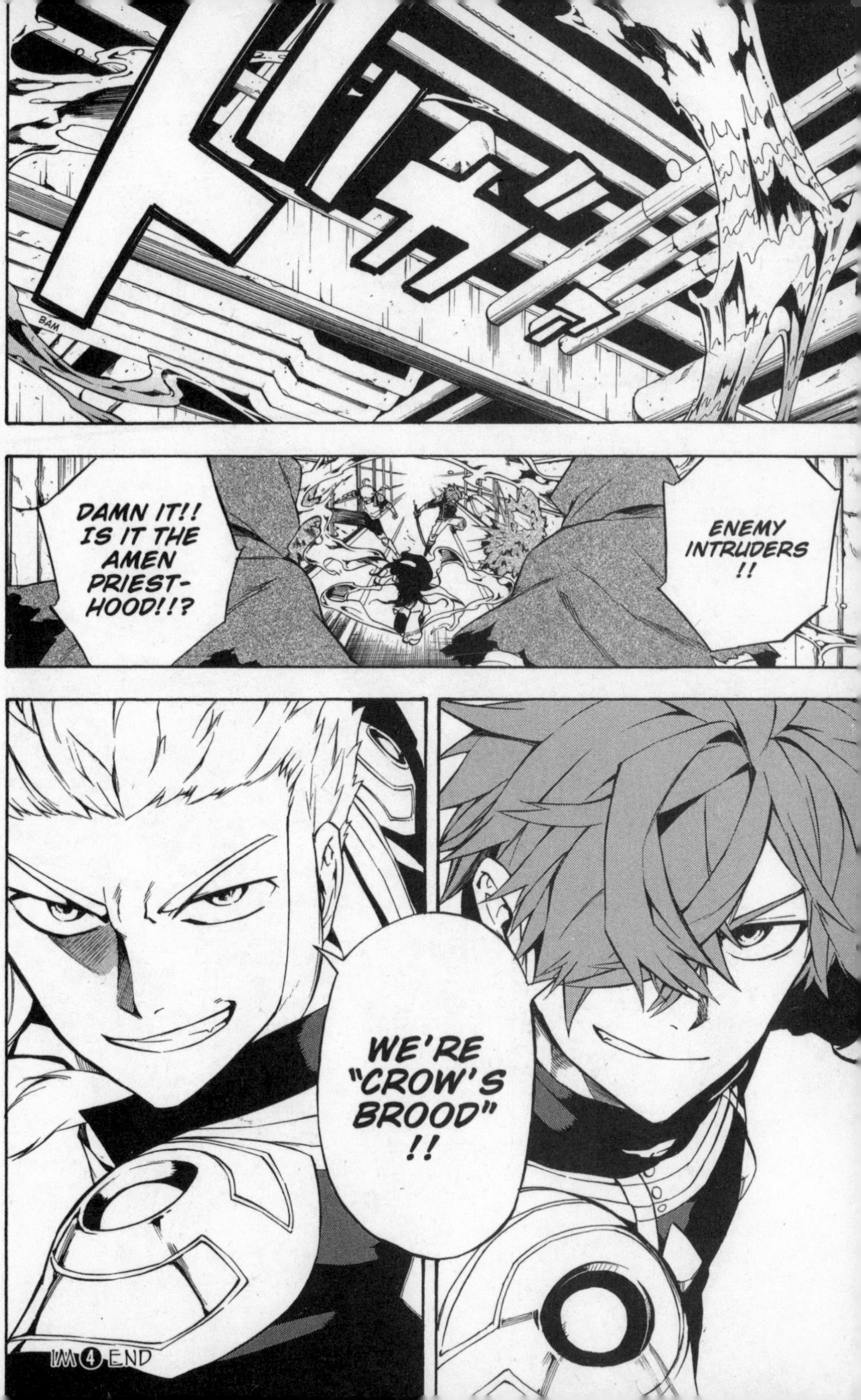
BAM
ENEMY INTRUDERS !!
DAMN IT!! IS IT THE AMEN PRIEST-HOOD!!?
WE'RE "CROW'S BROOD" !!
IM 4 END

EXTRA

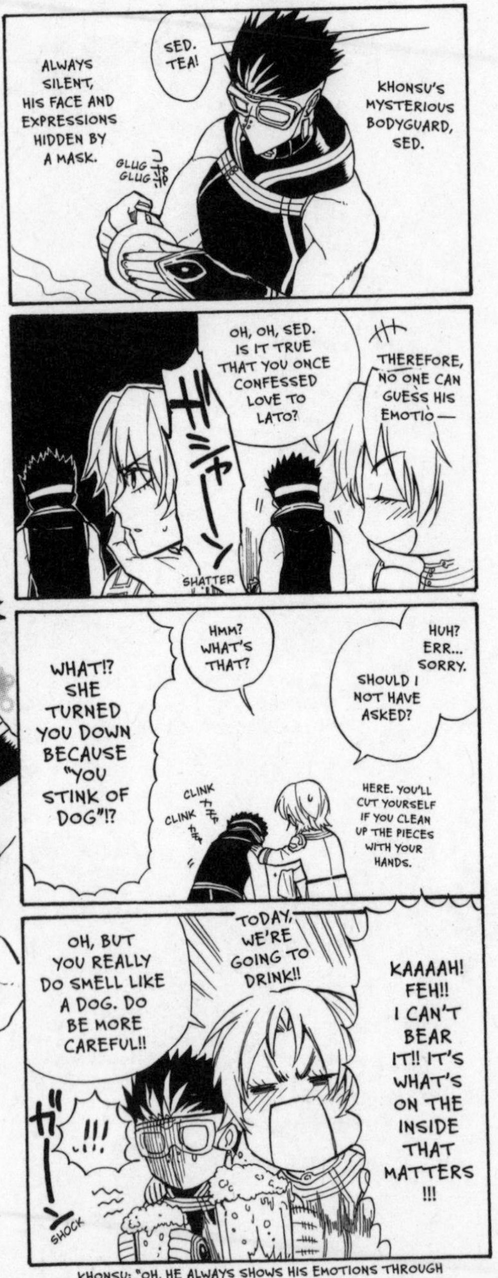
KHONSU'S MYSTERIOUS BODYGUARD, SED.
SED. TEA!
ALWAYS SILENT, HIS FACE AND EXPRESSIONS HIDDEN BY A MASK.
GLUG GLUG
THEREFORE, NO ONE CAN GUESS HIS EMOTIO—
OH, OH, SED. IS IT TRUE THAT YOU ONCE CONFESSED LOVE TO LATO?
SHATTER
HUH? ERR... SORRY.
SHOULD I NOT HAVE ASKED?
HMM? WHAT'S THAT?
WHAT!? SHE TURNED YOU DOWN BECAUSE "YOU STINK OF DOG"!?
HERE. YOU'LL CUT YOURSELF IF YOU CLEAN UP THE PIECES WITH YOUR HANDS.
CLINK
CLINK
KAAAAH! FEH!! I CAN'T BEAR IT!! IT'S WHAT'S ON THE INSIDE THAT MATTERS !!!
TODAY, WE'RE GOING TO DRINK!!
OH, BUT YOU REALLY DO SMELL LIKE A DOG. DO BE MORE CAREFUL!!
!!!
SHOCK

KHONSU: "OH, HE ALWAYS SHOWS HIS EMOTIONS THROUGH HIS MOVEMENTS. HE'S QUITE EASY TO READ!"

Special Thanks.

- Arisa Yukimiya
- Ui Kizuki
- Mai Kurozuki

SPECIAL HELP FROM:

- Chiinyo-san
- Bechika Hatoya-san

My editor,
Yuuichi Shimomura-sama

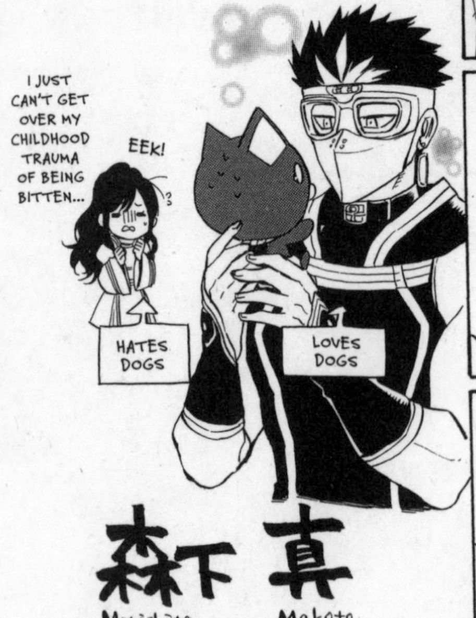
I JUST CAN'T GET OVER MY CHILDHOOD TRAUMA OF BEING BITTEN...
EEK!
HATES DOGS
LOVES DOGS

森下 真
Morishita Makoto

TEACH ME!! KHONSU-SENSEI!!

THE AMEN PRIESTHOOD

SO WHAT'S IT LIKE???

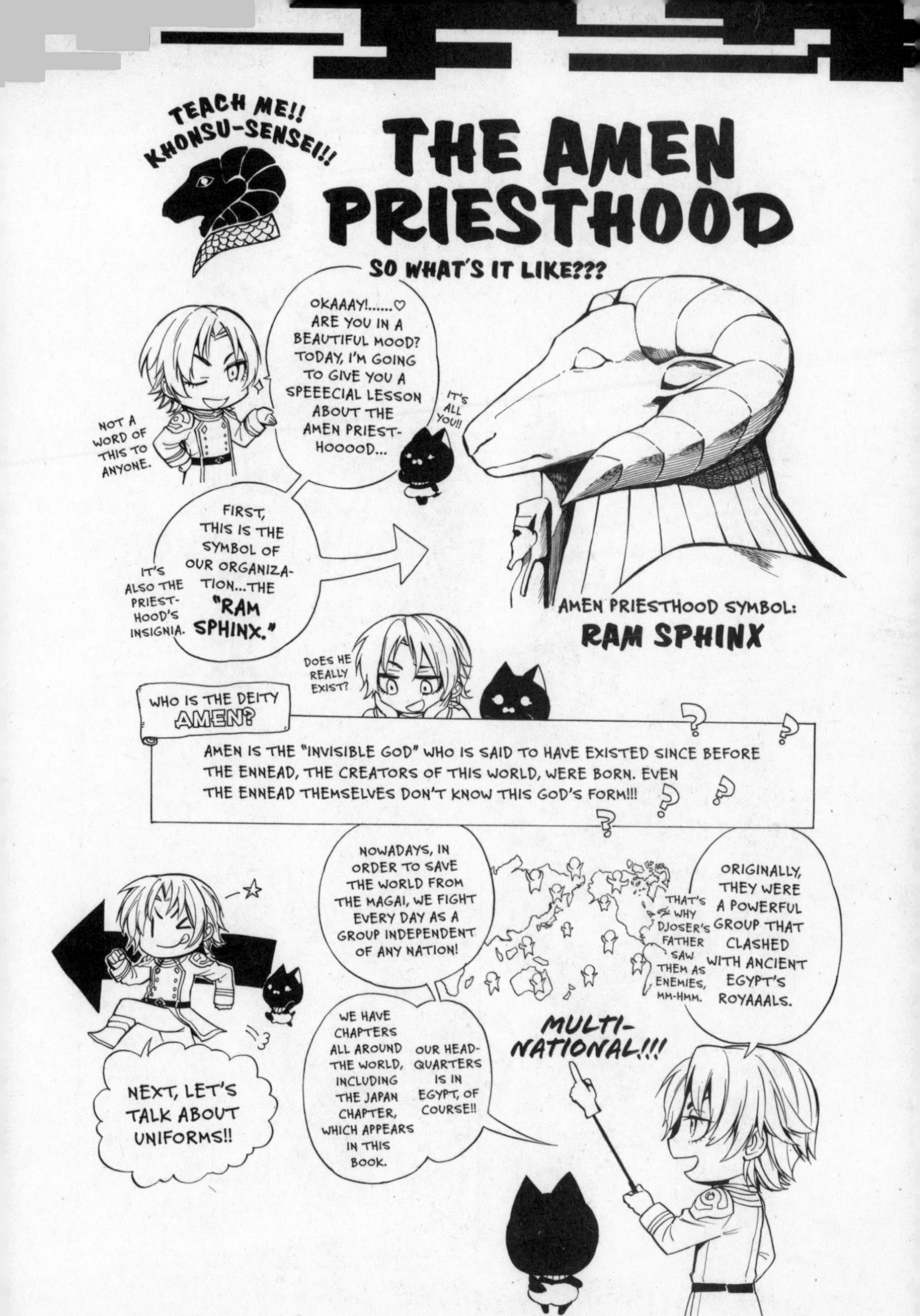

OKAAAY!......♡ ARE YOU IN A BEAUTIFUL MOOD? TODAY, I'M GOING TO GIVE YOU A SPEEECIAL LESSON ABOUT THE AMEN PRIEST-HOOOOD...
IT'S ALL YOU!!
NOT A WORD OF THIS TO ANYONE.
AMEN PRIESTHOOD SYMBOL:
RAM SPHINX
FIRST, THIS IS THE SYMBOL OF OUR ORGANIZA-TION...THE "RAM SPHINX."
IT'S ALSO THE PRIEST-HOOD'S INSIGNIA.
DOES HE REALLY EXIST?
WHO IS THE DEITY AMEN?
AMEN IS THE "INVISIBLE GOD" WHO IS SAID TO HAVE EXISTED SINCE BEFORE THE ENNEAD, THE CREATORS OF THIS WORLD, WERE BORN. EVEN THE ENNEAD THEMSELVES DON'T KNOW THIS GOD'S FORM!!!
ORIGINALLY, THEY WERE A POWERFUL GROUP THAT CLASHED WITH ANCIENT EGYPT'S ROYAAALS.
THAT'S WHY DJOSER'S FATHER SAW THEM AS ENEMIES, MM-HMM.
NOWADAYS, IN ORDER TO SAVE THE WORLD FROM THE MAGAI, WE FIGHT EVERY DAY AS A GROUP INDEPENDENT OF ANY NATION!
MULTI-NATIONAL!!!
WE HAVE CHAPTERS ALL AROUND THE WORLD, INCLUDING THE JAPAN CHAPTER, WHICH APPEARS IN THIS BOOK.
OUR HEAD-QUARTERS IS IN EGYPT, OF COURSE!!
NEXT, LET'S TALK ABOUT UNIFORMS!!

AMEN PRIESTHOOD UNIFORMS

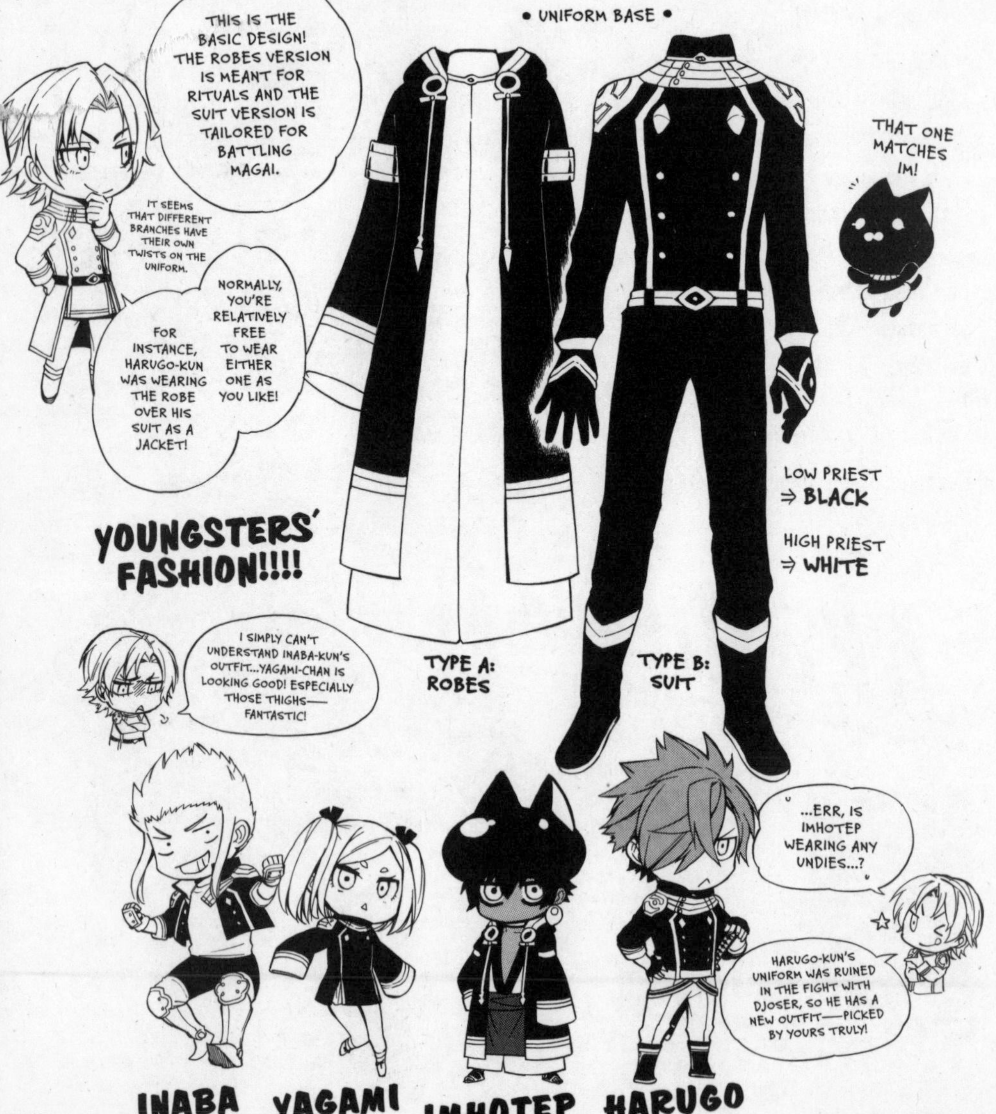
• UNIFORM BASE •
THIS IS THE BASIC DESIGN! THE ROBES VERSION IS MEANT FOR RITUALS AND THE SUIT VERSION IS TAILORED FOR BATTLING MAGAI.
IT SEEMS THAT DIFFERENT BRANCHES HAVE THEIR OWN TWISTS ON THE UNIFORM.
NORMALLY, YOU'RE RELATIVELY FREE TO WEAR EITHER ONE AS YOU LIKE!
FOR INSTANCE, HARUGO-KUN WAS WEARING THE ROBE OVER HIS SUIT AS A JACKET!
THAT ONE MATCHES IM!
TYPE A: ROBES
TYPE B: SUIT
LOW PRIEST ⇒ BLACK
HIGH PRIEST ⇒ WHITE
YOUNGSTERS' FASHION!!!!
I SIMPLY CAN'T UNDERSTAND INABA-KUN'S OUTFIT...YAGAMI-CHAN IS LOOKING GOOD! ESPECIALLY THOSE THIGHS—FANTASTIC!
...ERR, IS IMHOTEP WEARING ANY UNDIES...?
HARUGO-KUN'S UNIFORM WAS RUINED IN THE FIGHT WITH DJOSER, SO HE HAS A NEW OUTFIT—PICKED BY YOURS TRULY!
INABA
YAGAMI
IMHOTEP
HARUGO

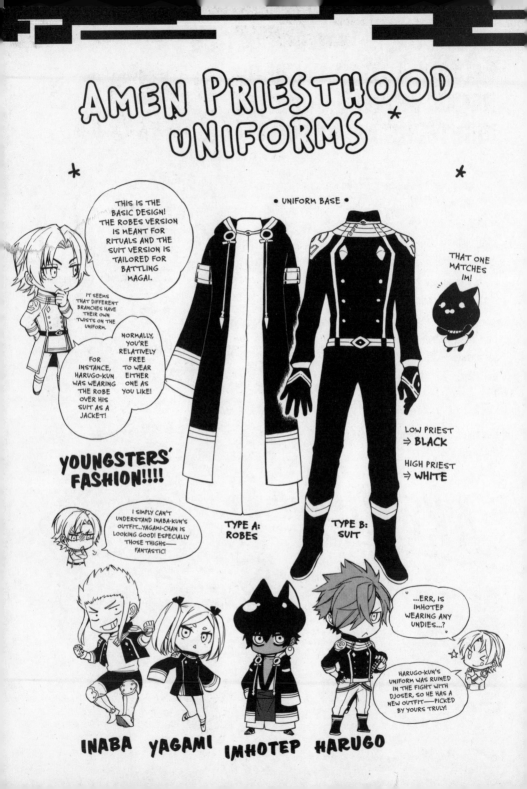

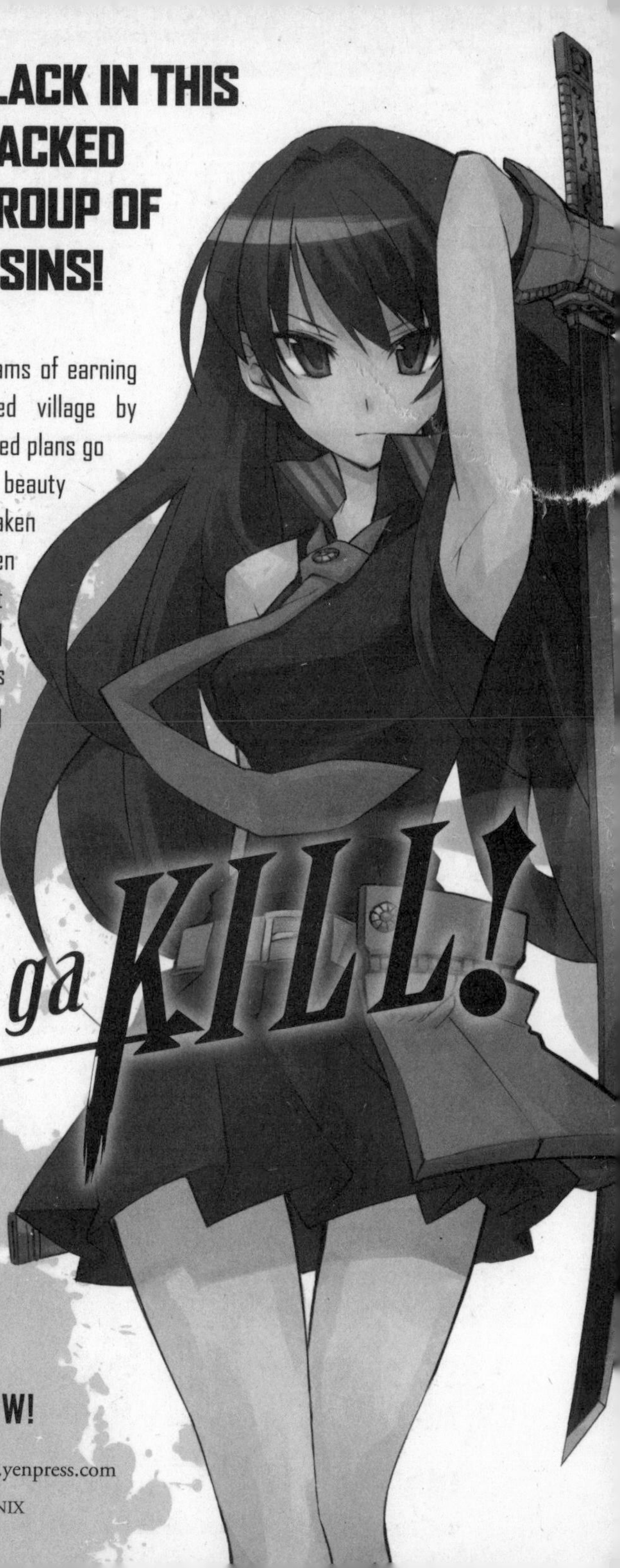

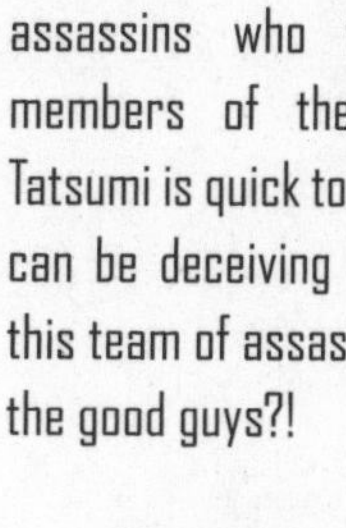

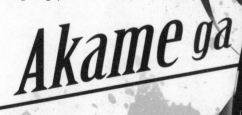

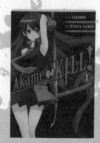

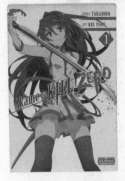

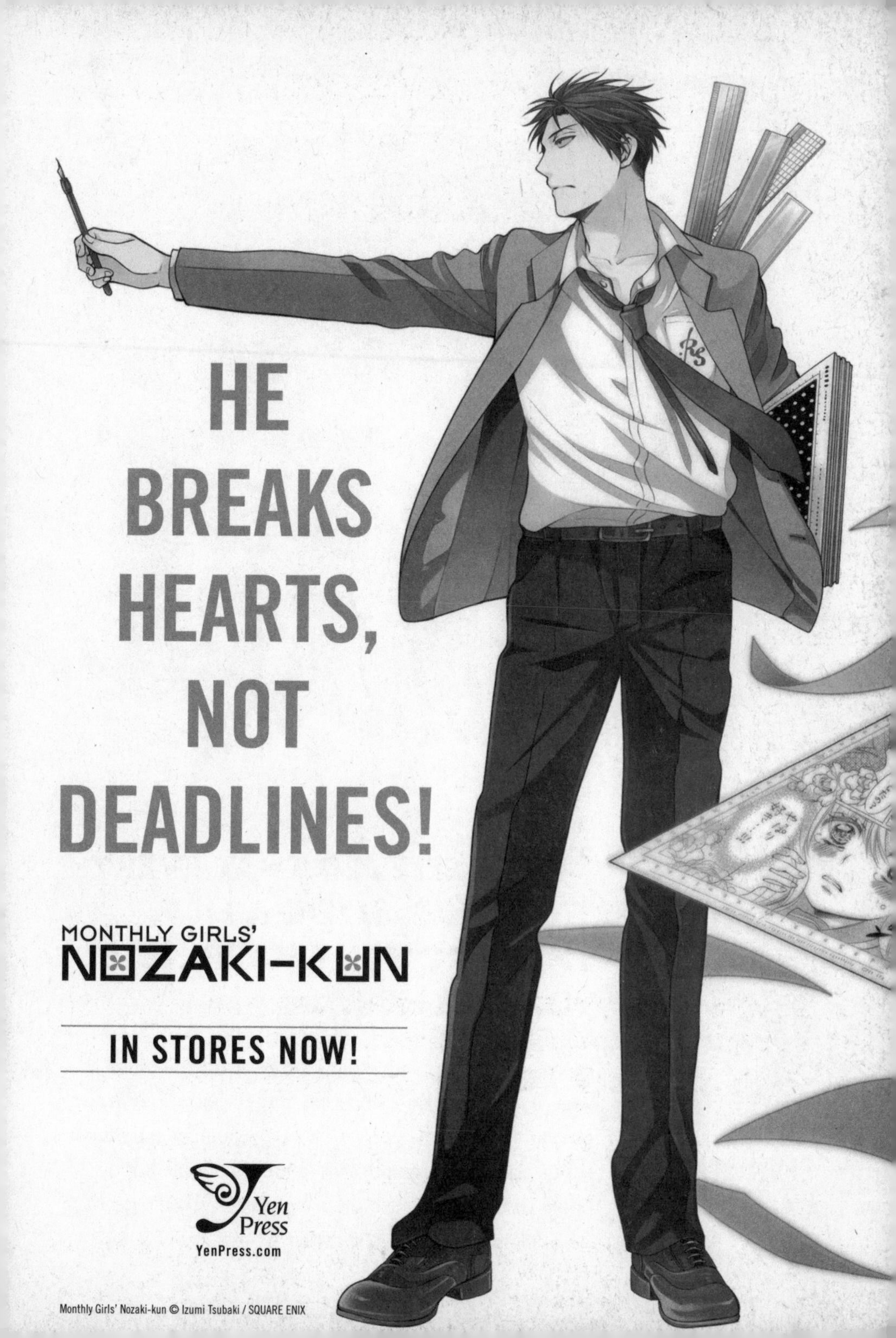

WELCOME TO IKEBUKURO, WHERE TOKYO'S WILDEST CHARACTERS GATHER!!

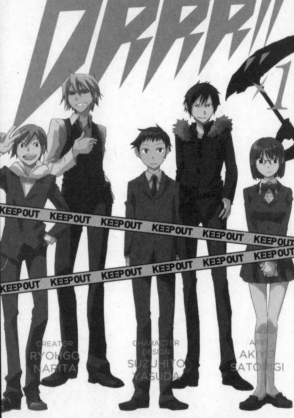

AS THEIR PATHS CROSS, THIS ECCENTRIC CAST WEAVES A TWISTED, CRACKED LOVE STORY...

AVAILABLE NOW!!

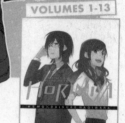

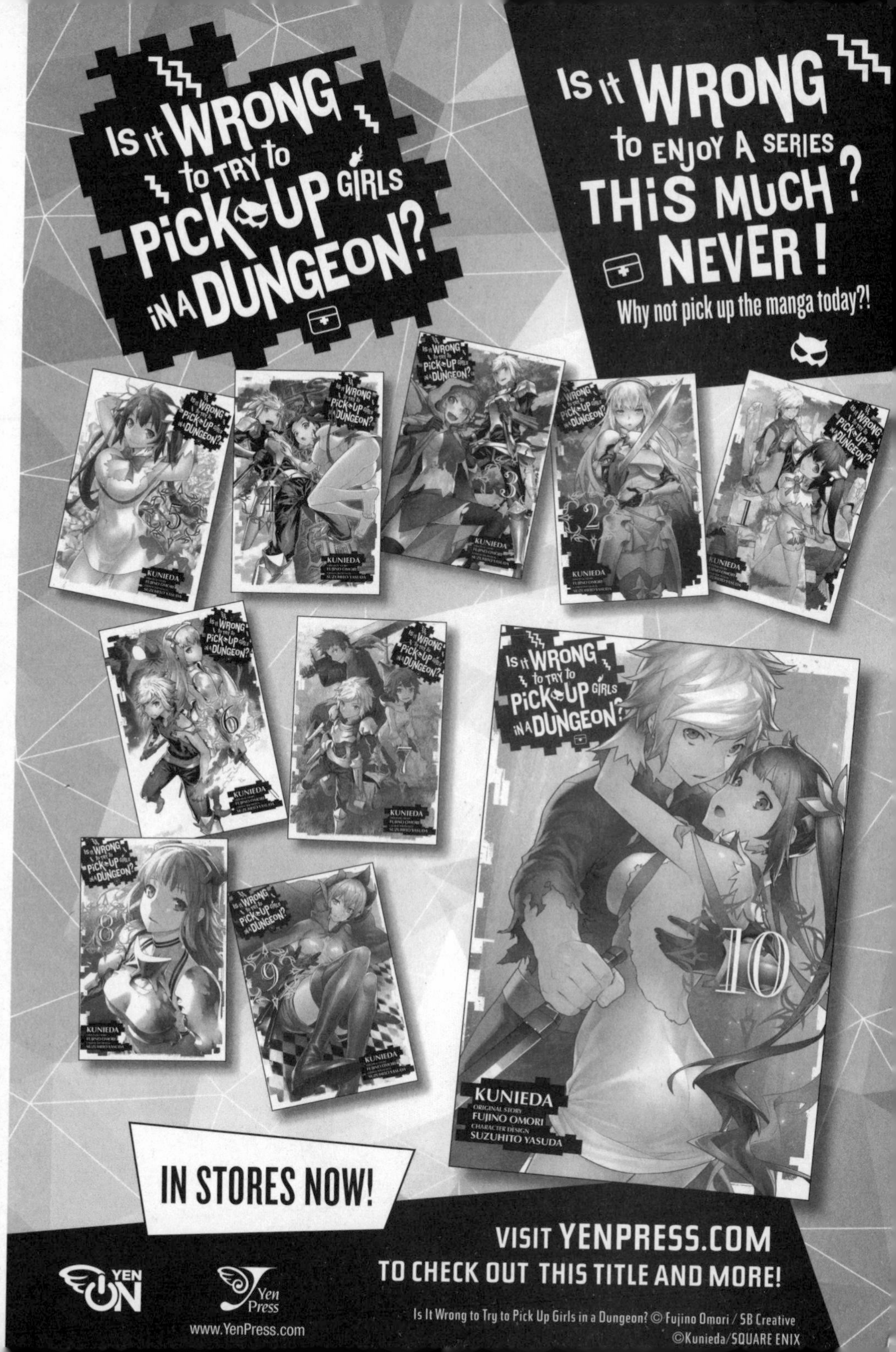
Is it WRONG to try to PiCK UP GIRLS iN A DUNGEON?
Is it WRONG to ENJOY A SERIES THIS MUCH?
NEVER!
Why not pick up the manga today?!
KUNIEDA
ORIGINAL STORY FUJINO OMORI
CHARACTER DESIGN SUZUHITO YASUDA
IN STORES NOW!
VISIT YENPRESS.COM
TO CHECK OUT THIS TITLE AND MORE!
YEN ON
Yen Press
www.YenPress.com
Is It Wrong to Try to Pick Up Girls in a Dungeon? © Fujino Omori / SB Creative
©Kunieda/SQUARE ENIX

HE DOES NOT LET ANYONE ROLL THE DICE.

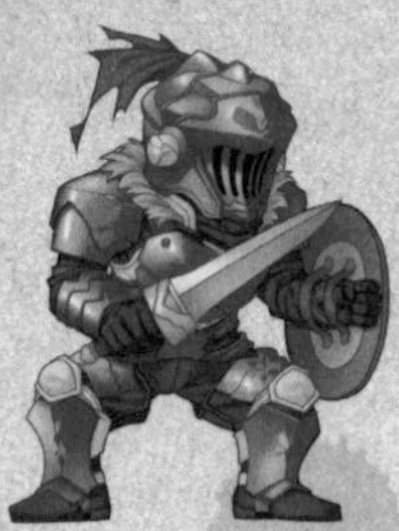

A young Priestess joins her first adventuring party, but blind to the dangers, they almost immediately find themselves in trouble. It's Goblin Slayer who comes to their rescue—a man who has dedicated his life to the extermination of all goblins by any means necessary. A dangerous, dirty, and thankless job, but he does it better than anyone. And when rumors of his feats begin to circulate, there's no telling who might come calling next...

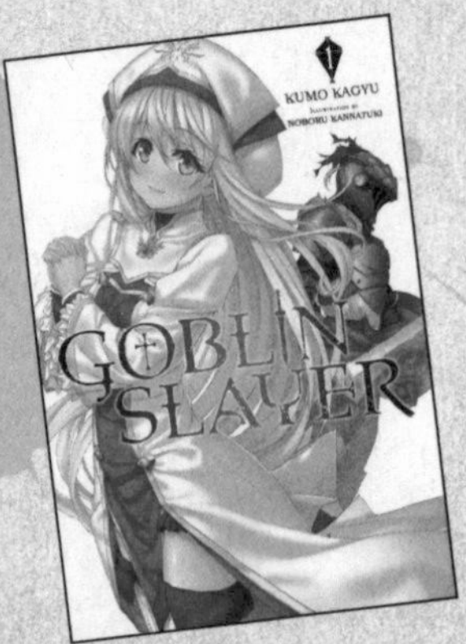

Light Novel V. 1-9 Available Now!

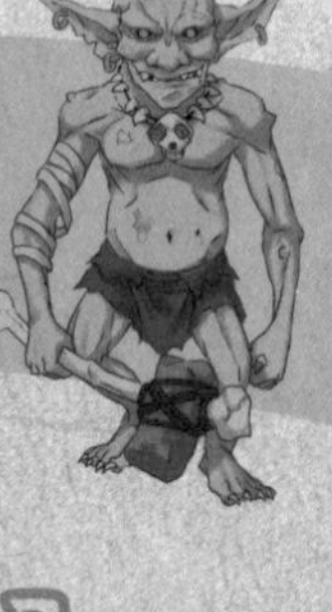

Check out the simul-pub manga chapters every month!

Yen Press   YEN ON
www.yenpress.com

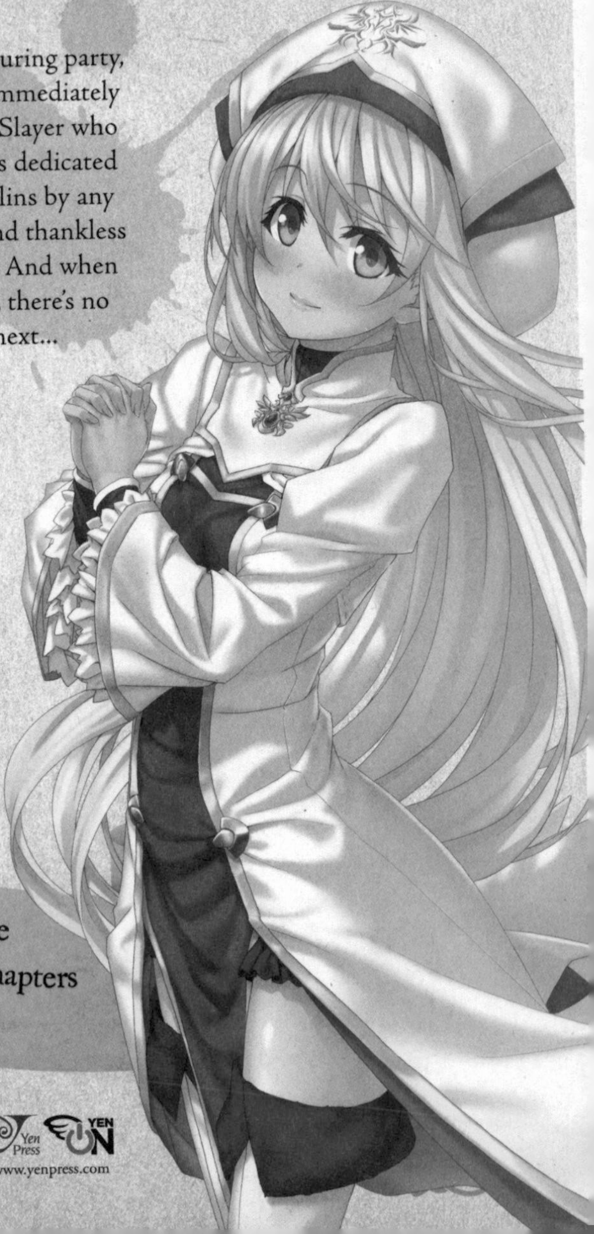

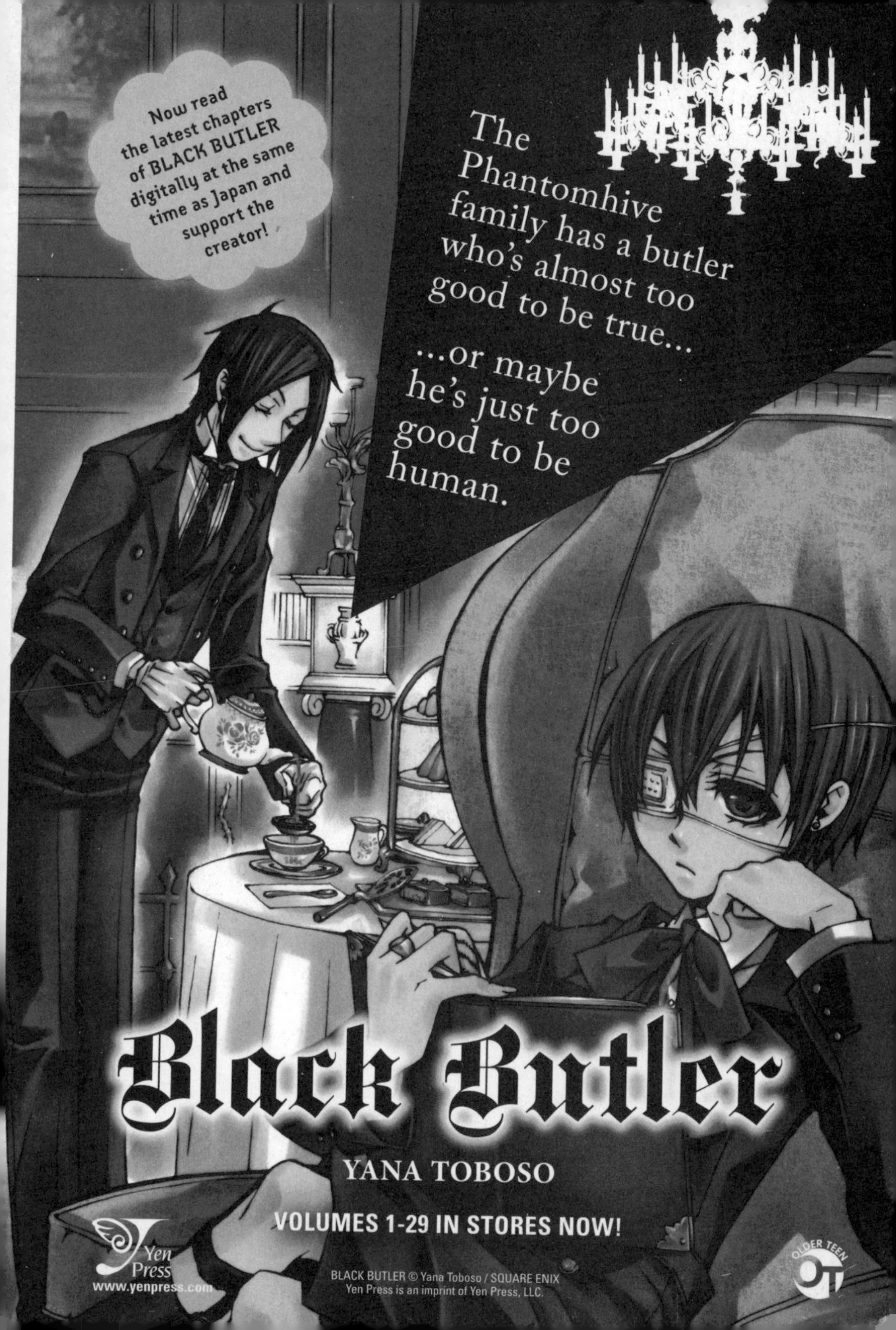
Now read the latest chapters of BLACK BUTLER digitally at the same time as Japan and support the creator!
The Phantomhive family has a butler who's almost too good to be true...
...or maybe he's just too good to be human.
Black Butler
YANA TOBOSO
VOLUMES 1-29 IN STORES NOW!
Yen Press
www.yenpress.com
BLACK BUTLER © Yana Toboso / SQUARE ENIX
Yen Press is an imprint of Yen Press, LLC.
OLDER TEEN
OT

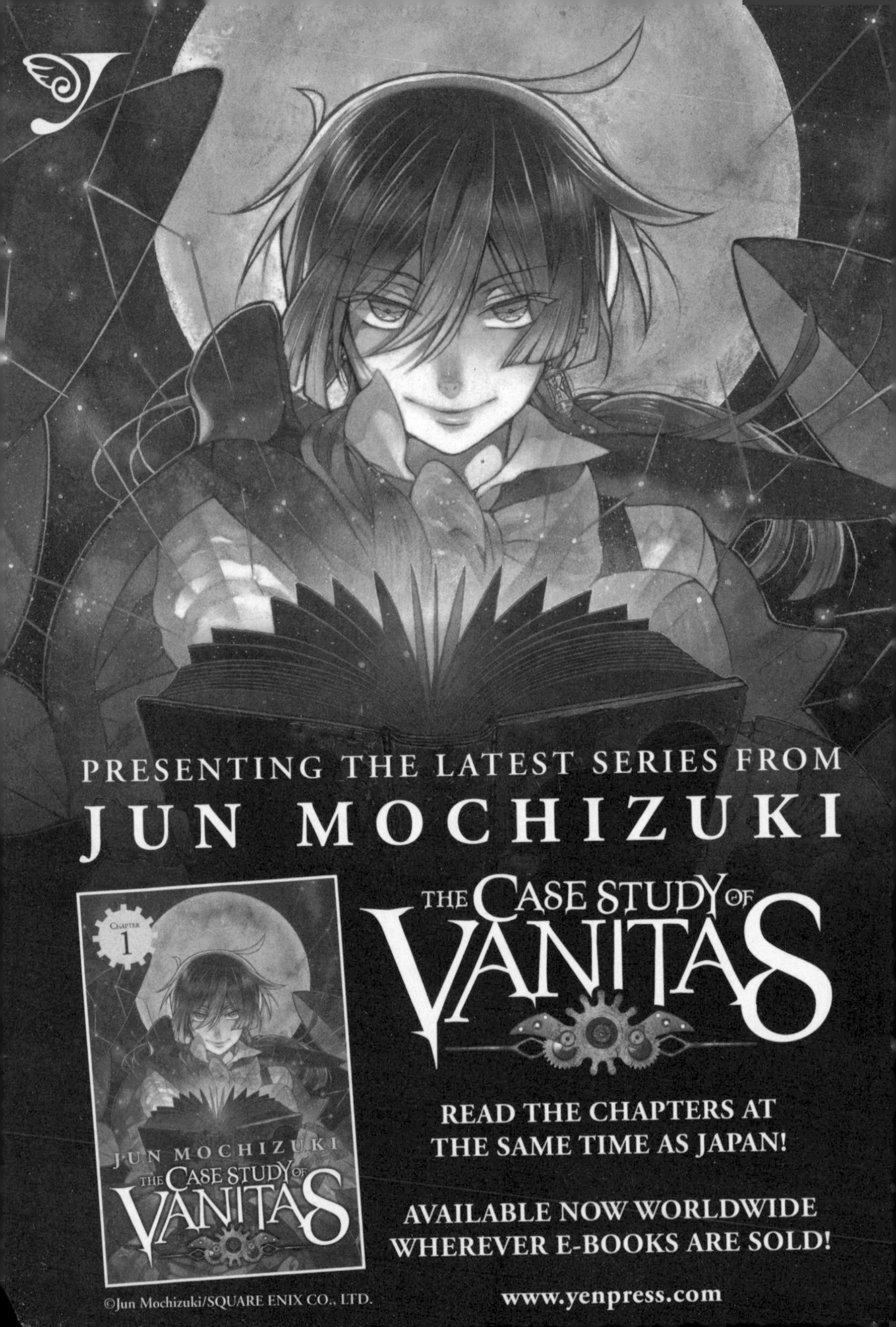
PRESENTING THE LATEST SERIES FROM
JUN MOCHIZUKI
CHAPTER 1
JUN MOCHIZUKI
THE CASE STUDY OF VANITAS
THE CASE STUDY OF VANITAS
READ THE CHAPTERS AT THE SAME TIME AS JAPAN!
AVAILABLE NOW WORLDWIDE WHEREVER E-BOOKS ARE SOLD!
©Jun Mochizuki/SQUARE ENIX CO., LTD.
www.yenpress.com

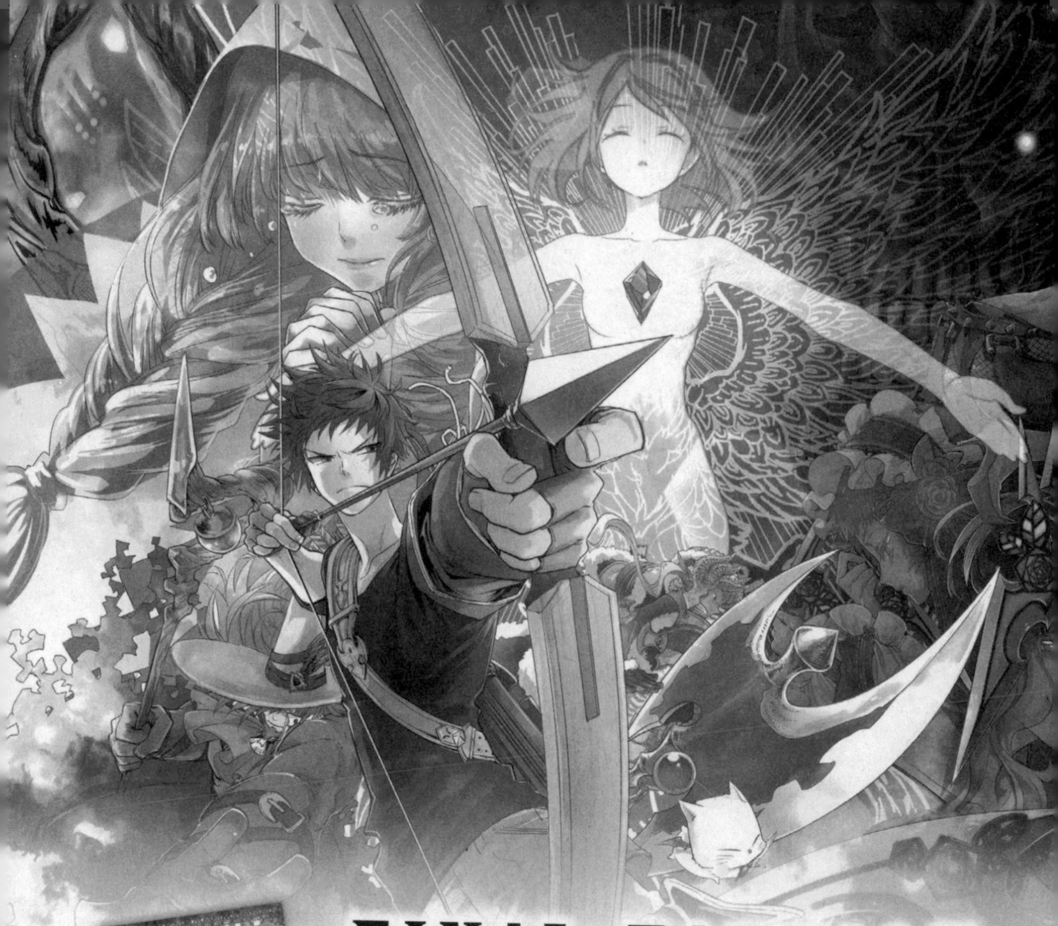

FINAL FANTASY

ファイナルファンタジー　ロスト・ストレンジャー

LOST STRANGER

Keep up with the
latest chapters in
the simul-pub
version! Available
now worldwide
wherever e-books
are sold!

For more information,
visit www.yenpress.com

Karino Takatsu, creator of
SERVANT × SERVICE, presents:

My Monster Girl's Too Cool For You

Burning adoration melts her heart...literally!

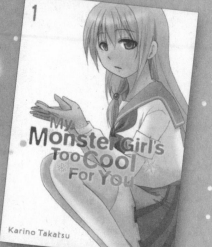

In a world where *youkai* and
humans attend school together,
a boy named Atsushi Fukuzumi
falls for snow *youkai* Muku Shiroishi. Fukuzumi's passionate feelings
melt Muku's heart...and the rest of her?! The first volume of an
interspecies romantic comedy you're sure to fall head over heels for
is now available!!

Yen Press

**Read new installments of this series every
month at the same time as Japan!**

CHAPTERS AVAILABLE NOW AT E-TAILERS EVERYWHERE!

YenPress.com

IM

Great Priest Imhotep

4

by MAKOTO MORISHITA

Translation: Amanda Haley
Lettering: Rochelle Gancio

IM Vol. 4 ©2016 Makoto Morishita/SQUARE ENIX CO., LTD.
First published in Japan in 2016 by SQUARE ENIX CO., LTD. English translation rights arranged with SQUARE ENIX CO., LTD. and Yen Press, LLC through Tuttle-Mori Agency, Inc., Tokyo.

English translation ©2017 by SQUARE ENIX CO., LTD.

Yen Press
150 West 30th Street, 19th Floor
New York, NY 10001

Visit us at yenpress.com ⚫ facebook.com/yenpress
twitter.com/yenpress ⚫ yenpress.tumblr.com
instagram.com/yenpress

First Yen Press Print Edition: August 2020
Originally published as an ebook in December 2017 by Yen Press.

Yen Press is an imprint of Yen Press, LLC.
The Yen Press name and logo are trademarks of Yen Press, LLC.

The publisher is not responsible for websites (or their content) that are not owned by the publisher.

Library of Congress Control Number: 2019953326

ISBN: 978-1-9753-1145-2 (paperback)

10 9 8 7 6 5 4 3 2 1

WOR

Printed in the United States of America